Cross-Cultural Counseling and Psychotherapy

(PGPS - 93)

Pergamon Titles of Related Interest

Cross-Cultural Counseling and Psychotherapy

Edited by
Anthony J. Marsella
Paul B. Pedersen
University of Hawaii

Pergamon Press
New York • Oxford • Toronto • Sydney • Paris • Frankfurt

Pergamon Press Offices:

U.S.A. Pergamon Press Inc., Maxwell House, Fairview Park, Elmsford, New York 10523, U.S.A.

U.K. Pergamon Press Ltd., Headington Hill Hall, Oxford OX3 0BW, England

CANADA Pergamon Press Canada Ltd., Suite 104, 150 Consumers Road, Willowdale, Ontario M2J 1P9, Canada

AUSTRALIA Pergamon Press (Aust.) Pty. Ltd., P.O. Box 544, Potts Point, NSW 2011, Australia

FRANCE Pergamon Press SARL, 24 rue des Ecoles, 75240 Paris, Cedex 05, France

FEDERAL REPUBLIC OF GERMANY Pergamon Press GmbH, Hammerweg 6, D-6242 Kronberg-Taunus, Federal Republic of Germany

Library of Congress Cataloging in Publication Data

Main entry under title:

Cross-cultural counseling and psychotherapy.

(Pergamon general psychology series ; v. 93)
   Based on a conference held in Honolulu in June 1979 and sponsored by the Culture Learning Institute of the East-West Center.
   Includes index.
   1. Counseling—Cross-cultural studies—Congresses.
2. Psychotherapy—Cross-cultural studies—Congresses.
I. Marsella, Anthony L. II. Pedersen, Paul, 1936-
III. East-West Center. Culture Learning Institute.
BF637.C6C73 1980   616.89'14   80-18472
ISBN 0-08-025545-0

To our children:

Laura Joy

Gianna Malia

and

Karen Britt

Kai Berndt

Jon Olaf

Table of Contents

Preface

The purpose of the present volume is to provide students, teachers, and professionals with a historical, conceptual, and applied resource for cross-cultural counseling and psychotherapy. Cross-cultural counseling and psychotherapy refers to those behavior change activities which involve clients and therapists from different ethnocultural traditions. It is an emerging specialty area in all of the major mental health professions. It would be incorrect to assume that cross-cultural counseling and psychotherapy, at its current state of development, represents a formal set of therapeutic procedures and activities. It does not! Ultimately, formal principles and procedures may emerge and become accepted. But this is unlikely without a concerted effort to organize our existing research and clinical knowledge.

Today, cross-cultural counseling and psychotherapy is more notable for its potential than its achievements. It challenges us to consider the possibility that our values, assumptions, and methods regarding behavior are culturally limited and, thus, factually suspect. And yet, it offers us the opportunity to extend our horizons to new limits of understanding and effectiveness. The present volume, then, is intended to be both an overview of our existing knowledge and a stimulus for new efforts!

As the editors of the original papers which comprise this volume, we have made an effort to capture the promise and the controversy which characterize cross-cultural counseling and psychotherapy today. The volume is organized into four main sections: *Foundations, Evaluation, Ethnocultural Considerations,* and *Future Perspectives.*

The *Foundations* section consists of three chapters.

Juris Draguns provides an overview of the problems in cross-cultural counseling and therapy, surveying the issues to identify important gaps in our knowledge about cross-cultural counseling. He also examines the role of indigenous therapies and the cultural bias inherent in formal counseling and therapy services, the role of Westernized assumptions in shaping mental health support systems, and the cultural adaptations of therapy systems. He notes that culturally different alternatives give rise to basic problems in delivering appropriate counseling and therapy to a culturally differentiated population. He also points out that the cultural definition of mental health and the effect of intercultural contact on mental health are important issues in cross-cultural counseling.

Norman Sundberg provides a summary of research findings on intercultural mental health. The findings point out shared patterns of emphasis in counseling and therapy to culturally different clients and also illuminate gaps in the research where more data is needed. A number of research hypotheses are identified which build on what we already know and which articulate the most important issues in developing the foundations of cross-cultural counseling therapy.

Frank Johnson reviews the importance of interaction rules for inter-cultural counseling and therapy, outlining the multidimensional context of therapy, wherein multiple factors complicate the ethnic and cultural dimension of therapy. He observes that the norms, values, assumptions, and ideologies which define a client's subjective culture are defined by very specific interaction rules which must be identified and acknowledged in order for counseling or therapy to be successful.

The second section, *Evaluation,* contains four chapters. These chapters approach the problem of evaluating cross-cultural counseling and psychotherapy from the vantage points of expectations, process variables, and statistical analyses. Each of the chapters provides the readers with a discussion of the alternative research strategies for examining the many variables that influence the cross-cultural counseling and psychotherapy encounter.

Arnold Goldstein reviews the effect of client expectancies and anticipations on all therapy, and particularly on cross-cultural counseling and therapy. He discusses *a conformity* prescription where the treatment is reformulated to fit the client. Research findings support greater emphasis on *reformity* as an approach to intercultural counseling and psychotherapy.

Derald Sue reviews the evaluation studies on process variables in cross-cultural counseling and therapy, with specific emphasis on the role of counselor credibility among culturally different clients. Credibility appears to be a more important predictor of success in counseling and therapy than theoretical orientations or the range of other alternative predictors. Other process variables are also included in his evaluation criteria.

Michael Lambert integrates research on cross-cultural counseling and therapy according to outcome measures of counseling effectiveness. The application of Western psychotherapeutic methods to non-Western cultures raises the question of the adequacy of existing guidelines for intercultural counseling and therapy outcomes. Relationship variables correlate with desired outcomes more frequently than any other therapist characteristic. He suggests that a "facilitative" relationship with the client may be the most important variable irrespective of cultural differences.

Martin Katz reviews alternative outcome variables for intercultural counseling and therapy systems demonstrating the importance of data-based conclusions which support the importance of matching culturally different clients with culturally specific mental health services. In the final analysis it is the outcome variables which determine the success of failure of an intervention.

The third section, *Cultural Considerations,* contains four chapters. Each chapter examines a different ethnocultural group. Carolyn Block describes working with black clients, Amado Padilla with Hispanic clients, Harry Kitano with Japanese-American clients, and Norman Dinges and his colleagues with Native American Indian clients.

These chapters were designed not only to inform the reader about issues of working with clients from the ethnocultural traditions represented, but also to provide knowledge culled from experience and research on suggested practices.

Carolyn Block reviews the literature on intercultural counseling and therapy related to the identity of a black client. She emphasizes the phenomenological aspects of transracial therapy, citing specific diagnostic issues for working with black clients. A therapist or counselor will need to alter white culture treatment modes for the black client. The problems she discusses are particularly relevant for the non-black therapist or counselor working with the black client.

Amado Padilla reviews the literature on Hispanic-Americans, sorting out those studies which most effectively define the guidelines for special needs of the rapidly increasing Spanish speaking minorities. He notes that the resistance by Hispanic clients to use of traditional mental health services relate directly to more effective incorporation of natural support systems within the Hispanic cultural perspective.

Harry Kitano describes the dilemma of Japanese-Americans seeking counseling when they are comfortable with neither the Japanese nor the American mode of mental health care. Problems of role identity, both as Americans and as Japanese, affect the definition of mental health problems and the effectiveness of counseling or therapy. New models of counseling and therapy will need to be developed to accommodate generations of Asian-Americans who choose to incorporate aspects of both Eastern and Western value systems in their life style.

Norman Dinges, Joseph Trimble, Spero Manson, and Frank Pasquale explore the broad range of alternative perspectives relevant to different Native American Indian cultures, reconciling theory and practice within the context of programmatic mental health services. The chapter draws on examples of collaboration between indigenous and dominant culture therapies, adaptations of Western principles in non-Western cultures, the adaptation of indigenous principles in isolated communities, and the gaps in research knowledge about an appropriately applicable mental health care delivery system.

The fourth and final section of the book, *Future Perspectives,* contains two chapters. These chapters provide a perspective for both the past and the future of the area.

Allen Ivey's chapter draws out the implications of eight basic assumptions in counseling and therapy for social policy issues. He proposes that cultural considerations can provide a more adequate conceptual base for counseling and therapy to emphasize primary prevention and match therapies with individuals and environments, thereby increasing counseling effectiveness across cultures.

Paul Pedersen reviews the alternative scenarios for developing interculturally sensitive mental health care for a culturally diverse population, emphasizing the importance of a harmonious scenario as the alternative to either an authoritarian or a chaotic process. Role identification and identity diffusion are the primary future issues in a comprehensive and eclectic system that includes Western as well as non-Western assumptions for defining the task of counseling and therapy in a culturally mixed world population. As we look toward the future we are all immigrants entering a host culture where we may expect an uncomfortable adjustment as we redefine and adapt our familiar views.

All of the chapters in the volume were originally presented at a conference on cross-cultural counseling and psychotherapy which was held at the East-West Center, Honolulu, Hawaii, in June 1979. The conference was sponsored by a project entitled "Developing Interculturally Skilled Counselors" (DISC) which was funded by a three year grant from the National Institute of Mental Health (T24-MH15552-01). Additional support was provided by the Culture Learning Institute of the East-West Center, Honolulu, Hawaii.

The Editors wish to express their appreciation to a number of people who helped make both the Conference and the volume possible: Kay James, DISC project secretary, provided extremely valuable support in coordinating the schedules and the limited resources for assembling the conference participants; Gary Kawachi, DISC project secretary, provided extensive secretarial support for coordinating and assembling the book chapters following the conference; the conference staff of the East-West Center Culture Learning Institute provided all the services necessary to insure efficiency and comfort; Jerry Frank, Psychology Editor at Pergamon Press, provided both encouragement and patience at just the right times. Lastly, we wish to thank our chapter authors for their cooperative spirit in responding to our suggestions on content and style. We hope this volume will provide a substantive starting place for all people seeking to increase their knowledge and skill in providing help to people from different ethnocultural traditions.

A.J.M./P.B.P.
Honolulu, 1979

Part I:
Foundations

Chapter 1

Cross-Cultural Counseling and Psychotherapy: History, Issues, Current Status

Juris G. Draguns

The range of the topic of this chapter is broad and its outer limits remain uncertain. My objective is to provide a brief overview of the major problems in the field of cross-cultural psychotherapy and counseling, without aspiring to either comprehensiveness or definitiveness. In the process of providing a survey of issues in this area of conceptualization, investigation, and clinical activity, I will attempt to separate that which we know from that which we do not know and indicate areas which, in my opinion, remain in need of investigation. At the same time, I will search for points of contact between issues and findings in research and practice of counseling and psychotherapy in its home milieu and the choices and dilemmas which confront the observer, evaluator, and practitioner of psychotherapy and counseling across cultures.

PSYCHOTHERAPY AND COUNSELING ACROSS CULTURES: NOT ONE FIELD BUT MANY

All of these goals are all the more difficult to attain because of the fragmented and complex status of psychotherapy and counseling across cultures. First, we have counseling and psychotherapy to deal with, two overlapping activities, one shading off into the other, yet each with its own distinct focus and, more important for the immediate issue at hand, its own periodicals and publication circuits which are only incompletely interpenetrated.

For the purpose of this chapter, counseling is construed as an activity that facilitates and fosters personal problem solving. Psychotherapy is principally concerned with changing persons, their characteristic modes of subjective experience and overt behavior, i.e., their personalities. It is obvious that no clear dividing line can be drawn between these two activities. Intrinsically, they probably share a greater degree of similarity than their quasi-independent existence suggests.

On the most general plane, the functions of psychotherapy and counseling are probably universal: to alleviate distress, to reintegrate the client into the culture, and to enable him or her to respond to cultural roles and to meet cultural expectations. As pointed out elsewhere (Draguns, 1975), culture is inevitably a silent participant in the enterprise of psychotherapy. This recognition is shared by Wachtel (1977, p. 3), a contemporary pioneer in reconciling and integrating behavioral and psychoanalytic therapy:

> Psychotherapy is not just a technical activity performed by a practitioner. Psychotherapies have existed throughout history, and they have always been rooted in philosophical views of human nature and man's place in the universe. The theories that guide psychotherapeutic efforts both reflect and shape the culture's view of human potential and the good life.

The other issue, that of heterogeneity of activities and services loosely subsumed under the heading of cross-cultural psychotherapy and counseling, can only be faced by addressing ourselves to differentiating these diverse activities (see Sundberg, in press; Wohl, in press). At the very minimum, the following semi-autonomous areas of practice, research, and writing can be distinguished.

Indigenous Psychotherapy

This provisional term refers to the gamut of verbal and interpersonal techniques designed for the alleviation of personal distress and for the induction of change of behavior which have been developed independently of the Western tradition of purportedly scientifically-based psychotherapy.

It is uncertain, at this point, whether psychotherapy is a pancultural universal, but it is certainly not a Western particular. A rich literature, descriptive for the most part, has come into being on what Collomb (1972) has called psychiatry without psychiatrists. A number of sources (Pedersen, Lonner, & Draguns, 1976; Prince, 1976, 1980; Sanua, 1966; Torrey, 1972a) are available on this subject. Indigenous psychotherapy, as it is practiced around the world, encompasses a great deal of variety and can be classified in a number of ways. Tseng and Hsu (1979) have proposed a four-fold division of healing systems into supernaturally, naturally, medically-physiologically, and sociopsychologically oriented ones. In a somewhat different manner, one could say that the cultural modes of explanation and intervention in the area of personal distress proceed from the four reference points of supernatural intervention, regularities or principles of nature, bodily functioning, and social interaction. Most cultures, if not all, gather and transmit knowledge on each of these four classes of phenomena and bring them selectively to bear upon counteracting human confusion, ineffectuality, and suffering. Illustrative and descriptive information has been accumulating on instances of such intervention in a great many cultures. Apart from the purely descriptive aspect of this body of writing, i.e., documentation, at various degrees of penetration and detail, on what is done, by whom, to whom, with what effect, this body of literature is germane to a number of issues.

First, one might ask, what light does the information extant on indigenous psychotherapy shed on the "basic ingredients" of psychotherapy (Strupp, 1973a), its "common factors" (Garfield, 1973), or on the necessary and sufficient conditions of personality change (Rogers, 1957)? To what extent and in what manner does the sum of the available descriptive data complement the information on this issue gathered intraculturally? Second, what knowledge we have on psychotherapy within the framework of other cultural traditions raises the question of the range of effective psychotherapeutic techniques, possibly beyond those available in our own culture.

Third, the powerful thrust toward the development of comprehensive mental health services throughout the world has stimulated the search for a way to integrate the services already there, indigenous and available, with those of the imported variety. Within the last decade, a body of writing has come into being on the delivery of mental health services beyond cultural frontiers (Higginbotham, 1976, 1979a, 1979b). The World Health Organization is currently engaged in a project in four developing countries around the world—Colombia, India, Sudan, and Senegal—on the development of community-based mental health services (Diop, Collignon, & Gueye, 1976). In these efforts, blending in of native psychotherapy is an important component.

Parallel, however, to the integration and incorporation of indigenous services into comprehensive mental health planning, there is a countertrend recently noted by Higginbotham (1979c) on the basis of observations in several countries of South East Asia. He reported that the skills and services of traditional practitioners are being eroded as the population is experiencing a rapid pace of modernization and urbanization. A similar development has been independently noted by Claver (1976) on the Ivory Coast of West Africa. Specifically, Claver (1976, p. 30) says: "The [traditional] healer does not have much to offer us. The new society has experienced upheavals which have provided the inhabitant of the Ivory Coast with a new *persona* which completely eludes the healer. He now remains the psychologist of an epoch left behind.''[1]

Fourth, the question has, on occasion, been asked of how the techniques and concepts of indigenous psychotherapies could be imported and fitted into the array of services in the West. As an example, a German psychologist, Ingeborg Wendt (1967), trained in Japan and immersed in the Japanese techniques of psychotherapy, suggested that it would be worthwhile to develop Morita-clinics in the West. More recently, we have heard suggestions of the value of the Hawaiian concept of ho'oponopono, a communal effort at helping solve an individual's problems (Nishihara, 1978), in the implementation of community-oriented intervention programs not limited to ethnic Hawaiians or the inhabitants of Hawaii. Better known, of course, and therapeutically used, or incorporated into psychotherapy, are Yoga, transcendental meditation, and Zen, all of which have been imported from outside of our cultural milieu. These instances, however, are few and far between; on the whole, the thrust of psychotherapeutic efforts has been in the other direction, i.e., toward the export of our psychotherapeutic concepts, techniques, and services to other cultures.

Western Psychotherapy and its Worldwide Extension

This brings us to the second variant of cross-cultural psychotherapy which involves the application of psychotherapy, as it has been developed in the West, in cultures outside of the Western tradition. A number of authors have addressed themselves to the integration of the yield from these endeavors (Draguns, 1975; Wohl, in press). Their conclusions are cautious and pessimistic. The possibility of exporting psychotherapy services is not denied; after all, we have seen the radiation of psychoanalysis from Vienna across borders and seas. Nonetheless, the range of usefulness of psychotherapeutic services outside of their cultural locale is circumscribed, unless they are adapted. As pointed out by a number of writers (Draguns, 1975; Wohl, in press), psychotherapy defies isolation from its cultural context. Moreover, culture pervades the conduct and experience of psychotherapy, and change in one's behavior and well being takes place in relation to cultural referents. The technique and rationale of Western psychotherapy is so impregnated with its cultural ethos that its application beyond the cluster of interrelated Western cultures has been called into question (Pande,

---

[1]Translated from French by the author.

1968). On the other side of the ledger, it could be argued that psychotherapy in the West rests on more general principles generic to psychotherapy regardless of cultural origins and locations (e.g., Torrey, 1972a). The provisional solution at which it is easy to arrive is that psychotherapy is an amalgam of the universal and culture-specific. Its application beyond the confines of a culture requires adaptation. In what way and to what extent can psychotherapy be accommodated to its clientele in a new and different culture?

Cultural Adaptations of Psychotherapy

This introduces the third major theme of cross-cultural psychotherapy: the nature and extent of its cross-cultural adaptibility. For the sake of convenience, let us consider it in terms of the therapist, the technique, and the client. One prerequisite with which it is difficult to disagree is that the therapist, as part of his expertise and competence, should know the culture within which he operates. Devereux (1969), for example, applied himself to a thorough study of the "Plains Indians," preparatory and concurrent to conducting psychotherapy with one of them. The psychotherapeutic interventions he undertook were informed by this knowledge, but his technique did not appreciably differ from what he might have done with a "standard" American client. In addition to relevant anthropological and cross-cultural psychological information, several other sources have been suggested. In reference to a great many American ethnic groups, Giordano and Giordano (1976) have provided valuable and specific information that the counselor or the therapist should keep in mind in initiating and maintaining contacts with members of these groups. Weidman (1975) in her work with members of other cultures in Miami, Florida, pioneered the concept of culture-broker, a well-informed intermediary whose inputs are brought to bear upon the therapy process. Least formally and most ubiquitously, the client remains the major source of information about those features of his or her cultural experience which might otherwise baffle the therapist. The limit of this mode of inquiry is that the individual, and not the culture, is the focus of all therapy (Draguns, in press); sessions should not degenerate into ethnographic data-gathering in its own right and for its own purpose nor to satisfy the therapist's curiosity. Rather, the referent always is: Is this information needed for therapy, and, if so, how?

The second major accommodation is in the therapist's technique as it is adapted to the client's culturally-based expectations (Higginbotham, 1979c). A continuity obtains between the existing roles and models outside of therapy and what takes place in therapy. Much has been written, for example, on the affinities of client-centered Rogerian therapy and the

American cultural ethos and its central themes of optimism, egalitarianism, and individualism (e.g. Meadow, 1964). Similar parallels can be drawn between Morita-therapy and non-therapy models of behavior in the Japanese culture (Cerny, 1967; Reynolds, 1976) and psychoanalysis in turn-of-the-century Vienna (Toulmin & Janik, 1973). More generally, the expectations and norms of the American middle class have suffused and pervaded the modes of intervention in psychotherapy and counseling. The extension and adaptation of these services to a variety of minorities historically outside of the American mainstream has generated a substantial and rapidly growing literature on changes in technique and relationship which these extensions require and entail (Abad, Ramos, & Boyce, 1974; Atkinson, Maruyama, & Matsui, 1978; Banks, Berenson, & Carkhuff, 1967; Peoples & Dell, 1975; Ruiz & Padilla, 1977; Smith, 1977; D. Sue & S. Sue, 1972; S. Sue & McKinney, 1975; Trimble, in press; Vontress, 1969, 1970, in press). What emerges as a common thread in the writings of therapy with Blacks, Mexican Americans, American Indians, and Asian Americans is the independent emphasis that writers of various persuasions and orientations place on activity, as opposed to reflection and passivity, as the recommended mode of intervention with these several groups.

A higher activity level is, to be sure, not the only technical adaptation recommended. Another important theme that pervades this body of literature is the importance of therapist-client compatibility. The most concrete, but perhaps not the most crucial, form that this compatibility takes is for both the therapist and the client to be members of the same minority group. It is not surprising that in several, although not all, of the studies on this topic a preference for such cultural or racial matching on the part of minority clients is documented. But this state of affairs does not exhaust the complexities of cultural and personal affinity of counselors and therapists.

Perhaps the more general, if subtler, conclusion from this body of clinical and research writings could be expressed as follows: Expect complications as the therapy or counseling process is extended across ethnic, racial, or subcultural lines; and do not attribute these complications exclusively or automatically to the client.

Several recent writers on this subject (e.g. Vontress, in press) are in agreement in emphasizing the countertransference reactions that therapy and counseling across a subcultural gulf often engender. Thus, therapists undertaking to treat members of minority groups should approach this task with a maximum of self-awareness and be prepared to deal with their own distortions of the therapy experience and relationship.

This principle is applicable *a fortiori* to therapy experiences across a cultural gulf in the restricted sense of the term: those situations in which the therapist and the client come from different countries, are native speakers of different languages, and carry with them the results of markedly different patterns of social learning. Yet, remarkably, little has been written about the personal and subjective experience of therapists operating outside of their cultural milieu and/or dealing with clients who are products of a different culture. Wintrob and Harvey (in press) have provided an articulate and frank account of their emotional and cognitive reactions while doing therapy in Liberia. Collomb (1973) has attempted to answer the question: What impels a mental health professional to offer services outside of his or her usual geographic and cultural milieu, and how may these motives interfere with his or her optimal functioning as a therapist? In the process, Collomb has presented a provisional typology of what might be called the cultural distortions of countertransference. On the basis of his observations, he has distinguished three attitudes that could be described as those of universalism, cultural uniqueness, and rejection of one's own culture of origin. In the first case, the sojourner proceeds on the assumption of the superiority and universal applicability of the Western body of psychiatric knowledge and technique. In Collomb's (1973) words, he or she is there "to contribute everything where nothing existed before."[2] The second attitude stands in stark contrast to the foregoing one and seeks to emulate the operations of the ethnologist with their emic emphasis; meaning is imposed only from within the culture in terms of indigenous categories. The third attitude is marked above all by the rejection of one's culture of origin, accompanied often, although not always, by the tendency to idealize the host culture and to gloss over the problematic features it might present. These three preliminary reference points are useful to keep in mind for both the actual practitioner of therapy or counseling across cultures and for the investigator concerned with therapist characteristics and their effect upon process and outcome in a different cultural setting.

Parenthetically, it should be mentioned that psychotherapy across culture lines is much more frequently practiced than explicitly recognized. Freud's famous case of wolf-man, a Russian nobleman treated for obsessive compulsive neurosis, must be reintroduced in this connection. Gardiner's (1971) recent volume containing Freud's (1953) original report as well as a unique, life-long follow-up by the wolf-man himself and by two psychoanalysts, does not focus on the specifically cultural features in this man's analysis. How many more individuals—minority group members, sojourners, immigrants, and others—are therapeutically treated across culture lines without either party to the transaction realizing the cross-cultural nature of their encounter? I suppose that therapists, being sensitive people, may recognize intuitively the cultural features of an individual's background which make a difference in psychotherapy and, yet, there are

---

[2]Translated from French by the author.

likewise a great many instances in which the cultural features go undetected and continue to complicate and obstruct psychotherapy. Jilek-Aal (1978) has recently alluded to the fact that these cultural features can, paradoxically, be most easily overlooked in members of other cultures who live in our own pluralistic societies. Working with English-speaking Salish Indians of Western Canada, she found that it was easier to gloss over important, yet unobtrusive, features of their cultural background than with members of a number of East African cultures she had investigated earlier. The other side of the coin is the heterogeneity of cultural background and identity of people sharing the same cultural label or designation. To extend this point, the problem of faulty second-language usage and the complications of communication and comprehension that they engender in psychotherapy are easily and readily recognized. More subtle and easily overlooked are the problems of using the individual's first language, readily understood by client and therapist alike, but in a different manner. Fleeting allusions, nuances of intonation and meaning can be lost upon the recipient unless he or she is attuned to the subtleties of a specific, cultural language usage (Vontress, in press). Of course, language usage can be idiosyncratic; more typically, however, its peculiarities are cultural - readily understood within the group, but lost upon the outsider. And they are rarely attended to, and still less frequently learned, by outsiders. The therapist is faced with the task of acquiring this sensitivity or with the danger of losing this information. George Bernard Shaw is reputed to have said that England and the United States are two nations separated by a common language. Such a barrier all too often obtains in cross-cultural psychotherapy.

This leaves the client. Therapy, even on its home grounds, requires the client's adaptation to the rules which the therapist explicitly knows, but only partially and incompletely reveals. This uncertainty about the therapy's *modus operandi* is, according to Strupp (1973b), one of its essential features. One may or may not agree with that. In therapy across culture lines, in any case, this ambiguity is magnified. The client has to come to grips with, and tolerate, this ambiguity; and must be prepared for the process of discovery of a new and different kind of human interaction and relationship that therapy entails. Some, but not all, candidates for this experience undertake the journey. They probably possess to a greater extent than their peers the ability to deal with the complex and the unexpected.

It would be a grave mistake to do psychotherapy in the same way with all the people designated Black, Mexican, or American Indian. Yet, the knowledge of the culture of one's clients provides the therapist with an entree and/or point of departure. The therapist's experience with a cultural group or the information on it in the relevant professional literature serve as sources of hypothesis, to be verified, discarded, and modified on the basis of information acquired in the course of psychotherapy.

Culture-Contact Situations

The fourth major concern of cross-cultural psychotherapy involves those situations in which culture is at least a part of the problem. A major share of the literature in this field is devoted to the maladaptation and stress of the culture contact situation. The problems of people removed from their cultural moorings—through migration, sojourn, involuntary displacement —occupy a great many culturally-oriented mental health professionals (Alexander, Klein, Miller, & Workneh, in press; Pedersen, Lonner, & Draguns, 1976; Taft, 1977) as does the phenomenon of culture shock. A considerable amount of information has come into being on how to help people who are casualties of intercultural mobility—distraught college students, confused immigrants, traumatized expellees and refugees, discouraged and dissatisfied Peace Corps volunteers. Attempts have been made to sketch a composite portrait of an individual who is least or most likely to succumb to this kind of stress (Pinter, 1969). Similarly, characteristics of host environments have been scrutinized to identify those features which render such an environment particularly stressful or unusually stress-free for newcomers (Taft, 1977). And, most important, a sizable literature has come into being on psychotherapy and counseling with individuals transplanted to a new cultural setting (Alexander et al., in press; Szapocznik, Scopetta, Aronalde & Kurtines, 1978; David, 1976). This body of writing provides practically relevant information for the professional involved in extending services to immigrants, sojourners, or returnees from intensive cross–cultural encounters.

Therapy and its Cultural Milieu

The fifth preoccupation of the culture and psychotherapy literature concerns the relationship between a culture and its therapeutic services. We have already skirted this problem under a different heading. What features of a culture are reflected in its therapeutic services? What kinds of models are implicitly emulated in the conduct of psychotherapy? In this area, we can only rely upon speculation. While the area of investigation is an important one, obstacles in the path of objective and systematic investigation of these variables are prodigious and major. Once again, one can only point to statements placing psychotherapy in its respective cultural context (Draguns, 1975; Neki, 1973; Wittkower & Warnes, 1974) and relating it to the needs, expectations, models, and opportunities experienced in that culture.

A fascinating issue concerns the generic relationship between psychotherapy and the cultural milieu in which it is practiced. Draguns (1975) speculated on a continuity model of such a relationship; simple cultures would be characterized by direct and straightforward modes of therapeutic intervention and complex, hierarchically organized cultures, by elaborate ritualized techniques. Tseng and Hsu (1979) recently articulated a different possibility: that of a compensatory relationship between cultural features and the characteristics of therapeutic intervention. Thus, in highly controlled and overregulated environments, psychotherapy may provide an avenue of release for feelings and emotions, a safety valve. By contrast, in underregulated or perhaps anomic settings, psychotherapy would be likely to emphasize external and social control, at the expense of self-expression. These two formulations open the possibility for testing differential hypotheses, a task that, as yet, has not been tackled.

What Is and Is Not Psychotherapy?

I have saved the major question to the end: What are the limits of psychotherapy as revealed by its multitudinous patterns of practice in a wide variety of cultures. For psychotherapy—and counseling—to be meaningful concepts, they should be differentiated from nonpsychotherapy and noncounseling. Two axes of differentiation can be proposed: psychotherapy (and counseling) as distinguished from other kinds of therapy and helpful services, e.g. noninterpersonal, somatic, and psychotherapy vs. antitherapy, to encompass, for lack of a better term, everything that is nontherapeutic. In this connection, does everything that is tried by way of social and verbal influence in a variety of cultures produce beneficial and therapeutic results? In principle and on a rational basis, one would be inclined to answer that question in the negative. Yet, as I have pointed out elsewhere (Draguns, 1975), I have seen only a minimum of careful, well documented accounts of therapy failures in other cultural settings. (See Claver, 1976, for a few brief illustrations of failures of indigenous therapeutic intervention on the Ivory Coast.) By contrast, we have heard a great deal about therapeutic successes by a wide variety of techniques of intervention. Does everything work, then, with at least some kinds of people? If it does not, what are the limits of therapeutic effects and counseling influence?

To elaborate on this problem, few contemporary American psychotherapists of whatever theoretical persuasion would disagree with these two statements: A therapist should not induce guilt in a client ("You should feel guilty about it") and he or she should not suppress a client's communications ("You should not talk about this"). Nonjudgmental attitude of the therapist and spontaneity on the part of the client are deeply ingrained and widely shared features of the therapy process. Yet, the two indigenously developed therapies of Japan, Naikan and Morita, are based on guilt induction and control and suppression of communication respectively. In the Naikan system, the client is admonished to think of all the ways in which he has wronged his mother (Tanaka-Matsumi, 1979) and, in the course of Morita therapy, what the client may say and when and how is elaborately restricted and ritualized (Reynolds, 1976). The contrast between Western expectations and Japanese therapy is stark. It is not surprising that, in Western observers, sophisticated in their understanding of therapeutic experience but new to the culture, the first confrontation with these techniques produces on occasion a kind of culture shock. My suspicion is that this reaction is more often experienced than documented. Here, in any case, is an excerpt from the reaction of a recent sophisticated and sympathetic Western psychiatric visitor: "Upon a European observer, Morita and Naikan therapies produce a highly unsettling effect. . . .In a Morita clinic, one has the feeling of observing people in monastic isolation; there is little to remind one of a medical or medical–psychological therapeutic institution. The atmosphere appears somber, paralyzing, almost ghostlike. . ." [Schepank, 1978, p. 265][3]

For all of the unusual nature of these trappings, documentation on Morita therapy indicates that this therapy works in a substantial proportion of cases on its home grounds. Does its effectiveness broaden our range of understanding of what is effective and permissible in psychotherapy? However, first let us address ourselves to the historical development of cross-cultural therapy.

HISTORY OF CROSS-CULTURAL PSYCHOTHERAPY AND COUNSELING

Since we are dealing not with one field but many, it is not easy to provide a historical overview. But this is not the only difficulty that must be confronted. Because the various points of contact between culture and psychotherapy arose rather inconspicuously, we lack obvious and clearcut historical landmarks. What follows, then, is, at best, a historical sketch; it should be replaced by a more definitive effort based on historical scholarship which I do not possess.

---

[3]Translated from German by the author.

Indigenous Psychotherapy

The origins of cultural orientation in psychotherapy and counseling can be traced to two kinds of culture contact situation: on the one hand, the anthropological and ethnographic study of remote, different and "primitive" cultures; and, on the other hand, the palpable, day-to-day experience of cultural variation in the modern pluralistic and complex Western societies, such as that of the United States. The origins of the first anthropological accounts of native healing go back to the nineteenth century; these are not necessarily limited to, nor focused upon, psychic healing as personal problem solving, although they include references to psychological problems and difficulties. What is noteworthy about these early accounts is that they are presented as ethnographic curiosities; their relevance, if any, to the understanding of the generic personal influence or personality or behavior-change process is certainly not in focus. It remained for the post-World War II generation of culturally-oriented psychiatrists—such as Kiev (1964) and Prince (1976)—to take the operations of native specialists seriously and to document them as instances of effective psychotherapy in different cultural milieus. As Torrey (1972b) more recently put it, we have something to learn from the witchdoctors; what we as modern counselors and psychotherapists could learn from them is to separate the effective ingredients from the incidental trappings in our own implementation of therapeutic services. This effort has culminated, at Torrey's (1972a) hands, in the whimsical and engaging formulation of therapeutic universals. Their details are recapitulated elsewhere in this chapter and are, in any case, widely quoted. While other experts on indigenous psychotherapy would come up with somewhat different lists (e.g. Prince, 1976, 1980 in press), they would not argue with the efforts toward establishing what is universal and what is culture-specific in psychotherapy.

Meanwhile, watching exotic therapists at work spawned a new issue and even a controversy that revolved around the psychological status of indigenous therapists. Were the shamans and witchdoctors, with their often dramatic access to altered states of consciousness, the madmen of their respective cultures who had found a socially useful niche? The idea was an attractive one from the point of view of radical cultural relativism and perhaps also, paradoxically, from that of colonialism. At this point, there is no need to recapitulate the vicissitudes of this notion; in light of current data, it is both empirically and conceptually untenable (see Boyer, Klopfer, Brawer, & Kawai, 1964; Fabrega & Silver, 1973). In this volume, Dinges, Trimble, Manson, and Pasquale carefully document and trace the origin, flowering, and demise of the "crazy shaman" notion, replaced on the current scene not only by curiosity and fascination with the indigenous healers' ministrations, but often with the willingness to integrate their practices and skills in modern mental health delivery of services.

Psychotherapy in Pluralistic Cultures

The second interface between culture and counseling and psychotherapy occurred under our very eyes and, yet, took place inconspicuously. Probably, for as long as psychotherapy and counseling have been practiced, these services have been delivered at least in some instances across culture lines. Freud's (1953) treatment of the wolf-man, elaborated upon elsewhere in this chapter, comes to mind in this connection. More relevant to the explicit recognition of cultural factors in the modern pluralistic American microcosm are a number of more recent American reports. Erikson (1950), in his classical contribution, also drew upon therapeutic and quasi-therapeutic situations beyond the mainstream of American culture. Seward (1956) illustrated her work on culture and personality with case studies of psychotherapy of Americans of a variety of cultural backgrounds. Abel (1956) addressed herself to the problem of the role of cultural factors among the American clientele in psychotherapy. Devereux (1951, 1953) ventured beyond the usual settings in which psychotherapy was conducted in order to undertake, and to report in detail, psychoanalytically-oriented psychotherapy with a "Plains Indian," not further identified in terms of nation or tribe in order to protect his privacy. All of these pioneering contributions have extended verbal psychotherapy to new groups of clients, demonstrated its effectiveness on the case level with new populations, and illustrated the serendipitous "fallout" of psychotherapy as an avenue of learning about the personal experience of another culture. On the current scene, there are approaches even more venturesome, involving not only the extension but the adaptation of the therapy technique and experience. These are discussed elsewhere in the chapter.

Trends in Counseling

Less conspicuously, a similar kind of progression has occurred in counseling. Wrenn's (1962) early paper sensitized counselors to the problem of cultural encapsulation and warned against the imposition of culturally alien goals, values, and practices upon counselees across cultural lines. The road traversed since then has been marked by a number of developments. One is struck, for one, by the large and increasing share of articles in counseling periodicals that deal with the issue of culture, either through research or the consideration of practical service delivery problems. Another development is the appearance of several books addressed to the issue of counseling across a cultural gulf (Atkinson, Morten, & Sue, 1979; Pedersen, Lonner, & Draguns, 1976; Walz & Benjamin, 1978). In contrast to cross-cultural psychotherapy, counseling across cultures has seen the development and growth of a modest amount of systematic, explicitly designed research. All of these developments can be expected to continue, if not necessarily to multiply.

From the Periphery toward the Center: The Relevance of Culture in Counseling and Psychotherapy

For a long time, the developments just recapitulated remained somewhere on the periphery of awareness of the majority of specialists in counseling and psychotherapy. Exporting psychotherapeutic and related services to new locations and populations and importing them from exotic cultures and remote sites were concerns for a small band of pioneers, barely noted by their colleagues at large. With the growth of cultural awareness and self-consciousness, the development of basic cross-cultural disciplines, and the efforts by a number of disadvantaged minorities to achieve equality of opportunity and status, this situation experienced a dramatic change, at least in the United States in the sixties and the seventies. Concurrent with these trends, the realization gained ascendancy that the delivery of psychotherapeutic and counseling services across a cultural gulf is much more frequent than had been generally thought. Pedersen (in press) has taken the position that, at least in the multicultural setting of the United States, crossing such a cultural gulf in the mental health field is the rule rather than the exception. Extending the concept of culture, Pedersen has maintained that the cultures of the counselor and of the counselee may be expected to differ, perhaps slightly, yet perceptibly, in most counseling encounters.

These developments have sparked the recommendations of the Vail Conference on Clinical Psychology, sponsored by the American Psychological Association (Korman, 1974). The knowledge of the cultures of one's clientele has been elevated to an ethical imperative. Henceforth, doing therapy or counseling without cultural sensitivity, knowledge, or awareness is not just problematic, it has been declared unethical. The implication of these recommendations is that the knowledge on therapy and culture has ceased being an esoteric field; instead, it has become a matter of direct and practical concern for the vast majority of clinical—and, by implication, counseling—psychologists in the pluralistic culture of the United States.

FINDINGS AND PROBLEMS: A BRIEF
AND SELECTIVE SURVEY

The major varieties of work on cross-cultural psychotherapy have, I believe, by now been identified and their progression has been sketched through time. What remains to be done is to take stock of the present state of knowledge in all of these areas of endeavor. Cross-cultural psychotherapy, as has been seen, is an extremely wide-ranging field encompassing the ministrations of native healers ("Witchdoctors") and of modern psychotherapists, applied to people around the world and across the block. Despite this heterogeneity, I will endeavor to identify general problems and principles which characterize this entire area.

From Speculation to Evidence

First and foremost, this is a field in which the disproportion of writings to findings is high. The problems of doing psychotherapy and counseling research across cultural lines are forbidding. It is, therefore, not surprising that little research has been done. In particular, our knowledge on the efficacy of various therapeutic interventions in non-Western cultures rests on descriptive, qualitative observations on the case level. We are, in this area, still at a prequantification, premethodological stage. Much has been said about variations in psychotherapy around the world constituting a laboratory of nature. If so, this laboratory remains underutilized. Specifically, four kinds of information are needed: (1) Intracultural data on the effects and consequences of various indigenous therapy techniques. This would involve the application of research designs developed in investigating the effects of therapy in this country and elsewhere and applying them outside of our cultural tradition. A start has been made in investigating the efficacy of Morita-therapy (Miura & Usa, 1970; Reynolds, 1976) and Naikan (Tanaka-Matsumi, 1979) in Japan, two procedures indigenous to their culture. yet developed and practiced by modern mental health professionals. Jilek-Aal (1978) has noted the effectiveness of the Salish Indian spirit dance in promoting therapeutic change in alcoholics and other patients of that cultural group. It induces regression through an altered state of consciousness, promotes the experience of death and rebirth, and provides the participant with a new identity reoriented toward the ideal of the Salish culture. The rationale and the procedure appear to be reminiscent of the fixed-role therapy of George Kelly (1955), except for the greater reliance on affective and regressive processes, and on altered states of consciousness. (2) Cross–cultural comparisons of effectiveness of various techniques of psychotherapy, varying and, in the ideal case, counterbalancing both culture

and psychotherapeutic technique. (3) Comparing the effectiveness of indigenous and extraneous psychotherapies in a given setting. I am aware of
the problems of equating the client populations here, since the use of traditional vs. modern approaches to therapy would come about as a result of
self-selection. Nonetheless, at least approximations of such a comparison
could still be attempted and executed. (4) Since native components of psychotherapy are increasingly being utilized, from Lambo's (1962; Erinosho,
1976) village model to the use of traditional healers within the Hispanic
populations of North American cities (Ruiz & Langrod, 1976), the effect of
using these indigenous mental health specialists upon outcome should be
investigated. Does the addition of healers of one's own cultural tradition
result in the enhancement of effectiveness of mental health services? Including this condition in a conventional outcome research design should
enable one to answer this question.

Active Ingredients of Psychotherapy and Counseling

Various authors have come up with distinct if overlapping lists of active
ingredients in psychotherapy on the basis of cross-cultural evidence. Torrey's (1972b) list is well known: naming and explaining the disorder, gratify-
ing the need for acceptance and warmth, exercising status and prestige,
communicating with the client, and conveying one's understanding.
Torrey's list, then, is dominated by nonspecific ingredients. What therapists
of diverse orientations and cultures share is the ability to generate perceptions of competence and concern in their clients. The therapist is on top of
the situation and is interested in the client. More daringly and generally,
Prince (1976, 1980) subsumes all psychotherapy anywhere under the
heading of mobilization of endogenous resources. The therapist's role,
regardless of technique, is catalytic. He enables the client to make use of his
or her existing assets and strengths. How the therapist accomplishes this
objective is a matter of cultural shaping. To judge from Prince's (1980) accumulated evidence, non-Western cultures have relied to a greater extent
than the West upon the induction of altered states of consciousness to bring
about these catalytic effects. This formulation ties in with Higginbotham's
(1977) recent emphasis upon expectations as a major factor in cross-cultural, as well as conventional intracultural therapeutic intervention (Goldstein, 1962). The question that remains to be answered is: what techniques
effectively satisfy the expectations for help aroused in different cultures?
Empirically, the descriptive information assembled on psychotherapy
around the world provides a part of the answer: the range of such techniques is wide. What we lack, at this point, is a more explicit, systematic,
and specific understanding of what techniques fulfill what expectations on

the basis of what kinds of culturally-mediated learning.

Outside of the cultural frame of reference, Mendel (1972) endeavored to formulate a more complex list of universals that cut across the peculiarities of psychotherapeautic practice of diverse orientations and lands. On the positive side, all psychotherapy involves hope, learning, relationship, and a here-and-now encounter. Negatively, psychotherapy inescapably fosters dependency, disorganization, passivity, and nonspontaneity. In terms of concrete operations, the universals in psychotherapy include confrontation, exploration of the past, exploring of new alternative behaviors, and trying them out in practice. Mendel's list is both more detailed and more concrete than Torrey's and Prince's cross-culturally inspired formulations. It is also presented on a different level from these two contributors' proposals. While Torrey and Prince are addressing themselves to the issue of what matters in psychotherapy, Mendel is principally concerned with the problem of what happens in psychotherapy. It is interesting and worthwhile to turn the tables; the formulations by Torrey and Prince were designed to bring cross-cultural therapeutic experience to bear upon the practice of psychotherapy on home grounds. Mendel's proposal might be tested for its actual universality by examining it in light of the cross-cultural descriptive evidence on psychotherapy.

What research on cultural variations of psychotherapy exists pertains, with but few exceptions, to cultural variations in this country. Moreover, it is lopsidedly weighted down toward the counseling end of the continuum of helpful interpersonal services. Even so, research on cultural, ethnic, and racial variations in the counseling and therapy practice lags much behind the amount of research effort expanded on the role of socioeconomic class in psychotherapeutic services (see Larion, 1973, 1974; for recent reviews). Is this a reflection of an implicit judgment by American psychotherapy researchers that, in the pluralistic American universe, class matters more than ethnicity in the response to, and utilization of, therapeutic resources? Abramowitz and Dokecki's (1977) review, based on analogue studies, seems to corroborate this impression; in the appraisal of individuals in the mental health setting at this time, in the United States, class lines exercise a greater effect upon the interviewer than do race and sex. But the basis for these conclusions remains restricted in time and in format. A more thorough research effort on the effects of ethnicity, race, minority status, and socioeconomic class, all of these variables being interrelated, is necessary in order to resolve this issue.

Similar Countries, Different Therapies: Unexplored Area of Research

What is lacking, at this time, is a substantial body of data on psychotherapeutic response across national lines in comparable and interrelated countries. Several observers (Sanua, 1966; Wittkower & Warnes, 1974) have remarked on the different styles of delivery and different rates of utilization of psychotherapeutic services in a number of related European and American nations. Moreover, statements have been made on the relationship of these impressionistic differences to the dominant values and the official ideologies of the countries in question (Wittkower & Warnes, 1974). But hard data on this problem are just not available. Nonetheless, it is precisely in the range of moderate and mild differences that definitive conclusions on the relationship of culture to therapeutic service delivery could be obtained. To expand on this notion, the parallel between the prevalence of authoritarian-totalitarian political regimes and the deemphasis of explorational, open-ended, insight-oriented therapy has repeatedly been noted in Germany, Japan, and the Soviet Union. Two of these countries have experienced an abrupt change in their political orientation, with a considerable cultural change in its wake. Have changes in the nature of psychotherapeutic services kept pace with these political and cultural transformations? Impressionistic data would suggest that this is indeed so, at least in part, but more systematic and objective information on this issue remains to be provided.

Within the United States, suggestions have been made (e.g. Albee, 1977) that the goals and the ethos of psychotherapy have been transformed as the values in the larger society have changed. The typical psychotherapy patient in Freud's day was a self-abnegating, repressed hysteric; at this time, he or she may have been replaced by a self-indulgent, yet lonely and alienated, narcissistic character (see Lasch, 1979).

Between the pluralistic microcosm of United States society and the exotic therapeutic practices of archaic small-scale cultures or of remote non-Western nations, there is a gap in our knowledge of the nexus which ties psychotherapy and culture. On the basis of writings in the available literature, it is more difficult to form an impression of psychotherapy in India or Japan than in the Netherlands or Switzerland.

Another challenge, as yet not systematically met, is the opportunity that the experience and investigation of cross-cultural psychotherapy affords for the study of subjective culture (Triandis, 1972). As pointed out elsewhere, (Draguns, in press), the observation of psychotherapy experiences provides an unusual, perhaps unique, chance to glimpse the subjective world of the members of another culture. One is reminded in this connection of the central role that material gleaned in psychotherapy played in the development and formulation of Western personality theories. The structure and content of the subjective world of individuals from another culture, eventually to be divided into that which is cultural and that which is personal, may be destined to play a similar role in shedding light on the culture within the person—the pattern of unspoken rules and implicit relationships which members of a culture share and harbor within themselves. This would constitute the "fallout" from cross-cultural psychotherapy in a variety of forms, the fortuitous basic-knowledge bonus from an essentially applied and clinical activity.

TWO UNIVERSAL AXES FOR CLASSIFYING CROSS-CULTURAL PSYCHOTHERAPY AND COUNSELING

Elsewhere (Draguns, in press) I observed that cross-cultural application of therapeutic services could be placed and evaluated on two axes: the emic-etic (Berry, 1969; Price-Williams, 1973) and the autoplastic-alloplastic (Vexliard, 1967).

Emic-Etic

On the former continuum, the descriptions of indigenous psychotherapy and the acceptance of claims of its effectiveness fall toward the emic end. Psychotherapy is embedded in its cultural context and is not extricated from it in the service of any kind of general or universal principles. At the etic extreme, there is the unspoken assumption that therapy as practiced in the West is universally applicable, albeit with some nonessential modifications. Few of the current observers of the scene of cross-cultural psychotherapy would hold these two extreme positions in their undiluted form. Many would gravitate, however, toward one of these two poles. The challenge to the practitioner as he ventures beyond his cultural milieu is how to strike the balance between the universal and the culturally specific, and how to switch from one frame of reference to the other, or how to combine the two. The field of counseling and psychotherapeutic services for the sojourners, especially the students, and for the cultural and ethnic minorities has been traditionally slanted toward the etic end of the continuum. The effect of the development of a body of writings, by therapists and counselors belonging to these minorities and endeavoring to develop a culturally fitting mode of delivering these services, has been to redress the balance in the emic direction. As D. Sue (1977) points, out, counseling services geared to a culturally distinct group have to be appropriate in process and in goals to be acceptable and effective. On the worldwide arena, Higginbotham's (1979c) development of an Ethno–Therapy and Culture Accommodation Scale, the results of which are taken into account before developing and initiating services, is the expression of a parallel trend. My prediction is that, in the years to come, we will hear a great deal more about these and similar developments, all of them intended to diversify psychotherapy and to make it more flexible. Ultimately, however, these steps in the emic direction raise the issue of the universals in psychotherapy on the plane of concepts, techniques, goals, and values. It is then that, once again, we will need to swing in the etic direction, but on a firmer, more solid basis, insured against the pitfall of mistaking our cultural base for the essentials of human culture.

Autoplastic-Alloplastic

Similar considerations pertain to the alloplastic-autoplastic axis. All of us respond to stimuli and situations by either changing ourselves (autoplastically) or the environment (alloplastically) and by combining these two operations in various proportions. To what extent are psychotherapy and counseling across cultures oriented to changing the individual as opposed to having him or her change the environment? Again, psychotherapy with international students, in particular, was characterized in the past by facilitating the process of accommodation to, and acceptance of, the host's culture norms. The possibility of extending the individual's "degrees of freedom"—his or her scope of choices—in the service of actively changing the environment was neglected and underemphasized. Recent developments (e.g. Alexander et al., in press) are designed to reverse this imbalance. Kitano and Matsushima (in press) have suggested that counseling traditionally has been directed at the individually, socially, and culturally deviant. Its implicit goal has historically been to bring about a greater degree of conformity to the norms of the dominant majority group. In the case of members of minority groups, the contemporary counselor or therapist faces a choice: to prepare the client for changing obstacles in the environment, or to equip him or her for a greater degree of accommodation to the social structure in its current state. In a pluralistic society, the increase in the individual's options also involves choices on the extent and nature of one's relationships, reference groups, and identity, especially in relation to one's ethnic or cultural group. Across the world, the psychotherapeutic and counseling services of both the modern and the traditional variety may vary in the extent to which they foster integration into a group as opposed to self-development. The task of future research is to ascertain how these goals are associated with differences in the social context, technique, and relationship of psychotherapy and counseling experiences.

Psychotherapy and Counseling as Special Experiences

Finally, to an unknown degree, the effectiveness of psychotherapy and counseling hinges on the discontinuous, different, and special character of these experiences as compared with everyday life. Cultures vary in how they make psychotherapy different, but I believe that all of them operate with that end in mind. The differences and similarities of special state induction may well be compared across cultures in relation to both antecedents and effects.

CONCLUSIONS

The basic goal of all of these endeavors is to foster the understanding of psychotherapeutic phenomena on a worldwide basis; the practical objective is the development of optimal therapeutic services for all cultures. As a final utopian goal, complete understanding of the nature of psychotherapy in relation to culture should enable us to develop services optimally effective for a particular culture. Obviously, we are miles away from these lofty goals. But the pursuit of new and increased knowledge about psychotherapy and its worldwide variations is justified by the hope and expectation of, at one time or another, producing this humane and desirable result.

On the basis of the brief overview provided here, we have seen that it would be a mistake either to gloss over or to exaggerate the culturally distinct features of psychotherapy and counseling. Obviously, a few worldwide features are discernible no matter by whom or where these services may be provided. Yet the culture contributes more than just the external and visible trappings. It is deeply embedded in the subjective experience of therapy and pervades the give-and-take that characterizes the therapy process. Disentangling the culturally unique and the humanly universal threads of these encounters will help us understand psychotherapy and counseling, culture, and the behavior of people in distress.

REFERENCES

Abad, V., Ramos, J., & Boyce, E. A model for delivery of mental health services to Spanish-speaking minorities. *American Journal of Orthopsychiatry*, 1974, *44*, 584-595.

Abel, T. Cultural patterns as they affect psychotherapeutic procedures. *American Journal of Psychotherapy*, 1956, *10*, 728-740.

Abramowitz, C.V., & Dokecki, P.R. The politics of clinical judgment: Early empirical returns. *Psychological Bulletin*, 1977, *84*, 460-476.

Albee, G.W. The Protestant ethic, sex, and psychotherapy. *American Psychologist*, 1977, *32*, 150-161.

Alexander, A.A., Klein, M., Miller, M., & Workneh, F. Psychotherapy and the foreign student. In P. Pedersen, J.G. Draguns, W.J. Lonner, & J. Trimble (Eds.), *Counseling across cultures.* (2nd ed.) Honolulu: University Press of Hawaii, in press.

Atkinson, D.R., Maruyama, M., & Matsui, S. Effects of counselor race and counseling approach on Asian Americans' perceptions of counselor credibility and utility. *Journal of Counseling Psychology,* 1978, *25,* 76-83.

Atkinson, D.R., Morten, G., & Sue, D.W. *Counseling American minorities: A cross-cultural perspective.* Dubuque, Iowa: Wm. C. Brown, 1979.

Banks, G., Berenson, B., & Carkhuff, R. The effects of counselor race and training upon counseling process with Negro clients in initial interviews. *Journal of Clinical Psychology,* 1967, *23,* 70-72.

Berry, J.W. On cross-cultural comparability. *International Journal of Psychology,* 1969, *4,* 119-128.

Carkhuff, R.R., & Pierce, R. Differential effects of therapist race and social class upon patient depth of self-exploration in the initial clinical interview. *Journal of Consulting Psychology,* 1967, *31,* 632-634.

Cerny, J. Zu den psychopathologischen und philosophischen Fragen der japanischen Neurosen-Psychotherapie nach der Morita-Konzeption (System Zen). *Aktuelle Fragen der Psychiatrie und Neurologie,* 1967, *6,* 66-81.

Claver,B.-G. Problèmes de guerissage en Cote d'Ivoire, *Annales Médico-Psychologiques,* 1976, *134*(1), 23-30.

Collomb, H. *Psychiatrie san psychiatres.* Cairo: Études Medicales, 1972. (cited in Higginbotham, 1979a).

Collomb, H. L'avenir de la psychiatrie en Afrique. *Psychopathologie Africaine,* 1973, *9,* 343-370.

David, K.H. The use of social learning theory in preventing intercultural adjustment problems. In P. Pedersen, W.J. Lonner, & J.G. Draguns (Eds.), *Counseling across cultures.* Honolulu: University Press of Hawaii, 1976.

Devereux, G. Three technical problems in psychotherapy of Plains Indian patients. *American Journal of Psychotherapy,* 1951, *5,* 411-423.

Devereux, G. Cultural factors in psychoanalytic therapy. *Journal of the American Psychoanalytic Association,* 1953, *1*(4), 629-635.

Devereux, G. *Reality and the dream: Psychotherapy of a Plains Indian.* Garden City, NY: Doubleday, 1969.

Diop, B., Collignon, R., & Gueye, E. Presentation de l'étude concertée de l'O.M.S. sur les stratégies pour l'extension pes soins de santé mentale. *Psychopathologie Africaine,* 1976, *12,* 173-188.

Draguns, J.G. Resocialization into culture: The complexities of taking a worldwide view of psychotherapy. In R.W. Brislin, S. Bochner, & W.J. Lonner (Eds.), *Cross-cultural perspectives on learning.* New York: Sage Publications, 1975.

Draguns, J.G. Counseling across cultures: Common themes and distinct approaches. In P. Pedersen, J.G. Draguns, W.J. Lonner, & J. Trimble (Eds.), *Counseling across cultures.* (2nd ed.) Honolulu: University Press of Hawaii, in press.

Erikson, E.H. *Childhood and society.* New York: Norton, 1950.

Erinosho, O.A. Lambo's model of psychiatric care. *Psychopathologie Africaine,* 1976, *12,* 35-44

Fabrega, H. Jr., & Silver, D.B. *Illness and shamanistic curing in Zinacantan: An ethnomedical analysis.* Stanford, CA: Stanford University Press, 1973.

Frank, J.K. Therapeutic factors in psychotherapy. *American Journal of Psychotherapy,* 1971, *24,* 359-361.

Freud, S. From the history of an infantile neurosis. In J. Strachey (Ed.), *The standard edition of the complete psychological works of Sigmund Freud,* Vol. 17, London: Hogarth, 1953.

Gardiner, M. (Ed.) *The wolf-man by the wolf-man.* New York: Basic Books, 1971.

Garfield, S. Basic ingredients on common factors in psychotherapy *Journal of Consulting and Clinical Psychology,* 1973, *41,* 9-12.

Giordano, J., & Giordano, G.P. Ethnicity and community mental health. *Community Mental Health Review,* 1976, *1,* No. 3, 4-14, 15.

Goldstein, A.P. *Therapist-patient expectancies in psychotherapy.* New York: Pergamon Press, 1962.

Higginbotham, H.N. A conceptual model for the delivery of psychological services in non-Western settings. *Topics in Culture Learning,* 1976, *4,* 44-52.

Higginbotham, H.N. Culture and the role of client expectancy in psychotherapy. *Topics in Culture Learning,* 1977, *5,* 107-124.

Higginbotham, H.N. Culture and the delivery of psychological services in developing nations. *Transcultural Psychiatric Research Review,* 1979, *16,* 7-27.[a]

Higginbotham, H.N. Culture and mental health services in developing countries. In A. J. Marsella, T. Ciborowski, & R. Tharp (Eds.), *Perspectives in cross-cultural psychology.* New York: Academic Press, 1979.[b]

Higginbotham, H.N. Cultural accommodation in the delivery of mental health services in three Asian countries. Unpublished doctoral dissertation, University of Hawaii, 1979.[c]

Jilek-Aal, W. Native renaissance: The survival and revival of indigenous therapeutic ceremonials among North American Indians. *Transcultural Psychiatric Research Review,* 1978, *15,* 117-148.

Kelly, G. *The psychology of personal constructs.* New York: Norton, 1955.

Kiev, A. (Ed.) *Magic, faith, & healing.* Glencoe, Ill.: Free Press, 1964.

Kitano, H., & Matsushima, H. Counseling Japanese-Americans. In P. Pedersen, J. Draguns, W.J. Lonner, & J. Trimble, *Counseling across cultures.* Honolulu: University Press of Hawaii, in press.

Korman, M. National conference on levels and patterns of professional training in psychology: Major themes. *American Psychologist,* 1974, *29,* 441-449.

Lambo, T. The importance of cultural factors in psychiatric treatment. *Acta Psychiatrica Scandinavica,* 1962, *38,* 176-179.

Larion, R.P. Socioeconomic status and treatment approaches reconsidered. *Psychological Bulletin,* 1973, *79,* 263-270.

Larion, R.P. Patient and therapist variables in the treatment of low-income patients. *Psychological Bulletin,* 1974, *81,* 344-354.

Lasch, C. *The culture of narcissism: American life in an age of diminishing expectations.* New York: Norton, 1979.

Meadow, A. Client-centered therapy and the American ethos. *International Journal of Social Psychiatry,* 1964, *10,* 246-260.

Mendel, W.M. Comparative psychotherapy. *International Journal of Psychoanalytic Psychotherapy,* 1972, *1*(4), 117-126.

Miura, M., & Usa, S. A psychotherapy of neuroses: Morita therapy. *Psychologia,* 1970, *13,* 18-34.

Neki, J.S. Gurú-chepā relationship: The possibility of a therapeutic paradigm. *American Journal of Orthopsychiatry,* 1973, *43,* 755-766.

Nishihara, D.P. Culture, counseling, and ho'oponopono: An ancient model in a modern context. *Personnel and Guidance Journal,* 1978, *56,* 562-566.

Pande, S.K. The mystique of Western psychotherapy: An Eastern interpretation. *Journal of Nervous and Mental Disease,* 1968, *146,* 425-432.

Pedersen, P. The cultural inclusiveness of counseling. In P. Pedersen, J.G. Draguns, W.J. Lonner, & J. Trimble (Eds.), *Counseling across cultures.* 2nd ed.) Honolulu: University Press of Hawaii, in press.

Pedersen, P., Lonner, W.J., & Draguns, J.G. (Eds.) *Counseling across cultures.* Honolulu: University Press of Hawaii, 1976.

Peoples, U.Y., & Dell, D.M. Black and white student preferences for counselor roles. *Journal of Counseling Psychology,* 1975, *22,* 529-534.

Pintér, E. Wohlstandsflüchtlinge. Eine sozialpsychiatrische Studie an ungarischen Flüchtlingen in der Schweiz. *Bibliotheca Psychiatrica et Neurologica,* 1969, No. 138.

Price-Williams, D. Psychological experiment and anthropology: The problem of categories. *Ethos,* 1974, *2,* 95-114.

Prince, R.H. Psychotherapy as the manipulation of endogenous healing mechanisms: A transcultural survey. *Transcultural Psychiatric Research Review,* 1976, *13,* 115-134.

Prince, R.H. Variations in psychotherapeutic experience. In H.C. Triandis & J.G. Draguns (Eds.), *Handbook of cross-cultural psychology.* Vol. 6. *Psychopathology.* Boston: Allyn & Bacon, 1980.

Reynolds, D.K. *Morita psychotherapy.* Berkeley: University of California Press, 1976.

Rogers, C.R. The necessary and sufficient conditions of therapeutic personality change. *Journal of Consulting Psychology,* 1957, *21,* 95-103.

Ruiz, P., & Langrod, J. Psychiatrists and spiritual healers: Partners in community mental health. In J. Westermeyer (Ed.), *Anthropology and mental health: Setting a new course.* The Hague: Mouton, 1976.

Ruiz, R.A., & Padilla, A.M. Counseling Latinos. *Personnel and Guidance Journal,* 1977, *55,* 401-408.

Sanua, V.D. Sociocultural aspects of psychotherapy and treatment: A review of the literature. In L.E. Abt, & B.F. Riess (Eds.), *Progress in clinical psychology.* New York: Grune & Stratton, 1966.

Schepank, H. Östliche Psychotherapieformen und ihre soziokulturellen Determinanten. *Zeitschrift fur psychosomatische Medizin and Psychoanalyse,* 1978, *24,* 258-284.

Seward, G. *Psychotherapy and culture conflict.* New York: Ronald Press, 1956.

Smith, E.J. Counseling Black individuals: Some stereotypes. *Personnel and Guidance Journal,* 1977, *55,* 390-396.

Strupp, H.H. On the basic ingredients of psychotherapy. *Journal of Consulting and Clinical Psychology,* 1973, *41,* 1-8.[a]

Strupp, H.H. Toward a reformulation of the psychotherapeutic influence. *International Journal of Psychiatry,* 1973, *11,* 363-365. [b]

Sue, D.W. Counseling the culturally different: A conceptual analysis. *Personnel and Guidance Journal,* 1977, *55,* 422-425.

Sue, D.W., & Sue, S. Counseling Chinese-Americans. *Personnel and Guidance Journal,* 1972, *50,* 637-644.

Sue, S., & McKinney, H. Asian-Americans in the community mental health care system. *American Journal of Orthopsychiatry,* 1975, *45,* 111-118.

Sundberg, N.D. Toward research evaluating cross-cultural counseling. In P. Pedersen, J.G. Draguns, W.J. Lonner, & J. Trimble (Eds.), *Counseling across cultures.* (2nd ed.) Honolulu: University Press of Hawaii, in press.

Szapocznik, J., Scopetta, M.A., Aranalde, M.A., & Kurtines, W. Cuban value structure: Treatment implications. *Journal of Consulting and Clinical Psychology,* 1978, *46,* 961-970.

Taft, R. Coping with unfamiliar environments. In N. Warren (Ed.), *Studies of cross-cultural psychology.* Vol. 1. London: Academic Press, 1977.

Tanaka-Matsumi, J. Cultural factors and social influence techniques in Naikan therapy: A Japanese self-observation method. *Psychotherapy: Theory, Research, and Practice,* 1979, *16,* 385-390.

Torrey, E.F. *The mind game: Witchdoctors and psychiatrists.* New York: Emerson Hall, 1972. [a]

Torrey, E.F. What Western psychotherapists can learn from witchdoctors. *American Journal of Orthopsychiatry,* 1972, *42,* 69-76.[b]

Toulmin, S.E., & Janik, A. *Wittgenstein's Vienna.* New York: Simon & Schuster, 1973.

Triandis, H.C. *The analysis of subjective culture.* New York: Wiley, 1972.

Trimble, J. Value differentials in dealing with American Indian students in a counseling situation. In P. Pedersen, J.G. Draguns, W.J. Lonner, & J. Trimble (Eds.), *Counseling across cultures.* (2nd ed.) Honolulu: University Press of Hawaii, in press.

Tseng, W.S., & Hsu, J. Culture and psychotherapy. In A.J. Marsella, R.G. Tharp, & T.J. Ciborowski (Eds.), *Perspectives on cross-cultural psychology.* New York: Academic Press, 1979.

Vexliard, A. Autoplastie et alloplastie, *Psychologia,* 1967, *10,* 56-68.

Vontress, C.E. Cultural barriers in the counseling relationship. *Personal and Guidance Journal,* 1969, *48,* 11-17.

Vontress, C.E. Counseling Blacks. *Personnel and Guidance Journal,* 1970, *48,* 713-719.

Vontress, C.E. Racial and ethnic barriers in counseling. In P. Pedersen, J.G. Draguns, W.J. Lonner, & J. Trimble (Eds.), *Counseling across cultures.* (2nd ed.) Honolulu: University Press of Hawaii, in press.

Wachtel, P.L. *Psychoanalysis and behavior therapy: Toward an integration.* New York: Basic Books, 1977.

Walz, G.R., & Benjamin, L. (Eds.) *Transcultural counseling: Needs, programs and techniques.* New York: Human Sciences Press, 1978.

Weidman, H. Concepts as strategies for change. *Psychiatric Annals,* 1975, *5,* 312-314.

Wendt, I.Y. Eine japanische Zen-Klinik in Westen. *Schweizerische Zeitschrift für Psychologie and ihre Anwendungen,* 1967, *24,* 366-370.

Winthrob, R.M. & Harvey, Y.K. The self-awareness factor in intercultural psychotherapy: Some personal reflections. In P. Pedersen, J.G. Draguns, W.J. Lonner & J. Trimble (Eds.) *Counseling across cultures.* (2nd ed.) Honolulu: University Press of Hawaii, in press.

Wittkower, E.D., & Warnes, H. Cultural aspects of psychotherapy. *American Journal of Psychotherapy,* 1974, *28,* 566-573.

Wohl, J. Can we export Western psychotherapy to non-Western cultures? In P. Pedersen, J.G. Draguns, W.J. Lonner, & J. Trimble (Eds.), *Counseling across cultures. (2nd ed.) Honolulu: University Press of Hawaii, in press.*

Wrenn, G.C. The culturally encapsulated counselor. *Harvard Educational Review,* 1962, *32,* 444-449.

Chapter 2

Cross-Cultural Counseling and Psychotherapy: A Research Overview*

Norman D. Sundberg

HOW BEST TO COUNSEL A STRANGER?

About the old fable of the blind men and the elephant, I have often wondered how the poor elephant feels about all those different views of its identity. Its self-perceptions and ideas about its role in life must be quite confused after all those blind therapists have worked on it. In our tackling of this gigantic topic of close human relationships across potentially hundreds of cultural and ethnic variations, not to mention individual variations, I hope we can come out with some kind of notion of the beast that will be sufficiently articulated and heuristic to allow useful action and research.

My principal purpose for this chapter is to stimulate readers to develop conceptual frameworks which are both practical and researchable. I am assuming that most readers will be concerned with a fundamental question: How am I and others to work with those clients who are very different from ourselves? More specifically, my aims are to define the area of search and review research of relevance to cross-cultural counseling and therapy, to

*The following people have contributed significant ideas or have critically read earlier drafts of this chapter, and I am very appreciative of their help: Belkis Bengur, Anthony J. Marsella, and Lonnie Snowden.

present a set of plausible and potentially researchable hypotheses growing out of the literature, and to raise some more general questions and issues about cross-cultural research in this important area.

THE SCOPE OF SEARCH

Ideally, I would like to spread the broadest of nets in the literature search. I would like to look at all helping behavior including not only formal arrangements with professionally designated therapists and counselors but also at natural helping in families and neighborhoods, folk treatments and services, and self-help groups. I believe that the greatest help we usually could make in any culture would be to enhance the natural problem-solving and helping activities already "in place" (Sundberg, 1979). But this community concern must be reserved for another discussion, another time and place, and I will only touch on it briefly again at the end. There is enough to do trying to feel one's way around the strange counseling and therapy elephant.

The terms "counseling" and "psychotherapy" have blurred boundaries even within the Western societies in which they have been professionalized. In other times and other cultures, the functions to which they refer have been served by priests, medicine men, shamans, and a variety of other healers and spiritual guides. Draguns (1975) has said, in delimiting a review, pyschotherapy consists of:

> modes of intervention that (1) involve differential and asymmetrical roles of at least two individuals, one distressed and the other allegedly equipped with expertise to remove or alleviate such distress, (2) by means of techniques that are principally verbal, interpersonal and psychological in nature, and (3) with the general objectives of bringing about relief, reorganization of adaptive resources, and personality change [p. 276].

We need to note also that clients may enter therapy with a limited amount of personal distress; the distress may be largely on the part of others, such as parents or legal authorities. With that proviso, Draguns' definition applies well to psychotherapy, but more needs to be added as we broaden the field to include counseling. Counseling to me implies developmental, educative, and career assistance as well as personal therapy. I would include interactions in which the client may have relatively little personal distress but may be at a point in normal development and decision making where consulting with a mentor or wise counselor and obtaining more information is of practical value. Life planning is part of counseling. I have found the simple three-fold division of purposes for counseling of Gilmore (1973, p. 44) quite useful: choice (such as whether to go to college, file a divorce, or change jobs), change (such as the need to acquire new social skills, give up smoking, alter one's daily routine of activities, or face a terminal illness), and confusion reduction (e.g., get a realistic view of one's abilities and vocational possibilities, reorient one's life while coming off drug dependence, or gain perspective on responsibility for an alcoholic husband). So, in this chapter, I will be using a broad view of counseling and psychotherapy and will use the labels interchangably.

Cross-cultural therapy does not have a long history. Morrow (1975) indicates that one of the earliest reports on interracial therapy was *Black Hamlet* by Sachs (1947)—a successful psychoanalysis of an African medicine man. Some early writers were pessimistic, however, about interracial therapy because of the biases that would interfere with transference.

The term "cross-cultural" or "transcultural" may be used in many different ways. The core meaning for me is that the client and the therapist are from very different backgrounds. Culture (following Segall, 1979) is a convenient label for knowledge, skills, and attitudes that are learned and passed on from generation to generation. Cultural transmission also occurs in a physical environment in which places and times have acquired special meanings; cultures offer a person some stimuli rather than others—certain "props" for the stage, and some behavior supports. For instance, if we know that a man is from North India and we know that area, we can guess with a certain probability that he has dealt mostly with people from his caste, that he has had to contend with very crowded buses, that he has seen a variety of people at work as he walked through the town's narrow lanes, and that he has been expected to be obedient to his parents and at the proper time submit to their choices for his occupation and marriage partner. Culture implies a way of life, that is often so engrained within people that they are not conscious of assumptions they make about themselves and others. The term "cross-cultural," thus, signifies a condition or concern for understanding the interaction of people of different cultural backgrounds—a deliberate attention to differences and similarities, and the recognition of them in whatever tasks in which the two people are engaged. Very commonly, this concern comes down to values, beliefs, norms, and life style differences.

Here I am using "cross-cultural" to include "cross-ethnic" too, that is, to cover relationships between therapists and clients who are of a different racial or subcultural background, even though they may reside in the same country or city, such as a white counselor with a black client or vice-versa. Paul Pedersen (1978) broadens the idea of cross-cultural to include almost all differences: "If we consider the value perspectives of age, sex role, life-style, socioeconomic status and other special affiliations as cultural, then we may well conclude that all counseling is to some extent cross-cultural [p.

480]." Statistically speaking at the present time, however, most cross-cultural research reports and most common therapy situations probably consist of a white, middle class, English-speaking therapist (often male) working with a black or Hispanic client in the United States or Great Britain. Many of these white middle class people are asking "How do I do therapy with a person so different—a stranger?" More and more, counselors of black, Hispanic, native American, or foreign backgrounds are also working with clients who are "different" and similar cross-matches are occurring frequently around the globe as we become mobile and interdependent.

In the following survey of the literature, I have emphasized recent studies in which client and therapist are from different cultural or ethnic backgrounds. I have not systematically searched for monocultural studies in non-Western countries, though research on such practices as yoga or Morita therapy may have interesting implications, and I will mention them briefly when discussing therapeutic processes. My principal interest was to locate research studies that measure effectiveness of counseling or psychotherapy in cross-cultural situations. However, of necessity, I have included other studies of client and therapist variables related to cross-cultural helping to serve as a basis for hypothesis formation.

THE CURRENT STATE OF RESEARCH—A REVIEW

In brief forecast of what is to come, I can say that the production of true cross-cultural research on therapeutic effectiveness is nearly zero. That is, there are extremely few studies which carefully and systematically vary cultural aspects of client, counselor, or process variables in observing outcome criteria. This finding is true for both correlational and experimental studies.

There are, however, a rather sizable number of reviews and books which provide interesting resources for research hypotheses. These are experience-based accounts, anecdotes, speculations, and theory but have little systematic cross-cultural research on therapy itself. For instance, Jerome Frank's classic, *Persuasion and Healing* (1974), and E. Fuller Torrey's *The Mind Game: Witchdoctors and Psychiatrists* (1972) persuasively demonstrate common and special features of psychotherapy throughout the world. From time to time there have been useful reviews of publications. Some of them (e.g. Sanua, 1966) combine cultural, ethnic, and socioeconomic aspects of treatment. Socioeconomic and class differences are often included in such reviews since ethnic minority status is frequently associated with poverty in the United States and possibly in many other countries. Lorion (1978) specifically reviews treatment of low income people. Several reviews and discussions covering cultural aspects of counseling, psychotherapy, and mental health services are included in articles or, chapters by Draguns (1975), Harrison (1975), Kinzie (1978), Prince (1980), S. Sue (1977), and Tseng and Hsu (1979), and in the following books: *Counseling American Minorities* (Atkinson, Morten, & Sue, 1979), *Understanding & Counseling Ethnic Minorities* (Henderson, 1979), *Minority Issues in Mental Health* (Jones & Korchin, in press), *Transcultural Research in Mental Health* (Lebra, 1972), *Counseling Across Cultures* (Pedersen, Lonner, & Draguns, 1976; Pedersen, Draguns, Lonner, & Trimble, 1980), another *Minority Issues in Mental Health* (Smith, Burlew, Mosley, & Whitney, 1978), and *Transcultural Counseling* (Walz & Benjamin, 1978). *Annual Review* chapters on student counseling, psychotherapy, and community psychology usually have short sections related to work with minority and low-income people (e.g. Cowen, 1973; Gomes-Schwartz, Hadley, & Strupp, 1978; Kelly, Snowden, & Munoz,1977; Krumboltz, Becker-Haven, & Burnett, 1979; Layton, Sandeen, & Baker, 1971; Pepinsky & Meara, 1973; and Whitely, Burkhart, Harway-Herman, & Whiteley, 1975). Howard and Orlinsky (1972) have provided a particularly well organized, culturally oriented review of psychotherapy. There are also many reviews of cultural aspects of psychopathology (e.g. Dohrenwend & Dohrenwend, 1974; Draguns, 1973; King, 1978; Marsella, 1979; and Strauss, 1979); and Garfield and Bergin (1978) have several references to race and other culturally relevant variables in their comprehensive overview of research in psychotherapy and behavior change. Acosta (1979), Padilla, Ruiz, & Alvarez (1975), and Sue and Sue (1977) explore barriers to effective cross-cultural counseling. These reviews and overviews have aided in the location of the few significant studies that there are, and have served to stimulate the formulation of hypotheses to be mentioned later on.

In preparing for this review I have looked through the most likely research journals from 1975 through 1979. As part of the search, I read first the article titles; if there was any indication of attention to cultural variables I read the abstracts and often the whole article. In the last five years, the four APA journals most likely to have reports on counseling and therapy, namely, the *Journal of Abnormal Psychology,* the *Journal of Consulting and Clinical Psychology,* the *Journal of Counseling Psychology,* and *Professional Psychology,* showed in only one to three percent of the articles any indication of cultural or ethnic material. Some of these were not research articles, but reports of programs or reviews. Among the research reports, the vast majority were on assessment techniques, such as the Wechsler Intelligence Scale for Children (WISC) or Minnesota Multiphasic Personality Inventory (MMPI); others were cross-cultural correlational or group difference studies unrelated to counseling or therapy. The number sampling populations other than the American was miniscule. Among the U.S. minorities, about half of the articles used Black samples, about 20 percent Hispanics, and only a very small number Asian-American; in the nearly total sample of titles and abstracts I read for these five years of APA journals, none were about Native Americans, or Indians.

Other journals, such as the *International Journal of Psychology* and the *Journal of Cross-Cultural Psychology*, are heavily involved in research using cultural variables, but they almost never report studies of counseling or therapy. The two major sources in psychiatry, the *Transcultural Research Review* and the *International Journal of Social Psychiatry,* also have a high proportion of culturally related articles, but again very few reports on cross-cultural psychotherapy per se, and nearly all of these are anecdotal or impressionistic.

None of over 100 culture-related articles I inspected closely in the four APA journals and the four cross-cultural journals in psychology and psychiatry had a controlled evaluation of the relation of cultural variables to counseling or psychotherapeutic outcomes or process "in vivo." The closest any research came to actual therapy experimentation was the use of simulation or analog. Three of the few experimental studies are outlined in Table 2.1. The authors are to be congratulated that they, at least, did systematic research on ethnic concerns, but the field as a whole certainly cannot be proud of its work record at trying to understand cultural influences in counseling and psychotherapy. Even in these three studies, the variations in findings suggest that the role of ethnic and cultural differences is not clear. None of the studies indicate the degree to which there were clear cultural differences other than the superficial skin color labels. More complete and systematic research must look into the client's dialect, life style, group affiliations, and reports of identification with minority culture, as well as the therapist's background and experience in cross-cultural therapy.

SELECTED CULTURAL FINDINGS OF RELEVANCE TO FUTURE RESEARCH

Clearly, we have little information from direct tests of cultural influences on therapy process and outcome. However, the wider cross-cultural research literature (some of it anecdotal and speculative) is available to furnish possible methods and contextual information and to suggest hypotheses. In this section, findings reported in previous reviews of research and recent studies will be covered under the following headings: Client/patient variables; counselor/therapist variables; client/therapist

Table 2.1

Examples of Recent Experimental Studies of Cross-Cultural Counseling

Reference	Subjects	Interviewers	Procedures	Measures of Effects	Significant Cultural Findings
Woods & Zimmer (1976)	12 black & 12 white female undergraduates	2 black and 2 white male counseling graduate students	Analog. Selective reinforcements for (1) positive, or (2) negative self-reference, or (3) yoked noncontingent comments.	Increase in positive or negative self-reference over baseline.	No effects of race on conditionability.
Merluzzi & Merluzzi (1978)	42 white undergraduates	2 black and 2 white female counseling graduate students	Analog. Interviewer roles varied for being (1) experts or (2) referents who were understanding and self-disclosing. Subjects randomly assigned by race, counselor roles, and internal vs. external locus of control.	Pre and post testing on attitudes toward procrastination, career planning; also cognitive-affective inventory.	Whites perceived as more expert. White referent role related to negative attitude toward procrastination on follow-up.
Casciani (1978)	48 white undergraduate volunteers	12 graduate students and mental health workers, equally male-female and black-white.	Simulation. Subjects observed video tape of counselor-model reading prepared script and responded to model's requests for 5 positive and 5 negative topics. Random assignment to conditions.	Responses coded for depth of self-disclosure, speech duration, and self-reference. Also post-experimental questionnaire on interview.	Black models rated more likeable. In general, very few race differences. White students as willing to disclose to blacks as to whites. Several sex differences, including more disclosure to same sex.

34

similarities; role, process, and technique variables; outcome and context variables; and the general settings of psychotherapy. In each of these sections, the primary concern will be to report empirical research employing cultural or socio-cultural elements supplemented by more speculative accounts related to research potentialities.

Client/Patient Variables

The largest amount of culture-relevant research has to do with client/patient variables. These sort themselves out into several major categories. One area of findings that will permeate much of the following discussion is sheer demography of the clientele.

Client demographic characteristics In the United States and probably many other countries, psychotherapy is used mainly with middle and upper class segments of the population and somatic therapies with lower class and less educated sectors. Such findings from the classic Hollingshead and Redlich study (1958) have been confirmed by later research (Lorion, 1978). In general, psychotherapy is chosen for Schofield's (1964) YAVIS people (Youthful, Attractive, Verbal, Intelligent, and Successful) and not for what might be called the QUOID people (Quiet, Ugly, Old, Indigent, and Dissimilar culturally). Howard and Orlinsky (1972) point out, however, that the community mental health movement has given increasing attention to working class, lower class, and indigenous people. Gomes-Schwartz et al. (1978) have an encouraging conclusion from their review: "Many of the recent studies on the effects of social class (or related dimensions such as educational level or income) have failed to confirm what had become almost stereotyped notions about the lower class patient's intrinsic unsuitability for therapy. In four studies social class variables were not related to remaining in therapy [p. 439]."

A somewhat different phrasing of the demographic problem is the question of the probability that different cultural groups will use mental health services in general and in comparison with other helping modalities. A large number of people in the United States and in other countries seek what might be called psychological services from folk resources, often religious or quasi-religious. For instance, there is a resurgence of American Indian use of indigenous therapeutic ceremonials (Jilek-Aal, 1978). In extensive reviews, Prince (1976, 1980) urges therapists to study and use the self–healing processes that exist in the culture, particularly altered states of consciousness induced by the suffering person or in folk practices. In the United States, Acosta (1979) contends that *curandero* use is not a significant factor among urban Chicanos. However, a student of mine, Maria Beals, found through interviewing migrants and recently settled farm workers that more use of *curanderos* and more belief in witchcraft existed than Chicanos were willing to say directly to mental health workers; her study was informal and a much more complete survey of rural people needs to be made. Webster and Fretz (1978) found that Asian-American, black and white students ranked several helping sources similarly; family and friends came first but the college counseling service was high on the list. Flores (1978) and others have demonstrated that mental health center personnel and policies responsive to bicultural and bilingual needs can attract clients. Acosta (1979) provides an analysis of barriers to Mexican–American usage of service, such as language problems and stereotypes among both caregivers and caretakers, and suggests research. Other chapters in this book look more extensively at usage of mental health services by minorities.

Client psychopathology and presenting problems The literature on psychopathology of ethnic groups in the United States and other countries is too voluminous to cover here and much of it is not directly related to psychotherapeutic considerations; readers who are interested are referred to reviews mentioned earlier. There seems to be some controversy about the importance of race as a factor in pathology, at least in the United States. One reviewer, King (1978), concludes "The central consistent finding was that race alone could not account for the prevalence of mental illness and seems not to be the primary etiologic factor when trying to account for differences in the rates of psychopathology [p. 413]." King also comes out strongly for a universalistic point of view, saying "There is strong evidence to point to a basic unity of man across cultures which is reflected in common personality types, common basic forms of psychological disturbance [p. 419]." Another comprehensive review (Warheit, Holzer, & Arey, 1975) states that low socioeconomic status is the most powerful predictor of poor mental health conditions, though, of course, Blacks and Spanish-Americans are disproportionately represented among the poor. Another study (Dohrenwend, 1973) found major life changes, which are often related to physical and mental breakdown, occur more frequently among the poor and women as compared with others. Raskin, Crook, & Herman (1975) found remarkable similarities between Blacks and Whites in core symptoms of depression when groups were controlled for age and social class differences, although Blacks showed more negativism and introjection of anger.

In contrast to some of the above conclusions, many have found strong cultural differences in expression of disorder, especially when they study non-Western societies. Marsella, Kinzie, & Gordon (1973) and Tanaka-Matsumi and Marsella (1976) even found domestic ethnic differences;

somatic expression of depression is more common among Chinese-Americans than among Japanese-Americans or Caucasians in Hawaii. Cross-cultural study of mental disorders is confused by measurement problems, such as variations in words for states of mind or feeling. Some cultures have few, if any, words for depression or shame, and others have many. Marsella and his colleagues (Marsella, 1980; Marsella, Murray & Golden, 1974) discuss a number of these research problems and recommend further research. Boucher (1979) has an interesting review of research on emotion and culture.

In regard to college student counseling problems, several studies (Benson & Miller, 1966; Johnson, 1971; Westbrook et al., 1978) have looked at ethnic and cultural differences. In general, many problems international students report are similar to those of fellow American students, such as academic work and finances; language mastery is a special problem for those coming from non-European and non–English-speaking countries (but, then, the English language is often a problem for American students too). Johnson urges that foreign students be thought of as students first. Westbrook and his colleagues found that the ranking of student problems was the same for black and white students. These studies, however, are generally of a rather superficial kind and do not go beyond a questionnaire given to students in classrooms; the more subtle nuances of cultural aspects of problem orientation require more refined studies. Even questionnaires, however, may show special problems and differences among foreign students, including those having to do with climate, communication with Americans, discrimination, homesickness, depression, irritability, and tiredness. In general, it would seem that the variety of problems cross–cultural counselors are likely to encounter implies a strong need for generic skills; in a time when therapy training seems to be more and more specialized, thought needs to be given to its utility for work with other-culture clients.

Client expectations Another extremely important area that has received considerable research attention has been reviewed by Higginbotham (1977). A number of studies he surveys (e.g., Arkoff, Thayer & Elkind, 1966; Tan, 1967) show that Asian–American students in contrast with American students expect therapy to be directive, nurturant, practical, and advice-giving. They often see a serious stigma in going to psychiatric services, but will go more often to counseling centers. Families try to avoid "losing face" and hide problems from public view. Fukuhara (1973) finds these student characteristics true in Japan also. Peoples and Dell (1975) believe, on the basis of their limited data, that preference for counseling style may be more important than race differences; both white and black students preferred an active as compared with a passive role in counselors shown on video. This expectancy was again confirmed with Asian-Americans, who rated directive counselors as more credible and approachable (Atkinson et al., 1978). Aronson and Overall (1966) found that lower class people, as compared with middle class, were more oriented toward treatment that was medical, directive, supportive, and in which they were passive; however, Lorion (1978) found no significant socioeconomic differences in understanding the process of psychotherapy and argues that such discrepancies in the United States may be diminished by widespread television viewing. Higginbotham (1977) states: "In short, there appears to be scattered yet consistent empirical support for the contention that clients approach therapy with well-defined and individually diverse role expectations, therapist preferences, forms of support anticipated, types of advice sought, or type of medical care desired [p. 111]."

Client preferences for therapists A closely related area of research is client preferences for ethnic or racial background of counselors or therapists. Harrison (1975) and Higginbotham (1977) give reviews of this topic. Part of the question has to do with satisfaction with actual client-counselor similarity and matching; that topic will be postponed to a later section. Here we will look only at noninteractional statements of preferences themselves. Harrison (1975) concluded on the basis of his research review that "counselees tend to prefer counselors of the same race, particularly if they are black counselees [p. 131]." Blacks appear to talk more in the presence of blacks. Higginbotham is less certain, however, and points to a recent study (Acosta & Sheehan, 1976) which found, in contrast to earlier studies with Mexican-American students, that they had as high a regard for Anglo professionals as those coming from their own ethnic group, and had a favorable attitude toward psychological services. The preference issue is far from settled. Studies show conflicting results, some in favor of similar-race counselors (e.g., Thompson & Cimbolic, 1978, who studied student preferences) and some in the opposite direction (Gamboa, Tosi, & Riccio, 1976), who found white delinquent girls preferred a black counselor for discussing personal-social problems). In conclusion, it seems likely that race by itself may not be of importance for many Americans in approaching a counselor, but there are sure to be individual differences in preference and other factors have not been clarified by the research so far; the relative importance of the counselor's race, age, sex, etc., is likely to be highly susceptible to local reputation and even national mass media effects.

Client interests, values, world views, work orientation, and attitudes There are a host of client variables of self-definition relative to the environment which seem important for cross-cultural counseling or therapy. It is inappropriate here to review this vast area, but I will simply illustrate with a few studies and ideas. For instance, it may be of use to counselors to know that black male inner city, secondary school students, as compared with whites, prefer occupations in the artistic, health, and welfare fields (Sewell & Martin, 1976). Inner city and suburban ninth graders were contrasted in another study of occupational preferences (Shappell, Hall, & Tarrier, 1971); both seemed to have a fairly realistic picture of the world of work, but their work values were different. Inner city youths were concerned with concrete extrinsic rewards, such as location and physical environment and time constraints; suburban youths expressed values for some intrinsic rewards such as personal satisfaction and also some extrinsic rewards such as opportunities for promotion and making friends. Another study (Hager & Elton, 1971) of low income groups showed that white college students were more interested in the physical sciences and blacks more interested in the social sciences.

Korman, Greenhaus, & Badin (1977, p. 185) concluded from their review that work values, reactions to work experiences, and job satisfaction show few consistent racial differences. Yankelovich (1974) suggests that the American work ethic may be going through a cultural shift into the postindustrial era, and Albee (1977) calls ours a "self-indulgent society" likely to be supplanted by the more hard-working Chinese and Japanese. However, more up-to-date data on such trends need to be obtained before any fundamental shift in values can be concluded. The Fear of Success scale and attendant hypotheses have spawned much research, but the clearly posited male-female differences seem to be blurred, and there seem to be strong cultural influences interacting with acceptance of traditional sex roles (Korman et al., 1977); black militant women have high fear of success but romantically attached black women do not. The popular topic of self-disclosure has received little cross-cultural attention, but one study (Dukro, Dukro & Beal, 1976) suggests the expected relation with mental healthiness does not occur among blacks.

A study in Miami (Szapocznik, Scopetta, Aranalde, and Kurtines, 1978) demonstrated, using a values orientation scale based on the well known Kluckhohn-Strodtbeck work, that Cubans preferred hierarchical social relations, subjugation to nature, and present time, and tended not to endorse idealized humanistic values; American adolescents, in contrast, preferred individuality in relationships, mastery over nature, and future times, and they endorsed idealized humanistic values. The authors suggest the therapeutic importance of using concrete, obtainable objectives in the near future and structural family therapy which manipulates dysfunctional interaction patterns.

Cross-cultural studies also suggest strong differences in word association (e.g., Chartier & Sundberg, 1969; Shaffer, Sundberg, & Tyler, 1969; Tanaka-Matsumi & Marsella, 1976) and choice patterns for work and leisure (e.g. Tyler, Sundberg, Rohila, & Greene, 1968). Derald Sue (1978) sees two fundamental factors running through much of this concern for work and world view, namely, internal vs. external locus of control or power and internal vs. external locus of responsibility. He outlines ways in which people differing on these factors need to be treated in cross-cultural counseling. Berman (1979a) in a relevant study has shown that white counselors' diagnoses tend to be individualistic and blacks' views put more nearly equal blame or credit on the individual and society.

Client acculturation and alienation The degree of identification and integration with the majority culture would seem to be an important variable in direct counseling and therapy and in mental health program planning, especially for defining cultural similarities and differences that go beyond skin color and language. Torres-Matrullo (1974) found that Puerto Ricans with low acceptance and adjustment to the majority American culture were inclined toward higher depression and less self-confidence and sense of self-control. Burbach and Thompson (1971), studying college freshmen, found that blacks scored higher than others on total alienation; blacks were higher than whites on powerlessness and normlessness, and higher than Puerto Ricans on social isolation; the researchers concluded that black students felt less in control of their lives than others. (It would be interesting to see if there have been changes since the turbulent late 1960s and early 1970s.) Guthrie (1980) presents a thorough review of alienation as it relates to psychopathology in various cultures.

Generational differences and length of stay of immigrant families also are interesting. For instance, among Asian-Americans (Connor, 1975) and Mexican-Americans (Buriel, 1975; Knight & Kagan, 1977; Knight, Kagan, Nelson, & Gumbiner, 1978), children varying in generation of upbringing in the United States clearly differ from one another; the later generations increase in similarity to general American norms and behavior patterns. Rather sadly, this means that later generation Chicanos seem to be less cooperative than earlier ones and become more competitive like their Anglo compatriots. Szapocznik, Scopetta, & Kurtines, (in press) outline a model of acculturation and show that behavioral and value changes are linear functions of time spent in the host culture; they also find age and sex differences in acculturation. Major conflicts arise from the fact that younger family members, especially males, acculturate faster than older members of the family. Naditch and Morrissey (1976), using role stress hypotheses, conclude from a study of Cuban adolescent refugees that high rates of mental illness relate to ambiguity about evaluations of role performances, especially regarding dating and expressions of sexuality. An interesting informal report of acculturation problems for American baseball players in Japan is presented in a recent *Sports Illustrated*; Whiting (1979) shows the clash between the American orientation to individualism and the Japanese cultural norm of "wa"—which is concern for team play, unity, and obedience to the coach and manager. Of general interest and relevance to acculturation is the review by King (1978); he finds mixed research evidence for an association between modernization and mental health in developing countries. Similarly, Smither and Rodriquez-Giegling (1979) question the concept of marginality and find degree of modernity not correlated with anxiety among Indo-Chinese refugees. Marsella (1978a) provides an excellent review of the effects of modernization on individuals in traditional societies; he ends by raising the question about the future: Do not highly developed societies with impending scarcities have a lot to learn from more "traditional" and less developed societies which get along on less and live more simply?

Counselor/Therapist Variables:

Next to client cultural variables in counseling and therapy, counselor variables have received the most attention. Still there is a surprising lack of recognition that counselors do vary a great deal, and many studies use only two or three counselors in studies of particular procedures or ethnic differences; the ecology of therapeutic contacts is not being represented. The following coverage of recent articles and reviews will present highlights, sampling major variables of importance.

Demographic characteristics As Howard and Orlinsky (1972) point out in their review, the personal statistics of American therapists are at sharp variance with those of clients and patients. Some professional helpers are from the upper middle-class though the greatest number have originated in lower middle-class families. These reviewers state "they are indeed a socioeconomic elite, but an *achieved* elite whose cultural marginality and status mobility tend to create a relativistic rather than Establishment-oriented value perspective. This no doubt helps them to assist their patients who are also (though perhaps in more personal ways) culturally marginal people [p. 626]." There are also differences in demographic characteristics of different forms of preferred psychiatric treatment (organic vs. psychological). The therapists are predominantly male and white, and they tend to come from Protestant and Jewish backgrounds. It would be interesting to repeat the Henry, Sims, and Spray (1971) study, from which most of these findings come, to see if there have been shifts in the intervening decade or so.

Therapist prejudice, and culture-related attitudes Therapist and counselor *attitudes,* especially *prejudice,* would seem to be related to effectiveness in counseling. However, Harrison's review (1975) of two studies found no significant relation of prejudice and dogmatism with supervisor's ratings of effectiveness; another study showed that high-prejudiced white therapists saw black patients a fewer number of times than low-prejudiced white therapists. Bloombaum, Yamamoto, & Jones (1968) carried out structured interviews with 16 practicing therapists; their racial and cultural attitudes reflected the same order of preference for social distance as found in the general population though statements of stereotypes were subtle.

Studies of labeling and attribution (Kelly et al., 1977) often present therapists with the same materials attributed to people of different backgrounds; this procedure usually produces different assessment results, not only for non-white people but also for elderly, female, and politically active "clients." Sandler, Holmen, & Schopper (1978) found significant differences across counselor ratings of female welfare recipients rated to ethnicity; for instance, counselors saw Mexican-Americans as less competitive and more apologetic and docile than blacks or Anglos; however, the recipients' own self-ratings did not differ across ethnic groups. Sometimes (Merluzzi & Merluzzi, 1978), counselors overcompensate for minority status; this is suggested by the finding that white graduate student counselors rated black-labeled case summaries more positively than white-labeled ones. Similar research procedures are often used in studies of *clinical judgment.* For instance, Di Nardo (1975) found that graduate students rating staged interviews consistently gave higher pathology ratings to lower-class than middle-class labeled clients. In an extensive review entitled "The Politics of Clinical Judgment," Abramkowitz and Dokecki (1977) concluded that evaluative prejudice is more circumscribed than many critics of mental health professionals have claimed; analog studies of race, sex, and value attributions have generally yielded no results or only mildly supportive ones, and practitioners' political values seem not to moderate patient labeling significantly. The use of indigenous paraprofessionals and the increase in minority American therapists may have changed the picture of prejudice and attribution problems somewhat in recent years. However, we cannot be sure that same-background people will be free of prejudice against their co-ethnic and co-cultural clients.

Therapist knowledge of other cultures Though knowledge of dialect or other-culture language seems of obvious importance for the success of cross-cultural therapy, there seem to be no research studies on that topic.

The same criticism applies to nonverbal communication and use of the physical environment. Likewise, there apparently is no research on therapists' knowledge of the culture of clients. Banks (1975), among others, recommends that the therapist wishing to work with black clients should recognize the heterogeneity of black culture and should become actively involved in the educational, political, and cultural life of different kinds of blacks. He suggests visiting barbershops, colleges, churches, bars, and other hangouts of black people. Other suggestions might be to read novels and biographies and become acquainted with the art, drama, and music of the other culture.

Therapist intercultural skills Competence in therapy with other-cultural people certainly requires assessment and communication skills. Assessment is a broader concept than testing, and testing is too broad a topic to take up at this point; interested readers are referred to discussions such as those by Butcher and Garcia (1978), Irvine and Carroll (1979), Lonner (1976), Snowden and Todman (in press), and several of the general books on minority issues mentioned earlier. More direct counseling skills have been studied by Berman (1979 a and b); she used ratings of black and white graduate students' written responses to videotaped client vignettes. Her findings were that blacks tended to use more active expression skills and whites more attending skills, such as reflection of feeling. There were no significant sex differences. Pedersen (1978) identifies four cross-cultural counselor skills which might be related to research as well as used in his intriguing training program, namely articulating the culturally relevant problems, anticipating culture-related resistance, diminishing defensiveness, and promoting recovery skills.

Other therapist attitudes and miscellaneous characteristics Kinzie (1978), calling on his experience in Malaysia and elsewhere, argues in favor of the social aspects of the medical model in intercultural work; he sees the value of the assumption that no one is to be blamed for the misfortune and the authoritative relationship implied for helping; he notes that the "sick role" is confirmed in almost all cultures. Whether a psychologist or other mental health worker should use the attitudes implied by the medical model is open to question. Merluzzi, Merluzzi, and Kaul (1977) did an interesting analog study with black and white interviewers assuming an expert role or a referent role (a warm, interested, self-disclosing role). Using undergraduate ratings as the dependent variable, they found a statistical interaction between race and role with the black-expert and the white-referent interviewers being more influential. These findings suggest some complexity in the use of the medical (or expert) role. Studies mentioned earlier also indicate questions about acceptance of feeling-oriented approaches in different cultural groups; direct advice giving may be expected and appropriate in many situations. Sue and Sue (1977) note that counselors who believe in the value of insight and in emotional and verbal expressiveness will have trouble with many cultural groups, including Asian-Americans. They also note that culture-inappropriate concepts of what constitute mental illness and disturbance may interfere with counseling. Sue and Sue recount cultural differences in eye contact, use of personal space, and other interactional components that the counselor needs to be aware of. Torrey (1972) points out the importance throughout the world of therapist skill in labeling the patient's problem and Frank (1974) notes the value of creating hope and confidence in the success of therapy.

Derald Sue (1978) has listed five characteristics of culturally effective counselors: (1) self-knowledge, especially regarding one's assumptions about good and bad behavior; (2) awareness of generic counseling characteristics and their relation to culture and class; (3) understanding of sociopolitical forces affecting clients, especially racism and oppression; (4) ability to share world views of clients and not be culturally encapsulated; and (5) mastery of an eclectic variety of skills and theories, and ability to choose which are appropriate for a particular client. Many of these proposals come down to a description of the counselor as a broadly trained and experienced human being with a commitment and interest in a pluralistic society. Banks (1975) notes that the competence of minority therapists depends on a full understanding of one's cultural roots, self-identity, and the relations of these to one's own psychodynamics. Jones and Seagull (1977) also emphasize cultural and self-knowledge for white therapists working with black clients. Bengur (1979) interviewed 12 counselors and therapists of various backgrounds about their effective and ineffective cross-cultural experiences. In general, it seems that counselors need to go through a period of decentering their own cultures and overcoming stereotypes of other-culture clients; they become more highly differentiated in their thinking as they learn from their clients about the client's culture-related attitudes and problems. The result of this process also leads them to an appreciation of the common human problems underlying many cultures and, then, the counselor can find within himself or herself ways of empathizing with the client's situation.

Client-Therapist Similarities

There have been many studies of client preferences for therapists, as mentioned earlier. Here, we will consider actual similarity and its effects. The results are far from conclusive, as suggested in some of the findings reported in table 2.1., discussed earlier, and by several reviewers (Harrison, 1975; Higginbotham, 1977; Parloff, Waskow, & Wolf, 1978). Few of these studies have used actual patient or client populations, and they are often single-interview or analog studies; sometimes there are no control groups. The careful review by Parloff et al. (1978) concludes that there is not much definitive information about effects of cultural matching or mismatching. They note that sex and socioeconomic status differences are also important to consider in similarity studies, and that therapist attitudes would seem to be particularly important. This ability to communicate and empathize with a similar-background person may be particularly important for blacks in these times (Harrison, 1975). Gomes-Schwartz et al. (1978) also conclude that "data indicate that the treatment style. . .or the therapist's competence and comfort in dealing with racial or class differences between himself and his patient. . .might be important influences on outcome [p. 439]." Likewise, the client's comfort with a person of different background is important, and it is often necessary in psychotherapy to deal with feelings about racial and cultural differences in the counseling pair. A rather interesting implication for matching arises from the study of lower-class black patients by Vail (1978); he found that race of therapist was not a significant correlate of remaining in treatment, but that patients remained longer with therapists of the opposite sex. In another chapter in this book, Goldstein presents many useful points about obtaining congruence between expectations and roles of the client and therapist.

Role Complementarity, Process, and Technique Variables

Closely intertwined with similarity and role considerations are interactional problems in cross-cultural therapy. Scholars of different cultures such as Torrey (1972), emphasize the necessity for patient belief in and acceptance of the therapeutic techniques. Yet, often the therapist is faced with "resistance." Montijo (1975), for instance, states that many Puerto Ricans shrink from assuming responsibility for their pathological actions. They believe in fate, luck, and malevolent actions of others. If they form a good, positive transference, the role relationship will probably be like that of a child confiding in a benevolent mother or father and asking for support. As mentioned earlier, Higginbotham (1977) indicates that many people from other cultures expect an active, authoritarian role on the part of the therapist while the patient takes a passive, dependent role. Obviously, these "images" of certain clientele must be checked against the real behavior of individuals and groups. Therapists are as subject to the development of cultural stereotypes as other people. Some research points out the errors of common stereotypes. For instance, Cole and Cole (1978) have shown that the image of the Mexican and Mexican-American as being fatalistic and having an external locus of control is not true, at least for university students; they perceive causation to be as much an internal matter as Anglo, Irish, and German students. Still, the general principle obtains, the therapist should expect that, in a pluralistic society, cultural backgrounds may contribute to role expectations, and it will be her or his responsibility to be aware of these and to take them into account in therapy.

As briefly stated earlier, there is debate (Gomes-Schwartz, et al., 1978) about whether the client should be systematically indoctrinated into the preferred participative-expressive role of the therapists or should be met on his or her own ground. That is, should the therapy be shaped to fit the procedural expectations of the client or the preferences and capabilities of the therapist? Howard and Orlinsky (1972) state that "the major *de facto* function of our psychotherapy activity is as a kind of higher education in the development of interpersonal skills and emotional capabilities [p. 658]" in most instances; the procedures are appropriate for middle and upper-class individuals from Western cultures but may not be for others. It may, incidentally, be true that the worldwide expansion of television will serve to provide more common transcultural understandings of therapy. It would seem that behavioral approaches in which more specific problem definition and directive guidance is exercised might be more appropriate for many other-cultural problems, but the acts of defining the behavioral problems and setting behavioral goals are in themselves in danger of being culture-bound.

Szapocznik, Scopetta, and King (1978) argue strongly that mental health services should study the cultural values and expectations of the client population and then select the treatment modalities which best fit. If we are to follow this line of development, we could profit well by a much more extensive knowledge of the folk therapeutics and systematic cultural therapies developed in other countries. Already, meditation and yoga are being added to therapists' armamentaria. As yet, most therapists have very little knowledge of such procedures as those used in Arab folk-healing (Sanua, 1979), Sufism (Nurbakhsh, 1978), Morita therapy (Reynolds, 1976), and Naikan therapy (Reynolds, 1977), to mention a few.

In addition to broadening the cross-cultural therapist's repertoire of treatments, it would seem important in training to help the therapists deal with content and problems particular to the cross-cultural situation. For instance, the therapist should develop ways of rather quickly understanding the cultural background of the client, learning about his or her culturally-related expectations for therapy, and dealing with unexpressed concerns about the differences between the therapist and the client. Discussing these differences may often be important for developing trust and overcoming reluctance of the client to participate fully in therapy (Banks, 1975).

One aspect of cross-cultural therapy that is seldom discussed is its poten-tiality for exploring the meaningfulness of the client's "roots." Jungian therapy emphasizes the exploration of self, especially in the second half of life. Therapists might find that clarification of background, ethnic identity, and cultural values may be very helpful for certain clients.

Cultural Aspects of Outcome and Context Variables

The many research considerations regarding outcome variables discussed by many authors (e.g., in Gelso, 1979; Garfield and Bergin, 1978; Hadley and Strupp, 1977; Smith and Glass, 1977) also apply to studies of cross-cultural effectiveness. Central to outcome studies are decisions about criteria; and, as Costello (1978) concludes from a cultural comparison of social com-petence, criterion variables must be studied for freedom from ethnic or cultural bias. One must ask whether chosen criteria favor one group vs. another, and who is making the judgments of successful outcomes. In the tripartite of interested parties (Strupp & Hadley, 1977; Hadley & Strupp, 1977), namely, the individual, society (including the family), and the mental health professional, cultural values may affect judgments by any or all. Szapocznik et al. (1978) have found that the study of the society, especially the ethnic or subcultural community being served, is an important first step. As briefly indicated earlier, their Value Orientations Scale, used for this purpose, consists of four factors: A Relationship Scale (from high values on individualism or autonomy to high preference for lineality or hierarchical relations), an Idealized Humanistic Scale (being for or against an egalitarian and growth-oriented life style), a Mastery of Nature and Future Orientation vs. Subjugation to Nature and Present Orientation Scale, and a Human Nature Scale (seeing human beings as basically evil or good). Although their assessment instrument may not be ideal, it does point the way toward an ex-amination of beliefs and assumptions underlying criteria for cultural aspects of adjustment. Higginbotham (1979) also has developed a rather elaborate and promising procedure, the Ethno-Therapy and Culture Ac-commodation Scale for gathering culture-specific mental health data.

Many of the people who seek cross-cultural therapy or counseling are bicultural or multicultural. If cultural values or criteria conflict, which should be used? Should the foreign student, for instance, be judged by suc-cess or feelings of success in the American setting, or in the setting to which he or she will return, or in both? There is, at present, little analysis and research on this problem. In looking for cultural aspects of assessment of outcomes, we need also to be developing contextual or situational assess-ment procedures. Cultural factors will impinge through the surrounding relations with family and peers and through the usage of the physical environment. Magnusson and Stattin (1978), studying anxiety in several cultures, concluded that comparisons are enhanced by studying both situational and personal aspects. Interactionism is likely to be a key goal for methodological development in assessment in coming years.

Another promising area for development of research is in regard to support groups and social networks (Brammer, 1978; Gottlieb, 1979; Hirsch, 1979). Boyd, Shuman, McMullan, & Fretz (1979) provide an illustration of a transition support group for black freshmen entering the stresses of college life. Whiteley et al. (1975) report the extensive study done by Astin et al. (1972) assessing the effectiveness of special programs designed to serve high risk college students, many of whom were from minority backgrounds. Among the findings were greater likelihood of persistence in larger, more selective (richer?) universities, and in two-year, well-structured programs; the effectiveness of financial support in the form of scholarships was also considerable. Discussion of criteria and effectiveness invariably lead us into analysis of the situations and systems within which therapy functions.

Cultural Aspects of Therapy Settings

The physical location and the social organization of mental health services will have symbolic meanings. The convenience of access and the interest and communication modes of staff will encourage or discourage utilization of an agency or cooperation with outreach. As mentioned earlier, utilization of services and continuation have been the subject of a number of studies, and cultural factors seem important for both of these (Kelly et al., 1977). In general, minority groups in the Unitead States underutilize mental health services, but findings are mixed (Andrulis, 1977; Genthner & Graham, 1976; Padilla et al., 1975; Sue, 1977; Sue & Kirk, 1975). Some combinations of certain services with certain minority groups result in good initial relations and follow-through; such interactions need to be studied more extensively. These considerations also need to be applied to the locus of treatment of foreign students. Yeh (1972) found, for instance, that the prognosis for treatment of paranoid manifestations among Chinese students was better if they returned to their home country.

What is the responsibility of communities for cross-cultural mental health services, and in what ways should that responsibility be expressed? Neki (1978) raises this question on an international scale and points out the variety of ways in which different countries provide services; of much importance, as he sees it, are the degree of affluence and the number and nature of the mental health professional cadre. He notes "that services, once instituted, generate their own need, and establish a negotiated order within themselves and within the administrative and economic structure of the respective communities so that their existence becomes self-perpetuating [p. 205]." Thus, mental health agencies and professionals promote culture change. Neki states that, in certain cultures, folk healers may be more effective than Western-trained professionals. Higginbotham (1979) also presents this view in an excellent review of cultural patterns of services in developing countries.

Stanley Sue (1977) points out that the ethic is becoming established in the United States that the mental health system is responsible for providing responsive, nondiscriminative services for all. Analyses by Sue and others show that psychotherapy is provided less often to minority and low income groups; questions arise like these: Is standard counseling or psychotherapy appropriate? What are the ways to be truly responsive to minorities and other-cultural groups? S. Sue (1977) urges strong support for three models of service delivery: Increased utilization of existing services; establishment of independent but parallel services in barrios, reservations, and ghettoes directly serving minority groups; and development of new forms of therapies and institutions more culturally appropriate. Padilla et al. (1975) also makes three recommendations: the training of paraprofessionals and professionals for adaptation to the minority culture, the use of culturally relevant family treatment, and the barrio service center providing a wide variety of financial and social services as well as counseling. In non-Western settings, Higginbotham (1979) identifies three existing models—the usual Western-type psychiatric approach, the public health approach modeled after the American community mental health movement, and the village system making use of indigenous healers and natural therapeutic elements. For further development, Higginbotham suggests following a four-point, culture-specific (emic) assessment program: (1) analysis of the culturally defined problem, particularly the local rules for assigning deviant labels and causation; (2) finding the norms for personal adjustment to assist in establishing therapeutic goals; (3) studying the expected tactics and sources of caring, the means of social influence in resocialization and healing; and (4) determining the expected community relationship with the agency, including the preferred kind of personnel, location, access of families, and ways of handling costs.

This large section on a variety of variables ends the review of the literature, which has particularly been oriented toward culture-related articles presenting research or suggesting research possibilities. We have moved quickly through a rather large and somewhat chaotic mass of findings and ideas. The remaining part of this chapter will now try to integrate ideas and comment on the literature.

A SET OF HYPOTHESES FOR CROSS—CULTURAL RESEARCH AND NEEDED METHODOLOGY

In an earlier review (Sundberg, 1976) I tried to arrive at a set of hypotheses or protohypotheses for research on the effectiveness of cross-cultural counseling and therapy. These hypotheses, which attempt to summarize and extend the available literature, are presented below.

The cultural meaning of entry: Entry into the counseling system will be affected by cultural background, acculturation, and socialization toward seeking help; therapist awareness of such cultural screening and the symbolic meaning of help-seeking will enhance the effectiveness of the counseling or therapy program.

Similarity of culturally relevant goals: The more similar the expectations of the intercultural client and counselor in regard to the goals of counseling, the more effective the counseling or therapy will be.

Congruent roles: Of special importance for effectiveness in intercultural counseling is the degree of congruence between counselor and client in their orientation toward dependency, authority, openness of communication, and other special relationships inherent in counseling and therapy.

Clarity about cultural understanding: The more the aims and desires of the client can be appropriately simplified or formulated as objective behavior or information (such as specific behaviors and university course requirements), the more effective the intercultural treatment will be.

Developing the Professional's Intercultural Understanding and Communication Skills

Understanding socialization: The more personal and emotion-laden the interaction becomes, the more the client will rely on words learned early in life, and the more helpful it will be for the therapist to be knowledgeable about socialization in the client's culture.

Communication sensitivity: the effectiveness of intercultural counseling and therapy will be enhanced by the treating person's general sensitivity to communications, both verbal and nonverbal, and by knowledge of communication styles in other cultures.

Knowledge of other-culture helping: Specific background and training in cross-cultural interactions similar to the counseling one and on understanding the day-to-day living problems in other relevant cultures as compared with one's own will enhance effectiveness of intercultural helping.

Developing the Client's Intercultural Attitudes and Skills

Cultural aspects of preparation for therapy: The less familiar the client is with the counseling or therapy process, the more the counselor/therapist or the treatment program will need to be sensitive to either adapting counseling style or instructing the client in the skills of communication, decision making, and transfer to outside situations.

Relating to the Client's Present and Future Environments

Comparison of assumptions and values: The effectiveness of intercultural helping will be increased by mutual knowledge of the values and assumptive frameworks of the culture of the client's origin in relation to the cultures of present and future fields of action.

Cultural identification and reference groups: Intercultural counseling of psychotherapy is enhanced by the knowledge of the client's degree of identification with the relevant cultures and the use of intercultural reference groups most important to the client.

Cultural adjustment and mastery: The effectiveness of intercultural counseling and therapy is increased by helper awareness of the process of adaptation to the stress and confusion of moving from one culture to another (system boundary crossing) and by consideration of the skills required to gain mastery over the new system.

Client's cultural plans: Effective counseling or therapy requires consideration of both the present living situation and the future arena of action, the focus to be determined by the goals and priorities of the client and an exploration of the bicultural or multicultural nature of these situations.

Universality, Group-Commonality, and Uniqueness in Intercultural Helping

Cross-cultural counseling universals: Despite great differences in cultural contexts and language, and in the implicit theory of counseling or therapeutic process, a majority of the important elements of intercultural helping are common across cultures and clients. These elements are likely to include such counselor characteristics as tolerance for anxiety in the client, a manifest positive flexibility in response to the client, a reasonable confidence in one's information and belief system, and an interest in the client as a person.

Culture-specific therapeutic techniques and assumptions: Culture specific modes of counseling will be found that work more effectively with certain cultural and ethnic groups than with others. Important variables in such studies will be degree of identification of the client with the contrast culture, degree of acculturation, communication styles, and belief systems.

Individually unique aspects: Intercultural helping will be effective to the extent that the counselor treats the client as a special individual with particular concerns and life history and with his or her own competencies and resources for "self-righting" within the life situation.

The intention is to point to those aspects of therapy which are particularly sensitive to cultural influences, but the reader will note that many may apply to all therapeutic situations. The 15 hypotheses are divided into five general sections, and I will comment briefly on needed development of operational methods for each section. Needless to say, it is not possible to go into great detail since a single section could easily make quite an extensive chapter in itself; so I will be very brief and selective. The aim is to suggest some possibilities for research.

Mutuality of Purposes and Helping Expectations

These hypotheses propose that cultural elements are involved in entering therapy, setting goals, establishing rapport and reciprocal roles, and using information and other sources. The assumption here is that if therapy is to continue there must be some commonly agreed upon explicit or implicit rationale and relationship. In order for research to test these hypotheses, it will be necessary to develop or find assessment procedures for comparison of client and therapist expectations, goals, and world views and orientations to therapy.

Research projects might compare cross-cultural counselors and clients on such orientations and expectations; for instance, studies might use Q-sorts properly expressed in dialect or language understandable to both parties. Experimental studies might compare various designs for arriving at mutual agreements and relate these to criteria of outcome in therapy. The last hypothesis favors clear cognitive or behavioral approaches to therapy and requires intensive study of common problems of the cultural clientele.

Dawis (1978) outlines a mode for cross-cultural counseling research emphasizing behavioral or interactional approaches and value orientations in adjustment.

Developing the Professional's Intercultural Understanding and Communication Skills

Hypotheses in this section emphasize the knowledge and competence needed for an effective transcultural therapist—particularly about cultural aspects of development, communication, and helping. Assessment instruments which would help with research on these hypotheses would include tests of knowledge of relevant cultures; ability to understand and if necessary use dialects, slang, and relevant languages; background experience in intercultural situations; willingness to observe and learn from other cultures, barrios, and ghettoes; interest and ability to raise hope and expectations for change in clients; empathy and ability to predict culturally-tinged reactions to situations; awareness of the costs to clients for participation in therapy in terms of time, money, possible acceptance of the "sick" or helpless role; and appreciation for the possibilities and problems of cultural marginality.

Research studies might investigate the hypothesis that intercultural competence requires a broad repertoire of skills and theories rather than a narrow one; development of assessment profiles or descriptive patterns of cultures, particularly in regard to elements of importance in counseling which could then be used to train and screen paraprofessionals and professionals; and correlation of measures of awareness of one's own culture with awareness and competence in working with others.

Developing the Client's Intercultural Attitudes and Skills

This hypothesis has to do with the using of opportunities in counseling and therapy. It presumes that there is a need for either (1) the development of the client's understanding and ability to use help, or (2) the modification of the usual therapeutic procedures. An important assessment technique for this purpose would be a test of acculturation or identification with the minority or other-culture; such a measure would probably rely heavily on language or dialect used in the home and the nature of most social contacts. Assessment of the client's knowledge and expectations about therapy, feelings of suspiciousness, trust, credibility of the agency or therapist, and a sense of helplessness or powerlessness in his or her living situation would be valuable. Procedures measuring skills for problem solving and change might be particuarly helpful, especially if they would then be used for continued treatment or training.

Studies might make use of role induction films or orientation programs for clients. Presumably, the more different the culture is from the culture of those offering treatment, the more difficult it would be to use the role induction approach and the more necessary it would be to develop different ways of presenting therapeutic programs.

Relating to the Client's Present and Future Environments

These hypotheses emphasize the importance of different and changing environments in psychotherapy, and the place of the client in systems of significance. They relate to congruence or incongruence of communities of interaction now and in the future, to reference groups, to processes or cultural adaptation of "culture shock", and to the client's choices of environments and awareness of their norms and values. It would be useful to have assessment devices for determining significant systems of interaction for the client, for analysis of the important elements in those systems, for a broad bandwidth of adjustment problems including financial and working matters as well as socio-emotional concerns, for choice and decision-making style of clients relative to various environmental situations and for profiling the important characteristics of various living situations.

Research on cultural aspects of reference groups and networks would seem to be particularly important. Again, one would expect that the therapist with multiple competencies or the agency with a variety of coordinated services would be most helpful. One would expect that comparison of cultural aspects of environments would produce high and low contrast cultures; and individuals would vary in their capabilities for adjustment in contrasting cultures. Of relevance would be a clarification of the degree to which a situation is oppressive or punishing for the other-culture client.

Universality, Group-Commonality, and Uniqueness in Intercultural Helping

These three hypotheses indicate that, with any counseling or therapeutic situation, each of the individuals involved share some things with all others, such as need for oxygen and food and a history of being a child; they share some things with some other people, such as a common cultural history of affiliation with a particular group; and in other ways, they are completely unique with their own personal histories, individual appearance, and so on. In regard to the latter component, it is well to remember the common statistical finding of great variation within groups; individual differences are typically much larger than group differences. Assessment devices might be developed which sort out these components and profile the commonalities and differences. For therapeutic situations, it might be well to train therapists to recognize these differences and to make optimal use of them. The inventorying of competencies in common with others as well as those which are unique may be of help in promoting the self-esteem and self-knowledge of the client.

GENERAL COMMENTS ON INTERCULTURAL THERAPY RESEARCH

As is apparent from the earlier part of this chapter, despite a fair amount of writing about cross-cultural counseling and psychotherapy, there is very little systematic research on therapy itself. Yet, as the world grows more interdependent and mobile, there is bound to be more and more need for understanding the cultural elements of this important area of human endeavor. Effectiveness of therapy is complex enough to study, but when one adds a vaguely defined variable like culture it becomes even more complex. The complexity undoubtedly is part of the reason for the rather weak research response to the challenge. This limited usage of cultural variables is also apparent in other parts of psychology, such as the developmental field (Laboratory of Comparative Human Cognition, 1979) where recent doubts about the cross-ethnic validity of the tests and measures which provide hard data add to the feeling of discouragement. It is just possible that the elaborate structure of current psychology built largely in the United States and English-speaking countries is quite ethnocentric (Diaz-Guerrero, 1977).

Of high priority in such cross-cultural research I would set such questions as these: What is the extent of usage of different kinds of intercultural therapy that exists now? How might we classify and describe these different kinds of techniques and theories and the variables that are of importance? What are the human problem-solving procedures that exist in cultural communities already, and how might they be strengthened? In cross-cultural therapy itself, how might we study the expectations of the involved parties and how they resolve their differences? Among current Western therapies, such as behavior therapy, gestalt, psychoanalysis, or family systems therapy, which can be adapted most readily to which cultural groups? How might indigenous people be more involved through training and other means in the mental health effort?

At the present time, the usual approach in the cross-cultural literature is for therapists to describe experiences in esoteric, overseas settings or in programs on reservations and ghettoes. Although such anecdotes and illustrations are interesting and valuable and should be continued, we need now to support moves toward (1) systematic field studies and analyses of behavior change and natural problem solving "in place," (2) careful evaluation of therapeutic programs with minorities and other cultures, (3) analog and simulation studies deliberately varying many of the culturally related variables mentioned in this and other chapters, and (4) experimental comparisons of different therapeutic processes based on cultural hypotheses. For such research, we will need to clarify much more carefully what the important dimensions of cultural differences and similarities are in order to use populations in which cultural variations can be measured. We must go beyond the simple use of skin color or nationality. We must develop a number of theoretical models, especially ones with a sensitivity to the ecology of human problems, possibilities, competence building, and helping processes (Barker & Barker, 1961; Bronfenbrenner, 1977; Kelly et al., 1977; Lamb & Rapin 1977; and Zimmer, 1978).

These are only a small sample of the many research questions and needs that arise when one enters this complex and fascinating field—trying to psychologically assist persons very different from oneself. . .strangers.

REFERENCES

Abramowitz, C.V., & Dokecki, P.R. The politics of clinical judgment: Early empirical returns. *Psychological Bulletin,* 1977, *84*, 460-476.
Acosta, F.X. Barriers between mental health services and Mexican Americans: An examination of a paradox. *American Journal of Community Psychology,* 1979, 7, 503-520.
Acosta, F.X., & Sheehan, J.G. Preferences toward Mexican-American and Anglo-American psychotherapists. *Journal of Consulting and Clinical Psychology,* 1976, *44*, 272-279.
Albee, G.W. The Protestant ethic, sex, and psychotherapy. *American Psychologist*, 1977, *32*, 150-161.
Andrulis, D.P. Ethnicity as a variable in the utilization and referral patterns of a comprehensive mental health center. *Journal of Community Psychology,* 1977, *5*, 231-237.
Arkoff, A., Thayer, F., & Elkind, L. Mental health and counseling ideas of Asian and American students. *Journal of Counseling Psychology,*1966, *13*, 219-228.
Aronson, H., & Overall, B. Treatment expectancies of patients in two social classes. *Social Work,* 1966, *11,* 35-41.
Astin, H.S., Astin, A.W., Bisconti, A.S., & Frankel, H.H. *Higher education and the disadvantaged student.* Washington D.C.: Human Services Press, 1972.
Atkinson, D.R., Maruyama, M., & Matsui, S. Effects of counselor race and counseling approach on Asian Americans' perceptions of counselor credibility and utility. *Journal of Counseling Psychology*, 1978, *25*,76-83.
Atkinson, D.R., Morten, G., & Sue, D.W. *Counseling American minorities: A cross-cultural perspective.* Dubuque, Iowa: Wm. C.Brown, 1979.
Banks, H.C. The black person as client and as therapist. *Professional Psychology*, 1975, *6*, 470-474.

Barker, R.G., & Barker, L.S. The psychological ecology of old people in Midwest, Kansas, and Yoredale, Yorkshire. *Journal of Gerontology*, 1961, *16*, 144-149.

Bengur, B. Interviews with counselors about effective and ineffective cross-cultural counseling. Paper, University of Oregon, Psychology Dept. 1979.

Benson, A.G., & Miller, R.E. A preliminary report on uses of the Michigan International Student Problem Inventory in research, orientation and counseling, developing a balanced program and evaluating potential for academic success of/for foreign students. Unpublished paper, Michigan State University, International Programs Office, May 1966.

Berman, J. Counseling skills used by black and white male and female counselors. *Journal of Counseling Psychology*, 1979, *26*, 81-84. (a)

Berman, J. Individual versus societal focus: Problem diagnoses of black and white male and female counselors. *Journal of Cross-Cultural Psychology*, 1979, *10*, 497-507. (b)

Bloombaum, M., Yamamoto, J., & Jones, Q. Cultural stereotyping among psychotherapists. *Journal of Consulting and Clinical Psychology*, 1968, *32*, 99.

Boucher, J.D. Culture and emotion. In A.J. Marsella, R.G. Tharp, & T.J. Ciborowski, (Eds.), *Perspectives on cross-cultural psychology*. New York: Academic Press, 1979.

Boyd, V.S., Shueman, S., McMullan, Y.O., & Fretz, B.R. Transition groups for black freshmen: Integrated service and training. *Professional Psychology*, 1979, *10*, 42-48.

Brammer, L.M. Informal helping systems in selected subcultures. *Personnel and Guidance Journal*, 1978, *56*, 476-479.

Bronfenbrenner, U. Toward an experimental ecology of human development. *American Psychologist*, 1977, *32*, 513-531.

Burbach, H.J., & Thompson, M.A. Alienation among college freshmen: A comparison of Puerto Rican, black and white students. *Journal of College Student Personnel*, 1971, *12*, 248-252.

Buriel, R. Cognitive styles among three generations of Mexican American children. *Journal of Cross-Cultural Psychology*, 1975, *6*, 417-429.

Butcher, J. N., & Garcia, R.E. Cross-national application of psychological tests. *Personnel and Guidance Journal*, 1978, *56*, 472-475.

Casciani, J.M. Influence of model's race and sex on interviewees' self-disclosure. *Journal of Counseling Psychology*, 1978, *25*, 435-440.

Chartier, G.M., & Sundberg, N.D. Commonality of word listing, predictability, originality and chucking: An analysis of American and Indian ninth-graders. *International Journal of Psychology*, 1969, *4*, 195-205.

Cole, D., & Cole, S. Locus of control in Mexicans and Chicanos: The case of the missing fatalist. *Journal of Consulting and Clinical Psychology*, 1978, *46*, 1323-1329.

Connor, J.W. Value changes in third generation Japanese Americans. *Journal of Personality Assessment*, 1975, *39*, 597-600.

Costello, R.M. Premorbid social competence construct generalizability across groups: Path analyses with two premorbid social competence components. *Journal of Consulting and Clinical Psychology*, 1978, *46*, 1164-1165.

Cowen, E.L. Social and community interventions. *Annual Review of Psychology*, 1973, *24*, 423-472.

Dawis, R.V. A paradigm and model for the cross-cultural study of counseling. *Personnel and Guidance Journal*, 1978, *56*, 463-466.

Diaz-Guerrero, R. A Mexican psychology. *American Psychologist*, 1977, *32*, 934-944.

Di Nardo, P.A. Social class and diagnostic suggestion as variables in clinical judgment. *Journal of Consulting and Clinical Psychology*, 1975, *43*, 363-368.

Dohrenwend, B.P. & Dohrenwend, B.S. Social and cultural influences on psychopathology. *Annual Review of Psychology*, 1974, *25*, 417-452.

Dohrenwend, B.S. Social status and stressful life events. *Journal of Personality and Social Psychology*, 1973, *28*, 225-235.

Draguns, J.G. Comparisons of psychopathology across cultures: Issues, findings, directions. *Journal of Cross-Cultural Psychology*, 1973, *4*, 9-47.

Draguns, J.G. Resocialization into culture: The complexities of taking a worldwide view of psychotherapy. In R.W. Brislin, S. Bochner, & W. J. Lonner (Eds.), *Cross-cultural perspectives on learning.* New York: Sage, 1975.

Duckro, R., Duckro, P., & Beal, D. Relationship of self-disclosure and mental health in black females. *Journal of Consulting and Clinical Psychology*, 1976, *44*, 940-944.

Flores, J.L. The utilisation of a community mental health service by Mexican-Americans. *International Journal of Social Psychiatry*, 1978, *24*, 271-275.

Frank, J.D. *Persuasion and healing.* (Rev. ed.) New York: Schocken, 1974.

Fukuhara, M. Student expectations of counseling: A cross-cultural study. *Japanese Psychological Research*, 1973, *15*, 179-193.

Gamboa, A.M., Tosi, D.J., & Riccio, A.C. Race and counselor climate in the counselor preference of delinquent girls. *Journal of Counseling Psychology*, 1976, *23*, 160-162.

Garfield, S.L., & Bergin, A.E. (ed.) *Handbook of psychotherapy and behavior change: An empirical analysis.* (2nd ed.) New York: Wiley, 1978.

Gelso, C. J. Research in counseling: Methodological and professional issues. *The Counseling Psychologist*, 1979, *8*(3), 7-35.

Genthner, R.W., & Graham, J.R. Effects of short-term public psychiatric hospitalization for both black and white patients. *Journal of Consulting and Clinical Psychology*, 1976, *44*, 118-124.

Gilmore, S.K. *The counselor-in-training.* Englewood Cliffs, N.J.: Prentice-Hall (formerly Appleton-Century-Crofts), 1973.

Gomes-Schwartz, B., Hadley, S.W., & Strupp, H.H. Individual psychotherapy and behavior therapy. *Annual Review of Psychology*, 1978, *29*, 435-472.

Gottlieb, B.H. The primary-group as supportive milieu: Applications to community psychology. *American Journal of Community Psychology*, 1979, *7*, 469-480.

Guthrie, G. Alienation and anomie. In H.C. Triandis & J.G. Draguns (Eds.), *Handbook of cross-cultural psychology.* Vol. 6. *Psychopathology.* Boston: Allyn & Bacon, 1980.

Hadley, S.W., & Strupp, H.H. Evaluations of treatment in psychotherapy: Naivete or necessity? *Professional Psychology*, 1977, *8*, 478-490.

Hager, P.C., & Elton, C.F. The vocational interest of black males. *Journal of Vocational Behavior*, 1971, *1*, 153-158.

Harrison, I.K. Race as a counselor-client variable in counseling and psychotherapy: A review of the research. *The Counseling Psychologist*, 1975, *5*(1), 124-133.

Henderson, G. *Understanding and counseling ethnic minorities.* Springfield, IL: Charles Thomas, 1979.

Henry, W.E., Sims, J.H., & Spray, S.L. *The fifth profession.* San Francisco: Jossey-Bass, 1971.

Higginbotham, H.N. Culture and the role of client expectancy in psychotherapy. *Topics in Culture Learning*, 1977, *5*, 107-124.

Higginbotham, H.N. Culture and the delivery of psychological services in developing nations. *Transcultural Psychiatric Research Review*, 1979, *16*, 7-27.

Hirsch, B.J. Psychological dimensions of social networks: A multimethod analysis. *American Journal of Community Psychology*, 1979, *7*, 263-278.

Hollingshead, A.B., & Redlich, F.C. *Social class and mental illness.* New York: Wiley, 1958.

Howard, K.I., & Orlinsky, D.E. Psychotherapeutic processes. *Annual Review of Psychology*, 1972, *23*, 615-668.

Irvine, S.H., & Carroll, W.K. Testing and assessment across cultures: Issues in methodology and theory. In H.C. Triandis and J.W. Berry (Eds.), *Handbook of cross-cultural psychology*. Vol. 2. *Methodology*. Boston: Allyn & Bacon, 1979.

Jilek-Aal, W. Native renaissance: The survival and revival of indigenous therapeutic ceremonials among North American Indians. *Transcultural Psychiatric Research Review*, 1978, *15*, 117-148.

Johnson, D.C. Problems of foreign students. *International Educational and Cultural Exchange*, 1971, *7*, 61-68.

Jones, A., & Seagull, A. A. Dimensions of the relationship between the black client and the white therapist: A theoretical overview. *American Psychologist*, 1977, *32*, 850-855.

Jones, E., & Korchin, S. (Eds.) *Minority issues in mental health*. New York: Holt, Rinehart and Winston, in press.

Kelly, J.G., Snowden, L.R., & Munoz, R.F. Social and community interventions. *Annual Review of Psychology*, 1977, *28*, 323-362.

King, L.M. Social and cultural influences on psychopathology. *Annual Review of Psychology*, 1978, *29*, 405-433.

Kinzie, J.D. Lessons from cross-cultural psychotherapy. *American Journal of Psychotherapy*, 1978, *32*, 510-520.

Knight, G.P., & Kagan, S. Acculturation of prosocial and competitive behaviors among second- and third-generation Mexican-American children. *Journal of Cross-Cultural Psychology*, 1977, *8*, 273-284.

Knight, G.P., Kagan, S., Nelson, W., & Gumbiner, J. Acculturation of second- and third-generation Mexican-American children: Field dependence, locus of control, self-esteem, and school achievement. *Journal of Cross-Cultural Psychology*, 1978, *9*, 87-98.

Korman, A.K., Greenhaus, J.H., & Badin, I.J. Personnel attitudes and motivation. *Annual Review of Psychology*, 1977, *28*, 175-196.

Krumboltz, J.D., Becker-Haven, J.F., & Burnett, K.F. Counseling psychology. *Annual Review of Psychology*, 1979, *22*, 533-564.

Laboratory of Comparative Human Cognition. Cross-cultural psychology's challenges to our ideas of children and development. *American Psychologist*, 1979, *34*, 827-833.

Lamb, D.H., & Rapin, L.S. An ecological model for categorizing and evaluating student development services. *Journal of Counseling Psychology*, 1977, *24*, 349-555.

Layton, W.L., Sandeen, G.A., & Baker, R.D. Student development and counseling. *Annual Review of Psychology*, 1971, *22*, 533-564.

Lonner, W.J. The use of Western-based tests in intercultural counseling. In P. Pedersen, W.J. Lonner, & J.G. Draguns (Eds.), *Counseling across cultures.* Honolulu: University Press of Hawaii, 1976.

Lonner, W.J. Issues in cross-cultural psychology. In A.J. Marsella, R.G. Tharp, & T.J. Ciborowski (Eds.), *Perspectives on cross-cultural psychology*. New York: Academic Press, 1979, 17-45.

Lorion, R.P. Research on psychotherapy and behavior change with the disadvantaged: Past, present, and future directions. In S.L. Garfield & A. E. Bergin (Eds.), *Handbook of psychotherapy and behavior change: An empirical analysis.* (2nd ed.) New York: Wiley, 1978.

Magnusson, D., & Strattin, H. A cross-cultural comparison of anxiety responses in an interactional frame of reference. *International Journal of Psychology*, 1978, *13*, 317-332.

Marsella, A.J. The modernization of traditional cultures: Consequences for the individual. In D.S. Hoopes, P.B. Pedersen & G.W. Renwick (Eds.), *Overview of intercultural education, training and research*. Vol. III. *Special research areas.* La Grange Park, IL:

Intercultural Network, SIETAR, 1978, 108-147 (a)

Marsella, A.J. Thoughts on cross-cultural studies on the epidemiology of depression. *Culture, Medicine and Psychiatry*, 1978, *2*, 343-357. (b)

Marsella, A.J. Cross-cultural studies of mental disorders. In A.J. Marsella, R.G.Tharp, & T.J. Ciborowski (Eds.), *Perspectives on cross-cultural psychology*, New York: Academic Press, 1979.

Marsella, A.J. Depressive experience and disorder across culture. In H. Triandis & J. Draguns (Eds.), *Handbook of cross-cultural psychology* Vol. 5. *Culture and psychopathology*. Boston: Allyn & Bacon, 1980.

Marsella, A.J., Kinzie, D., & Gordon, P. Ethnic variations in expression of depression. *Journal of Cross-Cultural Psychology*, 1973, *4*, 435-458.

Marsella, A. J., Murray, M.D., & Golden, C. Ethnic variations in the phenomenology of emotions: I. Shame. *Journal of Cross-Cultural Psychology*, 1974, *5*, 312-328.

Marsella, A.J. Tharp, R., & Ciborowski, T. (Eds.). *Perspectives on cross-cultural psychology. New York: Academic Press, 1979.*

Martindale, C. The therapist-as-fixed-effect fallacy in psychotherapy research. Journal of Consulting and Clinical Psychology, 1978, *46*, 1526-1530.

Merluzzi, B.H., & Merluzzi, T.V. Influence of client race on counselor's assessment of case materials. *Journal of Counseling Psychology*, 1978, *25*, 399-404.

Merluzzi, T.V., Merluzzi, B.H., & Kaul, T.J. Counselor race and power base: Effects on attitudes and behavior. *Journal of Counseling Psychology*, 1977, *24*, 430-436.

Montijo, J. The Puerto Rican client. *Professional Psychology*, 1975, *6*, 475-477.

Morrow, R.S. Introduction. Symposium: Ethnic differences in therapeutic relationships. *Professional Psychology*, 1975, *6*, 468-469.

Naditch, M.P., & Morrissey, R.F. Role stress, personality and psychopathology in a group of immigrant adolescents. *Journal of Abnormal Psychology*, 1976, *85*, 113-118.

Neki, J.S. An examination of the extent of responsibility of mental health services from the standpoint of developing communities. *International Journal of Social Psychiatry*, 1978, *24*, 204-219.

Nurbakhsh, D. Sufism and psychoanalysis: Part one: What is Sufism? and Part two: A comparison between Sufism and psychoanalysis. *International Journal of Social Psychiatry*, 1978, *24*, 204-219.

Padilla, A.M., Ruiz, R.A., & Alvarez, R. Community mental health services for the Spanish-speaking/surnamed population. *American Psychologist*, 1975, *30*, 892-905.

Parloff, M.B., Waskow, I.E., & Wolfe, B.E. Research on therapist variables in relation to process and outcome. In S.L. Garfield & A.E. Bergin (Eds.), *Handbook of psychotherapy and behavior change: An empirical analysis.* (2nd ed.) New York: Wiley, 1978.

Pedersen, P.B. Four dimensions of cross-cultural skill in counselor training. *Personnel and Guidance Journal*, 1978, *56*, 480-484.

Pedersen, P.B., Draguns, J.G., Lonner, W.J., & Trimble, J. (Eds.). *Counseling across cultures* (2nd ed.). Honolulu: University Press of Hawaii, 1980.

Pedersen, P.B., Lonner, W. J., & Draguns, J.G. (Eds.). *Counseling across cultures.* Honolulu: University Press of Hawaii, 1976.

Peoples, V. Y., & Dell, D.M. Black and white student preferences for counselor roles. *Journal of Counseling Psychology*, 1975, *22*, 529-534.

Pepinsky, H.B., & Meara, N.M. Student development and counseling. *Annual Review of Psychology*, 1973, *24*, 117-150.

Prince, R.H. Psychotherapy as the manipulation of endogenous healing mechanisms: A transcultural survey. *Transcultural Psychiatric Research Review*, 1976, *13*, 115-134.

Prince, R.H. Variations in psychotherapeutic procedures. In H.C. Triandis & J.G. Draguns (Eds.). *Handbook of cross-cultural psychology.* Vol. 6. *Psychopathology.* Boston: Allyn & Bacon, 1980.

Raskin, A., Crook, T.H., & Herman, K.D. Psychiatry history and symptom differences in black and white depressed inpatients. *Journal of Consulting and Clinical Psychology,* 1975, *43,* 73-80

Reynolds, D.K. *Morita psychotherapy.* Berkeley: University of California Press, 1976.

Reynolds, D.K. Naikan therapy—an experiential view. *International Journal of Social Psychiatry,* 1977, *23,* 253-263.

Sachs, W. *Black Hamlet.* Boston: Little, Brown, 1947.

Sandler, I., Holmen, M., & Schopper, A. Self versus counselor perceptions of interpersonal characteristics of female welfare recipients: A cross-cultural comparison. *Journal of Community Psychology,* 1978, *6,* 179-188.

Sanua, V.D. Sociocultural aspects of psychotherapy and treatment: A review of the literature. *Progress in Clinical Psychology,* 1966, *7,* 151-190.

Sanua, V.D. Psychological intervention in the Arab world: A review of folk treatment. *Transcultural Psychiatric Research Review,* 1979, *16,* 205-208.

Schofield, W. *Psychotherapy: The purchase of friendship.* Englewood Cliffs, N.J.: Prentice-Hall, 1964.

Segall, M.H. *Cross-cultural psychology.* Monterey, CA.: Brooks/Cole, 1979.

Sewell, T.E., & Martin, R.P. Racial differences in patterns of occupational choice in adolescents. *Psychology in the Schools,* 1976, *13,* 326-333.

Shaffer, M., Sundberg, N.D., & Tyler, L.E. Content differences on work listings by American, Dutch, and Indian adolescents. *Journal of Social Psychology,* 1969, *79,* 139-140.

Shappell, D.L., Hall, L.G., & Tarrier, R.B. Perceptions of the world of work: Inner city vs. suburbia. *Journal of Counseling Psychology,* 1971, *18,* 55-59.

Smith, M.L., & Glass, G.V. Meta-analysis of psychotherapy outcome studies. *American Psychologist,* 1977, *32,* 752-760.

Smith, W.D., Burlew, A.K., Mosley, M.H., & Whitney, W.M. *Minority issues in mental health.* Reading, MA: Addison-Wesley, 1978.

Smither, R., & Rodriguez-Giegling, M. Marginality, modernity and anxiety in Indochinese refugees. *Journal of Cross-Cultural Psychology,* 1979, *10,* 469-478.

Snowden, L., & Todman, P. The psychological assessment of blacks: New. and needed developments. In E. Jones & S. Korchin (Eds.), *Minority issues in mental health.* New York: Holt, Rinehart and Winston, in press.

Strauss, J.S. Social and cultural influences on psychopathology. *Annual Review of Psychology,* 1979, *30,* 397-416.

Strupp, H.H., & Hadley, S.W. A tripartite model of mental health and therapeutic outcomes: With special reference to negative effects in psychotherapy. *American Psychologist,* 1977, *32,* 187-196.

Sue, D.W. World views and counseling. *Personnel and Guidance Journal,* 1978, *56,* 458-462.

Sue, D.W., & Kirk, B.A. Asian-Americans: Use of counseling and psychiatric services on a college campus. *Journal of Counseling Psychology,* 1975, *22,* 84-86.

Sue, D.W., & Sue, S. Barriers to effective cross-cultural counseling. *Journal of Counseling Psychology,* 1977, *24,* 420-429.

Sue, S. Community mental health services to minority groups: Some optimism, some pessimism. *American Psychologist,* 1977, *32,* 616-624.

Sundberg, N.D. Toward research evaluating intercultural counseling. In P. Pedersen, W.J. Lonner, & J.G. Draguns (Eds.), *Counseling across cultures.* Honolulu: University Press of Hawaii, 1976.

Szapocznik, J., Scopetta, M.A., Aranalde, M. & Kurtines, W. Cuban value structure: Treatment implications. *Journal of Consulting and Clinical Psychology,* 1978, *46,* 961-970.

Szapocznik, J., Scopetta, M.A., & King, O.E. Theory and practice in matching treatment to the special characteristics and problems of Cuban immigrants. *Journal of Community Psychology,* 1978, *6,* 112-122.

Szapocznik, J., Scopetta, M.A., & Kurtines, W. Acculturation: Theory, measurement and clinical implications. *InterAmerican Journal of Psychology,* in press.

Tan. H. Intercultural study of counseling expectancies. *Journal of Counseling Psychology,* 1967, *14,* 122-130.

Tanaka-Matsumi, J. & Marsella, A.J. Cross-cultural variations in the phenomenological experience of depression: I. Word association studies. *Journal of Cross-Cultural Psychology,* 1976, *7,* 379-396.

Thompson, R.A., & Cimbolic, P. Black students' counselor preference and attitudes toward counseling center use. *Journal of Counseling Psychology,* 1978, *25,* 570-575.

Torres-Matrullo, C. Acculturation and psychopathology among Puerto Rican women in mainland United States. *Dissertation Abstracts International,* 1974, 35(6-B), 3041.

Torrey, E.F. *The mind game: Witchdoctors and psychiatrists.* New York: Emerson Hall, 1972.

Tseng, W.S., & Hsu, J. Culture and psychotherapy. In A.J. Marsella, R.G. Tharp, & T.J. Ciborowski (Eds.), *Perspectives on cross-cultural psychology.* New York: Academic Press, 1979.

Tyler, L.E., Sundberg, N.D., Rohila, P.K., & Greene, M.M. Patterns of choices in Dutch, American and Indian adolescents. *Journal of Counseling Psychology,* 1968, *15,* 522-529.

Vail, A. Factors influencing lower-class black patients remaining in treatment. *Journal of Consulting and Clinical Psychology,* 1978, *46,* 341.

Walz, G.R., & Benjamin, L. (Eds.) *Transcultural counseling: Needs, programs and techniques.* New York: Human Sciences Press, 1978.

Warheit, G.J., Holzer, C.E., & Arey, S.A. Race and mental illness: An epidemiological update. *Journal of Health and Social Behavior,* 1975, *16,* 243-256.

Webster, D.W., & Fretz, B.R. Asian-American, black and white college students' preferences for help-giving sources. *Journal of Counseling Psychology,* 1978, *25,* 124-130.

Westbrook, F.D., Miyares, J., & Roberts, J.H. Perceived problem areas by black and white students and hints about comparative counseling needs. *Journal of Counseling Psychology,* 1978, *25,* 119-123.

Whiting, R. You've gotta have "Wa." *Sports Illustrated,* 1979, *51*(13), 58-71.

Whiteley, J.M., Burkhart, M.Q., Harway-Herman, M., & Whiteley, R.M. Counseling and student development. *Annual Review of Psychology,* 1975, *26,* 337-366.

Woods, E., & Zimmer, J.M. Racial effects in counseling-like interviews: An experimental analogue. *Journal of Counseling Psychology,* 1976, *23,* 527-531.

Yankelovich, D. The meaning of work. In J.M. Rosow (Ed.), *The worker and the job.* Englewood Cliffs, NJ: Prentice-Hall, 1974.

Yeh, D.K. Paranoid manifestations among Chinese students studying abroad: Some preliminary findings. In W.P. Lebra (Ed.), *Transcultural research in mental health.* Honolulu: University Press of Hawaii, 1972.

Zimmer, J. Concerning ecology in counseling. *Journal of Counseling Psychology,* 1978, *25,* 225-230.

Chapter 3

Ethnicity and Interactional Rules in Counseling and Psychotherapy: Some Basic Considerations

Frank A. Johnson

Psychotherapy and counseling are extraordinarily complex operations. Even in a two-party therapeutic interaction, the moment-to-moment activity requires a complicated phenomenology of linguistic, paraverbal, semantic, and contextual factors merely to describe the interaction, let alone to "explain" the process. And, of course, psychotherapy is far more complex than even the most comprehensive, moment-to-moment description can portray. Characteristically, it consists of a *series* of encounters unfolding over a period of weeks, months, or years, where subtle and dramatic changes in behavior may take place.

As another aspect of complexity, it is obvious that the sequences of manifest actions occurring within the therapeutic encounter are in themselves only the most objective (i.e., observable) parts of the process. The subjective changes, although harder to record and measure, constitute a critical dimension of the therapeutic process. Also, the actions taking place within the therapeutic microcosm are themselves embedded in a social reality structure residing outside the confines of the office. This social reality extends far beyond the characteristics of the particular individual client and therapist. Such complexity is almost stupefying, and it is easy to understand why therapists as well as researchers and theoreticians focus on delimited conceptual characteristics of the therapeutic process, or resort to reductionistic terms to "explain" progress or change.

This chapter is written as an overview of communicational and contextual variables inherent in the therapeutic situation. Those particular variables related to ethnicity will be accentuated within the context of other important factors in the phenomenology of the therapist/patient interaction. The framework for this overview is social-interactional to facilitate the inclusion of social scientific as well as psychological levels of reference. Also by way of explanation, the simple term "psychotherapy" rather than the compound expression "counseling and psychotherapy" will usually be used throughout this chapter. Also in this presentation, therapeutic procedures, for reasons of economy and simplification, will by and large refer to a two-person situation.

The purpose of this chapter is to articulate the ways in which cultural variables affect the psychotherapeutic situation. The following outline will be used in specifying these articulations: (a) First, a descriptive outline of the psychotherapeutic process will be summarized, explicating generic factors held to account for the efficacy of therapeutic procedures irrespective of culture. (b) Second, social interactional factors (e.g., ideologies, value systems, and norms) will be discussed in relation to their ubiquitous and profound impact on the therapeutic situation. The potential negative effects on communication due to cross-cultural differences in values and norms will be developed through a discussion of "micronorms" which Erving Goffman (1967b) and others have defined as *interaction rules*. (c) Third, the effects of ethnicity on interaction rules in the therapeutic situation will be outlined by way of visualizing the mechanics through which cultural "fit" or "non-fit" affect the communicational process of therapist/patient interaction. (d) Finally, some reflections will be made on the positive effects of recent interest in cross-cultural variables in the fields of psychotherapy and counseling.

PSYCHOTHERAPEUTIC AND COUNSELING PROCEDURES

Needs for Specialized Services

Regardless of cultural context, psychotherapeutic procedures take place in a communicational matrix and operate as agencies for change, i.e., betterment or improvement. There is an expectation that the interventions of the therapist will change objective behavior—adaptation, adjustment, achievement, as well as subjective behavior — in terms of conflict resolution, diminution of symptoms, and increased understanding. Procedures vary between nations, societies, and cultures, as well as within societies and cultures themselves. Also, the definitions of deviance, normality, and abnormality vary significantly between cultures as well as within cultures and, for that matter, among social classes. Similarly, the belief that the psychotherapeutic procedure will "work" (i.e., positive expectancy), or the manner in which it will "work" shows a variation within the society — particularly according to the accessibility or opportunity for therapeutic interventions.

Of course, psychotherapy and counseling are merely formalized and socially authenticated procedures for problem resolution. Such procedures are sought by individuals who are defined by themselves or others as in need of extraneous, i.e., professional, assistance. By assumption, that need is present when naturally available resources inside and/or outside the client have been depleted, or found inadequate to intercurrent stresses or preoccupations. Within American psychology, psychiatry, and psychoanalysis, there has been an increasingly critical examination of the auspices under which counseling and psychotherapy are conducted. In the past, some of this criticism has pointed to the failure to consider factors related to the culture and/or class. These criticisms coincide with the recognition of increasing needs for therapeutic procedures among ethnic and nonethnic Americans. These needs have been particularly well stated by Levine (1976) and summarized by King (1978). Levine postulates that if industrial society maintains its present set of conditions — weak social structures, diffuse and rapidly changing values, vague adult gender roles — that the incidence of disorder will undergo a continuing and substantial increase [p. 420]. King has reviewed research literature examining cultural variables in regard to differential responses to the stress of changing conditions present in contemporary society.

> There is some evidence that groups with structures or rituals for relieving guilt, anxiety and grief, that allow children to deal with supportive adults, and provide status for women and elderly persons have low depression and psychological disorder. There is also clear evidence that individuals or groups that are unable to maintain some continuity of change, but still maintain cohesion through custom, language, worship, life-style and ceremonies, develop a buffering against the breakdown characterized by persons without roots [p. 418].

There are, then, indications of increasing need for counseling and therapeutic procedures, and this need is being expressed at a time when the differential effects of culture on psychological health and disability are becoming matters of common understanding. There is promise in this coincidence of increasing needs for service and acknowledgement of the importance of ethnicity. This promise could lead to a more sophisticated understanding of the process of psychotherapy and counseling; it should also lead to setting up more relevant and responsive services for ethnic clients. The

following section will look at some features which are generic to all psychotherapies. Later sections will examine some of the mechanics through which
culture is communicationally transacted in the therapeutic situation.

Some Cultural and Status Factors in the Therapeutic/ Counseling Situation

A number of outcome studies have looked into the quality of match (or
"fit") between therapist and client. (A particularly good review is included
in Luborsky, Auerbach, Chandler, & Choen, 1971.) In general, results from
this literature have uniformly shown that concordance in social class,
education, and ethnicity is correlated with positive outcome in therapeutic
situations. Despite the evidence of need for commonality between the participants, the therapeutic situation itself requires a calculated *asymmetry*
(i.e., imbalance) in the social roles, status, and objectives of the client and
therapist. In all cultures, the therapist is a culturally authenticated healer
whose social role is to provide help. Contrastingly, the client is identified as
a person present in the role of needing help. The primary intention of the
therapeutic encounter is to produce change (i.e., improvement and relief)
for the client. In an essay on comparative psychotherapies, Torrey (1972)
has put the healer/client role asymmetry in cross-cultural perspective, demonstrating that these qualities of expectation are indeed universal, although
the particulars are extremely varied according to cultural differences.

Since psychotherapy takes place in an interpersonal communicational
framework, certain specialized conditions (i.e., procedures, rules, customs)
are necessary to make the interaction process distinctive from similar communications between friends, advisors, teachers, and others. In all cultures,
the "healing" procedure takes place in a distinctive physical setting, again,
in order to differentiate the situation from similar but less auspicious encounters. Also, some form of confidentiality or "secrecy" about what is discussed is implicit, but often may be explicitly guaranteed. In contrast to
ordinary conversational situations, the procedure seeks out rather than
avoids areas of conflict, anguish, confusion, and heightened emotion. Also
unlike ordinary life situations, the procedure is not reciprocal in terms of
the ebb and flow of dialogue; the interaction is created to focus on the behavior and subjectivity of the client. Additionally, the situation fosters reflection and *in*action (during the encounter) rather than *re*action, although
some procedures, e.g., psychodrama or behavioral modification, may focus
on rehearsing particular actions. Psychotherapeutic procedures take place
in the context of "present," "past," and "future"; however, there are significant cross-cultural differences in orientation to this chronological spectrum.
Western psychotherapies characteristically stress past/present connections.

However, as Murase and Johnson (1974) described, two Japanese psychotherapeutic procedures — *Morita* and *Naikan* — only sparingly investigate the past. Contrary to Western traditions, concentration on the origins of ambivalence and replaying infantile conflicts would be regarded as "sick" — i.e., antithetical to Japanese cultural values, which extoll forgiving, forgetting, or even pretending to ignore the past in order to conduct contemporary relations. Kiev (1972) has also summarized a number of "culture specific syndromes" and contrasted these alongside analagous Western conditions. In treatment of these syndromes by an indigenous therapist, the emphasis on the past is often highly focalized and brief.

Two culturally contrasting situations described by Torrey (1972) illustrate some of these differences in regard to chronological as well as other dimensions.

First case (Western "middle class" psychotherapy): The psychiatrist looked thoughtfully at his patient. "You looked angry when you were just talking about your father. You often look angry when you talk about him. I wonder if something happened to you once that made you very angry at him." At this point the patient broke down sobbing, blurting out a forgotten history of neglect and deceit by a thoughtless father toward a little girl. Afterwards the patient felt better.

Second case (Psychotherapy with an "indigenous" healer): The witchdoctor stared solemnly at the small shells. They had landed in a pattern resembling the shape of a large animal. He picked one shell up and examined it minutely. "You have broken the taboo of your family. It has offended the sacred bear that protects your ancestors. That is why you are sick." The patient and her family breathed a sign of relief. It was as they had suspected. Now that they knew for certain what was wrong they could proceed with the necessary sacrifices. After these had been made, the patient began to get better [p. 70].

The above cases at once demonstrate cross-cultural similarities and differences. In terms of similarities, each case illustrates a culturally authenticated healer having an effective transaction with his client through a consensually acceptable "explanation" of the client's difficulty. This action results in the release of tension and the opportunity for change (i.e., "improvement"). The differences, of course, are that the cultural substantiation of the therapists are quite specific and the causal-motivational explanations are exceedingly culture-bound. (One can playfully imagine the effects of "switching" these causal explanations, where the American psychiatrist tells his patient that her family has offended a "sacred bear," or, alternatively, the witch doctor would stare into his client's eyes and state that her suffering was due to her father's diffidence ten years earlier.) Also, the Western psychotherapist's interpretation in terms of past transactions with the father implicitly ties his patient's contemporary performance to a series of past encounters. Contrastingly, the indigenous healer's explanation focuses on an accidental lapse in ceremonial behavior which only fleetingly implicates past performance.

Despite the superficial differences in techniques, cross-culturally as well as within the same culture, certain fundamentals pertain to all therapeutic situations. Marmor (1971) discussed some of these "basics" in the context of comparisons between behavior therapy and psychoanalysis. He lists the following as generic to both methods of treatment:

1. *Release of tension* through catharsis;
2. *Cognitive learning,* both through trial-and-error, as well as of the gestalt variety;
3. Reconditioning by *operant conditioning* (through implicit or explicit reward or punishment);
4. Identification with the therapist;
5. Repeated reality testing as an equivalent of practicing in the learning process (p. 483). (Author's italics)

Using Marmor's outline, these "basics" will be briefly reviewed with reference to some effects of culture and ethnicity on these fundamental common aspects of psychotherapeutic process.

Catharsis Globally, "catharsis" refers to the tension relief that accompanies the divulging and *sharing* of information in a specialized context of trust and intimacy. Regardless of variations in technique or cultural setting, the joint communication between therapist and client constitutes a process through which an "intersubjective consensus" is developed regarding the meaning of what has been told and said (Johnson, 1975). Berger and Kellner (1964) first drew attention to the significance of such consensus in their analysis of personality support systems developing between marital partners. Somewhat later, Berger and Luckman (1967) elaborated a broadened theory concerning the microsociological characteristics of the intimate sharing of communication which they defined as "the social construction of reality." By their definitions, continuous and intimate communications in therapeutic as well as in specialized nontherapeutic situations utilizes a process which they term "legitimation." They comment that:

The most important conceptual requirement for alternation (i.e., change in behavior) is the availability of a legitimating apparatus for the whole sequence of transformation. What must be legitimated is not only the new reality, but the stages by which it is appropriated and maintained (p. 159).

Regardless of cultural setting, the therapist reinforces (i.e., legitimates) interpretations and conclusions that have been implicit in the narrations of the patient. Obviously, the form of such legitimation varies according to the differences in method, differences in cultural setting, and the characteristics of the participants.

Learning It is universally accepted that aspects of the psychotherapentic process can be productively understood by analogy to education and learning. The literature on behavior modification is based on a detailed explanation of the therapeutic situation in terms of highly specialized characteristics of the learning process.

In a more metaphorical manner, Szasz (1963) has analyzed the psychotherapeutic process according to the concept of education, dividing the procedure into *protoeducational, educational,* and *metaeducational* activities. *Protoeducational* is analogous to learning at a "rote" or denotational level where a "teacher" is involved in the simple definition of objects in the material and social world. The *educational* aspects of psychotherapy are concerned with the cognitive (conscious) learning occurring during the procedure based on what both participants are saying or doing. At the next stage, *metaeducational* activity is described as the process of learning about learning. That is to say that a protoeducational level is concerned with *facts,* the educational level is concerned with *tactics,* while the metaeducational level is a way of understanding *strategies* of interaction in everyday life.

A less metaphorical analysis of the therapeutic situation is available through *semiotics.* As discussed by Reichenbach (1947, 1951), semiotics is the study of signs and sign-using behavior, including linguistic as well as extralinguistic aspects of language. By systematically including paraverbal aspects of communication, semiotic analysis readily subsumes cultural and ethnic implications. Semiotics, therefore, permits the relativistic, value laden aspects of communication to be operationally defined alongside more standardizable, objective variables. As Reichenbach (1947) states (quoted in Szasz, 1961):

> It should be clearly seen that the instrumental use of language falls into a category in which the predicates "true" and "false" do not apply. These predicates express a semantical relation, namely, a relation between signs and objects; but since instrumental usage is in pragmatics, i.e., includes the sign-user, it cannot be judged as true or false [p. 19].

Although this citation is from the perspective of operational philosophy and linguistics, it is identical to the conclusions of the anthropologists regarding the shifting relativity of meaning according to diverse cultural and subcultural variables. Attribution of meaning, causality, and "sense" in regard to sequences of behavior is acknowledged as arbitrary (i.e., relativistic), and is related to the fact that the predicates of "true" and "false" do not rigorously apply. Instead, such communicational symbols and signals can only be defined through *interpretation,* i.e., a negotiated agreement between the therapist and client concerning consensual meaning. An understanding of such arbitrary designation illuminates the relativistic aspects of everyday experience, and highlights the significance of the crucial act of legitimation, which operates between patient and therapist (Berger and Luckmann, 1967).

In terms of Torrey's "cases" (1972), it is not important to establish the *veridical truth* of whether a patient is despondent because of offending a sacred bear, or because of a father's coldness. Neither statement is absolutely "true" or "false," except insofar as each of them can be legitimated as a plausible and consensual explanation of current difficulties. Given this arbitrariness, the need for "fit" between therapist and client is one of the most critical variables in the psychotherapeutic situation. The potentiality for distortion or misunderstanding is evident based on ethnic, gender, and class biases and the shifting nature of what may be held to be "true" and authentic for different persons coming from different cultures or class settings.

Operant Conditioning Conditioning is generally acknowledged as a ubiquitous and essential factor in psychotherapy and counseling. This means that, regardless of the technique, "school" of psychotherapy, or culture in which the procedure occurs, a client is progressively conditioned through reinforcement and reward toward the acquisition of new understandings, insights, and techniques which can be applied to improved levels of performance and comfort. Since the principles governing reinforcement and conditioning are so widely understood, they do not require restatement here. However, from a cultural standpoint, our interest is drawn to the wide diversity of techniques, methods, rituals, and ceremonial performances that are used in various cultures to lead to the assimilation of new, learned behavior.

Relationship with Therapist The relationship with the healer is universally regarded as a prominent component in psychotherapy and counseling, although in some procedures the relational aspects may be intentionally or ceremonially minimized. Classically, the client/therapist relationship has been productively studied using the concepts of "transference" and "countertransference." Recently, the potentially coercive aspects of transference have been publicized, especially in regard to the treatment of women and ethnics in American society. (Of course, the whole issue of coercion is in itself an American cultural preoccupation stemming from the highly held mandates for individual liberty and "independence.") However, most other cultures not only accept the therapist as an authority figure — even with the potential for coercion — but find such a situation desirable and consistent with status relativity within the culture (Murase & Johnson, 1974). While the importance of the relational aspects of psychotherapy are generally acknowledged, the degree of importance and the explanations for such significance are, at times, hotly disputed. Some of this dispute may be based on class, cultural, or subcultural differences in the expectations connected to the therapist/patient interaction. However, other differences in viewpoint relate to disputes concerning the operational, theoretical explanation of the psychotherapeutic process, itself.

Reality Testing Reality testing in the therapeutic situation is described by Marmor as a form of "practicing" which has to do with adjusting and accommodating to newly discovered ways of thinking and behaving. Operationally, "reality testing" refers to a process through which the *social reality* is repeatedly defined and legitimated. As Reusch and Prestwood (1950) comment:

> In psychotherapy it is the repeated contact with the therapist, the experience of these self-regulatory processes, and the continuous reference to the social situation . . . roles and implementations which bring about change within the patient (p. 339).

Marmor uses the term "practicing" to indicate that this continued definition and redefinition of reality permits a rehearsal for anticipated actions within a social reality which is outside of the treatment situation. Of course, the extent and explicitness of such practicing varies, e.g., among procedures such as behavior modification, Zen, psychoanalysis, psychodrama, faith-healing, etc. Also, the definitions and judgments concerning social reality are stricken with considerations of value, ideology, and norms. Nevertheless, it is a central function of any therapeutic process to be able to identify and define variations in social reality that will leave the client open to seek more rational and constructive future actions. Here again, the need for a potentially close "fit" between therapist and patient is obvious. Without such commonality, decisions concerning "what to practice" or "how to practice" may lead to endless misunderstandings, arguments, and impasse.

The next section of this chapter will discuss interactional explanations of the therapeutic situation before returning to a consideration of ethnic and cultural factors in counseling and psychotherapy.

INTERACTIONAL ANALYSIS OF THE THERAPEUTIC SITUATION

Interaction Rules

Although many professional fields have historically contributed to the study of human behavior, the disciplines of psychology, sociology, social psychology, and anthropology have been foremost in generating scientific descriptions and explanations of human actions. Coming from different traditions and using separate methodologies, these fields have examined patterns identified as *personality systems,* patterns described as *social systems,* as well as patterns which constitute *cultural systems.* These fields have persistently sought to define concepts and constructs applicable to human behavior, and have worked to create identifiable *units of study* which are capable of validation, replication, and, of course, statistical manipulation. As in other sciences, successful attempts to refine concepts into precise and measurable units of study have been achieved at the expense of a progressive loss of total phenomenology of actual behavior. Various "field theories" have attempted to reduce this by enlarging the range of perspective, typically through the use of multiple (methodological) levels of analysis. A felicitous instance of such theory building occurred in the late 1950s when a multidisciplinary group of scholars published a book concerned with elaborating a "General Theory of Action" (Parsons & Shils, 1951). In this volume, Henry Murray elaborated a classification of *interaction.*

> The social scientist's "real entity" is a temporal unit of interacting processes, the simplest being a short interpersonal proceeding, (e.g.) the movements and words of the actor (the *Subject)* and reaction of the alter (the *Object).* In representing an interaction unit of this type . . . our model of the proceeding should include as much information of the Object's thought and speech as of the Subject's thought and speech [p. 435].

About the same time, Reusch and Prestwood (1950) published a theoretical scheme of "Interaction Processes and Personal Codification" in an attempt to develop a heuristic model capable of including multidimensional aspects involved in patient/therapist interaction. They felt that: "The maximum information necessary to understand an interaction process at any one time involve(s) at least 25 variables [p. 307]." These variables were expressed by them in a 5 x 5 matrix with one ordinate displaying "social situation," "self," "other," "us," and "they," and a coordinate which tabulated "needs," "goals," "emotions," "roles," and "interpersonal techniques." Their thesis was that, at any moment in time, a given static interaction could be described through the ways in which these 25 variables were or were not interacting at that moment. To complicate their model further, they added a time dimensional component which gave a cubed matrix (5 x 5 x 3), including the time dimensions of "anticipation," "action," and "evaluation." It was the opinion of these authors that "the effective therapeutic agent is found in the interaction process [p. 338]." Specifically referring to culture in regard to the efficacy of therapy, they concluded that:

The previously existing antagonism between subjective view of the self as expressed in fantasy life . . . and attributed objective view of what the patient thinks culture, rules, and generalizations are about, is gradually eliminated. Essentially, the patient learns that information about the self is obtainable only through other people and not through self–centered study [p. 342].

Although criticized for his limited methodological focus on the dramatization of human encounter, Erving Goffman has added to the understanding of the microsociological characteristics of human encounters. In a series of publications he has elaborated on the concept of interaction rules (1959, 1967a, 1967b, 1969, 1974). In a description of face-to-face interaction in naturalistic settings, Goffman [1967a] has identified the subject matter of interaction itself, as consisting of: "The glances, gestures, positionings, verbal statements that people continuously feed into the situation, whether intended or not [p. 91]."

Although the description of interaction rules is recurrent in a number of Goffman's writings, one of these can serve as a definition:

When in the presence of others, the individual is guided by a special set of rules. . . . Upon examination these rules prove to govern the allocation of the individual's involvement with the situation, as expressed through a conventionalized idiom of behavioral cues [1969, p. 243].

More recently, Lyman and Douglass (1973) have looked into ethnicity in terms of strategies of individual and collective impression management — again employing the concept of interaction rules.

At the group level of social organization, ethnic relations usually translate themselves into sets and series of strategic and tactical situations played out over time. . . . If a (idealized) state of nature is to be avoided, there must be a degree of accommodation and association to a set of rules governing interaction and relationships between the members . . . composing the plural social order [p. 334].

Johnson and Johnson (1975), in a study of ethnic interaction between Japanese Americans and Caucasians in Honolulu, examined ethnicity "as a function of distinctive interaction rules in encounters both within and outside the Japanese community [p. 452]." Utilizing the theoretical approach of symbolic interaction theory, they looked at interethnic interaction as characterized by a mutual lack of knowledge concerning the norms, subcultures, and ethnic groups. In this same report, "exchange theory" (Singleman, 1972) was used to explain encounters where the rewards might be too low or the costs too high to continue to communicate in an interethnic relationship. The social-psychological literature connected with "interpersonal attraction" also documents situations in which dissonant communicational interaction leads to the rapid development of stereotyped extremes in behaviors between interethnic participants (Levinger & Snoek,

1972).

The persistent effect of culture of origin on interaction rules was studied by Johnson and Marsella (1978), who concluded that status norms present in the Japanese language were still evident in third generation Japanese Americans who did not understand or speak Japanese. This would indicate that interaction rules connected with speech in the Japanese language continued to be imparted through family communication, but were currently expressed in the English language.

In a different vein, Hochschild (1979) has investigated the implicit interaction rules connected with the regulation of *feeling* in social situations. She described a process in the modulation of feelings using the concept of "emotion management" in the context of what she terms "feeling rules":

> A feeling rule shares some formal properties with other sorts of rules, such as rules of etiquette, rules of bodily comportment, and those of social interaction in general (Goffman, 1967b). A feeling rule . . . delineates a zone within which one has permission to be free of worry, guilt, or shame with regard to the situated feeling [p. 91].

Interaction rules, therefore, have been identified as definable units of study in a number of disciplines which examine human action and communicational process (sociology, social-psychology, psychiatry, linguistics, semiotics). Such rules are here defined as being connected to the simple expectations concerned with the moment-to-moment governance of interaction. In this sense, interaction rules operate as a "final pathway" through which the various norms, value systems and ideologies present in any culture are monitored and interpreted in light of actual or anticipated behavior.

Interaction Rules, Psychotherapy, and Stereotyping

The psychotherapist in any culture works to assist in the definition of subtle gradations of implicit rules governing behavior which derive from a vast array of norms, value systems, and ideologies present in the shared "assumptive worlds" of the patient and therapist (Frank, 1963). With ethnic clients, the complexity of simultaneously dealing with diverse sets of competing (i.e., culturally dystonic) interaction rules poses a special problem for both the therapist and the client. The psychotherapist's goal is to make implicit rules situationally explicit, and to assist in decoding the tactical and strategic significance of such rules. Clarification of these rules can lead to looking at a range of additional options pertaining to the client's present and future behaviors. It is very evident that differences in class, culture, or subculture between clients and their therapists may seriously interfere with this purpose and potentially lead to high levels of confusion, misunderstanding, or overt conflict. Of course, other variables in the characteristics of client and therapist may produce similar incongruency in the communication process. However, cultural differences — because of their pervasive effect on behavior — are particularly prone to lead to bias on the part of therapists and/or their clients.

The most significant hazard of cross-cultural psychotherapeutic procedures, however, is that the different backgrounds of the participants tend to reinforce stereotypical behavior in the other partner. This distortion is, however, in no sense peculiar to psychotherapy. Johnson and Johnson (1975) have described such interactional rule distortions between Japanese Americans in Honolulu and their Caucasian counterparts. Parallel intercultural distortions between mainland Japanese and Americans have been described by Bennett, Passim, and McKnight (1958). Similar reports concerning stereotyping are widely available describing relationships between various ethnic groups (Singleman, 1972; Lyman and Douglass, 1973).

What is consistently described is that, in the absence of cultural commonality, each partner in the situation begins to retreat defensively into the projection of an exaggerated stereotype of ethnic behavior toward the other person. In the context of Japanese American and Caucasian American communication, this tends to make some Japanese Americans appear increasingly quiet, reticent, or aloof in interethnic situations, while some Caucasian Americans become more loud, verbose, and directive. Such encounters may rapidly escalate to a mutually defensive quality. Each participant begins to sense a subjective discomfort and begins to feel inauthentic and uncomfortable. At the same time, each partner perceives the increasingly exaggerated behavior of the *alter* as confirming the normatively held ingroup ethnic stereotypes which exist in all cultures as boundary mechanisms.

The objectives of the communicational situation then deteriorate and interaction predictably moves toward evasion and closure rather than toward openness and continuation. Such consequences are particularly serious in the therapeutic situation. Given such cultural parataxis, it becomes very difficult for either the patient or the therapist to evaluate mood, level of self-esteem, or to seek a consensual understanding of the meaning within the interethnic communication. Although this may be uncomfortable for the therapist, the implications for the client extend far beyond discomfort — particularly in persons with moderate to severe disabilities. Parenthetically, one wonders how much of the spurious "increased pathology" seen in some interethnic situations can be attributed to a situationally increased *stress on the patient* (which magnifies disability), in addition to the usual explanation of the bias of the nonethnic therapist which readily leads to a false interpretation of disability.

Of course, the processes and effects of stereotyping in interethnic interactions has been productively studied and identified through the work of a

number of social scientists. Townsend (1979), in a recent comparison between stereotypes connected to ethnicity and mental illness, cited four
"traits" involved in the process of steteotyping:

1. [Stereotypes] are exaggerated and serve to dichotomize between the in-group and the
   out-group;
2. They are maintained through selective perception;
3. They erect high thresholds for "crossing";
4. They persist despite the flow of personnel across boundaries and despite campaigns to
   alter them [p.208].

Townsend's description of these traits depicts collective, social attitudes
of groups; however, they equally apply to direct interpersonal communication between individuals involved in cross-cultural encounters.

There are obvious parallels and connections between prejudices held by
in-groups (expressed in the form of "norms") and the communicational
dissonance and resultant dysphoria that occurs between individuals
(monitored through the effects of defensive "interaction rules"). The point
of this section is to emphasize that although the actual interethnic distortion
develops on the basis of collectively held stereotypical "norms," the actual
transaction is governed by interaction rules through which such explicit
norms implicitly guide (and distort) the encounter.

Other Variables Affecting Interaction

Although cultural variables have a powerful potential for affecting (and
disrupting) interpersonal encounters, there are a number of equally important variables which impact on the interaction rules. These will briefly be
described here, partly in order to place cultural differences in the perspective of being *one* of a number of interpersonal differences which affect accuracy and consensus in communicational situations.

In an article concerned with personality structure, George Devereux
(1952) described personality in terms of a set of *axes,* including *biological,
cultural, experiential,* and what might be called *characterological* factors.
Devereux's "axes" could be expanded to include *gender* and *social class*
variables, which also act as selective factors influencing both perception and
performance in human communication. The combination of each of these
complex variables can be analogized to a series of optical lenses, similar to
those used by ophthalmologists to determine needs for correction of visual
acuity. Analogically, these "lenses" of perception filter and change the subjective experience of encounter in the same way that lenses polarize,
magnify, or change real images. An additional and obvious assumption is
that there are reciprocal, two-dimensional differences in subjective
categorization which affect both perception and behavior ("input" and
"output") occurring within a two-person system.

Biological Variables

Biological variables can metaphorically be defined as the "wiring" of the organism. Obviously, differences in the capacity to perceive, conceive, "understand," and emote vary within the population according to biological determinants. Although always affected by opportunity, education, and experience, hereditarily determined potentialities are present which affect the capacity to manipulate quantitative and qualitative information and to comprehend varying degrees of complex analysis and interpretation of experience. Similarly, despite the role of experience, certain biological givens influence the character of individual expressiveness and emotionality. Needless to say, such differences in individual capacities have a strong impact on the perception of self and other as well as the differential perception of objective and social reality.

Gender Variables

Recently, the importance of sex roles has been highlighted in terms of potential distortion due to gender differences on communication and interaction, particularly in the psychotherapeutic situation. The implications of bias in the perception of gender has received belated — although excellent — review by social scientists, psychologists, and psychiatrists. Literature concerning the fact that gender recognition involves a consistently lowered estimation of women's behaviors has been ably summarized by Maccoby and Jacklin (1975). The potentially malignant nature of gender discrimination (that is, sexism) in the psychotherapeutic situation has also received belated but clear enunciation. However, the ubiquitous and unobtrusive ways in which gender affects communication has received less attention. The subtle implications of gender differences in communication have received descriptive study in social psychology and linguistics. These less conspicuous differences in verbal and paraverbal behavior due to gender differences of the participants are, therefore, often unrecognized. Furthermore, they are not particularly stressed in the training of clinicians in psychology and psychiatry and other counseling professions. Fortunately, however, the potentially more blatant communicational distortions in regard to treatment situations where, for example, the therapist and/or the client are identified as gay or lesbian, have begun to be incorporated in the training of psychotherapists.

Characterological Variation

The use here of the word "characterology" refers to typologies of manifest behavior which fall into certain agreed upon and recognized categories within any given culture. Characterology in this broad sense is not equivalent to character "pathology," but, rather, identifies the fact that certain ranges of behavior in any society are not idiosyncratic or unique, but cluster into patterns (styles) which are abstracted and inferred from the actual observed behavior. Furthermore, such behaviors in all cultures are "named" — scientifically as well as colloquially. In addition to categorizing manifest behavior, characterology is also concerned with subjective, cognitive style and the variations in the quality of subjectivity. Only in unusual instances would such clusters of behavior justify the use of the more stereotyped "pathologic" categories of "obsessive personality," "hysterical personality," etc.

The therapist's intuitive and explicit understanding of normative structure in his or her society is a measure of the accuracy and understanding of the characterology or reaction patterns of the client. An accurate sense of the ranges of character style is necessary in order to lead to plausible interpretations concerning motives, meaning, and impact on others of the individual's behavior. Also, the therapist's intuitive or cognitive grasp of his or her own characterology is extremely important in calibrating judgments concerning the essence of other persons' behavior and characterology. Finally, understanding the differences in cognition and experience attributable to the patient's characterology is essential in order to calculate the *timing* as well as the *content* of interventions made to improve the patient's understanding, or to direct the patient's behavior toward higher levels of performance and comfort.

Developmental Variables

Persons who are involved in a psychotherapeutic interaction are looking through the lens of their own present and past developmental stages. Differences in position in the life cycle decidedly affect world view and capacity to see objective phenomena, as well as the capacity to see the other person accurately in a two-person situation. Again, training in psychotherapeutic work has only recently accentuated the explicit importance of developmental stages, especially in forms that permit a broader definition of the significance of life stages within various subcultures. A regrettable tendency has been noted in terms of the earlier definition of stages according to a universal schema based mainly on the developmental sequences of males. Increasing specification of developmental stages and critical periods of "passage" permit a more accurate contextualization of individual disability.

Social Class Variables

As Gordon (1964), Valentine (1969), and others have indicated, social class position can be structurally viewed as a subcultural experience predicated on the verification of the individual's identity within a particular occupational and educational strata. As in ethnic differentiations, class participation at all levels is based upon the avoidance of behaviors and encounters that are characteristically associated with other class experience. In this sense, class levels operate identically to ethnic categorizations: as boundary mechanisms operating to regulate family relationships, friendship networks, courting, recreational patterns, usage of language, expectations, and, of course, opportunities. Class experience is intimately connected to socioeconomic security and power; hence, expectancies and assumptions are very different depending upon class positions. Needless to say, there are differential rates of incidence and prevalence of major mental disabilities, with the experience of higher rates of schizophrenia in persons who fall into the lower socioeconomic class. Also, the options available to persons within any society obviously vary radically at the extremes of class position. Failure to observe these factors in the therapeutic situation leads to serious distortion in communication.

Finally, attitudes about social class also function to exaggerate stereotypes in the same manner found in interethnic interaction. In fact, most negative ethnic stereotyping involves two factors: a selective exaggeration of *cultural* characteristics in the context of a distorted characterization of *social class* position.

DISCUSSION AND CONCLUSIONS

During the past three decades, the complex interrelationships between personality and culture have received increased scholarly attention. Although beset by methodological difficulties, theoreticians from psychology, anthropology, and sociology have continued to work toward conceptualizations capable of explaining human behavior at *personal, social,* and *cultural* levels. In this context, the attempt to understand and explain cross-cultural psychotherapy is a practical instance of the need for more succinct, scientific understanding of the multiple process variables in the treatment situation. This present decade promises to further such understanding, partly stirred by the increasing need for specialized procedures devised to enhance communication with ethnic clients.

Recently there has been a reawakening of interest in the relationship of cultural variables to personality variables in contexts dealing with mental health, disability, normality, and the process of psychotherapy. In two recent issues of *Annual Review of Psychology,* King (1978) and Strauss (1979) surveyed the literature regarding social and cultural influences on various dimensions of individual and group behaviors. Both reviewers stated that relatively few hard and fast conclusions have been reached, although a qualitatively rich, descriptive data base is available specifying significant intercorrelations and (statistical) interactions. Both authors point to problems concerning methodology involved in devising studies capable of scientifically determining factors which operate in a consistent, predictable manner. Future investigations will, of course, require increasingly complex multivariate analyses. The question is, however, which variables out of a myriad of factors should be left in (or out) in order to investigate the interrelationships between culture and personality in the context of the process of psychotherapy. (Reusch and Prestwood's, 1951, previously cited 25 variable matrix is useful in suggesting the numbers of factors necessary to subsume the therapeutic situation in a three-dimensional framework.)

The design of this present chapter has been to provide an overview of the psychotherapeutic situation and to incorporate factors concerned with ethnicity. Several sections have identified and described specific points where cultural and social class factors articulate with other variables in the psychotherapeutic process. A definition of *interaction rules* has been given to describe the mechanics of the moment-to-moment evaluative process which monitors and guides personal interaction. Interaction rules have been defined as being highly situation-specific, exceedingly nonexplicit, and relatively ungeneralized in contrast to "norms," The significance of "fit" in the shared understanding of ethnic variables between therapist and client has been presented in terms of the possible variations in interaction rules of two or more interethnic participants. Additionally, the mechanics of stereotyping have been summarized through citation of some of the literature concerned with "exchange theory," symbolic interaction, and "interpersonal attraction." Another objective has been to note and accentuate the linguistic, paraverbal, semantic, and contextual factors present in psychotherapeutic and counseling situations. Implicit in this presentation is the need to place cultural factors in the appropriate perspective of being *one of a number of salient factors* affecting communication, action, and meaning.

Various methods and schools of psychotherapy have unwittingly distorted the explanation of process through emphasizing particular variables which are held to be of ascendant importance by practicioners trained in those methods. It should be hoped that the new fields of Cross-cultural Psychotherapy and Counseling will not repeat the mistakes of earlier "methods" by retreating into defensively chauvinistic positions. A hint of this is already evident in the reductionistic notion held in some quarters that *only* ethnics can properly treat other ethnics (from the same subculture). Obviously, the issue of cultural "fit" has to do with the conscious comprehension and empathy concerning those specific cultural ingredients which characterize any culture. It also reflects the acquisition of skill and experience in some form of psychotherapeutic technique. Needless to say, merely being a professional who happens to be a member of an ethnic group does not necessarily confer unusual insights about his or her own culture of origin, or uniformly connote particular distinction as a psychotherapist. In the reverse direction, counseling professionals from outside of particular ethnic groups are not categorically disqualified from learning to deal with specialized ethnic populations.

Another potential problem in "ethnic", or for that matter conventional, counseling is that overaccentuating subcultural variables can become a way of avoiding other significant explanations of difficulties. For example, it may be difficult for both the patient and the therapist to strike a balance between the significance of the *micropolitical* aspects of the patient's life (the day-to-day relationships where ethnic biases are present) and the *macropolitical* realities of bias present in the larger society which are ubiquitously present but may not sufficiently explain particular events in the patient's life. Even if the therapist is of the same ethnic group as the patient, decisions about the interpretation of the subjective sense of oppression require a great deal of skill. Minimizing the significance of such effects on the patient clearly would be oppressive; on the other hand, heedlessly reinforcing such feelings might also constitute a way of ignoring other salient and parallel explanations.

Also, there is a clear danger in concentrating on specific ethnic status while ignoring the *bicultural* situation in which both the patient and the therapist must navigate. Although this applies in many countries, both North and South American societies are particularly pluralistic. In these situations, the importance of bicultural understanding is especially important. Concentrating on a limited ensemble of specific subcultural norms, the therapist and patient may ignore the reality that behavioral adjustment in a pluralistic society must take into account the understanding of complex normative systems which situationally fluctuate depending upon context (e.g., work situation vs. family situation vs. in-law situation, etc.). Also, an *overemphasis* on the cultural or subcultural "fit" between therapist and client may unintentionally promote an *illusion of commonality,* as if ethnic experience were uniform. It is obvious that, regardless of commonalities in gender, class, and ethnicity, there are striking variations in experience and subjectivity present within all subcultures.

Finally, the recent recognition of ethnicity as a salient variable in psychotherapeutic situations allows for the expansion of existing training models to include curriculum and supervision designed to train psychotherapists and counselors to use insights concerning ethnicity to enable productive change in their clients. The development of training programs to create specialists for particular ethnic populations is undeniably sound and effective. However, it is equally evident that such curriculum and training should be incorporated into existing programs in clinical psychology, psychiatry, counseling, and social work. One of the dangers in accentuating the development of new, highly subspecialized, paraprofessional therapists for ethnic populations is that this might set up a cadre of narrowly-trained practitioners whose very existence would remove the incentive for traditional professionals to assume responsibility for treatment of diverse persons within American society. What is needed is the simultaneous development of sophisticated programs in ethnic issues within currently existing, as well as newly organized, centers for training psychotherapists and counselors.

REFERENCES

Bennett, J.W., Passim, H., & McKnight, R. *In search of identity.* Minneapolis: University of Minnesota Press, 1958.

Berger, P., & Kellner, H. Marriage and the construction of reality. *Diogenes,* 1964, *46,* 1-25.

Berger, P.L., & Luchmann, P. *The social construction of reality.* Garden City, N.Y.: Anchor Books, 1967.

Devereux, G. Psychiatry and anthropology: Some research objectives. *Bulletin of the Menninger Clinic,* 1952, *16,* 167-177.

Frank, J. *Persuasion and healing.* New York: Schoeken Books, 1963.

Goffman, E. *The presentation of self in everyday life.* Garden City, N.Y.: Doubleday, 1959.

Goffman, E. *Behavior in public places.* New York: The Free Press, 1967. (a)

Goffman, E. *Interaction ritual.* Garden City, N.Y.: Doubleday, 1967. (b)

Goffman, E. *Strategic interaction.* Philadelphia: University of Pennsylvania Press, 1969.

Goffman, E. *Frame Analysis.* New York: Harper & Row, 1974.

Gordon, M.M. *Assimilation in American life.* New York: Oxford University Press, 1964.

Hoschschild, A.R. Emotion work, general rules and social structure. *American Journal of Sociology,* 1979, *85,* 551-575.

Johnson, C., & Johnson, F. Interaction rules and ethnicity. *Social Forces,* 1975, *54,* 425-466.

Johnson, F. Some problems of reification in existential psychiatry. In R.G. Geyer & D.R. Schweitzer (Eds.), *Theories of alienation.* Leiden: Martinus Nijhoff, 1975.

Johnson, R., & Marsella, A. Differential attitudes toward verbal behavior in students of

Japanese and European ancestry. *Genetic Psychology Monographs,* 1978, *97,* 43-76.

Kiev, A. *Transcultural psychiatry.* New York: The Free Press, 1972.

King, L.M. Social and cultural influences on psychopathology. *Annual Review of Psychology,* 1978, *29,* 405-433.

Levine, E.M. Psycho-cultural determinants in personality development. *Volta Review,* 1976, *78,* 258-267.

Levinger, G., & Snoek, J.D. *Attraction in relationship.* Morristown, N.J.: General Learning Press, 1972.

Luborsky, L., Auerbach, P., Chandler, M., & Choen, J. Factors influencing the outcome of psychotherapy. *Psychological Bulletin,* 1971, *75,* 145-185.

Lyman, S.M., & Douglass, W.A. Ethnicity: Strategies of collective and individual impression management. *Social Research,* 1973, *40*(2), 344-356.

Maccoby, E., & Jacklin, C. *Psychology of sex differences.* Stanford, Calif.: Stanford University Press, 1975.

Marmor, J. Dynamic psychotherapy and behavior therapy. *Archives of General Psychiatry,* 1971, *24,* 22-28.

Murase, T., & Johnson, F. Naikan, Morita and Western psychotherapy. *Archives of General Psychiatry,* 1974, *31,* 121-128.

Murray, H.A. Toward a classification of interaction. In T. Parsons & E.A. Shils (Eds.), *Toward a general theory of action.* New York: Harper & Row, 1951.

Parsons, T., & Shils, E.A. (Eds.) *Toward a general theory of action.* New York: Harper & Row, 1951.

Reichenbach, H. *Elements of symbolic logic.* New York: Macmillan, 1947.

Reichenbach, H. *The rise of scientific philosophy.* Berkeley, Calif.: University of California Press, 1951.

Ruesch, J., & Prestwood, A.R. Interaction processes and personal codification. *Journal of Personality,* 1950, *18,* 391-430.

Singlemann, P. Exchange as symbolic interaction: Convergences between two theoretical perspectives. *American Sociological Review,* 1972, *37*(4), 414-423.

Strauss, J.S. Social and cultural influences in psychopathology. *Annual Review of Psychology,* 1979, *30,* 397-416.

Szasz, T.W. *The myth of mental illness.* New York: Dell, 1961.

Szasz, T.W. Psychoanalytic treatment as education. *Archives of General Psychiatry,* 1963, *9,* 46-52.

Torrey, E.F. What Western psychotherapists can learn from witchdoctors. *American Journal of Orthopsychiatry,* 1972, *42,* 69-76.

Townsend, J.M. Stereotypes of mental illness: A comparison with ethnic stereotypes. *Culture, Medicine and Psychiatry,* 1979, *3,* 205-229.

Valentine, C.A. Culture and poverty: Critique and counterproposals. *Current Anthropology,* 1969, *10,* 181-201.

Part II
Evaluation

Chapter 4

Evaluating Expectancy Effects in Cross-Cultural Counseling and Psychotherapy

Arnold P. Goldstein

During the past few decades, investigators in broadly diverse areas of inquiry have pointed to the relevance of anticipation of future events as they influence the character of the events which subsequently ensue. Such expectancy effects have been demonstrated in studies of person perception, level of aspiration behavior, group problem solving, teacher evaluations, diagnostic appraisals, behavior under stress, stereotyping, labeling behavior, and in other domains. Much of this research has been summarized recently in Jones' (1977) very useful book, *Self-Fulfilling Prophecies.* Two other books, Jerome Frank's *Persuasion and Healing* (1961) and my own, *Therapist-Patient Expectancies in Psychotherapy* (Goldstein, 1962), both of which appeared in the early 1960s, brought this conclusion to the domain of counseling and psychotherapy. Counselor and client expectancies of several types, these early writings held, were important influences upon both in-counseling participant behaviors, and eventual counseling outcome. Let us be more specific. The expectancy research conducted in counseling and therapy contexts both before and since the publication of these early books has led to a number of reasonably reliable findings which we would now like to enumerate. These findings bear upon the two major types of expectancies which have emerged, prognostic and role. Prognostic expectancies are anticipations of client gain as a function of counseling, held by the client himself and by the counselor. Role expectancies relate more to anticipated in-therapy behaviors, and are expectations held by client and counselor regarding their own and each other's responsibilities, rights, and obligations regarding desired and desirable, as well as undesired and undesirable future in-therapy behaviors. With these two definitions in mind, the following are the major empirical conclusions which may be drawn with regard to expectancy effects in counseling and psychotherapy.

PROGNOSTIC EXPECTANCY FINDINGS

1. Client prognostic expectancy consistently correlates positively and significantly with duration of counseling and with client change. Whether the client expectancy-client change relationship is also directional, i.e., causal, seems likely but still somewhat equivocal.

2. Counselor prognostic expectancy for client change consistently correlates positively and significantly with a host of other counselor evaluations, i.e., his or her degree of liking of the client, and his or her ratings of client ego strength, social adjustment, capacity for insight, and motivation for treatment. Counselor prognostic expectancy correlates negatively with client defensiveness.

3. Counselor prognostic expectancy for client change appears to causally influence such change via a chaining process in which counselor prognostic expectancy directly influences such other counselor states and behaviors as commitment, interest and involvement, effort put forth, the amount of counselor talk, and the amount of actual treatment, all of which in turn appear to bear upon client change.

4. A triad of client role expectancies has been consistently identified:

A. Nurturant. Expect a guiding, giving, protective counselor who is neither businesslike, critical, nor expects the client to take on the major responsibility for the progress of counseling.

B. Model. Expect a well-adjusted, diplomatic counselor who neither judges nor evaluates his clients, but behaves mostly as a very permissive listener.

C. Critic. Expect a critical and analytical counselor who anticipates that his clients will assume considerable responsibility for the counseling process. It is anticipated that the counselor will be neither gentle nor indulgent.

5. Mutuality or congruence of client and counselor role expectations significantly influences the content, duration, and outcome of counseling.*

6. Congruence- and outcome-enhancing role expectancy structuring may

---

*Duckro, Beal, & George (1979), however, review a series of recent studies which provide only partial support for these purported consequences of congruent role expectations.

be accomplished successfully by means of role induction, anticipatory socialization, and related precounseling interview procedures.

Roles as Cultures

Very, very few of the several dozen studies whose combined findings we have just summarized involved counselors and clients differing in cultural or national background, at least in the traditional, anthropological sense of "cross-cultural." In a broader, more comprehensive and, we feel, more heuristic sense, a great many of these expectancy-in-counseling investigations are indeed cross-cultural. Brislin & Pedersen (1976) have cogently written of "roles as cultures." In their view, as well as in our own earlier focus on low income client populations, the term "cross-cultural counseling," with all it implies for expectational, communication, relationship, and related process concerns, applies not only to the circumstance of a counselor and his or her client coming from different nations, but fits equally well the more broadly defined cross-cultural circumstance of counselor and client differing in sex, age, race, and/or socioeconomic status. We stress our subscription to this "roles as cultures" notion here, because much of what we wish to offer in this paper as relevant to the study of cross-national, cross-cultural expectancies derives quite directly from research on cross-social class, cross-cultural expectancy research.

INCREMENTAL PRESCRIPTION BUILDING

A second notion which is central to our presentation is that of prescriptiveness. As has been observed by a number of investigators concerned with the study of counseling outcome, it is no longer appropriate to phrase our investigative outcome questions in the simplisitic and global terms of the early 1960s, in which the question asked was of the order, "Is counseling method A better than counseling method B?" Now, instead, investigators address more differential, prescriptive questions to their data, e.g., "Which treatment method, administered by which counselor, to which client, would yield which outcomes?" (Bergin, 1978; Goldstein, 1978; Goldstein & Stein, 1976; Kiesler, 1969). In this view, counseling researchers can contribute to the goal of increasing the rate of successful counseling outcomes by engaging in prescription-building studies in which potentially active and outcome-enhancing counselor, client, and counseling method characteristics are each identified, operationally defined, implemented and, especially, systematically combined in the form of different matches, and then evaluated for their outcome efficacy. It is this process of active ingredient identification, combination, and evaluation which lies at the heart of a prescriptive view of counseling research. It is this same prescription-building identification, combination, and evaluation sequence applied to the realm of cross-cultural counseling expectancies which we wish to focus upon in the present paper.

In this view, it is the task of the researcher concerned with cross-cultural counseling expectancies and their outcome relevance to speculate about counselor and client prognostic and role expectancies, study their separate impact and, when encouraged by these preparatory efforts, conduct the types of factorial, multivariate investigations which are the experimental designs we feel can optimally lead to clincally useful and empirically tested expectancy-matching prescriptions. Table 4.1 schematically presents the alternative factorial levels which constitute the tactical and operational definition of this research strategy. In it we present a scheme in which types of investigations are hierarchically arranged by number and type of participant expectancy dimensions differentiated, experimentally blocked upon, and factorially evaluated.

As can be seen in Table 4.1, the varibles represented are counseling method, client expectancies, and counselor expectancies. As one proceeds across the research levels described, none, one, two, and all three of these variables are factorially examined. In counseling and psychotherapy research in general, as well as that portion of it devoted to expectancy effects, the large majority of studies reported are nondifferential or unidifferential in design. While such research is a useful beginning, it is, we feel, this bidifferential and, especially, tridifferential level of investigative inquiry—in which the investigator experimentally blocks on all three variables of interest—that is most likely to yield the counseling method X client expectancy X counselor expectancy interaction effect information which we view as vital for advancing the efficacy of the counseling process.

This incremental, prescription-building research strategy is one in which potentially relevant categories of client and counselor expectancies are tentatively identified, their measurement operationalized, and their implementation reflected in factorial matching studies of the types described in table 4.1. This strategy contrasts sharply with the other approaches to therapeutic prescription-building we have described elsewhere as (1) trial and error, (2) semi-prescriptions, or (3) negotiated prescriptions (Goldstein & Stein, 1976). Bidifferential and tridifferential incremental prescription-building studies, as they have been implemented to date (largely with method, client, and counselor variables other than expectancies), have proven to be a research strategy of very considerable empirical payoff—experimental elaborateness and expense not withstanding (Bidifferential: Love, Kaswan, & Bugential, 1972; McLachlan, 1972; Weinman, Gelbart, Wallace, & Post,

Table 4.1. Expectancy Matching: An Incremental, Prescription Building Research Hierarchy*

Level 1. Nondifferential Research

Type 1A: Counseling A for clients with expectancy X.

Type 1B: Counselor with expectancy 1 for clients with expectancy X.

Level 2. Unidifferential Research

Type 2A: Counseling A versus counseling B for clients with expectancy X.

Type 2B: Counselor with expectancy 1 versus counselor with expectancy 2 for clients with expectancy X.

Type 2C: Counseling A for clients with expectancy X versus clients with expectancy Y.

Level 3. Bidifferential Research

Type 3A: Counseling A versus counseling B for clients with expectancy X versus clients with expectancy Y.

Type 3B: Counselor with expectancy 1 versus counselor with expectancy 2 for clients with expectancy X versus clients with expectancy Y.

Level 4. Tridifferental Research

Type 4A: Counseling A versus counseling B for clients with expectancy X versus clients with expectancy Y by counselors with expectancy 1 versus counselors with expectancy 2.

---

*This expectancy matching schema is adapted from a more general, parallel schema applicable to a full range of counseling process variables and participant characteristics, not only their counseling-relevant expectations. This more general schema is from Goldstein, A.P. & Stein, N. *Prescriptive Psychotherapies*. New York: Pergamon Press, 1976, p. 21.

1972; Yamamoto, James, Bloombaum, & Hattem, 1967. Tridifferential approximations: Blumberg, 1972; DiLoreto, 1971; Miller, Barrett, Hampe, & Noble, 1972; Stephens & Astrup, 1965).

PARTICIPANT EXPECTANCIES IN CROSS-CULTURAL COUNSELING

To begin implementing the research strategy we have just described, a first task is the identification of potentially active, therapeutic ingredients that will constitute the variables on which we will block in the factorial studies to be conducted. In the present instance, the variables of interest are client and counselor expectancies in the context of cross-cultural counseling. What are the expectational dimensions thus identified? Pedersen, Lonner, & Draguns (1976) comment:

> ...the foreign student may expect counselors to be more authoritarian—giving advice that recommends or demands specific behaviors in a parent-surrogate role—than most American counselors would find comfortable. Arkoff, Thavor & Elking (1966) further found a sample of Asian students strongly accepting those very coping techniques of increasing willpower, avoiding morbidity, and thinking pleasant thoughts, which American psychologists and students in the sample strongly rejected as being simplistic [p. 33].

Alexander, Workneh, Klein, & Miller (1976) similarly observe that the foreign student client "...often expects an authoritarian, supportive, directive role of his therapist and may see the absence of these qualities as the therapist's lack of concern [p. 92]." Consistent with our earlier promulgation of roles as cultures, and the specific view that the middle-class counselor seeking to assist a same-nationality client of lower socioeconomic status *is* engaging in cross-cultural counseling, it is of interest to note reference to these same participant role expectancies in social class contexts. Early research by Overall & Aronson (1963) and later efforts of our own (Goldstein, 1973; Goldstein, Sprafkin, & Gershaw, 1976) have yielded a social-class related distinction between guidance and participation expectations. Guidance expectations, apparently more characteristic of low income clients, are similar to the nuturant role expectancies described earlier. The client anticipates an active, initiating counselor who leads the counseling process, determines its content, and who spends most of his time and effort giving the client concrete advice, specific guidance, and suggested problem solutions. Participation expectancies, in contrast, involve anticipations in which the behavioral burden for determining and enacting the substance of the counseling will be born mostly by the client, or coequally by client and counselor. Consistent with the dominance of an insight-oriented, psychodynamic definition of psychotherapy and counseling in lay thinking in America, the client with participation expectancies anticipates exploring his personal history, examining dynamic forces within himself, feeling much, working hard, bearing considerable initiation responsibility and, in general, participating actively in the change process vis-a-vis a helper whose own behavior, at least in a relative sense, is either more passive or, at most, equal in activity level to the client's. Participation expectancies, it should be noted, are particularly characteristic of middle socioeconomic level clients. Alexander et al. (1976) comment in this regard:

> Much of American psychotherapy has within it, both in technique and values, the importance of stripping away the "style" of a patient, of confronting, of challenging, of laying open the patient's dynamics—all of which may constitute a disgrace for the foreign patient. . . . Being urged to do this by the person they sought out to help them save face is often more confusing to the patient than he or she can tolerate [p. 92].

We have made a similar point with regard to the negative consequences ensuing from a noncongruent match between a client with guidance role expectations and the typical American counselor or therapist with preference for clients with participation expectations. The fact that half of all therapies in community mental health centers in the United States, almost all of which involve middle class therapists and lower or working class clients, end in but one or two sessions stands, to us, as dramatic testament to the consequences of cross-cultural expectational mismatches.

In addition to the nurturant, model, critic role-expectancy triad we examined at the outset, and the guidance versus participation dichotomy just considered, there are a number of additional participant expectancy dimensions of clear potential relevance to cross-cultural contexts and the research strategy we have proposed. Stressing the perhaps obvious, but all important fact that expectancies are learned (and, importantly, can be unlearned), Sundberg (1976) observes:

> Not only in regard to goals but also in regard to the process and relationship in counseling do the client and the counselor have expectations that are implicit and explicit before their first meeting and that develop further as the counseling session progresses. Socialization for dependency, customs of restricting personal communications to the family circle, and attitudes toward social hierarchy are learned. Another important variable is contained in predispositions toward liking or disliking whatever the counselor symbolizes in the culture-of-origin or the culture-of-residence (priest, healer, parental figure, scientist, or outcaste) [p. 147].

Yet, other classes of counseling-relevant expectancies associated with various cultural and subcultural groups are proposed by Papajohn & Spiegel (1975). Table 4.2 presents their view of culture-associated value orientations vis-a-vis activity, interpersonal relationships, time, man-nature relationships, and human nature.

To the extent that such sets, expectancies, or values exist and find overt, behavioral expression, one can anticipate their respective influence upon the

Table 4.2 Value Orientation Modalities and Preferences: An Interpretative Key

Modalities	Value Orientation Preferences		
Activity	*Doing:* Emphasis is on activity measurable by standards conceived as external to the acting individual, i.e., achievement. (American core culture)	*Being:* Emphasis is on activity expressing what is conceived as given in the human personality, i.e., the spontaneous expression of impulses and desires. (Mexican rural society)	*Being-in-Becoming:* Emphasis is on the kind of activity which has as its goal the development of all aspects of the self as an integrated whole. (Classical Greek Society, Yoga, Gestalt psychology)
Relational	*Individualism:* Individual goals are preferred to group goals; relations are based on individual autonomy; reciprocal roles are based on recognition of the independence of interrelating members. (American core culture)	*Collaterality:* Individual goals are subordinated to group goals; relations are based on goals of the laterally-extended group; reciprocal roles are based on a horizontal, egalitarian dimension. (Italian extended family)	*Lineality:* Group goals are preferred to individual goals; relations on a vertical dimension are hierarchically ordered; reciprocal roles are based on a dominance-submission mode of interrelation. (British upper-classes)
Time	*Future:* The temporal focus is based on the future; emphasis is on planning for change at points in time extending away from present to future. (American core culture)	*Present:* The temporal focus is based on the present; the past gets little attention; the future is seen as unpredictable. (Italian and Latin American societies)	*Past:* The temporal focus is based on the past; tradition is of central importance. (Traditional Chinese society)
Man-nature	*Master-over-nature:* Man is expected to overcome the natural forces and harness them to his purpose. (American emphasis on technology to solve all problems)	*Subjugation-to-nature:* Man can do little to counteract the forces of nature to which he is subjugated. (Spanish rural society)	*Harmony-with-nature:* Man's sense of wholeness is based on his continual communion with nature and with the supernatural. (Japanese and Navaho Indian societies)
Human nature	*Evil:* Man is born with a propensity to do evil. Little can be done to change this state, so the only hope is for control of evil propensities. (Puerto Rican culture)	*Mixed:* Man has natural propensities for both good and evil behavior. *Neutral:* Man is neither good nor bad innately. He is shaped by the environment he is exposed to. (American core culture)	*Good:* Man is innately disposed to good behavior. Society, the environment, etc., corrupt him. (Neo-Freudians)

Source: Papajohn, J. & Spiegel, J. Transactions in families. San Francisco: Jossey-Bass, 1975, p. 269.

client's activity level, its content, and his activity expectations of the counselor; client-counselor relationship formation and quality; counseling duration; counseling goals; and much more. In fact, the value dimensions highlighted in Table 4.2 appear to us, as well as to Papajohn and Spiegel, to be important determinants of a great many aspects of human functioning. They conjure up an expectational network of major relevance to the cross-culture counselor and his attempt to fully comprehend his client's world, and help remediate its difficulties.

Other fertile sources of information and speculation regarding participants' expectancies in cross-cultural counseling contexts include Kiev (1964), Lebra (1976), and Seward (1956). A further paper, by Higginbotham (1977), is especially noteworthy in this regard. He systematically examines ethnographic accounts, studies of international students in the United States, and research on mental health services for minority group clients, and concludes, in a manner fully consistent with our own views, that ". . .pretherapy expectations are dramatically colored by cultural antecedants. . . [p. 109]."

RESEARCH TACTICS

We have, to this point, presented the outlines of an incremental, prescription-building research strategy, and made at least a beginning toward specifying the participant expectancy dimensions which might profitably constitute the ingredients examined when implementing such a strategy toward the goal of improving the efficacy of cross-cultural counseling. In doing so, there exist a number of design implementation and measurement concerns which might usefully be considered.

Cultural Representation

In the initial planning of cross-cultural counseling expectancy research (and probably almost all cross-cultural research), as well as in its subsequent stages of implementation and evaluation, the research team should include knowledgeable and sensitive representatives of all cultures under study. Draguns and Phillips (1972) have made a similar point in urging upon us the use of local healers as research consultants, as has Torrey (1972) in his recommendation that indigenous personnel be used in all mental health planning efforts.

Actuarial versus Deterministic Expectancy Effects

In a seminal paper titled *Expectancies in Applied Settings,* Wilkins (1978) has distinguished between predictive use of expectancies in counseling and psychotherapy as a function of their correlation with outcome (an actuarial effect), and the possibility that expectancies causally influence outcome (a deterministic effect). As we noted earlier, evidence supporting the former is substantial, the later, somewhat more equivocal. We will not replicate Wilkins detailed paper here. Suffice to observe that it should be studied carefully by anyone seeking to more unequivocally demonstrate the causal, directional implications for counseling outcome of participant expectancies. Wilkins (1978) offers a number of additional, important methodological notions. We would direct particular attention toward his explication of the need for fully independent expectancy and change measurement; the pitfalls of "instilled expectancy" studies, and especially the value of validity checks to discern whether the expectancy structuring "takes" in such research, and his paradigmatic description of how one might optimally approach the important problem of identifying the processes or mechanisms through which prognostic and related expectancy information affects clients' change. The counselor and client affective, cognitive, and behavioral mediators of this expectancy-outcome relationship are, at the present time, mostly a matter of informed conjecture.

Measurement Considerations

It is often the case in cross-cultural research that data is gathered by means of presentation to respondents of prepared questionnaires, surveys, structured interviews, or similar instruments implicitly or explicitly constituted to bear upon the investigator's formal or informal hypotheses. While such a tactic fits well the hypotheses testing, i.e., later stages of a research program, its use from the outset precludes an opportunity to discern respondent expectancies not anticipated by the investigator. We follow Jones (1977), therefore, in recommending against the utilization of fixed-response formats, preselected vocabularies, and similar measurement deterrents to respondent full expression, and, instead, urge the increased use, again early in one's cross-cultural research program, of free response approaches, open-minded interviews, and more phenomenological participant-observer investigative techniques.

As one, therefore, more freely and more fully gathers expectational data *from the expector's perspective,* one can more justifiably shift to predetermined measurement devices. To minimize, and in a sense partially compensate for, the inherent fallability of all such instruments and, correspondingly, benefit more fully from their respective strengths, we urge approximations to a multimethod, multilevel, multisource measurement strategy in which behavioral, self-report, other-report, and projective information is gathered from not only the participants themselves, but also such relevant figures as the client's family, the counselor's supervisor, independent interview-rating judges, and appropriate others.

For matters which, for the most part, reflect needs quite independent of the demands of good research (getting a thesis done, pressure to publish, etc.), most expectancy research has been conducted in the context of brief counseling, has focused on precounseling or early-counseling expectancies, has involved graduate student counselors and undergraduate clients (of the same cultural background), and has utilized primarily Rogerian or quasi-Rogerian techniques. Such singularity of focus quite obviously and severely limits our confidence in generalizing any expectancy effects which emerge. Instances of measurement, clients, counselors, and counseling methods must be sampled broadly as a means of enhancing such needed external validity.

Two additional measurement concerns are worthy of consideration. As Higginbotham (1977) notes, the timing of assessment is critical, and may directly influence the nature of the expectations reported by the client. As he comments:

> ...measurement at the beginning of treatment, after the treatment rationale has been given, may tap only the credibility of the rationale or reflect changes in expectancy that are not associated with the specific technique. Also, initial subject assessment may sensitize them to later procedures making them more critical and suspicious. Once treatment has begun or upon client termination, the expectancy report becomes a function of the actual change experienced, with those who have changed reporting higher expectancies of success [p. 118].

Multiple measurement of expectancies, of the types we have suggested above, and conducted at different therapeutic stages, appears to be the appropriate corrective step in minimizing this assessment pitfall.

Higginbotham (1977) also calls our attention to social desirability as a principal alternative hypothesis regarding what expectancy measures actually reflect, especially self-report measures. Both Frank (1961) and Friedman (1963) concur in this view, and warn that subsequent self-reports from the client regarding perceived change may artifactually be influenced by an attempt to make such reports consistent with the earlier expectancy prognostications. At least in part, this concern may be moderated by the type of shift urged above away from exclusive reliance on self-report measurement of client expectancies.

While we have thus far in this chapter concerned ourselves mostly with research considerations, the investigative strategy proposed and its tactical consequences seem to us to have significant implications for the operation of expectancy effects in both counseling practice and training. It is to these implications we now wish to turn.

IMPLICATIONS FOR PRACTICE

Early in our own work with low income client populations, it became valuable to us to distinguish between two philosophies of therapeutic practice. The first we termed a *conformity prescription.* a position in which the patient is required to conform to the therapeutic preferences, expectations, and treatment biases of the therapist. Here the stance is taken that the treatment approach one typically offers—which in America usually means verbal, insight-oriented psychotherapy—is the general treatment of choice. If it is not generally successful with any particular type of client, the fault lies with the client, not the treatment. After all, our outcome statistics with other, e.g., middle-class, patient samples are quite frequently positive; so it must be the case, this position holds, that the nonresponsive patients are deficient not only with regard to the problems which caused them to seek help, but also with regard to the skills one must have to participate meaningfully in the preferred therapy approach. They lack "good patient" skills. Steps must be taken, therefore, to teach these skills or otherwise enhance the person's ability to enter into the (unchanged) treatment and conform to its (unchanged) expectations, demands, and procedures. We must enhance his attraction to treatment and the counselor (Goldstein, 1971), restructure his role expectancies regarding his and the counselor's in-counseling behavior (Hoehn-Saric, Frank, Imber, Nash, Stone, & Battle, 1964), or otherwise seek to help the client fit the therapy.

Though there are important exceptions, the conformity prescription strategy has generally failed to yield positive treatment outcomes. In this regard, we might add that the value of expectancy-instilling, expectancy-structuring techniques, such as the role induction interview (Hoehn-Saric, et al., 1964) or the use of simulated results from precounseling test batteries (Goldstein, 1971), have not yet been examined in cross-cultural counseling contexts. It is possible that these techniques work best when the gap between counselor and client expectancies is relatively modest, or at least no greater than "moderate." This does not seem to be the case in much cross-cultural counseling, in which very substantial differences often appear to exist in the prognostic and, especially, role expectancy positions of client and counselor. This possibility, of course, is conjectural and awaits empirical examination.

The alternative view we have labeled a *reformity prescription.* Here, rather than seeking to have the client fit the treatment, the treatment is reformulated to fit the client. Client expectancies, characteristics, and preferences, more than those of his therapist, determine the course the therapeutic ship will take. In our work with low income clients, clients' reliance upon external authority or example as determinants of behavioral standards, preference for overt action over extended verbalization, responsiveness to immediate feedback, and need for rapid, real-life reinforcement for maintenance of newly acquired behaviors led to our development of a reformity prescription therapy, Structured Learning Therapy, whose components—respectively congruent with the client characteristics and expectancies just enumerated—are modeling, role playing, performance feedback, and transfer training. To do this for the low income patient is to do no more nor less than we do for the middle class patient—with his expectation he will focus upon his motivations and intentions, explore his inner dynamic world, empathically have to concern himself with the feelings of others—when we offer such a patient verbal, insight-oriented therapy. So, too, must we do for the client embarking on cross-cultural counseling. We must accurately and sensitively discern his or her expectancies, preferences, characteristics, and then formulate, offer, and evaluate counseling whose substantive procedures and contents are fully responsive to these dimensions.

The incremental, prescription-building viewpoint central to this paper emphasized that all three major components of the counseling process—method, client, and counselor—must be optimally matched for positive counseling outcomes to ensue. We have spoken thus far in this section on implications for practice, mostly about methods and clients, and would be remiss were we not to also address our thinking to the counselor. In our studies of low income clients, and in the research of many other individuals, it has become clear that the range of persons who can serve in useful helping capacities is broad indeed. Starting in major ways in the mid-1960s, and as part of the beginnings of the community mental health movement, large numbers of so-called paraprofessional, nonprofessional, neighborhood, and indigenous therapists entered the working force. Very considerable evidence exists in support of the therapeutic potency of many such persons, potency often greater than that demonstrated by so-called professional therapists (Durlak, 1979).

The paraprofessional or indigenous helper is often an individual from the same or similar geographic, ethnic, socioeconomic, and/or racial background as the bulk of the clients he seeks to help; and, as such, is likely to share values, expectations, subtleties of language, and definitions of psychological disorder, and its optimal means for remediation with them. Given the demonstrated counseling outcome relevance of counselor-client expectancy congruence, of shared counseling-relevant values and beliefs, certain recommendations clearly follow. One is the increased, but certainly not exclusive, use of conationals as counselors. In effect, this is a recommendation that those persons concerned with improving the overall efficacy of cross-cultural counseling devote increasing proportions of their time and effort to training conationals as counselors of the target client groups. We will have more to say about such training in the final section of this chapter.

A second recommendation, which hopefully will not appear inconsistent with the first since we feel both can proceed simultaneously, is one which also has implications for training. It is a recommendation which urges a counselor selection view consistent with Anthony and Carkhuff's (1977) notion of the "functional therapist." To them, the professional versus paraprofessional controversy is largely a pseudocontroversy. One's concern ought to be with the functional, pro-outcome skills of given counselors, and how such skills may be most effectively enhanced, and less upon more guild-relevant matters of degree of credentialing. We feel likewise with reference to selection of cross-cultural counselors. Conationals, nonconationals, professionals, paraprofessionals, indigenous, sojourners, and never-been-theres have potential for becoming *functional* cross-cultural counselors and, at this very early stage of this very young specialty, none, save perhaps the most volitionally encapsulated and monoculturally-oriented, ought be categorically ruled out. Following the tripartite research strategy we have been expounding, who works best with and expects what from whom, using which methods, can eventually be discerned by investigative means.

IMPLICATIONS FOR TRAINING

Earlier we spoke briefly about the possibility of increasing the positiveness of client prognostic expectancies and the congruence of counselor-client role expectancies by means of procedures explicitly designed for such purposes for clients, e.g., role induction, expectancy structuring, simulated testing, and so forth. Counselor prognostic expectancies may be enhanced, and client and counselor role expectancies may be made both more similar and more accurate by means of analogous procedures addressed to the counselor. To best discern the possible content of such expectancy-altering procedures, we refer the interested counselor-trainer to Brislin and Pedersen's book *Cross-cultural Orientation Programs* (1976). This comprehensive text describes, in careful detail, a large number of training programs already in existence which were designed to enhance the cross-cultural knowledge, skills, sensitivities, beliefs, and expectancies of diverse trainees —military, business, Peace Corps, educational, and other types of sojourners. The specific programs examined include cross-culturally-oriented Human Relations Training (Filla & Clark, 1973), Intercultural Communications Workshops (Hoopes, 1975), Reorientation Seminars (Brislin & Pedersen, 1976), Case Study Simulations (Kleitsch, 1971), Cross-cultural Coalition Training (Pedersen, 1973), and training utilizing either the Contrast-American Technique (Steward, Danielson, & Foster, 1969), the Culture Assimilator (Triandis, 1968), or Self-confrontation techniques (Haines, 1964).

It is our view that the diverse, cross-culturally-oriented didactic and experiential substance of these programs can judiciously be integrated with the more traditional theory and technique instruction constituting more usual counselor training. In addition, we would also suggest (1) the use of conationals of the target client population in the role of counseling practicum cotrainer, (2) the use of client-actors in such practica, simulating the target client population, and (3) participation of conationals as counselor trainees in such practica. While the task of altering participant expectancies in outcome-enhancing directions is not an easy one, adaptations of the formal, cross-cultural orientation programs listed above, and implementation of the practica suggestions we have offered, are at minimum a reasonable beginning.

SUMMARY

Existing evidence increasingly suggests that client and counselor expectations regarding the counseling process and outcome dynamically influence the actual course of the process and the quality of the outcome. These conclusions appear to be operative whether counseling occurs within or across cultural perspectives. How to harness this potentially potent, outcome-enhancing effect is currently only a partially answered research question. We have proposed in this chapter that researchers turn more actively to an incremental, prescriptive research strategy, one in which participant expectancies and counseling methods are successively grouped into promising trials and examined for their outcome potency. This strategy demands heightened sensitivity by both researcher and practitioner to the sources, nature, and likely consequences of client expectancies in the context of cross-cultural counseling. The research problems existing when either implementing this research strategy or engaging in other studies of cross-cultural counseling are neither minor nor few in number. But this research effort promises considerable therapeutic benefit, and currently seems clearly worth pursuing.

REFERENCES

Alexander, A.A., Workneh, F., Klein, M.H. and Miller, M.H. Psychotherapy and the foreign student. In P. Pedersen, W.J. Lonner, & J.G. Draguns (Eds.), *Counseling across cultures*. Honolulu: University Press of Hawaii, 1976,

Anthony, W.A., & Carkhuff, R.R. The functional professional therapeutic agent. In A.S. Gurman & A.M. Razin (Eds.), *Effective psychotherapy: A handbook of research*. New York: Pergamon Press, 1977.

Bergin, A. & Lambert, W. The evaluation of therapeutic outcome. In S.L. Garfield & A.E. Bergin (Eds.), *Handbook of psychotherapy and behavior change*. New York: Wiley, 1978.

Blumberg, R.W. Therapist leadership and client dogmatism in a therapy analogue. *Psychotherapy: Theory, Research & Practice.* 1972, *9*, 132-138.

Brislin, R.W., & Pedersen, P. *Cross-cultural orientation programs*. New York: Gardner Press, 1976.

DiLoreto, A.O. *Comparative psychotherapy: An experimental analysis*. Chicago: Atherton-Aldine, 1971.

Draguns, J.G., & Phillips, L. *Culture and psychopathology: The quest for a relationship*. Morristown, N.J.: General Learning Press, 1972.

Duckro, P., Beal, D., & George, C. Research on the effects of disconfirmed client role expectations in psychotherapy: A critical review. *Psychological Bulletin,* 1979, *86*, 260-275.

Durlak, J.A. Comparative effectiveness of paraprofessional and professional helpers. *Psychological Bulletin,* 1979, *86*, 80-92.

Filla, T., & Clark, D. Human relations resource guide on inservice programs. St. Paul, Minn., State Department of Education, 1973.

Frank, J.D. *Persuasion and healing*. Baltimore: Johns Hopkins University Press, 1961.

Friedman, H.J. Patient expectancy and symptom reduction. *Archives of General Psychiatry,* 1963, *8*, 61-67.

Goldstein, A.P. *Therapist-patient expectancies in psychotherapy*. New York: Pergamon Press, 1962.

Goldstein, A.P. *Psychotherapeutic attraction*. New York: Pergamon Press, 1971.

Goldstein, A.P. *Structured learning therapy: Toward a psychotherapy for the poor*. New York: Academic Press, 1973.

Goldstein, A.P. (Ed.) *Prescriptions for child mental health and education*. New York: Pergamon Press, 1978.

Goldstein, A.P., & Stein, N. *Perspective psychotherapies*. New York: Pergamon Press, 1978. York: Pergamon Press, 1976.

Goldstein, A.P., & Stein, N. *Prescriptive psychotherapies*. New York: Pergamon Press, 1978

Haines, D. Training for culture contact and interaction skills. Air Force Systems Command, Wright-Patterson Air Force Base, AD611022, December 1964.

Higginbotham, H.N. Culture and the role of client expectancy in psychotherapy. In R.W. Brislin & M.P. Hammet (Eds.), *Topics in culture learning*. Honolulu: East-West Center, 1977.

Hoehn-Saric, R., Frank, J.D., Imber, S.D., Nash, E.H., Stone, A.R., & Battle, C.C. Systematic preparation of patients for psychotherapy. I. Effects on therapy behavior and outcome. *Journal of Psychiatric Research*, 1964, *2*, 267-281.

Hoopes, D. Editorial, *Communique,* January-March 1975, *5*, 3-4.

Jones, R.A. *Self-fulfilling prophecies*. Hillsdale, N.J.: L. Erlbaum, 1977.

Kiesler, D.J. A grid model for theory and research. In L.D. Eron & R. Calahan (Eds.), *The relation of theory to practice in psychotherapy.* Chicago: Aldine, 1969.

Kiev, A. *Magic, faith and healing.* Glencoe, Ill.: Free Press, 1964.

Kleitsch, R. The active case study. Unpublished manuscript, 1971.

Lebra, W.P. (Ed.) *Culture-bound syndromes, ethnopsychiatry, and alternate therapies.* Honolulu: University of Hawaii Press, 1976.

Love, L.R., Kaswan, J., & Bugental, D.E. Differential effectiveness of three clinical interventions for different socioeconomic groupings. *Journal of Consulting and Clinical Psychology,* 1972, *39,* 347-360.

McLachlan, J.F.C. Benefit from group therapy as a function of patient-therapist match on conceptual level. *Psychotherapy: Theory, Research & Practice,* 1972, *9,* 317-323.

Miller, L.C., Barrett, C.L., Hampe, E., & Noble, H. Comparison of reciprocal inhibition, psychotherapy, and waiting list control for phobic children. *Journal of Abnormal Psychology,* 1972, *79,* 269-279.

Papajohn, J., & Spiegel, J. *Transactions in families.* San Francisco: Jossey-Bass, 1975.

Pedersen, P. A cross-cultural coalition training model for educating mental health professionals to function in multicultural populations. Paper presented at the Ninth International Congress of Anthropological and Ethnological Sciences, Chicago, September 1973.

Pedersen P., Lonner, W.J., & Draguns, J.G. *Counseling across cultures.* Honolulu: University Press of Hawaii, 1976.

Overall, B., & Aronson, H. Expectations of psychotherapy in patients of lower socio-economic class. *American Journal of Orthopsychiatry,* 1963, *33,* 421-430.

Seward, G. *Psychotherapy and culture conflict.* New York: Ronald Press, 1956.

Stephens, J.H., & Astrup, C. Treatment outcome in "process" and "nonprocess" schizophrenics treated by "A" and "B" types of therapists. *Journal of Nervous and Mental Disease,* 1965, *140,* 449-456.

Stewart, E., Danielson, J., & Foster, R. Simulating intercultural communication through role playing. HumRRO Technical Report 69-7, May 1969.

Sundberg, N.D. Toward research evaluating intercultural counseling. In P. Pedersen, W.J. Lonner, & J.G. Draguns (Eds.), *Counseling across cultures.* Honolulu: University Press of Hawaii, 1976.

Torrey, E.F. *The mind game: Witchdoctors and psychiatrists.* New York: Emerson Hall, 1972.

Triandis, H. An analysis of cross-cultural interaction and its implications for training. Conference on Research in Cross-cultural Interaction, Office of Naval Research, 1968.

Weinman, B., Gelbart, P., Wallace, M., & Post, M. Inducing assertive behavior in chronic schizophrenics: A comparison of socioenvironmental, desensitization and relaxation therapies. *Journal of Consulting and Clinical Psychology,* 1972, *39,* 246-252.

Wilkins, W. Expectancies in applied settings. In Gurman, A. & Razin, W. (Eds.), *Effective psychotherapy.* N.Y.: Pergamon Press, 1979.

Yamamoto, Jr., James, Q.C., Bloombaum, M., & Hattem, J. Racial factors in patient selection. *American Journal of Psychiatry,* 1967, *124,* 630-636.

Chapter 5

Evaluating Process Variables in Cross-Cultural Counseling and Psychotherapy*

Derald Wing Sue

A basic assumption underlying counseling and psychotherapy is that the relationship which the counselor/therapist establishes with a client can either enhance or negate the process. When the emotional climate is negative, and when misunderstanding or little trust exists between the counselor and client, counseling can be both ineffective and destructive. Yet, if the emotional climate is realistically positive, and if trust and understanding exist between the parties, the two-way communication of thoughts and ideas can proceed with optimism. This latter condition is often referred to as rapport and sets the stage for other essential conditions to occur. What a counselor says or does in the sessions (approach and strategy) can either enhance or diminish his or her credibility and attractiveness. A counselor who is perceived as highly credible and attractive is more likely to elicit (a) trust, (b) motivation to work/change, and (c) self-disclosure.

Theories of counseling and psychotherapy attempt to outline an approach designed to make them effective. It is my contention that cross-cultural counseling cannot be approached through any one theory. There are several reasons for such a statement. First, theories of counseling are composed of philosophical assumptions regarding the nature of "man" and

---

*Parts of this chapter are based upon a forthcoming text (Sue, D.W. *Cross-Cultural Counseling: Theory and Practice,* New York: John Wiley & Sons, in press).

a theory of personality (Corsini, 1979; London, 1964; Patterson, 1973). These characteristics may be highly culture bound. What is the "true" nature of people is a philosophical assumption. What constitutes the healthy and unhealthy personality is also debatable and varies from culture to culture. Furthermore, theories of counseling have, often, failed to agree among themselves as to what constitutes desirable outcomes in counseling. A theory of counseling should, obviously, predict conditions under which counseling will be effective. A major difficulty in predicting effective counseling is the lack of agreement by the profession regarding desirable counseling outcomes. Past failures to determine unequivocably the effects of therapy can be traced mainly to this lack of agreement. Until we are able to agree upon desirable outcomes, it will be difficult to compare and evaluate the effectiveness of different methods of counseling. For example, the psychoanalytically oriented counselor uses *insight,* the behaviorist uses *behavior change,* the client-centered person uses *self-actualization,* and the rational-emotive person uses *rational cognitive processes.* The potential for disagreement is increased even further when the counselor and client come from different cultures.

Second, psychotherapy and its theoretical influences have been seriously questioned as to their overall effectiveness. Objections to therapy can be listed as follows: (1) Psychotherapy has not proven its effectiveness as a treatment modality; (2) it has been oversold as a form of treatment; and (3) much time, effort, and money are being wasted by practitioners and clients in psychotherapy (Eysenck, 1952; Rachman, 1971; Scriven, 1975; Teuber & Powers, 1963). I shall not go into all the complexities of this controversy, but will only point out what seems evident from the responses of other investigators (Bergin, 1971; Chartier, 1971; Garfield & Bergin, 1971; Razrin, 1971; Sloane, Staples, Cristol, Yorkston, & Whipple, 1975; Strupp, 1971). Psychotherapy may be valuable, but the most meaningful issue concerns the match between therapist, client, and situation.

Third, theories of counseling are also composed of a body of therapeutic techniques and strategies. These techniques are applied to clients with the hope of effecting change in either behaviors or attitudes. A theory dictates what techniques are to be used and, implicitly, in what proportions. For example, it is obvious that client-centered counselors behave differently from rational-emotive ones. Using Ivey and Anthier's (1978) microcounseling paradigm, it is possible to characterize the former as using mostly attending skills (e.g., paraphrasing, reflection of feelings, minimal encouragement) while the latter uses more influencing skills (e.g., expression of content, interpretation, giving advice). The fact that one school of counseling can be distinguished from another has implications. In the first place, it suggests a certain degree of rigidity in working with culturally different clients who might find such techniques offensive or inappropriate (Sue, 1977, 1978). The implicit assumption is that such techniques are applicable to all populations, situations, and problems. They are imposed according to the theory and not based upon client needs and values. As professionals, we often label ourselves as Freudians, Skinnerians, Gestaltists, or Rogerians without realizing how we have oversimplified the world.

Fourth, regardless of the counseling approach a counselor may espouse the counselor's impact on the client will be dependent on the client's perception of the counselor's credibility and attractiveness. Furthermore, regardless of the role the counselor assumes, traditional or activist, the influence the counselor wields on the client's behalf will be a function of the credibility he or she attains with the client, and significant others in the client's environment. Perceived counselor expertness, trustworthiness, and attractiveness, then, are viewed as central to any counseling role and should be heavily employed as process criteria.

As this chapter is concerned with evaluating process variables in cross-cultural counseling and therapy, the above points lead to several conclusions. I will be more concerned with counselor verbal/nonverbal behaviors and skills than of a specific theory of counseling. Regardless of the theoretical orientation, it seems important that we concentrate on identifiable communication/counseling skills and their effects in the cross-cultural counseling situation. Additionally, while counseling outcome is an important element in research and theory, it will be my preference to concentrate on how change occurs (process) rather than *what* change *results* (outcome) from counseling. The approach of this chapter will be fourfold. First, we will conceptualize counseling as a social influence process and delineate conditions that seem to affect credibility and attractiveness in cross-cultural counseling. Second, we will discuss process barriers to effective cross-cultural counseling and how they interact with cultural and sociopolitical influences. Third, evidence will be presented to indicate that counseling individuals from different cultures dictates not the same approach, but a differential one consistent with their life style. Fourth, possible research directions in evaluating process variables in cross-cultural counseling will be suggested.

COUNSELING AS A SOCIAL INFLUENCE PROCESS

Strong (1968) has conceptualized counseling as an interpersonal influence process in which the counselor attempts to influence the client's attitudes and behaviors. Drawing parallels between the dynamics of opinion change research and the counseling process, Strong has suggested that the counselor's influence on the client is a function of the client's perception of the counselor as expert, trustworthy, and attractive (socially acceptable). Counselors who are so perceived will exert more influence on their clients than counselors who are perceived as inexpert, untrustworthy, or unattractive. There is a sufficient number of counseling analog studies to support this contention (Atkinson & Carskaddon, 1975; Barak & LaCrosse, 1975; Merluzzi, Merluzzi, & Kaul, 1977; Schmidt & Strong, 1971; Spiegel, 1976; Strong & Schmidt, 1970). Using social influence theory as a means to analyze counseling not only has empirical validity and concentrates on process variables, but seems to be equally applicable to all approaches. Regardless of the counseling orientation, the counselor's effectiveness depends on his or her perceived expertness, trustworthiness, and attractiveness.

Most of the studies mentioned have dealt exclusively with a white population. Thus, findings that certain attributes contribute to a counselor's credibility and attractiveness may not be so perceived by culturally different clients. It is entirely possible that credibility as defined by credentials indicating specialized training may only mean to a black client that the white counselor has no knowledge or expertise in working with blacks. This statement is based on the fact that most training programs are geared for white, middle-class clients and are culturally exclusive. Our focus in this section will be to outline the various ways clients perceive their counselor's attempt to influence them, and then to discuss the dimensions of counselor expertness, trustworthiness, and similarity as they relate to the culturally different client.

Psychological Sets of Clients

Credibility and attractiveness of the counselor is very much dependent on the psychological set or frame of mind of the culturally different client. We all know individuals who tend to value rational approaches to solving problems and others who value a much more affective (attractiveness) approach. It would seem reasonable that a client who values rationality might be more receptive to a counseling approach which emphasizes a counselor's credibility. Thus, understanding a client's psychological set may facilitate the counselor's ability to exert social influence in counseling. Collins (1970) has proposed a set of conceptual categories which we can use to understand people's receptivity to pressures for change. We will apply them here with respect to the counseling situation. These five hypothetical "sets" or "frames of mind" are elicited in clients for a number of different reasons. Race, ethnicity, and the experience of discrimination often affects the type of "set" that will be operative in a minority client.

The Problem-Solving Set: Information Orientation In the problem-solving set, the client is concerned with obtaining correct information (solutions, outlooks, skills) that has adaptive value in the real world. The client accepts or rejects information from the counselor on the basis of this perceived truth or falsity; is it an accurate representation of reality? The processes tend to be rational and logical in analyzing and attacking the problem. Past experience has taught us that some people are more likely to provide accurate and helpful (credible) information than others. Minorities have learned that many whites have little expertise when it comes to their life styles and that the information and suggestions they give are likely to be white solutions or labels.

The Consistency Set People are operating under the consistency set whenever they change an opinion, belief, or behavior in such a way as to make it consistent with other opinions, beliefs, and behaviors. This principle is best illustrated Festinger's *A Theory of Cognitive Dissonance* (1957). Most of us operate under the assumption that the world is consistent. For example, since counselors are supposed to help, we naturally believe that they would not do things to hurt us. The rules of the consistency set specify that "good people do good things" and "bad people do bad things." It is important to note that the consistency set states that people are not necessarily rational beings but rationalizing ones. It is entirely possible that a white counselor who is perceived to be a product of socialization in a white society is perceived as a racist. Thus, all of their counseling behaviors may be perceived similarly.

The Identity Set In the identity set, the individual generally desires to be liked or similar to a person or group which they hold in high esteem. Much of our identity is formed from those reference groups to which we aspire. We attempt to take on their characteristics, beliefs, values, and behaviors because they are viewed favorably. An individual who identifies strongly with a particular group is likely to accept those beliefs, and conform to behaviors dictated by the group. If race or ethnicity constitutes a strong reference group for a client, then a counselor of the same race or ethnicity is likely to be more influential than one who is not.

The Economic Set In the economic set, the person is influenced because of perceived rewards and punishments the source is able to deliver. In these cases, the client may decide to change his or her behavior because the counselor holds greater power. The major problem with the use of rewards and punishments to induce change is that, while it may ensure behavioral compliance, it does not guarantee private acceptance. Furthermore, for reward and coercive power to be effective, the counselor must maintain constant surveillance. Once the surveillance is removed, the client is likely to revert back to previous modes of behavior. For culturally different clients, counseling which primarily operates on the economic set is most likely to prevent trust, rapport, and self-disclosure.

The Authority Set Under this set, some individuals are taught that position gives them a legitimate right to prescribe attitudes and/or behaviors. In our society, we have been conditioned to believe that certain authorities have the right to demand compliance. Mental health professionals, like counselors, are thought to have a legitimate right to recommend and provide psychological treatment to disturbed or troubled clients. It is this psychological set which legitimizes the counselor's role as a helping professional. Yet, for many minorities, it is exactly the roles in society which are perceived to be instruments of institutional racism.

None of the five sets or frames of reference are mutually exclusive. These sets frequently interact, and any number of them can operate at the same time. For example, it is possible that you are influenced by a counselor who you find highly credible. It is also possible that you like the counselor or find him or her very attractive. Are you accepting his or her influence because the counselor is credible (problem-solving set), attractive (identification set), or both?

It shoud be clear at this point that the characteristics of the influencing source (counselor) are all important in eliciting types of change. In addition, the type of set placed in operation often dictates the permanency and degree of attitude change. For example, the primary component in getting *compliance* (economic and authority sets) is *power* which the person holds over you; the ability to reward or punish. In *identification* (identity set) it is the *attractiveness* or liking of the counselor; and in *internalization* (problem-solving and consistency sets), credibility or truthfulness is important. While these sets operate similarly for both majority and minority clients, their manifestations may be quite different. Obviously, a minority client may have great difficulty identifying (identification set) with a counselor from another race or culture. Also, what constitutes credibility to a minority client may be far different from that of a majority client. I will have more to say about this point in the later sections.

Counselor Credibility

Credibility (which elicits the problem solving, consistency, and identification sets) may be defined as the constellation of characteristics that make certain individuals appear worthy of belief, capable, entitled to confidence, reliable, and trustworthy. Hovland, Janis, and Kelley (1953) identify two components of credibility: expertness and trustworthiness. *Expertness* is an *ability* variable while *trustworthiness* is a motivational one. Expertness depends on how well informed, capable, or intelligent others perceive the communicator (counselor). Trustworthiness is dependent upon the degree to which people perceive the communicator (counselor) as motivated to make nonvalid assertions. In counseling, these two components have been the subject of much research and speculation (Barak & Dell, 1977; Barak & LaCrosse, 1975; Dell, 1973; LaCrosse & Barak, 1976; Spiegel, 1976; Sprafkin, 1970; Strong, 1968; Strong & Schmidt, 1970). The weight of evidence supports our commonsense belief that the counselor who is perceived as expert and trustworthy can influence clients more than one who is lower on these traits.

Counselor Expertness Clients often go to a counselor not only because they are in distress and in need of relief, but because they believe the counselor is an expert; he or she has the necessary knowledge, skills, experiences, training, and tools to help (problem-solving set). Perceived expertness is typically a function of (a) reputation, (b) evidence of specialized training, and/or (c) behavioral evidence of proficiency/competency. For culturally different clients, the issue of counselor expertness seems to be raised more often than in going to the counselor of one's own culture and race. As mentioned previously, the fact that counselors have degrees and certificates from prestigious institutions (authority set) may not enhance perceived expertness. This is especially true of clients who are culturally different and aware that institutional racism exists in training programs. Indeed, it may have the opposite effect by reducing credibility. Neither is reputation expertness (authority set) likely to impress a minority client unless a favorable testimony comes from someone of their own group.

Thus, behavioral expertness or demonstrating your ability to help a client becomes a critical form of expertness in cross-cultural counseling (problem-solving set). Sue (1978) believes that using counseling skills and strategies appropriate to the life values of the culturally different client are crucial. Studies conducted by Atkinson, Maruyama, and Matsui (1978) and Berman (1979) seem to support this contention. These studies will be discussed in more detail in a later section.

In many ways, behavioral manifestations of counselor expertness override other considerations. For example, many counselor educators claim that specific counseling skills are not as important as the attitude one brings into the counseling situation. Behind this statement is the belief that universal attributes of genuineness, love, and unconditional positive regard are the only things needed. Yet, the question remains, how does the counselor communicate these things to a culturally different client? While a counselor may have the best of intentions, it is possible that his or her intentions might be misunderstood.

Counselor Trustworthiness Perceived trustworthiness encompasses such factors as sincerity, openness, honesty, or perceived lack of motivation for personal gain. A counselor who is perceived as trustworthy is likely to exert more influence over a client than one who is not. In our society, certain roles such as ministers, doctors, psychiatrists, and counselors are presumed to exist to help people. This assumption is accepted until proven otherwise. With respect to minorities, self-disclosure is very much dependent upon this attribute. Because counselors are often perceived by minorities to be "agents of the establishment," trust is something that does not come with the role (authority set). Indeed, it may be the perception of many culturally different clients that counselors cannot be trusted unless otherwise demonstrated. Again, the role and reputation you have as being trustworthy must be demonstrated in behavioral terms. More than anything else, challenges to the counselor's trustworthiness will be a frequent theme blocking further exploration/movement until it is resolved to the satisfaction of the client. Many minorities often use the "prove to me that you can be trusted" ploy which is most difficult for most counselors to handle. It is difficult because it demands self-disclosure on the part of counselors; something which counselor training programs have taught us to avoid. It places the focus on the counselor rather than on the client and makes many uncomfortable.

To summarize, expertness and trustworthiness are important components of any counseling relationship. In cross-cultural counseling, however, the counselor may be presumed to possess either. The counselor working with a minority client is likely to experience severe tests of his or her expertness and trustworthiness before serious counseling can proceed. The responsibility for proving to the client that you are a credible counselor is likely to be greater when working with a minority than a majority client. How you meet the challenge is important in determining your effectiveness as a cross-cultural counselor.

Counselor Attractiveness

Social-psychological (Bryne & Nelson, 1965; Dabbs, 1964; Mills & Aronson, 1965) and counseling analog studies (Barak & Dell, 1977; Schmidt & Strong, 1971) suggest that communicators (counselors) are able to influence others more effectively if they appear attractive to them. It is important to note that attractiveness and credibility are often associated with one another. For example, I might like a person or find him or her attractive because he or she is logical and trustworthy. However, interpersonal attraction is more likely to be the result of similarity. It appears that interactions with people who are similar to us tend to be rewarding because it validates our convictions (identification and consistency sets). Likewise, if we are strongly attracted to someone (liking), they are more likely to have influence over us. When people are dissimilar to us there is the possibility that they will disagree with our beliefs, attitudes, and/or opinions (consistency set). Not only may this fear be present in counseling, but there is the real possibility that the counselor will not understand or misinterpret the motives/behaviors/beliefs of the culturally different client.

An important question that must be asked is "Does the counselor have to share the cultural, racial, and class backgrounds of his or her clients to be effective?" This is a difficult question to answer and even the research in this area is inconclusive. Several authors (Banks, 1971; Kincaid, 1969; Vontress, 1971, 1972) argue strongly that successful interracial counseling is highly impossible because of the cultural/racial barriers involved. Studies which indicate that (a) black clients prefer black counselors (Harrison, 1975; Wolkon, Moriwaki, & Williams, 1973) and Asian-Americans prefer Asian-Americans (Atkinson et al., 1978), (b) there is a higher rate of return of black clients to black counselors (Heffernon & Bruehl, 1971), (c) a greater understanding of black clients by black counselors is often exhibited (Bryson & Cody, 1973), (d) there is greater depth of self-exploration of black patients treated by black therapists (Carkhuff & Pierce, 1967), (e) higher ratings of counselor effectiveness is given to black counselors by black clients (Banks, Berenson, & Carkhuff, 1967; Gardner, 1972), and (f) greater behavioral change follows counseling of black students by black counselors seems to support the proposition that counselor-client racial similarity enhances the likelihood of success in counseling. While nearly all of these studies deal with blacks, similar claims may be made for other racial groups as well. Yet, others (Aspy, 1970; Arbuckle, 1972; Cimbolic, 1973; Jones & Jones, 1972) claim that well trained and sensitive counselors of another race may be able to establish effective counseling relationships with their clients. For example, type of issue (education/vocation vs. personal problems) operating (Johnson, 1977), sex of counselor (Bryson, Bardo, and Johnson, 1975), counselor experience, (Cimbolic, 1972), and counselor style (Peoples & Dell, 1975) may be more important than race. Other important influences such as cultural identity (Atkinson, Morten, & Sue, 1979; Jackson, 1975) and world views (Sue, 1978) are important. Thus, a question as to whether a culturally different counselor can work with a client is too simplistic to answer.

Whether a counselor can work effectively with a person from a different culture or race depends on many factors of which racial and attitudinal similarity-dissimilarity are two important ones. The nature of the problem, counselor experience, counseling style, and degree of ethnic racial consciousness are just a few of the important variables that need to be considered. Yet, it cannot be denied that membership group and attitudinal similarity tends to enhance attractiveness and increase the probability of identification (identity set). In general, a person similar to you may be able to exert greater influence than one who is dissimilar. A counselor's similarity to the client may lead the client to initially view the counselor as an appropriate person to seek assistance from. In cross-cultural counseling, the counselor may be unable to use the client's identification set (membership-group similarity) to induce change. At times, racial dissimilarity may prove to be so much of a hindrance as to render counseling ineffective. Cross-cultural counseling by virtue of definition implies major differences between the client and counselor. How these differences may be bridged, and under what conditions the counselor will be able to work effectively with a culturally different client, are the key questions.

PROCESS BARRIERS TO EFFECTIVE CROSS-CULTURAL COUNSELING

I have repeatedly emphasized how counseling and therapy may be viewed legitimately as a process of interpersonal interaction and communication. For effective counseling to occur, the counselor and client must be able to appropriately and accurately send and receive both verbal and nonverbal messages. While breakdowns in communication often occur among members who share the same culture, the problem can be worsened among people of different racial or ethnic backgrounds. Misunderstandings that arise from cultural variations in communication may lead to alienation and/or an inability to develop trust and rapport. This may result in early termination of counseling or treatment as evidenced by the studies conducted by Sue and McKinney (1975) and Sue, McKinney, Allen, and Hall (1974). What they found was that Asian-Americans, Blacks, Chicanos, and Native Americans terminated counseling after only one contact at a rate of approximately 50 percent in contrast to a 30 percent rate for Anglo clients. In a previous article, Sue (1977) hypothesized that it was the inappropriateness of interpersonal interactions, that happens between counselor and client, which may account for these premature termination rates. Padilla, Ruiz, and Alvarez (1975), while referring to a Latin population, identified three factors that hinder the formation of a good counseling relationship: (a) A language barrier that often exists between the counselor and client, (b) class-bound values which indicate that counselors conduct treatment within the value system of the middle-class, and (c) culture-bound values that are used to judge normality and abnormality in clients. All three of these variables seem to interact in such a way as to seriously hinder and distort communications. As I have discussed these factors thoroughly in previous articles (Sue, 1977, 1978, in press), I will only summarize them here.

Within the Western framework, counseling is a white, middle-class activity that holds many values and characteristics different from Third World groups. Most theories of counseling and psychotherapy share common characteristics. These generic characteristics of counseling seem to be intimately rooted in the basic values of United States society. While different schools of counseling vary from one another, they do hold basic common assumptions.

First, counselors often expect their clients to exhibit some degree of openness, psychology mindedness, or sophistication. Most theories of counseling place a high premium upon verbal, emotional, and behavioral expressiveness and the attainment of insight. These are either the end goals of counseling or the medium by which "cures" are effected. Second, counseling is traditionally a one-to-one activity that encourages clients to talk about or discuss the most intimate aspects of their lives. Individuals who fail or resist doing this may be seen as resistant, defensive, or superficial. Third, the counseling situation is often an ambiguous one. The client is encouraged to discuss problems, whereas the counselor listens and responds. Relatively speaking, the counseling situation is unstructured and forces the client to be the primary active participant. Patterns of communication are generally from client to counselor.

Four other factors identified as generally characteristic of counseling are: (a) A monolingual orientation, (b) emphasis on long-range goals, (c) distinction between physical and mental well being, and (d) emphasis on cause-effect relationships. With respect to the first, the use of good standard English is predominantly the vehicle by which communication occurs. To individuals who might not speak or use English well, the lack of bilingual counselors is a serious handicap to accurate communication. Furthermore, since counseling is generally isolated from the client's environment and contacts are brief (a 50 minute session once a week), it is by nature aimed at seeking long-range goals and solutions.

Another important and often overlooked factor in counseling is the implicit assumption that a clear distinction can be made between mental and physical illness or health. Contrary to this Western view, many cultures may not make a clear distinction between the two. Such a separation may be confusing to the Third World client and cause problems in counseling. As Sue

(1977) has shown, all of these generic charactistics of counseling can clash or prove antagonistic to the values held by Asian-Americans, Blacks, Chicanos, and Native Americans.

In working with persons from minority cultural backgrounds, the counselor must take into consideration the interaction of class, language, and culture factors on verbal and nonverbal communication. Because counseling is a white, middle-class activity, the counselor must guard against possible misinterpretations of behaviors and be aware that many aspects of counseling may be antagonistic to the values held by the client. Counselors tend to respond according to their own conditional values, assumptions, and perspectives to reality without regard for other views. Counselors need to become culturally aware, to act on the basis of a critical analysis and understanding of their own conditioning, that of their clients, and the sociopolitical system of which they are a part.

Sue (1978) also makes a strong case for the concept of locus of responsibility when working with the culturally different client. In essence, this dimension measures the degree of reponsibility or blame placed upon the individual or system. In the case of many blacks, their lower standard of living may be attributable to their personal inadequacies and shortcomings; or, the responsibility for their plight may be attributed to racial discrimination and lack of opportunities. The former orientation blames the individual while the latter explanation blames the system. Such terms as person-centered or person-blame indicate a focus upon the individual. Those who hold a person-centered orientation (a) emphasize the understanding of a person's motivation, values, feelings, and goals; (b) believe that success or failure is attributable to the individual's skills or person inadequacies; and (c) believe that there is a strong relationship between ability, effort, and success in society. In essence, these people adhere strongly to the Protestant ethic that idealizes rugged individualism. On the other hand, situation-oriented or system-blame people view the social cultural environment as more potent than the individual. Social, economic, and political forces are powerful; success or failure is generally dependent upon the social economic system and not necessarily personal attributes. Avis and Stewart (1978) point out that a person-centered problem definition has characterized counseling. Definitions of mental health, the assumptions of vocational guidance, and most counseling theories stress the uniqueness and importance of the individual. As a result, the onus of responsibility for change in counseling tends to rest on the person. Caplan and Nelson (1973), in discussing the causal attribution of social problems, state that Western society tends to hold individuals responsible for their problems. Such an approach has the effect of labeling as deviant that segment of the population (racial and other minorities) that differs in thought and behavior from the larger society. Defining the problem as residing in the person enables society to ignore situationally relevant factors and to protect and preserve social institutions and belief systems.

It is apparent from earlier discussions that the ultimate success of cross-cultural counseling depends on the counselor's (a) flexibility in using techniques appropriate not only to the cultural group but the individual as well, and (b) ability to accurately handle the person-blame system-blame distinction. Such a counselor will generally hold high credibility and attractiveness with a culturally different client. We now turn to a discussion of these factors.

USE OF DIFFERENT SKILLS IN
CROSS-CULTURAL COUNSELING

One of the main assumptions of this chapter is that credibility and attractiveness are intimately related to a counselor's ability in cross-cultural counseling to use counseling strategies appropriate to the life styles of their culturally different clients, and to accurately identify the locus of responsibility. This latter term is most closely related to a diagnostic focus. With respect to the former, Sue (1977) makes a strong case that different cultural groups tend to require different counseling communication process interactions. Because groups and individuals differ from one another, the blind application of techniques to all situations and all populations seems ludicrous. In the interpersonal transactions between the counselor and the culturally different client, what is needed are differential approaches consistent with the life experiences of the client. It is ironic that, in this particular case, *equal treatment in counseling may be discriminatory treatment.* Counselors need to understand this train of thought. In the past, Third World groups have pointed to studies revealing that minority clients are given less preferential forms of treatment as a means of proving discriminatory health practices. Somewhere along the line, a confusion occurred in which to be treated differently was akin to discrimination. The confusion centered around the distinction between equal access and opportunities vs. equal treatment. Third World groups may not be asking for equal treatment so much as equal access and opportunity. This dictates a differential approach in counseling which is truly nondiscriminatory. Differential is not necessarily preferential. To identify relevant processes in cross-cultural counseling, Sue (1977) proposed a conceptual model to approach this task. He lists several conditions which are important. First, there must be a knowledge of minority group cultures and experiences. Second, we must make clear and

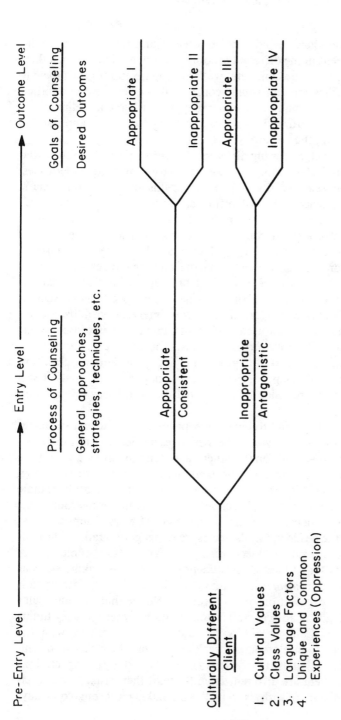

Fig. 5.1. Four conditions in counseling the culturally different

Source: Sue, D.W., Counseling the culturally different: A conceptual analysis. *Personnel and Guidance Journal, 1977, 7,* 422-425.

115

explicit the generic characteristics of counseling and the particular value assumptions inherent in the different schools of thought. Third, when these two aspects of our work are complete, we can compare and contrast them to see which approaches are consistent, conflictual, or new to one another. Figure 5.1 reveals four conditions which may arise when counseling a person from a different culture. This schema is proposed as one approach to looking at counseling the culturally different.

At the preentry level, culturally different clients inherit a whole constellation of cultural and class values, language factors, and life experiences. Likewise, the counselor is also a product of his or her culture, class, language, and experiences. This will influence the counseling activity as well as the particular school of counseling which is chosen by the counselor. Upon entering the process of counseling, counselors choose a general approach, style, or strategy in working with clients. All theories of counseling rely heavily on some basic techniques in the therapeutic session. Closely linked to the actual process of counseling are certain implicit or explicit goals: insight, self-actualization, behavior change, or specific goals such as studying better, dealing with aggression, how to interview for jobs, etc. As can be seen in figure 5.1, a culturally different client may be exposed to one of four conditions: (1) appropriate process, appropriate goals; (2) appropriate process, inappropriate goals; (3) inappropriate process, appropriate goals; and (4) inappropriate process, inappropriate goals. I will not go into the goals dimension of this model, but will focus briefly upon the process distinctions.

Conditions (1) and (2) tend to have appropriate and consistent strategies and techniques with the life styles and experiences of the culturally different client. Conditions (3) and (4), on the other hand, tend to have inappropriate or antagonistic process elements. For example, an appropriate process in counseling is illustrated by the following example. Suppose a black male student from the ghetto is failing in school and getting into numerous fights with other students. He can be treated in a variety of ways. Supposing that the student lacks the academic skills necessary to get good grades. The constant fighting is the result of peers teasing him about his "stupidity." A counselor who is willing to *teach* the student study and test-taking skills as well as *give advice* and *information* may be using an appropriate process consistent with the expectations of the student. Notice that this particular activity (teaching, giving advice, etc.) is not traditionally seen as a legitimate part of counseling. Calia (1968) points out that, in working with the culturally different, counselors must break away from their narrow definitions of counseling activities. Lorion (1974) concludes that the expectations of the lower-class client are different from those of therapists. Lower-class clients are concerned more with "survival" and making it through on a day-to-day basis. They expect immediate, concrete suggestions and advice. Getting job interviews for clients, teaching specific educational skills, and helping clients to understand and fill out unemployment forms may be the desired and preferred help. Thus, a counselor who uses counseling strategies which make sense to the client (consistent with his or her values) will be an effective and helpful one.

An example of an inappropriate process can also be given with respect to Native Americans. Trimble (1976) states that many Native Americans tend to view the person as harmonious with nature and that manipulation and active mastery of the environment is not perceived as desirable. Anglos, however, are concerned with controlling and mastering the physical environment: the more nature is controlled the better. Native American clients exposed to counselors who stress individual responsibility for changing and mastering the environment are, in effect, asking their clients to violate a basic value. For example, Gestalt approaches emphasize a body of technique used to be confrontive and controlling, actions which may prove embarassing to Indian clients. Two empirical studies (Atkinson, Maruyama, Matsui, & 1978; Berman, 1979) seem to support the contention that credibility and attractiveness may be dependent upon the counselor's use of appropriate counseling strategy.

Sue and Sue (1972) have made a strong case that Asian-American clients who may value restraint of strong feelings and believe that intimate revelations are to be shared only with close friends may cause problems for the "insight" or "feeling" oriented counselor. It is entirely possible that such techniques as reflection of feeling, asking questions of a deeply personal nature, and making depth interpretations may be perceived as lacking in respect for the client's integrity. The process of insight into underlying processes may not be valued by an Asian-American client. For example, some Asian-American clients who come for vocational information may be perceived by counselors as needing help in finding out what motivates their actions and decisions. Requests for advice or information from the client are seen as indicative of deeper, more personal conflicts. Although this might be true in some cases, the blind application of techniques that clash with cultural values seriously places many Asian-Americans in an uncomfortable and oppressed position. Atkinson, Maruyama, and Matsui (1978) tested this hypothesis with a number of Asian-American students. Two tape recordings of a contrived counseling session were prepared in which the client's responses were identical but the counselor's responses differed from being either directive or nondirective. Their findings indicated that counselors who use the directive approach were rated more credible and approachable than those using the nondirective counseling approach. Asian-Americans seem to prefer a logical, rational, structured counseling approach over an affective, reflective, and ambiguous one. This study indicates that counselors who work with certain Asian-Americans need to be aware that continual focus on affect through the use of reflection and summarization of feelings may actually reduce effectiveness and credibility. Most counselor training programs teach a core of counseling techniques that have been found to be effective with white, middle-class clients but not necessarily so with minority populations.

In another important study, Berman (1979) found similar results with a black population. The weakness of the previous study was that there was failure to compare equal responses with a white population. Berman's study compared the use of counseling skills between black and white male and female counselors. Berman's study used a video tape of culturally varied client vignettes which were viewed by black and white counselor trainees. They responded to the question "What would you say to this person?" The data was scored and coded according to a microcounseling taxonomy which divided counseling skills into attending and influencing ones. The hypothesis made by the investigator was that black and white counselors would give significantly different patterns of responses to their clients. Data supported the hypotheses. Black males and females tended to use the more active expression skills (directions, expression of content, and interpretation) with greater frequency than white counselor trainees. White males and females tended to use a higher percentage of attending skills. Berman concluded that race appears to be a major factor in the counselor's choice of skills, that black and white counselors appear to adhere to a distinctive style of counseling. Again, the implication for credibility and attractiveness of the culturally different counselor and its implications for counselor training programs are great. It is apparent that most training programs tend to emphasize the more passive attending skills. However, counselors so trained are ill-equipped to work with culturally different clients who might find the more active approach more relevant to their own needs and values. In a deeper analysis of these findings, Berman (1979) concludes that the more active style of the black counselors tends to include practical advice and allows for the introjection of a counselor's values and opinions. She concludes that "this style could well be preferred by minority counselors since its active stance would be likely to promote social change, rather than simply adhering to the status quo."

In the same study, Berman also investigated the diagnostic focus of black and white counselor trainees. What she found was that white counselors of both sexes were likely to focus their problem diagnosis in individual rather than in societal terms. For black counselors, however, results showed that diagnoses were evenly distributed between individual and societal focus. These findings are highly consistent with Sue's (1978) distinction between individual and system focus, and individual and system blame. In the society where individualism prevails, it is not surprising to find that white counselors tend to view their client's problems as residing within the individual rather than in society. Likewise, for minorities who have been the victims of oppression and discrimination, the focus upon societal factors may be evidence of their minority status and experience in the United States.

RESEARCH DIRECTIONS IN EVALUATING PROCESS VARIABLES IN CROSS-CULTURAL COUNSELING

Basic to the thesis of this chapter is the belief that effective cross-cultural counseling occurs when the counselor and client are able to appropriately and accurately send and receive both verbal and nonverbal messages. When the counselor is able to engage in such activities, his or her credibility and attractiveness will be increased. The process variables that are manifested in the counseling context may either enhance or negate the effectiveness of cross-cultural counseling. It appears imperative that we begin the much needed task of identifying relevant counseling practices for special groups. No one mode of counseling will be appropriate for all populations and situations. Thus, several research directions are proposed.

1. The evaluation of cross-cultural helping effectiveness can only come about when relevant process scoring systems are developed. While it may be beneficial to study necessary counseling conditions such as empathy, warmth, and genuineness (Carkhuff, 1969; Truax & Carkhuff, 1967), the rating scores used to measure these attributes have been criticized on methodological and theoretical grounds (Bergin & Suinn, 1975; Chinsky & Rappaport, 1970; Gormany & Hill, 1974; Rappaport & Chinsky, 1972). An alternative means of studying process variables would be to focus on specific verbal behaviors and skills. A number of response taxonomies have been proposed to analyze counselor behaviors (Danish & D'Angelli, 1976; Goodman & Dooley, 1976; Hill, 1978). Most of these taxonomies fail to deal with the possible cultural appropriateness or inappropriateness of helper behaviors. The one exception is the system proposed by Ivey and Authier (1978). Not only do they deal with cultural influences in the helping process, but they classify the focus of counseling responses used by the counselor. For example, is the response made by the counselor focusing on the helpee, helper, dyad or group, other people, topic, or the cultural-environmental-contextual area? As we have seen, this is an important dimension to consider with respect to minorities in America. The locus of responsibility as perceived by the counselor and by the culturally different

client can often be at odds with one another. With some modifications, systems such as that proposed by Ivey and Authier may offer us a valuable instrument by which to evaluate process variables in cross-cultural counseling.

2. A most fruitful area in evaluating process variables in cross-cultural counseling seems to be investigating counseling and communication styles with respect to individual counselor trainees, theoretical orientations, and ethnicity. Using a taxonomy system such as Ivey and Authier's, we can begin to do several things. First, in counselor training programs, for both inservice and preservice, we may be able to have trainees go through a series of simulated or real counseling sessions in which their counseling-communication styles are systematically scored. This will allow trainees to receive direct feedback about the skills that they use in counseling. I have often been impressed with how much a discrepancy exists between what counselors say they do and their theoretical orientation as opposed to what they actually do in counseling. This can start the necessary process of self-exploration and understanding of one's communication style and personal impact on others. Also, it may identify major areas in which the counselor tends to need upgrading of skills appropriate to other clients.

Second, it seems important that we begin to investigate what differences, if any, theoretical orientations have with respect to the process of counseling. Again, using a taxonomy system it may be possible to identify major differences in schools of counseling and therapy with respect to skills and language. Several investigators (Hill, Thames, & Rardin, 1979; Meara, Shannon, & Pepinsky, 1979) have investigated stylistic complexity of the language and counselor responses across three theoretical orientations. They have found major differences to exist with respect to language and counselor style. Watching Carl Rogers, Fritz Perls, and Albert Ellis (Shostrom, 1977) counsel the same client in 35 minute interviews, they were able to note these differences. Meara, Shannon, and Pepinsky (1979) conclude that Rogers taught his client to be her "feeling self"; Perls taught her to be her "fighting self"; and Ellis taught her to be her "thinking self." The study by Hill, Thames, and Rardin (1979) also found significant differences with respect to counselor response styles. Rogers, for example, mainly encouraged, restated, and reflected. Perls tended to be much wider in his repertoire of responses than either Rogers or Perls. Perls used mostly direct guidance, information, interpretations, open questions, minimal encouragers, closed questions, confrontations, approval-reassurance, and nonverbal references. Ellis was the most active of the three counselors using mostly information, direct guidance, minimal encouragers, interpretations, closed questions, and restatements. All three of the behaviors of the counselors tended to be consistent with their theoretical orientations.

Third, it seems important on the basis of earlier discussions concerning race and counseling style that we also begin to identify how various minority populations perceive variations in the counseling process. For example, studies similar to Berman (1979) might be used across a number of different groups (Asian-Americans, blacks, Chicanos, Native Americans, and whites). Several questions which might be asked are these: Do race and ethnicity affect a culturally different client's receptivity to counseling style? Do counseling and communication styles vary with respect to race and ethnicity?

These questions and the above discussions have important implications not only for counselor training, but for a possible match between a counselor and a culturally different client. If we assume that communication styles which are congruent and consistent with each other tend to result in more positive and beneficial changes, then this area of research must be undertaken. Communication styles with respect to individuals, theoretical orientations, and ethnicity can be closely analyzed with respect to a behavioral response category system such as that proposed by Ivey and Authier 1978).

3. Another major area of important research should deal with ethnicity and race as a function of perceived trustworthiness, expertness, and attractiveness in counseling styles. Various ethnic groups could be identified and correlates of behavioral trustworthiness, behavioral expertness, and behavioral attractiveness might be investigated with respect to each of the groups. Since counseling can be conceptualized as a social influence process, these three dimensions and how the various groups perceive them in counseling will be of great importance. For example, which behaviors enhance or decrease credibility and attractiveness can be systematically determined.

There are many other areas of investigation in dealing with process variables that can be carried out. For example, I am intrigued with how minority identity development theory and the theory of world views might be correlated with process variables in cross-cultural counseling. For example, Sue (1978) states that it is highly probable that problem definitions and specific counseling skills are differentially associated with a particular world view. One of the major reasons why Third World clients may prematurely terminate counseling is that counselors may not only differ in world view, but employ counseling skills inappropriate to their client's life styles. We drastically need research into all of the above areas. I will leave you with only this question: Are there specific counseling goals, techniques, and skills best suited for working with various populations? Implications for counselor training and practice are immense.

REFERENCES

Arbuckle, D.W. The counselor: Who? What? *Personnel and Guidance Journal,* 1972, *50,* 785-790.

Aspy, D.N. Empathy—congruence—caring are singular. *Personnel and Guidance Journal,* 1970, *48,* 637-640.

Atkinson, D.R., & Carskaddon, G. A prestigious introduction, psychological jargon, and perceived counselor credibility. *Journal of Counseling Psychology,* 1975, *22,* 180-186.

Atkinson, D.R., Maruyama, M., & Matsui, S. Effects of counselor race and counseling approach on Asian Americans' perceptions of counselor credibility and utility. *Journal of Counseling Psychology,* 1978, *25,* 76-83.

Atkinson, D.R., Morten, G., & Sue, D.W. *Counseling American minorities: A cross-cultural perspective.* Dubuque, Iowa: Wm. C. Brown, 1979.

Avis, J.P., & Steward, L.H., College Counseling: Intentions and change. *The Counseling Psychologist,* 1976, *6,* 74-77.

Banks, G. The effects of race on the one-to-one helping interviews. *Social Service Review,* 1971, *45,* 137-146.

Banks, G., Berenson, B., & Carkhuff, R. The effects of counselor race and training upon counseling process with Negro clients in initial interviews. *Journal of Clinical Psychology,* 1967, *23,* 70-72.

Barak, A., & Dell, D.M. Differential perceptions of counselor behavior: Replication and extension. *Journal of Counseling Psychology,* 1977, *24,* 288-292.

Barak, A., & LaCrosse, M.B. Multidimensional perception of counselor behavior. *Journal of Counseling Psychology,* 1975, *22,* 471-476.

Bergin, A.E. The evaluation of therapeutic outcomes. In A.E. Bergin and S.L. Garfield (Eds.), *Handbook of psychotherapy and behavior change: An empirical analysis.* New York: Wiley, 1971.

Bergin, A.E., & Suinn, R. Individual psychotherapy and behavior change. *Annual Review of Psychology,* 1975, *26,* 509-556.

Berman, J. Counseling skills used by black and white female counselors. *Journal of Counseling Psychology,* 1979, *26,* 81-84.

Bryne, D., & Nelson, D. Attraction is a linear function of proportion of positive reinforcements. *Journal of Personality and Social Psychology,* 1965, *1,* 659-663.

Bryson, S., Bardo, H., & Johnson, C. Black female counselor and the black male client. *Journal of Non-White Concerns in Personnel and Guidance,* 1975, *3,* 53-58.

Bryson, J., & Cody, J. Relationship of race and level of understanding between counselor and client. *Journal of Counseling Psychology,* 1973, *20,* 495-498.

Calia, C.F. The culturally deprived client: A reformulation of the counselor's role. In J.C. Bentley (Ed.), *The counselor's role: Commentary and readings.* Boston: Houghton Mifflin, 1968.

Caplan, N., & Nelson, D.S. On being useful: The nature and consequences of psychological research on social problems. *American Psychologist,* 1973, *28,* 199-211.

Carkhuff, R.R. *Helping and human relations.* New York: Holt, Rinehart & Winston, 1969. 2 vols.

Carkhuff, R.R., & Pierce, R. Differential effects of therapist race and social class upon patient depth of self-exploration in the initial clinical interview. *Journal of Consulting Psychology,* 1967, *31,* 632-634.

Chartier, G. A-B therapist variable: Real or imagined? *Psychological Bulletin,* 1971, *75,* 22-23.

Chinsky, J.M., & Rappaport, J. Brief critique of the meaning and reliability of "accurate empathy" ratings. *Psychological Bulletin,* 1970, *73,* 379-382.

Cimbolic, P. Counselor race and experience effects on black clients. *Journal of Consulting and Clinical Psychology,* 1972, *39,* 328-332.

Cimbolic, P.T. Group effects on black clients' perception of counselors. *Journal of College Student Personnel,* 1973, *14,* 296-302.

Collins, B.E. *Social psychology:* Reading, Mass: Addison-Wesley Publishing Co., 1970.

Corsini, R.J. *Current psychotherapies.* (2nd ed.) Itasca, Ill.: Peacock, 1979.

Dabbs, J.M. Self-esteem, communicator characteristics, and attitude change. *Journal of Abnormal and Social Psychology,* 1964, *69,* 173-181.

Danish, S.J., & D'Angelli, A.R. Rationale and implementation of a training program for paraprofessionals. *Professional Psychology,* 1976, *7,* 38-46.

Dell, B.M. Counselor power base, influence attempt, and behavior change in counseling. *Journal of Counseling Psychology,* 1973, *20,* 399-405.

Eysenck, H.J. The effects of psychotherapy: An evaluation. *Journal of Consulting Psychology,* 1952, *16,* 319-324.

Festinger, L. *A theory of cognitive dissonance.* Evanston, Ill.: Row & Peterson, 1957.

Gardner, W.E. The differential effects of race, education and experience in helping. *Journal of Clinical Psychology,* 1972, *28,* 87-89.

Garfield, S., & Bergin, A.E. Personal therapy, outcome and some therapist variables. *Psychotherapy: Theory, Research and Practice,* 1971, *8,* 251-253.

Goodman, G., & Dooley, D.A. A framework for help intended communication. *Psychotherapy: Theory, Research and Practice,* 1976, *13,* 106-117.

Gormany, J., & Hill, C. Guidelines for research in Carkhuff's training model. *Journal of Counseling Psychology,* 1974, *21,* 539-547.

Harrison, D.K. Race as a counselor-client variable in counseling and psychotherapy: A review of the research. *The Counseling Psychologist,* 1975, *5,* 124-133.

Heffernon, A., & Bruehl, D. Some effects of race of inexperienced lay counselors on black junior high school students. *Journal of School Psychology,* 1971, *9,* 35-37.

Hill, C.A. Development of a counselor verbal response category system. *Journal of Counseling Psychology,* 1978, *25,* 461-468.

Hill, C., Thames, T., & Rardin, D. Comparison of Rogers, Perls, and Ellis in the Hill counselor Verbal Response Category System. *Journal of Counseling Psychology,* 1979, *26,* 198-203.

Hovland, C.I., Janis, I.L., & Kelley, H.H. *Communication and persuasion.* New Haven: Yale University Press, 1953.

Ivey, A., & Authier, J. *Microcounseling: Innovations in interviewing, counseling, psychotherapy, and psychoeducation.* (2nd ed.) Springfield, Ill.: Charles C. Thomas, 1978.

Jackson, B. Black identity development. *ME FORM: Journal of Educational Diversity and Innovation,* 1975, *2,* 19-25.

Johnson, H.N. A survey of students' attitudes toward counseling at a predominantly black university. *Journal of Counseling Psychology,* 1977, *24,* 162-164.

Jones, M.H., & Jones, M.C. The neglected client. In R. Jones (Ed.), *Black psychology.* New York: Harper & Row, 1972.

Kincaid, M. Identity and therapy in the black community. *Personnel and Guidance Journal,* 1969, *47,* 884-890.

LaCrosse, M.B., & Barak, A. Differential perception of counselor behavior. *Journal of Counseling Psychology,* 1976, *23,* 170-172.

London, P. *Modes and morals of psychotherapy.* New York: Holt, Rinehart & Winston, 1964.

Larion, R.P. Patient and therapist variables in the treatment of low-income patients. *Psychological Bulletin*, 1974, *81*, 344-364.

Meara, N., Shannon, J., & Pepinsky. H. Comparison of the stylistic complexity of the language of counselor and client across three theoretical orientations. *Journal of Counseling Psychology*, 1979, *26*, 181-189.

Merluzzi, T.V., Merluzzi, B.H., & Kaul, T.J. Counselor race and power base: Effects on attitudes and behavior. *Journal of Counseling Psychology*, 1977, *24*, 430-436.

Mills, J., & Aronson, E. Opinion change as a function of the communicator's attractiveness and desire to influence. *Journal of Personality and Social Psychology*, 1965, *1*, 173-177.

Padilla, A.M., Ruiz, R.A., & Alvarez, R. Community mental health services for the Spanish-speaking surnamed population. *American Psychologist*, 1975, *30*, 892-905.

Patterson, C.H. *Theories of counseling and psychotherapy*. (2nd ed.) New York: Harper & Row, 1973.

Peoples, V.Y., & Dell, D.M. Black and white student preferences for counselor roles. *Journal of Counseling Psychology*, 1975, *22*, 529-534.

Perls, F. *Gestalt therapy verbatim*. Lafayette, Ca.: Real People's Press, 1969.

Rachman, S. *The effects of psychotherapy*. New York: Pergamon Press, 1971.

Rappaport, J., & Chinsky, J.M. Accurate empathy: Confusion of a construct. *Psychological Bulletin*, 1972, *77*, 400-404.

Razrin, A.M. A-B variable in psychotherapy: A critical review. *Psychological Bulletin*, 1971, *75*, 1-21.

Schmidt, L.D., & Strong, S.R. Attractiveness and influence in counseling. *Journal of Counseling Psychology*, 1971, *18*, 348-351.

Scriven, M. "First, the roses. . . ." *APA Monitor*, 1975, *6*, 2-3.

Shostrom, E.M. (Producer). *Three approaches to psychotherapy*. Santa Ana, Ca.: Psychological Films, 1977. (Film)

Sloane, R., Staples, F., Cristol, A., Yorkston, N., & Whipple, K. *Psychotherapy versus behavior therapy*. Cambridge, Mass.: Harvard University Press, 1975.

Spiegel, S.B. Expertness, similarity, and perceived counselor competence. *Journal of Counseling Psychology*, 1976, *23*, 436-441.

Sprafkin, R.P. Communicator expertness and changes in word meaning in psychological treatment. *Journal of Counseling Psychology*, 1970, *17*, 191-196.

Strong, S.R. Counseling: An interpersonal influence process. *Journal of Counseling Psychology*, 1968, *15*, 215-224.

Strong, S.R., & Schmidt, L.D. Expertness and influence in counseling. *Journal of Counseling Psychology*, 1970, *17*, 31-37.

Strupp, H.H. *Psychotherapy and the modification of abnormal behavior*. New York: McGraw-Hill, 1971.

Sue, D.W. Counseling the culturally different: A conceptual analysis. *Personnel and Guidance Journal*, 1977, *55*, 422-425.

Sue, D.W. Eliminating cultural oppression in counseling: Toward a general theory. *Journal of Counseling Psychology*, 1978, *25*, 419-428.

Sue, D.W. *Cross-cultural counseling: Theory and practice*. New York: John Wiley, in press.

Sue, D.W., & Sue, S. Counseling Chinese-Americans. *Personnel and Guidance Journal*, 1972, *50*, 637-644.

Sue, S., & McKinney, H. Asian-Americans in the community mental health care system. *American Journal of Orthopsychiatry*, 1975, *45*, 111-118.

Sue, S., McKinney, H., Allen, D., & Hall, J. Delivery of community mental health services to black and white clients. *Journal of Consulting and Clinical Psychology*, 1974, *42*, 794-801.

Teuber, J., & Powers, E. Evaluating therapy in a delinquency prevention program. *Proceedings of the Association of Nervous and Mental Diseases,* 1963, *3,* 138-147.

Trimble, J.E. Value differences among American Indians: Concerns for the concerned counselor. In Pedersen, P., Lonner, W.J., & Draguns, J.G. (Eds.), *Counseling across cultures.* Honolulu: East West Center Press, 1976.

Truax, C., & Carkhuff, R.R. *Toward effective counseling and psychotherapy: Teaching and practice.* Chicago: Aldine, 1967.

Vontress, C.E. Racial differences: Impediments to rapport. *Journal of Counseling Psychology,* 1971, *18,* 7-13.

Vontress, C.E. The black militant as a counselor. *Personnel and Guidance Journal,* 1972, *50,* 576-580.

Wolken, G.H., Moriwaki, S., & Williams, K.J. Race and social class as factors in the orientation toward psychotherapy. *Journal of Counseling Psychology,* 1973, *20,* 312-316.

Chapter 6

Evaluating Outcome Variables in Cross-Cultural Counseling and Psychotherapy*

Michael J. Lambert

This chapter deals with the implications of empirical investigations of psychotherapy for the practice of cross-cultural psychotherapy. First, the status of empirical knowledge concerning the general effects of psychotherapy will be described. This will be followed by a discussion of the variables that predict and cause positive and negative changes in patients. The importance of the therapist's theoretical orientation, attitude, technique, personality, and the ways the therapist contributes to the change process will be considered. The characteristics of patients (e.g., sex, degree of disturbance, etc.) that have been shown to relate to outcome will be summarized. Studies that have tried to examine the interaction of patient variables (such as locus of control) with therapist variables (such as directiveness) will also be summarized. The reader's attention will then be drawn to methods of assessing improvement in patients. Finally, the meaning of these results for cross-cultural psychotherapy will be considered along with empirical research related to cross-cultural psychotherapy outcomes.

The emphasis in this chapter is on the application of traditional Western therapies to persons whose cultural background is in some ways different. The effects of non-Western indigenous therapies (e.g., Morita Therapy, Naikan Therapy, Mudangs, Shamans, Bomohs) will not be considered. Empirical research on these methods employed both within their host culture and across cultures is scarce. For samples of the methods employed

---

*Parts of this chapter are based on reviews of psychotherapy recently published by Allen Bergin and myself (Bergin & Lambert, 1978), and on a more recent review—*The Effects of Psychotherapy*, Vol. 1 (Lambert, 1979) and Vol. II (Lambert, in preparation).

and results achieved, the interested reader should read summaries by Lebra (1976) or Yanagida (1977). This literature is directly related to the present endeavor and, although not discused, should be considered a rich source of documentation of both the similarities and differences between diverse people's solutions to problems of mental health.

Before moving on to the issues of research, it may be helpful to know the bias and background from which I am working. Over the past six years, I have made an intense study of psychotherapy outcome literature. I have been interested mainly in applications with adults who have neurotic and personality disorders. I have been most interested in empirical research involving controlled study of the outcomes of counseling and psychotherapy. As a practicing therapist, I have participated in the process of therapy. I have a belief in the efficacy of a variety of psychotherapeutic methods and hope to discover, through experimental and empirical methods, the causal relationships that seem to govern stability and change in human behavior. I believe scientific methods will aid in the discovery of effective methods of helping people when they are disturbed. Although the methodologies of science sometimes seem ill suited to the study of human interaction, these methods represent one important and often neglected point of view.

In the following paragraphs, I will attempt to integrate what I have learned from studying a great deal of the psychotherapy research literature with what I know about cross-cultural applications of psychotherapy.

The application of Western psychotherapeutic techniques to persons from a variety of cultures raises many interesting and important issues. Not only are there many ethnocentric cultural factors that enter into psychotherapy, but its evaluation is plagued by difficulties in defining psychopathology (see Marsella, 1979), agreeing upon definitions of acceptable outcome, and accurately understanding the meanings conveyed in different styles of communicating.

The application and study of psychotherapy from the broad perspective of cultural similarities and differences promises to be enriching although difficult and frustrating. Eventually, it will allow us to examine questions of critical importance such as the universality of laws of growth and change. To what extent are the diverse practices consumed under the heading of psychotherapy effective across cultures? Which might be offered like penicillin or polio vaccine? Will we find that the treatments labeled as psychotherapy are so culture bound, so much an art form, that little generalization is possible? What answers to these and related questions can be drawn from past studies of psychotherapy outcome?

IS PSYCHOTHERAPY EFFECTIVE?

Few issues in the area of psychotherapy have generated as much debate as

the question of the general effectiveness of psychotherapy. The accumulated mass of empirical data is a testimony to the importance and interest
researchers and clinicians have shown in answering the question: Is
psychotherapy effective?

There are conflicting conclusions drawn by past reviewers of this body of
American and Western European material. However, there is now considerable agreement about many of the major conclusions, which can be
derived from this literature. These will be summarized and placed into an
historical perspective before moving on into more current material.

Crucial contributors to debates over the efficacy of psychotherapy have
been published by Eysenck (1952, 1960, 1966) and more recently, by
Rachman (1973). As they reviewed the outcomes of therapy, the Eysenck-
Rachman surveys purported to show that about two-thirds of all neurotics
who enter psychotherapy improve substantially within two years as do an
equivalent proportion of neurotics who have never entered therapy! This
misleading and, in my opinion, inaccurate conclusion is still occasionally
quoted.

Eysenck (1952) originally based his claim on the percent improvement in
8,053 cases from 24 outcome studies published between 1927 and 1951.
These data were reprinted in 1961, 1965, and 1966 without modification.
Bergin (1971) has been the most thorough in his critique of the data in question. He has pointed out that the results of the original studies are open to
numerous interpretations and that, because of the ambiguity of the data,
different percentages of improvement can be tabulated and defended. He
showed that Eysenck was very stringent in his criterion of improvement and
seemed to be especially biased against psychoanalytically oriented psychotherapy. Nevertheless, Bergin (1971) concluded that, despite all the difficulties encountered in drawing sound conclusions from the studies
published prior to 1952, psychotherapy has been shown to have a modestly
positive effect.

When the results of studies published up to 1969 were added to those
already considered (Bergin, 1971), it became even clearer that the outcome
of psychotherapy was beneficial for about two-thirds or more of the patients seeking treatment. This outcome for psychotherapy is favorable when
contrasted to the improvement shown in patients who do not receive psychotherapy.

The empirical evidence which suggests the rate at which patients improve
without psychotherapy has been summarized by Lambert (1976). His
baseline was obtained by pooling the results of studies which included
follow-up data on patients who: (a) had never sought treatment but had
been identified in epidemiological studies; (b) had sought treatment but
were held on a waiting list; or (c) had sought but refused treatment once it

became available. Examining outcomes from 13 studies and over 700 neurotic patients, the median number showing improvement was 43 percent. A review of the empirical evidence strongly favors the position that patients with neurotic disorders improve in the absence of formal psychotherapy. This phenomenon is perhaps poorly named "spontaneous remission" and is undoubtedly the culmination of a wide variety of forces at work within the individual and existing naturally in the environment.

The median rate of spontaneous improvement quoted, while more accurate than a two-thirds estimate, is, nevertheless, unreliable. The evidence discussed indicates that reported rates of spontaneous improvement may vary from 0 to 90 percent at follow-up. This great diversity makes the use of such data unsatisfactory for the purpose of replacing a no-treatment control group. To be considered effective, psychotherapy patients should show improvement which exceeds improvement in appropriate control groups of similar patients using equivalent criteria. Such comparisons will probably result only when control groups are created randomly from the relevant population which is concurrently treated and when identical criterion measures are applied.

In answer to the question, "Is psychotherapy effective?," researchers and most current reviewers, with the exception of Eysenck and Rachman, have been in general agreement. Psychotherapy has been shown to be more effective than no therapy in controlled comparisons using a variety of outcome variables. To verify this conclusion, the interested reader should consult the following exhaustive and overlapping reviews: Bergin, (1971); Bergin and Lambert (1978); Bergin & Suinn (1975); Kellner (1975); Lambert (1979); Luborsky, Chandler, Auerbach, Cohen, & Bachrach (1971); Luborsky, Singer, & Luborsky (1975); Meltzoff & Kornreich (1970); Roback (1971); Smith and Glass (1977). As Korchin (1976) has put it, "Anyone with the patience of Job and the mind of a bank auditor is cordially invited to look again at the accumulated mass of material and settle the issue for himself."

In addition to the modestly positive effects of psychotherapy, the empirical literature gives support to several other conclusions. Included here is the tendency for more well-designed studies to produce more impressive results, more experienced therapists to have greater positive effects, different therapies to have equivalent outcomes, treatment duration to be unrelated to positive personality change, and a significant relationship between outcome and certain client and therapist traits. Not at all insignificant in a discussion of cross-cultural psychotherapy is the discovery of the "deterioration effect" (cf. Bergin, 1966; Lambert, Bergin, & Collins, 1977) and the general conclusion that some attempts to help persons in distress result in increased suffering, more intense symptoms, and other negative consequences. Consider now some of the more specific issues related to psychotherapy outcome.

WHAT CAUSAL AGENTS ARE IMPLICATED IN THE POSITIVE AND NEGATIVE EFFECTS OF PSYCHOTHERAPY?

Current research on psychotherapy outcome has moved well beyond studying the question: Is psychotherapy effective? Contemporary research designs frequently involve one of the following strategies:

1. Comparative studies in which two or more competing treatments are applied to a suitable and often homogeneous population of patients with the purpose of identifying the *most effective treatment.*
2. Factorial studies in which two or more treatments are applied to clients who are separated on the basis of organismic variables such as sex, or some personality trait. The intention is to identify *what treatment works best with which type of patient.* Do patient organism variables interact with treatment procedures to provide an ideal combination?
3. Dismantling studies in which a treatment of known value is examined with various components of the treatment missing. *What aspects of treatment are necessary* and sufficient for constructive change?

These types of research designs are very likely to lead to a further specification of causal relationship in the application of counseling techniques to patients. Some interesting findings have emerged from these research methods. A critical issue for cross-cultural psychotherapy is the relative importance of technique versus the therapeutic relationship in determining the outcome of psychotherapy, the types of treatments that might interact with specific cultural learnings, the relationship of client variables to outcome, and so forth.

Of What Importance is the School of the Therapist or the Use of Specific Therapy Techniques in Determining Outcome?

Under the broad question of "which treatment is more efficacious?" are more meaningful and productive questions. Which specific procedure obtains which results, with which patients, in what amount of time, and are these differential results equally enduring? These more specific questions do not set up a win-lose situation and, therefore, serve the more mature interests of inquiry.

Several past reviews have summarized the research on comparative studies. Meltzoff and Kornreich's (1970) is one such review. The authors list at least 38 studies that they believe represent the research relevant to the issue of differential outcome. They summarize as follows:

> There is hardly any evidence that one traditional school of psychotherapy yields a better outcome than another. In fact, the question has hardly been put to a fair test. The whole issue remains at the level of polemic, professional public opinion, and whatever weight that can be brought to bear by authoritative presentation of illustrative cases. . .there is no current evidence that one traditional method is more successful than another. . .[p.200].

Roback (1971), in a brief and overlapping review that considered outcomes in insight versus non-insight therapies, concluded there was no significant difference between behavior therapy and insight therapy outcomes. Lambert and Bergin (1973) and Bergin and Suinn (1975) contrasted the empirical evidence on outcomes of humanistic and behavioral approaches and, like Meltzoff and Kornreich (1970), concluded that neither had demonstrated a clear superiority, but that behavioral techniques appeared to have the advantage with some restricted problems.

"Everyone has won and so all must have prizes," concluded the Dodo bird in *Alice in Wonderland*; and Luborsky, Singer, and Luborsky (1975) agreed that this verdict also applied to the various forms of psychotherapy that have been put to an empirical test. They published a detailed review of more than 100 comparative studies, some of which overlapped with the review of Meltzoff and Kornreich (1970). They presented data on comparisons between time-limited versus unlimited therapy, drugs versus psychotherapy (in numerous combinations), client-centered versus other psychotherapy, and behavior therapy versus other psychotherapy. This review is most relevant to our focus because it was similarly concerned with adult outpatients, patients instead of recruited subjects, and types of problems that excluded simple habit disorders.

Luborsky's conclusions were similar to those already mentioned: "Most comparative studies of different forms of psychotherapy found insignificant differences in proportions of patients who improved by the end of psychotherapy."

The Temple Study typifies current studies of a comparative sort (Sloane, Staples, Cristol, Yorkston, & Whipple, 1975). It involved more than 90 outpatients seen at the Temple University Health Sciences Center. Diagnostic and demographic information are reported in detail, and the study patients were typical of those usually seen clinically.

By diagnostic category, the majority (two-thirds) were judged neurotic, with the remaining patients (one-third) considered to have personality disorders. Patients, such as those with severe depression, who required medication were not included in the study.

Patients were assigned to short-term analytically oriented psychotherapy, behavior therapy, or to a minimal treatment wait-list group. The groups receiving each treatment were matched with respect to sex and severity of symptoms but otherwise were randomly assigned to treatment groups.

The therapists in the study were six white males: five psychiatrists, and one clinical psychologist. Three were behavior therapists and three were psychoanalysts. All were considered good therapists by their peers and enjoyed excellent professional reputations (e.g., Joseph Wolpe, Arnold Lazarus). A list of stipulative definitions for each treatment method was drawn up and agreed to by the therapists. Tape recordings of the fifth interview were made to provide an independent assessment of therapist activities.

Assessment procedures included standard psychological tests: Minnesota Multiphasic Personality Inventory (MMPI); Eysenck Personality Inventory; California Psychological Inventory; the Target Symptoms technique; the Structured and Scaled Interview to Assess Maladjustment; reports by informants who had known the patient for an average of 12 years; as well as ratings by the therapist, client, and an independent assessor.

Outcome was assessed after four months of treatment and again one year after commencing treatment. Both treatment groups, as well as the wait-list control group, improved significantly on target symptoms, but the behavior therapy and psychotherapy groups had improved significantly more than the wait-list group. There were no differences between behavior therapy and psychotherapy on any of the target symptoms as rated by an independent assessor whose knowledge of the design was kept as blind as possible. On estimates of general functioning at work, in social situations, and the like, the groups also improved but did not differ from each other in amount of improvement. With respect to global outcome, the independent assessor rated 80 percent of the behavior therapy and psychotherapy groups as improved, whereas only 48 percent of the waiting controls were judged improved. On general adjustment, 93 percent of the group receiving behavior therapy were rated as significantly improved, whereas 77 percent of the psychotherapy and wait-list patients were rated as significantly improved.

All three groups maintained their improvement at follow-up. The general trend was for improvement to continue and for the patients in the wait-list group gradually to improve and to approach or equal the therapy groups. While this last finding supports the notion that therapy accelerates change that is otherwise going to occur in the absence of psychotherapy, it is confounded by the fact that only eight of the original 30 wait-list subjects could be considered untreated during the eight months between treatment and follow-up.

There are a few exceptions to the general trend pointing to a failure of current techniques to have unique effects. The treatment of fears and phobias seems to be one such exception. These classic neurotic disorders, in their most incapacitating forms, are present only in low proportions (2.2 percent) in the normal population (Agras, Chapin, & Oliveau, 1972). Similarly, they are not common in clinic populations. They are among the neurotic disorders that have the lowest rate of spontaneous recovery and can remain unimproved over years or decades (Lambert, 1976). Nevertheless, phobias can be treated effectively with improvement rates much higher than the low spontaneous remission rates would imply.

Gelder and Marks (1968); Gelder, Marks, and Wolfe (1967); Gillan and Rachman (1974); Hand, Lamontagne, & Marks (1974); Marks (1971); and Mathews, Whitehead, Hackman, Julier, Bancroft, Gath, & Shaw (1976) provide substantial evidence that treatments which involve patient exposure to the fear-evoking stimuli result in substantial improvement. Furthermore, the authors have included followup studies which suggest that these improvements are maintained at followup two to four years after treatment.

A variety of treatment approaches have been applied with a wide range of phobic disorders. This is probably the area of clearest superiority for behaviorally-oriented treatments. These have included: flooding, systematic desensitization, relaxation training, thought stopping aversion relief, behavioral rehearsal, and implosion. These behavioral techniques have been contrasted with insight-oriented psychotherapy, rational emotive psychotherapy, relationship therapy, group therapy, autogenic training, hypnosis, and "counseling." (Allen, 1971; DiLoreto, 1971; Gelder & Marks, 1966, 1968; Karst & Trexler, 1970; Mitchell & Ng, 1972; Paul, 1967).

It appears that a variety of diverse techniques have reduced phobias, including those based upon anxiety reduction, e.g., desensitization, or upon heightened arousal, e.g., flooding. An element common to the diverse successful approaches is exposure to the fear-provoking stimuli. This factor rather than relaxation or high anxiety is probably the necessary or salient feature of the variety of treatments that have been successful with these conditions (Marks, 1978).

Exposure in *vivo* appears more effective than exposure in fantasy. Emmelkamp and Wessels (1974) is illustrative of research in this area. They studied agoraphobics who were given four 90-minute sessions, three times weekly of either a) exposure in vivo; b) exposure in fantasy for 45 minutes followed by 45 minutes exposure in *vivo;* or c) exposure in fantasy with a therapist present. Outcome was best with in *vivo*, then in *vivo* with fantasy, and finally in fantasy only. A remaining question is the extent to which self-exposure versus therapist-assisted exposure is necessary for substantial improvement.

Other important variables that promote successful treatment appear to be high patient motivation which insures that the patient will execute therapeutic operations, and a therapist who behaves in such a way as to influence motivation and proper completion of treatment directives.

While it seems that phobias improve after exposure, some additional understanding is needed to increase effective treatment. Symptom substitution does not occur in unusual proportions in the behavioral treatments of phobia, but occasionally preexisting depressive states return and must be dealt with. Furthermore, some patients improve without exposure—either "spontaneously" or with the use of drugs (Hafner & Marks, 1976). Also, some patients who carry out treatment procedures properly and are continuously exposed to phobic objects do not improve. Therefore, the results of behavioral treatments are not yet as predictable as might be hoped, although they are more predictable than other treatment procedures with phobias.

It is expected (I am not aware of controlled cross-cultural tests on this topic) that the basic techniques will reduce phobias if applied properly to persons from highly diverse cultures. This speculation has not been adequately tested.

Future researchers, interested in studying culture and psychotherapy, would do well to study interventions that can be shown to be mediated primarily by technical procedures. In terms of treatment strategies, this would include mainly behavioral methods such as desensitization and flooding with highly specific fears. A treatment of related use may be biofeedback-mediated relaxation and self-control strategies with psychophysiological disorders. A possible research strategy would match cross-cultural patients on symptomology and apply several competing treatments over a short period of time. Using appropriate control groups, this strategy might maximize the impact of treatment and the possible presence of interactions between treatment methods and culture.

Another area in which specific techniques seem to be uniquely effective includes the treatment of certain sexual dysfunctions (e.g., premature ejaculation, female orgasmic dysfunction). Some non-Western indigenous therapies, such as Morita therapy, have also been tested with empirical methodology (see Kora, 1965; Reynolds, 1976), but their specific or unique effects are unknown and they also await appropriate adaptations and possible cross-cultural application. Much work needs to be completed before the active ingredients of treatment are agreed upon completely. Specific therapy techniques can rarely be prescribed on the basis of empirical research and even so, it seems quite reasonable to conclude that technique variables are not nearly as important as patient characteristics and therapist relationship variables in predicting psychotherapy outcome.

I have tried to illustrate in Fig. 6.1 and 6.2 what I personally consider the current state of affairs (as reflected by empirical research) in this area.

The figures suggest that therapist and client variables are the primary determinants of psychotherapy outcome, that many of the determinants have not as yet been clearly identified, or the strength of some may be even stronger than we assume. Figure 6.2 also suggests that therapist relationship factors may have their strongest influence on those people who are in the central area of the highly disturbed/slightly disturbed continuum.

Figures 6.1 and 6.2 ignore many common sense conclusions that have been drawn about therapy outcome. They represent, therefore, a rather conservative position. For example, they do not reflect the behavioristic assumption that techniques are highly effective in facilitating change. Nor do they reflect the client-centered belief that the therapist-offered relationship variables are necessary and sufficient conditions of change. The conclusions that are presented in figures 7.1 and 7.2 are limited by the problems inherent in applying scientific methods to complex human interactions. They have the advantage of relying upon a fairly well substantiated body of literature and are, therefore, to be taken more seriously than personal opinion. At the same time, future research may demonstrate that the Western literature as represented in these figures does not generalize to cross-cultural psychotherapy.

At the present time, cross-cultural psychotherapy research is at a pre-methodological level. Most of the literature on outcome (see Walz and Benjamin, 1978; Yanagida, 1977) continues to be on the level of descriptive case reports.

In order to understand the implications of outcome research for cross-cultural psychotherapy, we must examine some of the patient and therapist variables that have been related to the process and outcome of therapy. The reader should, however, be aware that the design of most of the studies in this area precludes us from drawing cause-effect relationships.

What Patient Variables Contribute to Psychotherapy Outcome?

There are many patient variables that have been correlated with psychotherapy outcome. A few general conclusions have resulted from empirical studies with these variables.

1. It is doubtful that demographic characteristics of patients such as sex, age, IQ, and marital status can be used effectively to help in the selection of particular types of treatment or as gross screening criteria for assignment to psychotherapy.

2. Severity of maladjustment, complexity of symptoms, and similar variables are highly useful in predicting outcome. These factors interact with the type and source of ratings used to determine outcome and,

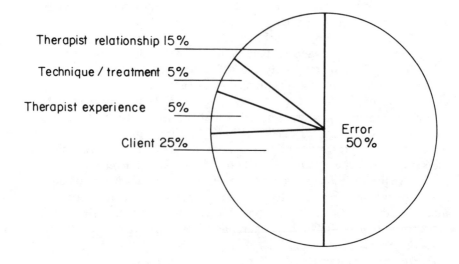

Fig. 6.1. The relative contribution of client, therapist,
and technique variables to psychotherapy outcome

Client: Included here would be such variables as age, sex, socioeconomic level IQ, marital status, diagnosis, motivation, ego strength, interaction with environmental factors, therapy readiness, degree of disturbance, duration of symptoms prior to seeking treatment. Some of these are overlapping variables but each considered separately interacts with treatment variables to produce outcome.

Therapist relationship variables: Includes therapist offered conditions such as empathy, genuiness, warmth, and respect.

Therapist experience: Includes unspecified variables such as poise, confidence, good judgment, accurate expectations, personal maturity, and even relationship skills.

Technique and treatment variables: Includes specified procedures which are clearly delineated and distinguishable from other procedures. Included would be diverse methods such as assertive training, EMG feedback, gestalt therapy, cognitive behavior therapy. In general, it represents the conclusions drawn from comparative studies.

Error term: Represents unaccounted components of outcome such as measurement error (e.g., since most outcome measures have reliabilities which do not exceed .80, 35% error could be due to this level of reliability).

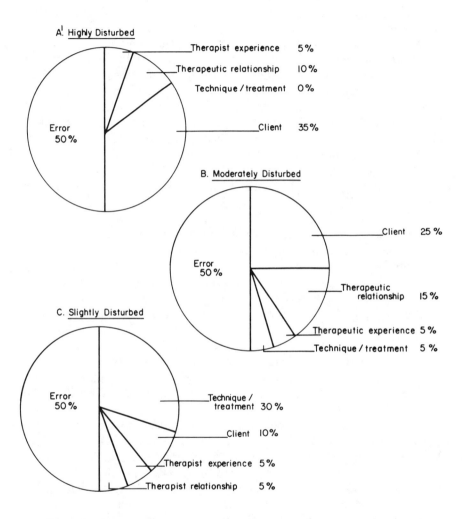

Fig. 6.2. The relative contribution of client, therapist, and technique variables to psychotherapy outcome in patient populations that differ in degree of psychological disturbance

---

*A ignores the effects of drugs on psychotic disorders.

therefore, do not show a simple relationship to indexes of change. The general conclusion that these variables predict outcome masks the need for specificity in research into outcome. For example, acute onset is more predictive of outcome in schizophrenia than it is in neurotic disorders. With sexual inadequacy on the other hand, *severity of specific symptoms* (e.g., primary inorgasmia versus secondary inorgasmia) along with *general marital adjustment* are more clearly related to outcome than is the nature of the onset of the disorder and, therefore, the former factors provide the best criteria for assignment of therapy. The same factors do not predict outcome across all types of problems and across all methods of treatment. Degree of maladjustment and the like are multidimensional rather than unidimensional variables. They must be well defined and can be expected to correlate highly with some measures of change and interact with some methods of treatment (Garfield, 1978; Horwitz, 1974).

3. The patient's expectation of the therapist's role performance influences dropout rates. When programs have been employed to modify the patient's expectations, they have been effective in reducing premature termination. Having therapists change their typical role behavior with some clients has had the same effect. Given the magnitude of the problem of premature termination, results of studies in this area continue to offer considerable challenge to the appropriateness of traditional treatments and the efficacy of delivery systems. The interested reader may wish to read a current review by Higginbotham (1977) on the topic of expectations. This review integrates a great deal of diverse literature on cross-cultural psychotherapy and presents a model that explains the impact of expectancies on outcome.

4. Ego strength, although somewhat difficult to define and multidimensional in nature, is a variable of modest predictive power. Its interaction with specific types of treatment has been elaborated upon by Horwitz (1974) and Kernberg (1973).

5. There is considerable agreement among *clinicians* that well-motivated patients are much more likely to have positive outcomes. Motivation, however, has proved difficult to study because it is not fixed. Some patients who begin well-motivated quickly lose their motivation, while those who are perceived as poorly motivated initially can become highly motivated after only a few sessions. The term motivation, in actuality, implies not only interest in changing, *but a desire to change in ways that are congruent with the goals and values of the therapist.* Perhaps this variable is confused with such things as the presence of a "working alliance." At any rate, past research has not unequivocally demonstrated the necessity of motivation for successful outcome (Rosenthal & Frank, 1958; Ross & Mendalsohn, 1958; Shapiro, Struening, Shapiro, & Barton 1976) though at times it does appear to be highly related to positive personality change.

6. The growing sophistication in research methods and statistical procedures is providing researchers with the opportunity to test more complex hypotheses. As yet, however, it is not possible to form ideal matches of therapist, therapy, and patient. Some exciting attempts at matching such as that undertaken in the Indiana Project (Berzins, 1977) are promising, but have not resulted in findings that can be applied clinically. The matching strategy has not really added much to our understanding of therapy outcome, but still cannot be thrown out. Some patients are helped by some methods while others are not, and it seems as if it should be possible to identify these patient subgroups and direct them into the appropriate treatment. As our ability to measure behavior change and relevant dimensions of personality increases and key characteristics of patients are identified, we may be able to optimize the pairing of patient, therapist, and therapy. So far, dimensions of a patient's personality such as "locus of control" and dominance show some relationship to *preference* for the style of the therapist, but no consistent relationship with outcome. Future researchers will need to continue to try to identify the interactions that may predict and cause a positive psychotherapeutic outcome. Hopefully, the research conducted will flow from theoretical formulations about characteristics of patients that provide a systematic basis for proposing and testing meaningful questions.

7. The general trend of evidence has suggested that patients from lower socioeconomic strata do not profit from the traditional psychotherapies to the extent that middle and upper class patients do (Heitler, 1976; Lorion & Cowen, 1976; Terestman, Miller, & Weber, 1974). They are less often accepted for dynamically oriented psychotherapy (Jones, 1974), appear more symptomatic (Derogatis, Yevzeroff, & Wittelsberger, 1975), and have appreciably higher dropout rates (Baekeland & Lundwall, 1975).

The traditional reasons for excluding these patients from psychotherapy rests on their generally inaccurate expectations for role performance by the therapist (offering advice and expecting high therapist directiveness). Also, the values of the traditionally middle class therapists are thought to make for unsuitable matches. These plausible explanations lack clear empirical support.

The rather consistent finding that higher dropout rates are associated with socioeconomic status are less uniform when this term is broken down into occupation, education, and other factors (e.g., Fiester & Rudestam, 1975; Pope, Geller & Wilkinson, 1975). Some studies support the idea that educational status is related to outcome (Bloom, 1956; Hamburg, Bibring, Fisher, Stanton, Wallerstein, Weinstock, & Harrard, 1967; McNair, Lorr, Young, Roth, & Boyd, 1964; Sullivan, Miller, & Smelzer, 1958). But many of these studies used only therapist ratings of outcome rather than a combination of measures.

The study by Wold and Steger (1976) is typical of others in this area. They studied 279 consecutive patients who applied for treatment over a seven-year period. Forty percent of all clients failed to return after the initial interview. Premature termination was predicted by *ethnicity,* treatment assigned, income, education, intake by paraprofessionals, diagnosis (psychosis), and assignment for diagnostic testing. This study supports some of the earlier findings in this area such as the idea that socioeconomic status and race lead to early termination.

The general status of characteristics of patients and outcome of psychotherapy are considered in several current reviews (Garfield, 1978; Gomes-Schwartz, Hadley, & Strupp, 1978; Lambert, 1979: Luborsky et al., 1971), that suggest the variety of results which have been obtained from studies that have included correlational analyses.

8. Concern has been expressed about the effects of possible therapist biases and stereotypes with regard to the dimension of racial differences. Also, some have questioned the impact of the absence of shared experiences and values which are clear in these cross-cultural matchings. A sufficient number of studies have been reported to have generated a few reviews of racial effects (Harrison, 1975; Jones, 1978; Lorion, 1978; Sattler, 1977). Very little support has been found for the concept of ideal racial matching in therapy. There is considerable evidence that whites can be helpful to blacks (Heffernon & Bruehl, 1971), but also that blacks leave therapy with whites at higher ratios than expected. There are not enough controlled outcome studies comparing the relative effects of black and white therapists with black and white clients to draw conclusions about comparative effects of these matchings. In most cases, the nul hypothesis has been accepted when studies involve real patients. Analog studies, on the other hand, tend to find effects due to race. More systematic research on racial pairings is needed.

Some evidence suggests that it is therapist comfort and competence in working with class and racial differences that make success more likely (Deykin, Weissman, Tanner, & Pursoff, 1975; Sloane et al., 1975). Still, there are many studies which have not found a relationship between social class, race, and outcome (Cole, Branch, & Allison, 1962; e.g., Rosenthal & Frank, 1958).

Which Therapist Variables Contribute to Psychotherapy Outcome?

Several therapist characteristics, qualities, and activities have been identified as contributing to positive and negative outcome. In fact, many clinicians believe these qualities to be the most important determinants of patient improvement. Therapist variables such as warmth, honesty, self-disclosure, empathic communication, specific personality characteristics, and personal adjustment are among those that have received the greatest attention in empirical studies. The identification of therapist variables that influence outcome has led to greater specification in training programs and attempts to select training candidates on the basis of these variables.

Relationship skills The most extensively studied therapist variables have been those identified by the client-centered school as "necessary and sufficient conditions" for patient personality change: accurate empathy, non-possessive warmth, positive regard, and therapist congruence or genuineness. Virtually all schools of therapy accept the notion that therapist relationship variables are important for significant progress in psychotherapy and, in fact, fundamental in the formation of a working alliance. Rogers (1959) made these therapist attitudes explicit and stated their hypothesized relationship to constructive personality change with near-mathematical precision.

A widely growing body of research has generally supported the importance of therapist relationship qualities. This research was initially summarized by Truax and Carkhuff (1967) in an excellent book. Additional studies were added for a later review—Truax and Mitchell (1971). The concepts have been broadened and redefined by Ivey (1971) and his colleagues. The studies quoted included treatment of inpatients, outpatient neurotics, children, and juvenile delinquents. Few people questioned the results although there was some skepticism about the strength of the relationships and the sufficiency of them to foster change in the absence of techniques.

Mitchell, Bozarth, & Krauft (1977) updated the Truax and Mitchell review of 1971. Their conclusions are more tentative and guarded with regard to the actual impact of therapist-offered conditions. Wilson and Evans (1977) conceptualized the place of the therapist-patient relationship in behavior therapy. Gurman (1977) elaborated on the importance of measuring therapist-offered conditions by assessing the *patient's perception* of the relationship. He feels this approach is more in line with client-centered theory than the rating of audio-taped therapy sessions by trained judges. Lambert and DeJulio (1977) reviewed evidence that had been offered in support of systematic training in therapist interpersonal skills. They found this area to be well behind psychotherapy literature and not as supportive of the value of this type of training program as some people believe. Lambert, DeJulio, and Stein (1978) reviewed research related to the claims of the client-centered school and suggested that research results only show modest support for the client-centered hypothesis.

Modest though the research support may be, there is still a well accepted and experimentally substantiated body of evidence that suggests the quality of the relationship as defined by these therapist-offered conditions, and as experienced by the patient, correlates with and perhaps produces positive outcomes. A corollary finding is that low levels of these relationship variables have been found to be associated with patient deterioration. In fact, our review of the causes of patient deterioration (Lambert, Bergin, & Collins, 1977) suggests that relationship variables are far more important in patient worsening than the misapplication of techniques.

Therapist sex Past research has not indicated that patients fare better under male or female therapists (Geer & Hurst, 1976; Grantham, 1973; Pardes, Papernik, & Winston, 1974; Scher, 1975; Sullivan, Miller, & Smelser, 1958). Two studies have suggested females seeing females had a poorer outcome (Meyer & Freeman, 1976; Mintz, O'Brien, & Luborsky, 1976), and one showed the opposite trend (Hill, 1975). Despite the apparent concern among feminists that male therapists may be harmful and inappropriate in helping women, there is little support in the empirical literature for such statements.

Therapist experience The qualifications of the therapist as determined by type of training, the inclusion of personal therapy as a part of training, professional affiliations, and even the necessity for training have all received attention in the research literature.

There is no evidence to suggest that a person from one professional discipline is more effective than another in employing psychotherapy. Like professional discipline, the personal therapy of the therapist, as well as the type of training received, have not demonstrated differential effects on patient outcome (Lambert, 1979).

The experience of the therapist is perhaps the strongest variable of those concerned with qualifications. It is a generally accepted idea that experience increases the ability of the therapist to treat patients. It seems likely that this rather gross variable is tapping numerous qualities that may be assumed to increase with age and experience, e.g., confidence, security, integration, flexibility, and knowledge. One would assume that this variable would show a strong relationship to outcome.

In fact, Luborsky et al. (1971) list experience as one of the few therapist factors having a reliable relationship to outcome. Bergin (1971) and Meltzoff & Kornreich (1970) have also indicated that the empirical evidence does favor the experienced clinician. These three reviews were rather exhaustive of studies that included this variable in their analyses.

Auerbach & Johnson (1977) have provided a more recent review of literature pertaining to the relationship of experience and therapeutic outcome. Their review *was not* supportive of the belief that experience is *highly* related to outcome. They did, nevertheless, find experienced therapists more likely to have positive outcomes. Five of eleven studies reviewed favored experienced therapists, with the remaining studies showing no difference or favoring the inexperienced therapists (Barrett-Lennard, 1962; Brown, 1970; Cartwright & Vogel, 1960; Fiske, Cartwright, & Kirtner 1964; Fiske & Goodman, 1965; Grigg, 1961; Katz, Lorr, & Rubenstein, 1958; Luborsky, in preparation; Myers & Auld, 1955; Scher, 1975; Sullivan, Miller, & Smelser, 1958). Few studies, however, have sought to include this as a major outcome variable. Thus, random assignment to either experienced or inexperienced therapists has rarely been done. Frequently, assignment to one or the other group has been biased.

Let me summarize now some of the major findings of empirical studies before turning to the implications for cross-cultural applications.

1. Traditional psychotherapy and behavior therapy as typically applied in the United States, Canada, Great Britain, and Western Europe is generally effective. It accelerates the recovery of patients beyond the results of "spontaneous remission."

2. Very few psychological disorders are uniquely responsive to specific treatment approaches. With but a few exceptions, we cannot prescribe psychological treatments and improve the likelihood of patient recovery. Specific techniques have not been demonstrated to be especially powerful in producing positive change in clients.

3. In contrast to the above conclusions is the relatively important contribution of the personal qualities and relationship skills of the therapist. The therapist's attitudes, as perceived by the patient, are correlated with positive and negative changes in diverse client types as measured by a variety of outcome measures.

4. Client characteristics have been shown to predict outcome, most notably, patient symptom complexity or intensity, motivation, and expectations. There is also strong support for the notion that class, racial, and ethnic group differences result in *unsatisfactory termination* of many clients although the relationship to improvement is less clear.

MEASURING OUTCOME IN CROSS-CULTURAL PSYCHOTHERAPY

As more studies are undertaken to demonstrate the generality of psychotherapy procedures, measurement issues will perhaps become clearer. At this point, there is a great deal of evidence regarding the generality of traditional psychological tests to new cultures. Most authors emphasize the lack of generality and the inadequacies of psychological tests (see Brislin, Lonner, & Thorndike, 1973; Lonner, 1976). However, the methods of assessment that apply to cross-cultural psychotherapy do not seem to differ greatly from the guidelines that already exist for assessing outcome within the United States.

Before turning to specific recommendations, let me highlight some issues of relevance (see also Bergin & Lambert, 1978; Bergin & Strupp, 1972) to outcome measurement. The earliest studies of outcome relied upon gross and somewhat poorly defined judgments of improvement. Frequently, only one source for these judgments was obtained—usually the therapist. It has become obvious that gross categorization of improvement into three to five categories or levels of improvement is not a very helpful approach to understanding change. They simply do not represent the actual complexity of psychotherapy outcome.

On the other hand, studies using multiple criterion measures (e.g., Mylar & Clement, 1972; Ross & Proctor, 1973; Wilson & Thomas, 1973) to assess behavioral treatment used to reduce seemingly simple fears may result in a decrease in behavioral avoidance of the feared object while not affecting the self-reported level of discomfort associated with the feared object. Likewise, a physiological indicator of fear may show no change in response to a feared object as a result of treatment while improvement in subjective self-report will be marked. Gross ratings of outcome ignore these and similar complexities that are at the heart of the truth they are meant to illuminate.

Not only has it proved too simple to gather change data through gross outcome ratings from a single point of view, but a few other general procedures are inadequate for assessing outcome and suggest the need for some general guidelines in outcome research. First, *changes in both behavior and internal states are important:* Malan (1976) and his associates, for example, have devised an assessment of internal or dynamic change as opposed to symptomatic or behavioral change. In their analysis, an assessment is made initially and at termination or follow-up to see if the patient has handled situations which were initially predicted to be the cause of regression and symptom formation. That is, to be considered improved on dynamic criteria, the patient must increase his capacity to cope with specific stress-precipitating events. In their study, the spontaneous remission rate for untreated subjects was between 33 and 50 percent on dynamic criteria as opposed to 60 to 70 percent on symptomatic criteria.

A second impression is that *traditional personality assessment procedures appear less promising than situation specific measures.* Currently, there is considerable skepticism about the value of personality assessment. This skepticism comes from various quarters including: (1) the popularity of behavioral approaches and corresponding lack of interest in standard assessment methods that lead to assigning people to diagnostic categories, identifying static traits, or elaborating upon internal dynamics; (2) the humanistically-derived belief that the testing and diagnostic enterprise is itself an unhelpful way of relating to persons seeking help; and (3) the belief that personality tests do not work very well and have unimpressive validity coefficients because they largely measure personality traits to the exclusion of situational variables (see Mischel, 1972). I would view attempts to adopt personality tests to diverse cultures unhelpful since they are less than adequate even in their culture of origin.

The practice of assessing situation-specific *behaviors* rather than global qualities which are viewed as signs or indirect manifestations of important general tendencies (e.g., that human movement in Rorschach responding indicates creativity or impulse control) should be emphasized. Assessments should attempt to measure situation-specific behavior, such as social anxiety related to skill deficiency in heterosexual relationships rather than traditional personality traits, especially those measured by projective tests.

A third consideration is the growing trend toward tailoring criteria to fit the individual patient. The possibility of tailoring change criteria to each individual in therapy is being mentioned with increasing frequency, and this practice has proved helpful in resolving several problems associated with outcome research.

A procedure which is receiving widespread attention and increased use is *Goal Attainment Scaling* (GAS) (Kiresuk & Sherman, 1968). Goal attainment scaling requires that a number of mental health goals be set up prior to treatment by one or a combination of clinicians, client, and/or a committee assigned to the task. For each goal specified, a scale with a graded series of likely outcomes, ranging from least to most favorable, is devised. These goals are formulated and specified with enough precision that an unfamiliar observer can determine the point at which the patient is functioning at a given time. The procedure also allows for transformation of the overall goal attainment into a standardized score.

Using this method for the treatment of anorexia nervosa, for example, one goal could be the specification and measurement of weight gain. A second goal could be reduction of depressive symptoms as measured by a scale(s) from a standardized test such as the Beck Depression Inventory. The particular scale examined could be varied from patient to patient and, of course, other specific types of diverse measures from additional points of view could also be added. Naturally, such a procedure allows for the specification of goals that are consistent with the values of clients from a variety of cultures. Thus, this procedure is in many ways ideal for cross-cultural studies.

GAS suffers because it is only a framework for structuring the statement of goals and does not assure that the individualized goals which are specified will be much more than poorly defined, subjective decisions by patient or clinician. Goals are often not only difficult to state, but written at various levels of abstraction. GAS, therefore, adds little that improves evaluation procedures except a framework directed toward more individualized, behaviorally oriented, observable outcome indexes upon which there has been prior agreement by those concerned.

To summarize the measurement of outcome, the following recommendations seem worthy of note.

1. Use multiple outcome measures that reflect change as seen by the many participants who are involved: the patient, the therapist, significant others not participating in treatment, and expert judges.
2. Use multiple outcome measures that reflect the vantage point of the person (sense of well being), the mental health profession (ideal mental health within the person's culture), and society (grade point average, antisocial behavior, etc.). For an elaboration of this concept, the interested reader should study Strupp and Hadley (1977).
3. Avoid projective tests altogether.
4. Avoid standardized personality tests.
5. Consider the use of symptom check lists which give frequency and intensity of specific symptoms, mood scales, and depression indexes.
6. Emphasize behavioral observations—observable behavior can be one source of stable data.

IMPLICATIONS FOR
CROSS-CULTURAL PSYCHOTHERAPY

Dyadic and small group interactions that are designed to benefit persons who are currently disturbed and could be diagnosed as having a psychological disorder rely upon certain healing principles.

The first implication of empirical research is that the host of methods loosely referred to as psychotherapy is helpful within cultures. One would expect that portions of the treatments would be effective with the entire human family.

A second implication is that very few specific methods have been found to be uniquely effective. The most reasonable place to begin cross-cultural research is with these few techniques. The reduction of fears or the treatment of sexual dysfunctions may provide the simplest place to observe the generality of specific methods.

Psychotherapy outcome research has emphasized the importance of client or patient variables: expectation, degree of disturbance, and the like. Also of considerable importance is the development of a facilitative relationship or working alliance. At least partially dependent on the therapist and his or her abilities, the quality of the relationship is definitely related to positive outcomes. This facilitative interpersonal climate is thought to result from the ability of the therapist to understand the client and to adequately communicate this understanding.

Cross-cultural psychotherapy, unfortunately, has its most serious problems in those very areas of interaction that have been demonstrated to affect psychotherapy outcome. Cross-cultural therapy implies a situation where the participants are most likely to show discrepancies between their shared assumptions, experiences, beliefs, values, expectations, and goals. From the research already quoted, it is obvious that this situation, at its extreme, sets up conditions that are most unfavorable for successful psychotherapy. This view is supported by the subjective reports of many clinicians involved in cross-cultural psychotherapy, as well as the limited cross-cultural research conducted in this domain.

Among the most notable difficulties is the client's inaccurate or inappropriate perception of the therapist's role. Thus, there will often be a discrepancy between what the patient expects (e.g., to take a passive-dependent role) and what the therapist interprets as the most beneficial role (e.g., to *facilitate* self-exploration, problem or feeling clarification, insight). Montijo (1975), for example, discussed the problems of Puerto Rican clients and emphasized the blocking that occurs as a result of differing expectations on the part of the psychotherapy participants. Also included in his discussion were problems resulting from feelings of powerlessness, fatalism, mistrust, superstition, externalization of control, and submission to authority figures. He suggests that, in general, these patients make the therapist overly responsible for treatment and refuse to acknowledge the presence of unconscious motivations (to look for other than surface reasons is to imply "bad faith").

A cross-cultural study that has demonstrated a great sensitivity to client expectations and therapist behaviors was published by Szapocnik, Scopetta, & King (1978). These authors chose to develop a special treatment based upon the unique needs of the Cuban immigrant population they were serving (as opposed to modifying client expectations to fit into existing treatments). They developed a culturally sensitive treatment (a treatment built on a set of therapeutic assumptions that complement the patient's basic values) that emphasized the family, and an active directive therapist who takes considerable responsibility for a treatment that has a crises- or problem-solving orientation, but minimizes the need for clients to interact in the social environment outside of the family. From their point of view, the best suited client for this crises-oriented, family therapy is one whose problems are related to acculturation in the new environment. The authors report that a study of the effectiveness of this approach with Cuban immigrants is under way but provide no comparative outcome data related to reducing premature termination.

Tan (1967) studied counseling expectancies in 200 students from the United States, England, and five Asian countries, and 62 graduate students in counseling at two American universities. The Asian groups appeared similar in their authoritarian orientation and expectancies—respect for elders and authority figures, submission, and nurturance. Those who had been in the United States longer were more similar to American students.

In a similar study, Fukuhara (1973) compared samples of 185 Japanese and 72 United States college students to determine expectancies toward counseling. He found that Japanese students saw the counseling service primarily as providing an advice-giving function. In contrast, U.S. college students saw counseling as a psychological service involving more personal involvement on the part of the counselor.

This same theme was emphasized by Wax and Thomas (1961) as they discussed the difficulties often inherent when whites work with American Indian clients. They suggest that, in general, forms of social or interactional control and influence are viewed by the Indian as out of the realm of proper behavior or action and that Indian clients frequently react with disgust, fear, or bewilderment at such interventions.

The major implication of research on client variables is that attempts must be made to help clients develop accurate expectations for therapy, help therapists develop more flexible assumptions about ways of being helpful, or to develop alternative forms of treatment.

In addition to expectation for role performance, the clients of cross-cultural therapy do not always find themselves motivated to change in ways that are congruent with a white or middle-class therapist's goals and value system. Although they may be motivated to seek treatment, they probably do not share as many valued directions of change as participants from the therapist's cultural background.

These problems, along with other barriers to counseling, have been discussed elsewhere (Abramowitz & Dokecki, 1977; Hastings, 1977; Kahn, Lewis, & Galvez, 1974; Pedersen, Lonner, & Draguns, 1976; Rome, 1971; Stratton, 1975; Sue & Sue, 1977; Todd & Shapira, 1974; Vassiliou & Vassiliou, 1973; Vontress, 1974; Wittkower & Warnes, 1974a,b).

At this point, there is little evidence to suggest that the client variable severity of disturbance acts any differently in cross-cultural therapy than psychotherapy in general. However, the level of environmental supports available to clients in cross-cultural psychotherapy may be quite low, making these patients more vulnerable to psychotherapy influence. This highlights the importance of a final point which is, perhaps, the central implication of psychotherapy research for cross-cultural psychotherapy.

The outcome of cross-cultural psychotherapy as with intracultural applications is highly dependent on the ability of the therapist to form a facilitative relationship with the client. In the ideal form of this facilitative relationship, the client will experience being warmly received, deeply accepted, and fully understood. If the therapy relationship deviates too far from this ideal, the client will break off the relationship prematurely or possibly even have a deteriorative experience. The fact that few therapist variables other than relationship variables correlate with outcome, coupled with the obvious and frequently mentioned difficulty in understanding and communicating this understanding of client meanings, suggest the possibility that cross-cultural psychotherapy is contraindicated in most circumstances.

Research evidence has not greatly clarified the circumstances when this would be true. It would, however, appear unwise to offer more than supportive help when serious communication problems exist in the relationship. Also, it seems quite likely that therapists who are unfamiliar with a particular culture, who are not experienced with the client's background, should not undertake a psychotherapy relationship. It would appear more appropriate to rely upon environmental manipulations such as the use of selected but possibly untrained persons from the client's home culture, or activities that reduce environmental stresses or remove the symptom triggers.

On the other hand, there is little reason to avoid psychotherapy when the clinician is able to develop an adequate relationship early in the process of therapy. Ordinarily, "experience" has been defined by years of experience or number of patient contacts. This is not an adequate way of defining experience in cross-cultural psychotherapy. More properly defined in terms of experience with the client's culture, this variable probably would show a much stronger relationship to outcome in cross-cultural counseling than in intracultural counseling.

At this point, there is little if any systematic research on the effects of special training procedures used to develop intercultural counseling skills. Attempts are under way and the future appears promising for empirical research in this area. Pedersen (1979a, b), for example has elaborated a model and developed a creative program of training in basic intercultural counseling skills. Initial studies show trainees to be enthusiastic and satisfied with the training, although there are not as yet data showing that this training has any effect on counseling outcome or even premature termination rates.

SUMMARY AND CONCLUSIONS

Over four decades of research into the effects of psychotherapy have resulted in some important discoveries. We can be assured that traditional therapies rest on a growing body of empirical research. They facilitate recovery from a symptomatic and painful mode of living and produce results that exceed those obtained without such intervention.

It is the hope of researchers to discover the causal relationship between the wide range of activities loosely referred to as psychotherapy and positive behavioral and "personality" changes. The scientific approach will seem especially worthwhile if it results in the discovery of procedures that are universally helpful across persons from diverse cultures. So far, this is more of a hope than a reality. We have, as yet, not been able to find many procedures that are uniquely effective with specific problems within groups of people with a similar cultural background.

We know that patient history, mental state, attitude and the like have a powerful effect on treatment outcome. These variables must be carefully controlled in cross-cultural research. It is also clear that the therapist has an impact on outcome. More specifically, therapist attitudes are implicated in both positive and negative outcomes. This seems to be especially true within moderately disturbed client populations. There is little doubt that, when the patient experiences the therapist as respectful, understanding, and congruent, positive change is more likely.

This latter conclusion is the most important conclusion for cross-cultural psychotherapy. Unlike some medical procedures, psychotherapy is mediated by a human relationship. The quality of the relationship is so dependent on the accurate communication of meanings that most therapies could not proceed past an initial interview without this accurate understanding. Since cross-cultural applications are likely to place barriers between the participants, it is an undertaking that should occur with caution. This is especially true where discrepancies exist between therapist assumptions and client expectations.

In North America, there has been an interest in the application of traditional therapies to persons who show class and racial differences. These "cross-cultural" matchings show that psychotherapy can be applied effectively when important discrepancies in background characterize the relationship between therapists and patients. Nevertheless, many problems have been noted in these matchings with the most characteristic being premature withdrawal from therapy.

The measurement of changes in psychopathology present some additional problems for cross-cultural psychotherapy research. At the same time, cross-cultural studies should be able to take advantage of advances made in methods of measuring changes that have emerged in the last 10-20 years. These emphasize the measurement of specific, and often behavioral, changes rather than gross improvement, the use of outcome ratings from multiple sources, the use of more symptomatic measures rather than theoretical constructs, and the like.

The rather serious tone of this chapter which emphasizes the dangers of cross-culture psychotherapy, coupled with the crises that often make alternatives unavailable, suggests the need for research into the effects of cross-cultural psychotherapy. This research might address some of the following questions:

1. What type of training will most effectively increase the likelihood of positive outcomes?
2. How could paraprofessionals be selected and trained to aid in the provision of services?
3. What are the strengths and limitations, or in what ways can paraprofessionals be used as adjuncts to treatment?
4. What types of pretherapy training or role induction procedures for patients and therapists are most effective?
5. Do the same patient variables predict outcome across diverse cultures?
6. Are the relationship variables critical in diverse cultures? Are they communicated in similar ways? Does their importance vary according to client variables or cultural variables?
7. What variables predict outcome in cross-cultural counseling? Therapist experience? Cognitive flexibility? Degree of shared subjective culture? Knowledge of early socialization experiences? Client predispositions, such as dependence, openness to feelings, etc.?

The possibilities are endless and, of course, promise to be highly informative and exciting. Hopefully, the research that is to come will build upon, rather than duplicate, the existing knowledge. This seems especially likely if this research does not duplicate the errors of the past. For example, it is tempting and much easier to study static variables such as socioeconomic status, sex, experience, race, etc., than the actual process of therapy. However, it is the process that is so closely linked with causality. It is the process that must be examined if we are to understand the principles of stability and change. We need to know, for example, not just that experienced or uniquely trained therapists produce the greatest good, but just how it is that this result is obtained. It is a privilege to be involved in such an important endeavor.

The application of cross-cultural psychotherapy calls for an experienced clinician whose education has included significant exposure to the culture of his or her client. A research application involving this select group seems to be called for immediately. In addition, research on the generalization of the utility and specific effects of fear reduction stratagies seems to be a hopeful and initial area to explore in cross-cultural psychotherapy research.

REFERENCES

Abramowitz, C.V., & Dokecki, P.R. The politics of clinical judgment: early empirical returns. *Psychological Bulletin,* 1977, *84,* 460-476.

Acosta, F.X., & Sheehan, J.G. Preferences toward Mexican-American and Anglo-American psychotherapists. *Journal of Consulting and Clinical Psychology,* 1976, *44,* 272-279.

Agras, W.S., Chapin, H.N., & Oliveau, D.C. The natural history of phobia: Course and prognosis. *Archives of General Psychiatry,* 1972, *26,* 315-317.

Allen, G.J. Effectiveness of study: Counseling and desensitization in alleviating test anxiety in college students. *Journal of Abnormal Psychology,* 1971, *77,* 282-289.

Auerbach, A.II., & Johnson, M. Research on the therapist's level of experience. In A.S. Gurman and A.M. Razin (Eds.), *The effective psychotherapist: A Handbook of research.* New York: Pergamon Press, 1977.

Baekeland, F., & Lundwall, L. Dropping out of treatment, A critical review. *Psychological Bulletin,* 1975, *82,* 738-783.

Barrett-Lennard, G.T. *Relationship inventory: Experimental form OSS-42.* Unpublished manuscript, Waterloo, Ontario: University of Waterloo, 1973.

Bergin, A.E. Some implications of psychotherapy research for therapeutic practice. *Journal of Abnormal Psychology,* 1966, *71,* 235-246.

Bergin, A.E. The evaluation of therapeutic outcomes. In A.E. Bergin and S.L. Garfield (Eds.), *Handbook of psychotherapy and behavior change.* New York: Wiley, 1971.

Bergin, A.E., & Lambert, M.J. The evaluation of therapeutic outcomes. In S.L. Garfield and A.E. Bergin (Eds.) *Handbook of Psychotherapy and Behavioral Change,* 2nd edition, New York: Wiley, 1978, pp. 139-190.

Bergin, A.E., & Strupp, H.H. *Changing frontiers in the science of psychotherapy.* Chicago: Aldine-Atherton, 1972.

Bergin, A.E., & Suinn, R.M. Individual psychotherapy and behavior therapy. *Annual Review of Psychology,* 1975, *26,* 509-556.

Berzins, J.I.: Therapist-patient matching. In A.S. Gurman, and A.M. Razin (Eds.), *Effective psychotherapy: A handbook of research.* New York: Pergamon Press, 1977.

Bloom, B.L. Prognostic significance of the under-productive Rorschach. *Journal of Projective Techniques,* 1956, *20,* 366-371.

Brislin, R.W., Lonner, W.J., and Thorndike, R.M. *Cross-cultural research methods.* New York: Wiley, 1973.

Brown, R.D. Experienced and inexperienced counselors' first impressions of clients and case outcomes: Are first impressions lasting? *Journal of Counseling Psychology,* 1970, *17,* 550-558.

Cartwright, R.D., & Vogel, J.L. A comparison of changes in psychoneurotic patients during matched periods of therapy and no therapy. *Journal of Consulting Psychology,* 1960, *24,* 121-127.

Cole, N.J., Branch, C.H., & Allison, R.B. Some relationships between social class and the practice of dynamic psychotherapy. *American Journal of Psychiatry,* 1976, *118,* 1004-1012.

Derogatis, L.R., Yevzeroff, H., & Wittelsberger, B. Social class, psychological disorder, and the nature of the psychopathological indicator. *Journal of Consulting and Clinical Psychology,* 1975, *43,* 183-191.

Deykin, E., Weissman, M., Tanner, J., & Prusoff, B. Participation in therapy: A study of attendance patterns in depressed outpatients. *Journal of Nervous and Mental Disorders,* 1975, *160,* 42-48.

DiLoreto, A.O. *Comparative psychotherapy: An experimental analysis.* Chicago: Aldine-Atherton, 1971.

Emmelkamp, P.M.G., & Wessels, H. Flooding in imagination vs. flooding in vivo: a comparison with agoraphobics. *Behavior Therapy,* 1974, *5,* 606.

Eysenck, H.J. The effects of psychotherapy: An evaluation. *Journal of Consulting Psychology,* 1952, *16,* 319-324.

Eysenck, H.J. *Handbook of abnormal psychology.* London: Pitman, 1960.

Eysenck, H.J. The effects of psychotherapy. In H.J. Eysenck (Ed.), *Handbook of abnormal psychology.* New York: Basic Books, 1961.

Eysenck, H.J. The effects of psychotherapy. *International Journal of Psychiatry,* 1965, *1,* 97-178.

Eysenck, H.J. *The effects of psychotherapy.* New York: International Science Press, 1966.

Fiester, A.R., & Rudestam, K.E. A multivariate analysis of the early dropout process. *Journal of Consulting and Clinical Psychology,* 1975, *45.* 528-535.

Fiske, D.W., Cartwright, D.S., & Kirtner, W.L. Are psychotherapeutic changes predictable? *Journal of Abnormal Psychology,* 1964, *69,* 418-426.

Fiske, D.W., Goodman, G. The post therapy period. *Journal of Abnormal Psychology,* 1965, *70,* 169-179.

Fukuhara, M. Student expectations of counseling: A cross-cultural study. *Japanese Psychological Research,* 1973, *15,* 179-193.

Garfield, S.L. Research on client variables in psychotherapy. In S.L. Garfield, & A.E. Bergin (Eds.), *Handbook of psychotherapy and behavior change.* (2nd ed.) New York: Wiley, 1978.

Geer, C.A., & Hurst, J.C. Counselor-subject sex variables in systematic desensitization. *Journal of Counseling Psychology,* 1976, *23,* 295-301.

Gelder, M.G., & Marks, I.M. Severe agoraphobics: A controlled prospective trial of behavior therapy. *British Journal of Psychiatry,* 1966, *112,* 309-319.

Gelder, M.G., & Marks, I.M. A crossover study of desensitization in phobias. *British Journal of Psychiatry,* 1968, *114,* 323-328.

Gelder, M.G., Marks, I.M., & Wolff, H.H. Disensitization and psychotherapy in the treatment of phobic states: A controlled inquiry. *British Journal of Psychiatry,* 1967, *113,* 53-73.

Gillan, P., & Rachman, S. An experimental investigation of behavior therapy in phobic patients. *British Journal of Psychiatry,* 1974, *124,* 392.

Gomes-Schwartz, B., Hadley, S.W. & Strupp, H.H. Individual psychotherapy and behavior therapy. *Annual Review of Psychology,* 1978, *29,* 435-471.

Grantham, R.J. Effects of counselor, sex, race, and language style on black students in initial interviews. *Journal of Counseling Psychology,* 1973, *20,* 553-559.

Grigg, A.E. Client response to counselors at different levels of experience. *Journal of Counseling Psychology,* 1961, *8,* 217-233.

Gurman, A.S. The patient's perception of the therapeutic relationship. In A.S. Gurman & A.M. Razin (Eds.), *Effective psychotherapy: A handbook of research.* New York: Pergamon Press, 1977.

Hafner, J., & Marks, I.M. Exposure in vivo of agoraphobics: The contributions of diazepam, group exposure and anxiety evocation. *Psychological Medicine,* 1976, *6,* 71-88.

Hamburg, D.A., Bibring, G.L., Fisher, C., Stanton, A.H., Wallerstein, R.S., Weinstock, H.T., & Harrard, E. Report of ad hoc committee on central fact-gathering date of the American Psychoanalytic Association. *Journal of American Psychoanalitic Association,* 1967, *15,* 841-861.

Hand, I., Lamontagne, Y., & Marks, I.M. Group exposure (flooding) in vivo for agoraphobics. *British Journal of Psychiatry,* 1974, *124,* 588.

Harrison, I.K. Race as a counselor-client variable in counseling and psychotherapy: A review of the research. *The Counseling Psychologist,* 1975, *5,* 124-133.

Hastings, J. Adaptation problems of Asian migrants. *Australian & New Zealand Journal of Psychiatry,* 1977, *11,* 219-221.

Heffernon, A., Bruehl, D. Some effects of race of inexperienced lay counselors on black junior high school students. *Journal of School Psychology,* 1971, *9,* 35-37.

Heitler, J.B. Preparatory techniques in initiating expressive psychotherapy with lower-class, unsophisticated patients. *Psychological Bulletin,* 1976, *83,* 339-352.

Higginbotham, H.N. Culture and the role of client expectancy in psychotherapy. In R.W. Brislin & M. Hamnett (Eds.) *Topics in culture learning,* Vol. 5. Honolulu: East-West Center, 1977.

Hill, C.E. Sex of Client and sex and experience level of counselor. *Journal of Counseling Psychology,* 1975, *22,* 6-11.

Horwitz, L. *Clinical prediction in psychotherapy.* New York: Aronson, 1974.

Ivey, A.E. *Microcounseling: Innovations in interviewing training.* Springfield, Ill.: Charles C. Thomas, 1971.

Jones, E. Social class and psychotherapy: A critical review of research. *Psychiatry,* 1974, *37,* 307-320.

Jones, E.E. The effects of race on psychotherapy process and outcome: An exploratory investigation. *Psychotherapy: Theory, Research and Practice,* 1978, *15,* 226-236.

Kahn, M.W., Lewis, J., & Galvez, E. An evaluation study of a group therapy procedure with reservation adolescent Indians. *Psychotherapy: Theory, Research And Practice,* 1974, *11,* 239-242.

Karst, T.O., & Trexler, L.D. Initial study using fixed role and rational-emotive therapy in treating public-speaking anxiety. *Journal of Consulting and Clinical Psychology,* 1970, *34,* 360-366.

Katz, M.M., Lorr, M., & Rubenstein, E.A. Remainder patient attributes and their relation to subsequent improvement in psychotherapy. *Journal of Consulting Psychology,* 1958, *22,* 411-413.

Katz, M.M., Lowery, H.A., & Cole, J.O. Behavior patterns of schizophrenics in the community. In M. Lorr (Ed.), *Explorations in typing psychotics.* New York: Pergamon Press, 1967.

Kellner, R. Psychotherapy in psychosomatic disorders: A survey of controlled outcome studies. *Archives of General Psychiatry,* 1975, *32,* 1021-1028.

Kernberg, O.F. Summary and conclusion of psychotherapy and psychoanalysis. Final report of the Menninger Foundations's Psychotherapy Research Project. *International Journal of Psychiatry,* 1973, *11,* 62-77.

Kiresuk, T.J., & Sherman, R.E. Goal attainment scaling: A general method for evaluating comprehensive community mental programs. *Community Mental Health Journal,* 1968, *4,* 443-453.

Kora, T. Morita therapy. *International Journal of Psychiatry,* 1965, *1,* 611-618.

Korchin, S.J. *Modern clinical psychology: Principles of intervention in the clinic and community.* New York: Basic Books, 1976.

Lambert, M.J. Spontaneous remission in adult neurotic disorders: A revision and summary. *Psychological Bulletin,* 1976, *83,* 107-119

Lambert, M.J. *The effects of psychotherapy.* Vol. 1. Montreal: Eden Press, 1979.

Lambert, M.J., & Bergin, A.E. Psychotherapeutic outcomes and issues related to behavioral and humanistic approaches. *Cornell Journal of Social Relations,* 1973, *8,* 47-61.

Lambert, M.J. Bergin, A.E., & Collins, J.L. Therapist-induced deterioration in psychotheraphy. In A.S. Gurman & A.M. Razin (Eds.), *Effective psychotherapy: A handbook of research.* New York: Pergamon Press, 1977.

Lambert, M.J., & DeJulio, S.S. Outcome research in Carkhuff's Human Resource Development Training Programs: Where is the donut? *Counseling Psychologist,* 1977, *6,* 79-86.

Lambert, M.J., DeJulio, S.S., & Stein, D.M. Therapist interpersonal skills: Process, outcome, methodological considerations and recommendations for further research. *Psychological Bulletin,* 1978, *85,* 467-489.

Lebra, W. *Culture-bound syndromes, ethnopsychiatry and alternate therapies,* Honolulu: University of Hawaii, 1976.

Lonner, W.J. The Use of Western-based tests in intercultural counseling. In P. Pedersen, W.J. Lonner, & J.G. Draguns (Eds.), *Counseling across cultures.* Honolulu, Hawaii: University Press of Hawaii, 1976.

Lorion, R.P. Research on psychotherapy and behavior change with the disadvantaged: Past, present, and future directions. In S.L. Garfield & A.E. Bergin (Eds.), *Handbook of psychotherapy and behavior change:* An empirical analysis. (2nd ed.) New York: Wiley, 1978.

Lorion, R.P., & Cowen, E.L. Comparison of two outcome groups in a school-based mental health project. *American Journal of Community Psychology,* 1976, *4,* 65-73.

Luborsky, L., Chandler, M., Auerbach, A.H., Cohen, J., & Bachrach, H.M. Factors influencing the outcome of psychotherapy: A review of quantitative research. *Psychological Bulletin,* 1971, *75,* 145-185.

Luborsky, L. Who benefits from psychotherapy? In preparation. (Described in "Research on the therapist's level of experience". In, *Effective psychotherapy: A handbook of research,* A.S. Gurman, A.M. Razin (Eds.), New York: Pergamon Press, 1977.

Luborsky, L., Singer, B., & Luborsky, L. Comparative studies of psychotherapies. *Archives of General Psychiatry,* 1975, *32,* 995-1008

Malan, D.H. *Toward the validation of dynamic psychotherapy: A replication.* New York: Plenum Press, 1976.

Marks, I. Phobic disorders four years after treatment: A prospective follow-up. *British Journal of Psychiatry,* 1971, *118,* 683-688.

Marks, I. Behavioral psychotherapy of adult neurotics. In S.L. Garfield & A.E. Bergin (Eds.), *Handbook of psychotherapy and behavior change.* New York: Wiley, 1978.

Marks, I.M., Gelder, M.G., & Edwards, J.G. A controlled trial of hypnosis and desensitisation for phobias. *British Journal of Psychiatry,* 1968, *114,* 1263.

Marsella, A.J. Cross-cultural studies of mental disorders. In A.J. Marsella, R. Tharp, & T. Ciborowski (Eds.), *Perspectives on cross-cultural psychology.* New York: Academic Press, 1979.

Mathews, A.M., Whitehead, A., Hackman, A., Julier, D., Bancroft, J., Gath, D., & Shaw, P. The behavioral treatment of sexual inadequacy: A comparative study. *Behavior Research & Therapy,* 1976, *14,* 427.

McNair, D.M., Lorr, M., Young, H.H., Roth, I., & Boyd, R.W. A three-year follow-up of psychotherapy patients. *Journal of Clinical Psychology,* 1964, *20,* 258-264.

Meltzoff, J., & Kornreich, M. *Research in psychotherapy.* New York: Atherton Press, 1970.

Meyer, R.G., & Freeman, W.M. A social episode model of human sexual behavior. *Homosexuality,* 1976, *2,* 15-20.

Mintz, J., O'Brien, C.P., & Luborsky, L. Predicting the outcome of psychotherapy for schizophrenics. *Archives of General Psychiatry,* 1976, *33,* 1183-1186.

Mischel, W. Direct versus indirect personality assessment: Evidence and implication. *Journal of Consulting Clinical Psychology,* 1972, *38,* 319-324.

Mitchell, K.M., Bozarth, J.D., & Krauft, C.C. A reappraisal of the therapeutic effectiveness of accurate empathy, nonpossessive warmth, and genuineness. In A.S. Gurman & A.M. Razin (Eds.), *Effective psychotherapy: A handbook of research.* New York: Pergamon Press, 1977.

Mitchell, K.R., & Ng, K.T. Effects of group counseling and behavior therapy on the academic achievement of test anxious students. *Journal of Counseling Psychology,* 1972, *19,* 491-497.

Montijo, J. The Puerto Rican client. *Professional Psychology,* 1975, *6,* 475-477.

Myers, J.K., & Auld, F. Some variables related to outcome of psychotherapy. *Journal of Clinical Psychology,* 1955, *11,* 51-54.

Mylar, J.L., & Clement, P.W. Prediction and comparison of outcome in systematic desensitization and implosion. *Behavior Research and Therapy,* 1972, *10,* 235-246.

Pardes, H., Papernik, D.S., & Winston, A. Field differentiation in inpatient psychotherapy. *Archives of General Psychiatry,* 1974, *31,* 311-315.

Paul, G.L. Insight versus desensitization in psychotherapy two years after termination. *Journal of Consulting Psychology,* 1967, *30,* 283-289.

Pedersen, P., Lonner, W.J., & Draguns, J.G. *Counseling across cultures.* Honolulu: University Press of Hawaii, 1976.

Pedersen, P.B. *Basic intercultural counseling skills.* Honolulu: DISC, 1979.a

Pederson, P.B. *Basic intercultural counseling skills: Part II, a workbook.* Honolulu: DISC, 1979.b

Pope, K.S., Geller, J.D., & Wilkinson, L. Fee assessment and outpatient psychotherapy. *Journal of Consulting and Clinical Psychology,* 1975, *43,* 835-841.

Rachman, S. The effects of psychological treatment. In H. Eysenck (Ed.), *Handbook of abnormal psychology.* New York: Basic Books, 1973.

Reynolds, D.K. *Morita psychotherapy.* Berkeley: University of California Press, 1976.

Roback, H.B. The comparative influence of insight and non-insight psychotherapies on therapeutic outcome: A review of the experimental literature. *Psychotherapy: Theory and Research Practice,* 1971, *8,* 23-25.

Rogers, C.R. A theory of therapy: personality, and interpersonal relationships as developed in the client-centered framework in psychology: A study of science. In: S. Koch (Ed.), *Formulations of the person and the social context.* New York: McGraw-Hill, 1959.

Rome, W.A. Some limitations of psychotherapy in Papua and New Guinea. *New Guinea Psychologist,* 1971, *3,* 40-41.

Rosenthal, D., & Frank, J.D. The fate of psychiatric clinic outpatients assigned to psychotherapy. *Journal of Nervous and Mental Disorders,* 1958, *127,* 330-343.

Ross, M. & Mendalsohn, F. Homoexuality in college. *Archives of Neurological Psychiatry,* 1958, *80,* 253-263.

Ross, S.M., & Proctor, S. Frequency and duration of hierarchy item exposure in a systematic desensitization analogue. *Behavior Research and Therapy,* 1973, *11,* 303-312.

Sattler, J.M. The therapeutic relationship under varying conditions of race. In A.S. Gurman & A.M. Razin (Eds.), *The effective psychotherapist: A handbook.* New York: Pergamon Press, 1977.

Scher, M. Verbal activity, sex, counselor experience, and success in counseling. *Journal of Counseling Psychology,* 1975, *22,* 97-101.

Shapiro, A.K., Struening E., Shapiro, E. & Barten, H. Prognostic correlates of psychotherapy in psychiatric outpatients. *American Journal of Psychiatry,* 1976, *133,* 802-808.

Sloane, R.B., Staples, F.R., Cristol, A.H., Yorkston, N.J., & Whipple, K. *Short-term analytically oriented psychotherapy vs. behavior therapy.* Cambridge, Mass.: Harvard University Press, 1975.

Smith, M.L., & Glass, G.V. Meta-analysis of psychotherapy outcome studies. *American Psychologist,* 1977, *32,* 752-760.

Stratton, J.G. Cross-cultural counseling: A problem in communication. *Psychiatric forum,* 1975, *5,* 15-19.

Strupp, H.H., & Hadley, S.W. A tripartite model of mental health and therapeutic outcomes: With special reference to negative effects in psychotherapy. *American Psychologist,* 1977, *32,* 187-196.

Sue, D.W., & Sue, S. Barriers to effective cross-cultural counseling. *Journal of Counseling Psychology,* 1977, *24,* 420-429.

Sullivan, P.L., Miller, C., & Smelzer, W. Factors in length of stay and progress in psychotherapy. *Journal of Consulting Psychology,* 1958, *22,* 1-9.

Szapocznik, J., Scopetta, M.K., and King, O.E. Theory and practice in matching treatment to the special characteristics and problems of Cuban immigrants. *Journal of Community Psychology,* 1978, *6,* 112-122.

Tan, H. Intercultural study of counseling expectancies. *Journal of Counseling Psychology,* 1967, *14,* 122-130.

Terestman, N., Miller, J.D., & Weber, J.J. Blue-collar patients at a psychoanalytic clinic. *American Journal of Psychiatry,* 1974, *131,* 261-266.

Todd, J.L., & Shapira, A. U.S. and British self-disclosure, anxiety, empathy, and attitudes to psychotherapy. *Journal of Cross-Cultural Psychology,* 1974, *5,* 364-369.

Truax, C.B., & Carkhuff, R.R. *Toward effective counseling and psychotherapy: Training and practice.* Chicago: Aldine, 1967.

Truax, C.B., & Mitchell, K.M. Research on certain therapist interpersonal skills in relation to process and outcome. In A.E. Bergin & S.L. Garfield (Eds.), *Handbook of psychotherapy and behavior change.* New York: Wiley, 1971.

Vassiliou, G., & Vassiliou, V. Subjective culture and psychotherapy. *American Journal of Psychotherapy,* 1973, *27,* 42-51.

Vontress, C.E. Barriers in cross-cultural counseling. *Counseling & Values,* 1974, *18,* 160-165.

Walz, G.R., & Benjamin, L. *Transcultural counseling: Needs, programs and techniques.* New York: Human Sciences Press 1978.

Wax, R.H. & Thomas, R.K. American Indians and white people. *Phylon: Atlanta University,* *12,* 1-8.

Wilson, G.L., & Evans, I.M. The therapist-client relationship in behavior therapy. In A.S. Gurman, A.M. Razin (Eds.), *Effective psychotherapy: A handbook of research,* New York: Pergamon Press, 1977.

Wilson, G.T., & Thomas, M.G.W. Self- versus drug-produced relaxation and the effects of instructional set in standardized systematic desensitization. *Behavior Research and*

Therapy, 1973, *11,* 279-288.

Wittkower, E.D., & Warnes, H. Cultural aspects of psychotherapy. *Psychotherapy & Psychosomatics,* 1974, *24,* 303-310.a

Wittkower, E.D., & Warnes, H. Cultural aspects of psychotherapy. *American Journal of Psychotherapy,* 1974, *28,* 566-573.b

Wold, P., & Steger, J. Social class and group therapy in a working class population. *Community Mental Health Journal,* 1976, *12,* 335-341.

Yangida, E.H. Culture and psychotherapy. In A.J. Marsella (Ed.) *Culture and psychopathology annotated bibliography.* Honolulu: Queen's Medical Center, 1977.

Chapter 7

Evaluating Drug and Other Therapies Across Cultures

Martin M. Katz

INTRODUCTION

The purpose of this paper is to review experience in the field of clinical research which may be relevant to the problems of evaluating drug and other treatments across cultures. Despite more than 25 years of research on the psychotropic drugs and several crossnational clinical trials, it is safe to state that a truly sound study of the efficacy of a drug treatment across diverse cultures has yet to be carried out. There are important methodological reasons why this is so. I will attempt to examine the more critical ones, and to make some recommendations concerning their resolution during the course of this paper.

As a clinical investigator, I am somewhat in awe of the magnitude of an evaluation task that requires comparing the efficacy of a drug or psychological treatment across different cultures. This feeling is based on several years of experience in attempting to study the influence of culture on psychological processes, particularly on the perception of abnormality and how that relates to clinical practice, generally. It specifically has to do with the fact that the influence of culture has, on the one hand, certain more obvious effects in the clinical situation, e.g., the expectations and the nature of the interaction of the doctor and the patient can be wholly different in one culture than in another. From another perspective, culture can have effects which are more subtle in their impact on the clinical process, e.g., the clinician, in addition to being professional, is, at a more basic level, a representative or "product" of his own culture; thus, culture influences the manner in which he perceives or experiences the "reality" of the clinical situation.

In a study some years back (Katz, Cole, & Lowery, 1969), we had a practical example of these influences at work in two national settings; the research dealt only with the issue of diagnosis, the first step in the clinical interaction process. In that study, large audiences of experienced British and American psychiatrists, approximately 40 in each group, viewed a filmed diagnostic interview of an American patient. They were asked to judge the extent to which a range of *affects* and *symptoms* were present, and then to indicate a diagnosis. The findings reflected the influence of culture on the act of diagnosis at two levels: (1) The more "obvious"; there was clear preference in each group for certain diagnostic categories over others, i.e., two-thirds of the Americans diagnosed the case as schizophrenic, *no* British psychiatrist did so. More than half of the British group assigned the category of "affective disorder," a qualitatively different classification. (2) At the more "subtle" level, the threshold for perceiving such emotions as depression, apathy, and hostility were lower in psychiatrists from one national setting than from the other. When the level of psychopathology seen generally by the two groups was controlled, the British saw significantly more depression in the patient than the Americans did; the Americans saw more apathy.

To interpret these results against the background of the cross-cultural framework adopted here, one might say that the British were generally less sensitive to the emotions of apathy and hostility in a patient from a different national background. Such important insensitivities or misreadings of emotions are very likely to occur in everyday practice in such interethnic situations. From the standpoint of the intercultural problems to be confronted in any major investigation in this area, one can ask whether these perceptions or interpretations can be changed easily, possibly through discussions, or whether they will require intensive "experiential" training. I gather that that is one of the prime issues confronting the Developing Interculturally Skilled Counselors (DISC) Program in Hawaii.

We have all been aware that the role of psychotherapy in the treatment of the severe mental disorders, the psychoses, has undergone serious changes over the past 25 years. It is fair to say that as regards the most complex of mental disorders, that of schizophrenia, the primary treatments in most all clinical settings in the West today are the psychotropic drugs. In the more recent past, the situation has become much the same in the treatment of certain major classes of the depressive disorders.

There are many reasons for this turn of events. Those in the research field like to think that the principal force influencing current treatment practices is scientific evidence; that is, that the drugs in fact have been demonstrated to be effective, if not superior to other forms of treatment for these condi-tions. The evidence is certainly accumulating that that is the case, if one notes the impact of the NIMH Collaborative Study (1964), and the Veterans Administration (Casey, Lasky, Klett & Hollister 1960) and May (1968) studies over these years. The evidence to support the efficacy of psychotherapy in schizophrenia is sparse and limited to highly specialized, primarily milieu approaches (Keith, Gunderson, Reifman, Buchsbaum, & Mosher, 1976). We are, in fact, almost completely dependent on the ex-perience of experts in this sphere — as against hard evidence.

The picture as regards the role of psychotherapy in treatment of the ma-jor depressive disorders is more promising of late. The work of Beck (1976) and of Lewinsohn (1974) with the newer cognitive and behavior therapies have demonstrated effectiveness with important subclasses of the condition. This issue of the role of psychotherapy in schizophrenia will be returned to later when work is described on the combining of drug and a psychosocial approach, in an important recent evaluation effort in clinical research.

More central to the purpose of the chapter, however, is the problem of *how* a treatment is evaluated across cultural settings — how it is ac-complished when this treatment is a *drug* and *not* a psychological therapy.

THE DRUG MODEL

The evaluation of a "physical" treatment is quite a bit simpler than that of a psychological, more easily managed generally, for reasons that are obvious to those who work in that field of mental health. First, the definition of what one is calling "treatment" can be defined operationally in physical or quantitative terms. The mere fact that we can define clearly what it is (the nature of the chemical agent), how much is being administered (dosage), and for how long — and the fact that the attributes associated with the therapist (his "personality," his approach, and the length and quality of his training) can be relegated to minor roles in this transaction — makes the task of the researcher very much lighter.

There are, moreover, other considerations which ease the burden of evaluation. Early investigational trials with such drugs usually lead to a more focused view of what actually is affected in the psychological condi-tion of the patient and what one can expect to happen once the treatment begins. Usually the goals are more limited, e.g., one expects certain symp-toms to be affected more than others, there is less expectation that the entire personality will undergo change, or that a restructuring of the patient's ex-periential life will ensue. These limited expectations simplify the task of evaluation; we predict changes in mood, the disappearance of certain symptoms or deviant behaviors, the return of other behaviors. Thus, finding or creating methods to measure such aspects is more feasible.

Despite the apparent simplicity of the evaluation criteria, prior to the introduction of psychotropic drugs few instruments of the type required were available. It was only in response to the demand in the early 1950s for hard evidence about these "new" treatments that such instruments began to be developed. Actually, the clinical research field owes much of the impetus for the development of its current methodology to the introduction of drugs and to the persistent demands for answers on these critical public health questions.

It strikes me that, despite the fact that the models for drug evaluation are by nature simpler than those required for assessing the various forms of psychotherapy, their structure, the methodology developed for the task, and the experience with solving the tactical problems in drug evaluation should have important carry-over for the assessment of psychological treatments. Further, if one has in mind the even more complex task of evaluating a psychotherapy across diverse cultural settings, then the models provided in the drug area may be a highly useful place to start.

It will be useful, then, to consider how simpler forms of treatment would be evaluated in the cross-cultural framework, i.e., to indicate how the technical problems would be defined, how they would be approached (if not solved), and what might be required in a study that would compare efficacy of a specific treatment across cultural settings.

The prime technical problems, basic to investigation in the field of clinical research, which have to be solved in the attempt to evaluate a treatment are to characterize in operational terms, (1) the nature, i.e., the psychopathologic and social phenomena of the clinical condition under study; and (2) the quality of change which is expected to occur as a function of treatment. These are central issues in clinical research *generally,* and not easily solved when one is working within only one cultural setting. In viewing these problems against a cross-cultural framework, we deal with a quite different perspective, and must use, as has been pointed out, a different set of lenses. Ken Sanborn and I have had some experience with these problems in Hawaii, and I would like to turn to a description of two studies which explore these issues.

To investigate how a drug brings about its effects or how the environment contributes to the etiology and expression of a specific psychiatric disorder, a highly detailed picture of the nature of that clinical condition is required at the outset. Another way of saying that is: one has to be able to define and to measure the dimensions of a disorder in order to be able to estimate the influence of a social factor, or to gauge the impact of an experimental intervention. If one wishes to assess the effects of a new treatment on neurotic depression, he or she obviously does not have to resolve all issues concerning its etiology. Nevertheless, the fact that we are seriously limited in our understanding of the nature of severe mental disorder complicates our approach to the most pragmatic of evaluation issues in this field.

DEFINING PSYCHOPATHOLOGY: THE HAWAII MULTIETHNIC STUDIES

As regards the basic phenomena, we have learned from studies of the interaction of culture and psychosis that ethnic groups can differ markedly in the behavioral and affective expression of what appears to be the same underlying psychopathology (Enright & Jaeckle, 1963); further, that psychosis can take a certain shape in the eyes of the "clinical professional," and appear quite differently to the community in which the patient lives (Katz, Sanborn, Lowery, & Ching, 1978).

We say of psychosis, then, that it is both a *clinical* and a *sociological* phenomenon. Not only do we define it differently in the frameworks of the hospital and of the community, but we use different language in our work to describe it in each setting, e.g., "symptoms" in one framework and "social deviance" in the other.

I will describe the application in research of the *clinical* and *sociological* vantages with the results of an extensive study of the interaction of ethnicity and psychopathology conducted in Hawaii. One objective of that program was to investigate the nature of psychosis through comparative studies of the forms which it takes in different ethnic groups. It involved two phases: (1) a clinical and social study of all patients from selected ethnic groups entering Hawaii's one state hospital who were diagnosed as severe functional psychiatric disorders; (2) a community study of social and symptomatic behavior which involved a sample of some 1,200 Hawaiians, representative of all ethnic groups in the population of the island of Oahu, none of whom had had any previous psychiatric contact.

In the patient study, the intention was to compare samples of Hawaii-Japanese, Hawaii-Caucasians, Part-Hawaiians, and Hawaii-Filipino psychotics, to determine whether their symptom patterns and social behavior could be distinguished and whether valid characterizations of their overall psychopathology could be developed. Some 300 patients were studied both in the hospital and from the vantage of the community over a period of two years.

The results of that study were not always consistent across the two settings, but certain results were very striking. If we compare the patterns of symptomatology for the Japanese and the Caucasians, as observed and rated by the clinical professionals, i.e., psychiatrists and psychologists, in a standard clinical interview, then we derive results illustrated in figure 7. 1.

The two ethnic groups differ from each other on a number of factors. Their symptom profiles resemble, in fact, mirror images, when we applied a discriminant function analysis to these data, the major distinguishing feature, as reflected in figure 7.1, was found to be the depression-anxiety factor. The Caucausians (who included a large proportion of Portuguese) were very high on this affect symptom scale; the Japanese low. A detailed analysis of the other major characteristics of these profiles is presented in Katz, Sanborn, and Gudeman (1969). In general, it can be said that the Caucasians, with their other major peak on belligerence, present a more "affective" picture; the Hawaii-Japanese, a more schizoid, withdrawn pattern.

It is clear, also, when we review the results of the parallel community study in the case of a particular ethnic group, that the behavior of the patients appear to be different in that setting and in the hospital situation. These differences in the perception of significant others and of the professionals and how the patients are described to behave have important implications for treatment and for determining the elements of successful intervention.

It is obviously important to treat the major symptoms of psychosis, e.g., the hallucinations, but, as far as the community and the patient's chances of remaining there are concerned, presence or absence of major signs of psychopathology may be less critical than that of disturbance in certain social behaviors which have a more significant meaning in that culture.

` In this second phase of the Hawaii Study, we were interested in determining whether comparable differences between the ethnic groups could be found when behavior in a more natural setting (the community) was the basis for analysis, and when another type of observer (one from the same ethnic group but other than a mental health professional) was used. In following up the clinical findings of the ethnic Japanese-Caucasian comparisons, we studied the behavior of representative "normals" in the Hawaiian community. We do that on the kinds of variables measured in the scales — *Relatives' Rating of Symptoms and Social Behavior Form* of the Katz Adjustment Scales (KAS) (Katz & Lyerly, 1963).

In order to examine how the *ethnic community defines mental disorder,* how each group identifies and then defines psychosis, we determine the discrepancy between the pattern of observed behavior in normals (Sanborn & Katz, 1979) (as described by members of their own ethnic group) from that pattern that was observed by significant others in the patient sample.

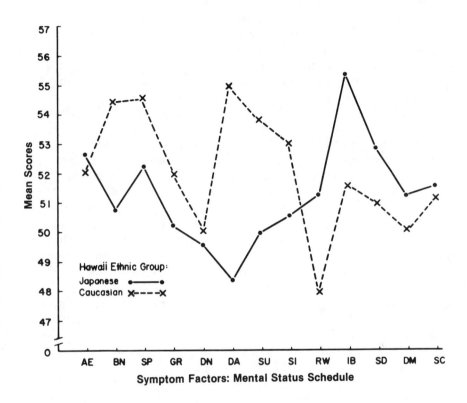

Note: AE = agitation/excitement; BN = beligerence/negativism; SP = suspicion/persecution/hallucinations; GR = grandiosity; DN = denial of illness; DA = depression/anxiety; SU = suicide/self-mutilation; SI = social isolation; RW = retardation/emotional withdrawal; IB = inappropriate/bizarre; SD = speech disorganization; DM = disorientation/memory

Fig. 7.1. Hawaii-Japanese and Hawaii-Caucasian Functional Disorders: Patterns of Symptomatology in the Hospital. From Katz, M.M., Sanborn, K.O., and Gudeman, H. Characterizing differences in psychopathology among ethnic groups in Hawaii. In: *Social Psychiatry,* F. Redlich (ed.), Baltimore: Williams and Wilkins, 1969.

We call these derived discrepancy profiles the patterns of "social deviance," reflecting its social community rather than clinical orientation.

We have calculated these for the Japanese and for the Caucasians, and the results are presented in figure 7.2. In examining them, we found that the peaks for the Japanese were *suspiciousness, negativism, anxiety,* and *bizarreness,* a pattern that described highly *anxious, paranoid behavior;* and for the Caucasians, a more contained pattern generally, where "expansiveness" and "helplessness" were somewhat prominent. When only lower class men were compared, the "helplessness" pattern was more distinct, reflecting a more depressed picture.

It appears that the symptoms or behavior changes which the Hawaii-Japanese community identified as being most associated with mental disorder or most characteristic of those who are eventually hospitalized (or are most disturbing to the ethnic community) are suspiciousness, anxiety, agitation, and negativism. These findings are based on the same patients that the clinicians described as severely schizoid with "blunted affect." The characteristic most associated with mental disturbance in the Hawaii-Caucasian man is *helplessness* — the factor most associated in our previous analyses of patient groups with depression. It seems as if depression has a special or more serious meaning for the Caucasians than for other groups, i.e., their community has less tolerance for it; it is associated with "severe mental disorder." It is not, apparently, a prominent concern of the Japanese; it does not result, if it exists to any serious degree at all, in hospitalization or in people being actually removed from the community.

It is clear that the community is not always in agreement with the professionals as to what constitutes mental disorder, and the relative significance, "meaning," of various critical behaviors, nor should they be.

There are also subtle differences in the social and the clinical frameworks which appear when contrasting ethnic groups, but of which we still know very little. Reducing the withdrawal, seclusiveness, and the "blunted affect" of the schizophrenic patient of Japanese background may achieve the clinician's goals. Unless the "suspiciousness," the distrust of others, is reduced, however, the community which initially identified this as a critical concern is likely to see that the patient does not remain long out of the hospital.

This research permits us to look closely at these two frameworks, the *clinical* and the *sociological,* and to identify with more precision the nature of the differences in perceptions and definitions of psychosis.

The relevance of this to the more general problem of evaluation, as I see it, is the following:

1. We need a multivantaged analysis of the patient, which includes the clinical, ethnic, and the sociological perspectives.
2. We need, therefore, a multifaceted definition of adjustment which will speak to the complexity of the concept of psychopathology.

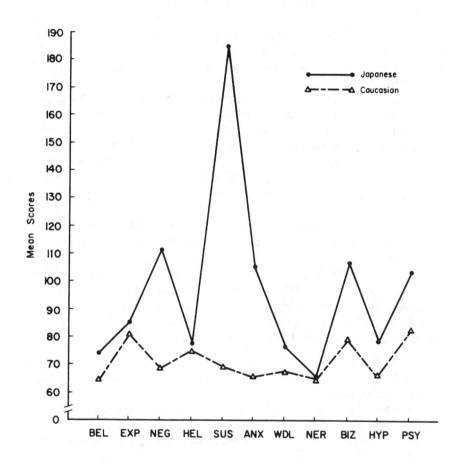

Note: BEL = belligerence
EXP = Verbal expansiveness
NEG = negativism
SUS = suspicious
ANX = anxiety
WDL = withdrawal/retardation

HEL = helplessness
PSY = general psychopathology
NER = nervousness
BIZ = bizarreness
HYP = Hyperactivity

Fig. 7.2. Ethnic Group Comparisons On Relatives' Ratings Of Social Behavior (KAS): Patterns Of Social Deviance.

TREATMENT STUDIES: CLINICAL AND SOCIAL ASSESSMENT

Some years back, when the psychotropic drugs were first introduced and appeared to offer tremendous promise in the treatment of psychosis, the National Institute of Mental Health was commissioned to carry out national clinical trials of their efficacy, focusing on the major mental disorder, schizophrenia. In view of all the prior experience with other somatic and with complex psychotherapeutic techniques, evaluating the efficacy of as apparently simple a treatment as a drug should not, as we noted, have presented any major problems. It was expected that the design and the methods for assessing new treatments would have already been worked out. However, they were not. Very few reliable scales adaptable to large studies and capable of elaborating the critical aspects of schizophrenia were actually available. (Those that were turned out to need further work. Special scales had to be developed for the assessment of patient behavior in the interview and on the ward. Self-report scales designed to be sensitive to drug effects were, also, only in the formative stage at that time.)

Given that both the "acute" effects of the treatment, i.e., immediate relief of the major symptoms, and its long-term impact were at issue, measures of the adjustment of patients after their return to the community were also necessary. An effective scheme for evaluation in large-scale treatment trials was evolved which included techniques which provided:

1. A quantified analysis of the major dimensions of psychopathology as judged and estimated by psychiatrists and psychologists. (Inpatient Multidimensional Psychiatric Scale)
2. A profile of symptomatic and social behavior on the ward as judged by the nurse. (Ward Behavior Scale)
3. Self-report data in the form of an evaluation of "mood." (Clyde Mood Scale)
   Finally, for purposes of assessing the quality of adjustment over the long-term and from the vantage of the patient's community,
4. A set of scales to be completed by a "significant other" in the patient's family and by the patient himself were developed. (Katz Adjustment Scales)

I will describe the primary criteria which guided the development of the adjustment scales because, over the years, we have put them to many uses, one of which I have already described; and they have been reasonably successful in providing a more systematic, measurable analysis of the patient's behavior against the standards — the conceptions, the perceptions, and the attitudes of the social community in which he lives.

With the community as the setting, we set out in the NIMH Collaborative Program to develop objective measures of:

1. Clinical psychopathology
2. Social behavior
3. Social performance
4. Person adjustment
5. Social adjustment

We would use a "significant other" and the patient as the prime sources of information.

I cannot go into detail as to how all of these facets were measured, but the approach is based on both the definitions of "psychopathology" and of "social deviance" which, as I noted, are critical to studies of clinical outcome.

There is the need to know the extent and nature of the former patient's current psychopathology as reflected in his social behavior; what his level of comfort or personal "distress" is as a function of the current psychopathology; how well he is performing in those social activities expected of someone in his role in the family and in the community (social performance); how satisfied he is with his level of performance (defined as "personal adjustment"); how "adjusted" he is from the standpoint of his family's expectations; and how satisfied they are with his level of performance ("social adjustment").

This comprehensive view of a patient's adjustment in the community attempts, therefore, to take into account both an *objective* analysis of the signs of psychopathology in terms of his social behavior and role performance, and the *subjective* attitudes of the family and the patient toward how well he is functioning.

In seeking examples of how these various techniques are applied, their peculiar strengths in assessing the somatic and the psychosocial therapies from the clinic to the community, I call attention to the followup phase of the NIMH Study and the more extensive analysis of the predictors and course of post-hospital adjustment in Michaux, Katz, Kurland, & Gansereit (1969). The more recently published Hogarty, Goldberg, & Schooler studies (1974) of combined drug and psychotherapy is, however, exemplary of how the problems confronting extensive evaluation programs of this type are resolved. The design calls for comparison of the efficacies of a new drug treatment and of a psychosocial approach (a social casework procedure) — "major role therapy" (MRT) on the course of ex-schizophrenics seen in a community outpatient situation. The project was designed with unusual care, having the necessary placebo controls and, thus, permitting an evaluation of the efficacy of the drug and MRT, each alone, and in combination, and both over the short-term (at six months) and over the long-term, i.e., at 18 months to two years following initiation of the treatment.

The care in selecting methods allows specific comparisons of the treatments on:

1. "symptom" dimensions as judged by the professionals,
2. "psychopathology and disturbed social behavior" as reported by (a) relatives and (b) judged by social workers in the community,
3. "social performance" as judged by relatives and patients,
4. "social adjustment" as derived from relative's ratings of performance and their expectations.

It deals, in other words, with both the clinical and the sociological frameworks for analyzing the short and long-term values of a drug and a psychosocial treatment. Its conclusions after two years provide the kind of comprehensive evaluation necessary if such studies are to have any impact on the future treatment practice of community mental health facilities.

We learn that, as expected:

1. Drug treatment is clearly effective in stemming relapse and reinstitutionalization during a period of two years following discharge.
2. Surprisingly, MRT has no effect on relapse rate during the first six months. It has a slight additive effect at two years with the drug and with placebo.
3. There are no interactive effects of drug and MRT at twelve months.
4. However, in later stages, at 18 and 24 months, when only the "sturdier" plabeco patients remain, (a) definite interactive effects favoring *drug and MRT* over drug alone occur, and (b) in interaction with placebo, MRT actually detracts, is worse than placebo alone.
5. At *18 months,* the interactive effects of *drug and MRT* and the potentially deleterious effects of this particular form of psychotherapy in the absence of drug (i.e., in surviving placebo patients only) are evident on social behavior and performance and on "symptomatology"; but *only* in the framework of the community (in the eyes of the significant other), not in the patient's own report or in the judgments of professionals. (With one exception, the social worker's judgment of his relations at home.)
6. Most all differences in social behavior and symptoms detected at 18 months by relatives were even more strongly evident at 24 months.
7. At two years, clear differences in clinical symptomatology were reported by both the professionals *and* patients, signifying superior improvement on *drug and MRT;* and in the placebo patients (no MRT), on *anxiety and depression* and in *thought disorder.*

These findings were in accord with those at 18 months reported by the "significant other." The two-year clinical data, therefore, confirms the earlier judgment based on the community ratings that the patients on combined drug and MRT were doing better than patients on the other treatments.

In reviewing the implications of this study, one notes that:

1. Improvement in the patient was more easily seen in *overt social behavior* before it was initially experienced or reported by the patient and was likely to be more visible, more observable, in the community than in the clinical interview.

2. The changes contributed by this particular form of psychosocial therapy, MRT, appear much later in the process and again are more visible within the "social framework" than through the eyes of the professional. (They are also changes in the sociological framework, not in the clinical.) In other words, if we were to rely strictly on clinical judgment, we would have arrived at different conclusions at 18 months, *all negative,* concerning the effects of the psychosocial treatment.

3. Further, as indicated in the ethnic studies, the relative importance of a facet of behavioral or affective change varies as a function of the framework, clinical or sociological, in which it is viewed. Improvement which is initially detected in the social framework, however, looks as if it is predictive of patients being later seen as "improved" by the clinicians.

These results reflect the multifaceted quality and meaning of the phenomena of mental disorder and reinforce the necessity for a multivantaged view of patient behavior.

CONCLUSIONS AND SUMMARY

In developing a strategy for evaluating psychological treatments across cultures, it is apparent that one must confront and somehow resolve several major technical problems in clinical and in cross-cultural research. There is, first of all, the issue of diagnosis. I have indicated how cultural variations in perception of clinicians can add to the already formidable problem of achieving reliability in any clinical setting. In this realm, we have, over the past few years, seen some significant advances through the application of the Research Diagnostic Criteria (RDC) (Spitzer, Endicott, & Robino, 1978), and the use of structured interview schedules, e.g., the Present State Examination (Wing, Cooper, & Sartorius, 1974). The former contributes to operationalizing the guidelines for diagnosis, and the latter has been used successfully in crossnational clinic research. They improve the situation markedly, but do not completely resolve the perceptual issue. The investigator must consider other solutions for this problem.

The second issue has to do with the fact that the nature and the impact of mental illness on the family and the community is likely to vary across cultures. Certain aspects of this condition are, as described in the Hawaiian Study, likely to be "salient," more disturbing than other elements. The goals of treatment will then vary across cultures. Investigators must be cognizant of that, and prepared to select or design their measures of outcome in accordance with the relative influences of the community and the clinical situation in that culture.

Finally, there is the problem about when and how to measure outcome, since the kind of change created by one type of treatment is likely to be different than that created by another. It is clear that drug treatment and psychotherapy proceed at a different pace and result in different patterns of change. Examples of how that happens are described through a comparative treatment study. One can see that developing a strategy for evaluating psychotherapy confronts formidable obstacles. Nevertheless, the goal is of high significance and the problems appear solvable.

In conclusion, mental illness is a clinical, an ethnic, and a sociological phenomenon. The clinic may hold different values and different goals of treatment than those held by the community. In the research sphere, we are only beginning to understand the concepts of psychopathology and social deviance and to articulate the influence of the different value frameworks of various ethnic and social groups on these concepts in American society. These differences in conception must be pursued and their results begin to have an impact on our way of assessing mental disorder across cultures and of treating it in the community.

REFERENCES

Beck, A.T. *Cognitive therapy and the emotional disorders.* New York: International Universities Press, 1976.

Casey, J.F., Lasky, J.J., Klett, C.J., & Hollister, L.E. Treatment of schizophrenic reactions with phenothiazine derivatives. *American Journal of Psychiatry,* 1960, *117,* 97-105.

Enright, J., & Jaeckle, W. Psychiatric symptoms and diagnoses in two sub-cultures. *International Journal of Social Psychiatry,* 1963, *9,* 12-17.

Hogarty, G.E., Goldberg, S.C., & Schooler, N.R. Drug and sociotherapy in the aftercare of schizophrenic patients. *Archives of General Psychiatry,* 1974, *31,* 609-618.

Katz, M.M., Cole, J.O., & Lowery, H.A. Studies of the diagnostic process: The influence of symptom perception, past experience, and ethnic background on diagnostic decisions. *American Journal of Psychiatry,* 1969, *125,* 109-119.

Katz, M.M., & Lyerly, S.B. Methods of measuring adjustment and social behavior in the community: I. Rationale, description, discriminative validity and scale development. *Psychological Reports Monograph,* 1963, *13,* 503-535.

Katz, M.M., Sanborn, K.O., Lowery, H.A., & Ching, J. Ethnic studies in Hawaii: On psychopathology and social deviance. In L.C. Wynne, R.L. Cromwell, & S. Matthysse. (Eds.), *The nature of schizophrenia: New approaches to research and treatment.* New York: Willey, 1978.

Katz, M.M., Sanborn, K.O., & Gudeman, H. Characterizing differences in psychopathology among ethnic groups in Hawaii. In F. Redlich (Ed.), *Social psychiatry,* Baltimore: Williams & Wilkins, 1969.

Keith, S.J., Gunderson, J.G., Reifman, A., Buchsbaum, S., & Mosher, L.R. Special Report: Schizophrenia, 1976. *Schizophrenia Bulletin,* 1976, *2,* 509-565.

Lewinsohn, P.M. A behavioral approach to depression. In R.J. Friedman & M.M. Katz (Eds.), *The psychology of depression: Contemporary theory and research.* Washington, D.C.: Winston-Wiley, 1974.

May, P.R.A. *Treatment of schizophrenia.* New York: Science House, 1968.

Michaux, W.W., Katz, M.M., Kurland, A.A., & Gansereit, K.H. *The first year out: Mental patients after hospitalization.* Baltimore: Johns Hopkins Press, 1969.

NIMH-PSC Collaborative Study group Effectiveness of phenothiazine treatment of acute schizophrenic psychoses. *Archives of General Psychiatry,* 1964, *10,* 246-261.

Sanborn, K.O., & Katz, M.M. Multiethnic Studies of Normality in Hawaii. Unpublished manuscript, Honolulu, Hawaii, 1979.

Spitzer, R.L., Endicott, J., & Robins, E. Research diagnostic criteria: Rationale and reliability. *Archives of General Psychiatry,* 1978, *35,* 837-844.

Wing, J.K., Cooper, J.E., & Sartorius, N. *Measurement and classification of psychiatric symptoms.* London: Cambridge University Press, 1974.

Part III
Ethnocultural Considerations

Chapter 8

Black Americans and the Cross-Cultural Counseling and Psychotherapy Experience

Carolyn B. Block

This discussion of treatment issues for black patients is primarily focused on factors observed in the extensive treatment of black child and adult patients in individual psychotherapy in both community mental health and private practice settings. This discussion will be presented in four parts: a historical overview of the relationship between the mental health professions and black Americans, a review of the research literature on clinical intervention and race, discussion of process variables related to the transracial therapy situation, and specific assessment, diagnostic, and treatment issues for black patients in transracial psychotherapy experiences. The focus of the discussion will be the black patient — nonblack therapist since this continues to be the most frequent cross-cultural dyad found in counseling and psychotherapy involving black patients. While reference is made to the black patient or the black experience for convenience in description, neither of these terms should be taken to imply that black cultural experiences are monolithic in nature.

BLACKS AND THE MENTAL HEALTH SYSTEM: HISTORICAL TRENDS

Mental Health Practice and the Black Client

In the psychological and psychiatric literature of the first half of this century, blacks were depicted as persons of limited cognitive, emotional, and social abilities who were or should be content with their low social status because of their relative immaturity compared to the dominant, white culture (Thomas & Sillen, 1972). This emphasis on immaturity and innate limited abilities led white clinicians and researchers to diagnose higher rates of hysteria and impulsive character disorders among blacks (Green, 1914; Hunt, 1947). Following World War II, when there were large numbers of black servicemen treated by white psychiatrists, the clinical literature on blacks shifted to a focus on their suspicion, hostility, and distrust of white therapists and their preoccupation with racial issues (Adams, 1950; St. Clair, 1951). These characteristics were interpreted either as resistances which greatly limited possibilities for successful psychodynamic treatment or as manifestations of early psychotic processes with diagnoses such as incipient paranoia, uncontrolled aggressive reactions, and chronic schizophrenia. With the advent of the civil rights movement in the 1960s, the clinical literature on the black patient shifted to an acceptance of the need of blacks to develop different defenses and coping styles to handle their special environmental realities. Racial consciousness, anger, and distrust could now be viewed as appropriate, adoptive behavior (Grier & Cobbs, 1968). The development of the community mental health center movement with its special emphasis on more accessible community based services for the underserved populations precipitated a focal concern on the development of mental health services to meet the needs of black patients. Black Americans were now sought after and encouraged to be treated in mental health services.

Black Cultures and Mental Health Services

This history of the changes in the clinical assessment of black patients has had a corresponding history of the understanding of mental health and psychiatric services by black individuals and family systems who were the recipients of these treatment approaches. This history has greatly influenced present treatment expectancies and behaviors of contemporary black patients in psychotherapy. Before 1965, for example, the black experience with mental health or psychiatric services was largely limited to emergency treatment and state mental hospitalization. Those few black patients seeking outpatient treatment were often refused or discouraged since they were thought by the clinical establishment to be unmotivated, nonintrospective, impulse ridden, or too concerned with reality (racial) issues. Since outpatient services were deemed unsuitable, psychiatric services were usually offered or forced upon blacks at times of acute dysfunctioning, especially when this dysfunctioning was viewed as dangerous to the patient, other persons, and/or the property of others. As a result, blacks perceived psychiatric service as necessary only during "nervous breakdowns," after all other physical resources had failed. Moreover, since they dealt with such acute dysfunctioning, such treatments were experienced as lengthy, severe, primitive, and usually involving involuntary confinement. Thus, from a black cultural viewpoint, a black person had to be insane to see a "shrink" since the resultant services were often harsh and lengthy.

With the advent of both the civil rights movement and the community mental health movement, there have been some changes in the roles and view of mental health services by the black culture as well. Some black patients, once intimidated by the white authority of traditional psychiatry, began to express and demand their rights to different treatment modalities. However, a substantial proportion of the black culture continues to view mental health and counseling services with considerable suspicion and wariness. Therefore, when a black female crosses the threshold of a public or private mental health setting, it must be appreciated that she is making a different statement by her presence. She is stating that, despite her own awareness of the negative history of the black experience in mental health, she has come to the realization that her problems are within herself and that they are so disturbing that she is willing to risk treatment in a historically negative and fearful setting. The risk is greatly multiplied when the therapist is not of her own race.

The decision to seek psychotherapy flies in the face of culturally revered coping styles within the black community. The black culture stresses early in life the ability to "do it." Emphasis is placed on the active — managing difficult situations without showing stress. The black culture places great emphasis and acclaim on being able to do difficult tasks with "no sweat." It is sanctioned to seek help and assistance for environmental needs within the family structure and through certain social agencies but, intrapsychically, the predominant goal is to be able to handle things alone or at least within one's family. Therefore, to admit to an intrapsychic problem that cannot be handled by oneself and to seek someone else's assistance on such personal concerns is a very different statement by a black person entering treatment. For example, in many American Jewish families, it is expected that one should seek a "shrink" at least once in a lifetime and that many persons in the same family will seek psychiatric help. This is hardly the expectation in a black family. Yet, today there are clearly more members of the black community seeking mental health and psychiatric services.

Given that the black person has now come to define his problems in emotional and psychological terms and presents himself to a mental health/psychiatric setting, what are the kinds of services he can expect to receive? Can a system of treatment developed in an alien, European culture, based on studies of persons of that culture, and performed by that alien culture be expected to have significant, positive effects for the black patient?

Contemporary Service Delivery and the Black Patient

Despite the recent development of community-based mental health centers, outpatient services and outreach programs, black Americans continue to be underrepresented in mental health treatment. Several studies have noted that blacks continue to receive a higher proportion of crisis intervention and inpatient services and considerably less long-term outpatient psychotherapy (Mayo, 1974b; Sue, 1977).

Warren, Jackson, Nugaris, & Farley (1973) and others (Griffith, 1977; Hughes, 1972; Jackson, 1976; Sue, McKinney, Allen, & Hall, 1974; Yamamoto, James, & Palley, 1968) found that black or other minority patients were seen in treatment for significantly shorter periods of time, tended to discontinue therapy before a mutual termination could be reached, or were more likely to be treated by paraprofessionals. Several studies have noted the effect of social class on type and length of psychotherapy (Jones, 1974; Schneiderman, 1965). A majority of blacks do fall in the lower socioeconomic groups. However, when education, income, and type of service are controlled, more than half of black patients discontinue treatment after an initial session (Sue, 1977). In a study of psychiatric inpatients by a private hospital, Steinberg, Pardes, Bjork, & Sporty (1977) found that when populations are controlled for level of diagnosis, black patients consistently had shorter hospital stays than white patients. Each of these studies of black patients in treatment demonstrates that, even under community mental health services, black American patients continue to be underserved in the patterns of mental health care. Though there are other factors which could contribute to these treatment service patterns, one central factor is the predominant involvement of non-black therapists in the diagnosis, disposition, and treatment of black patients.

CLINICAL INTERVENTION AND RACE

There is a growing body of psychological research on transracial psychotherapy. Several research studies have extensively documented the differential effects of black and white interviewers, experimenters, or testers on interview responses (Riess, Schwartz, & Cottingham, 1950), I.Q. test performance (Sattler, 1970), manual dexterity test performance (Katz & Greenbaum, 1963), and even the galvanic skin response (Bernstein, 1965) on black subjects. There is some evidence, too, that black and white experimenters and testers have differential effects on white subjects (Allen, Dubanoski, &

Stevenson, 1966; Riess, Schwartz, & Cottingham, 1950). The preponderance of research evidence supports the notion of a "race effect" in psychotherapy.

Most studies of the effects of race and treatment have been based on initial interview assessments. The majority of these studies concluded that blacks responded more favorably to black therapist/counselors. Some studies indicated that racial and social class similarity were positively related to a patient's depth of self-exploration, i.e., lower and middle class blacks showed less self-disclosure than middle class whites (Banks, 1972; Wolkon, Moriwaki, & Williams 1973). A series of studies looking at the differential effects of race versus degree of experience of therapist unearthed more complex findings. Banks, Berenson, and Carkhuff (1967) found that race was more important than degree of experience in working with black patients in the initial interview session; Cymbolic (1972) found that, after the initial interview, the degree of experience of the therapist was more important than race; and Gardner (1972) reported that both race and experience were of primary importance for black patients in therapy. A number of other studies have shown that blacks prefer black therapists and counselors (Banks et al., 1967; Grantham, 1973; Wolkon et al., 1973), achieve and engage in greater self-exploration (Banks, 1972), and feel they are better understood (Bryson & Cody, 1973) by black therapist/counselors than by white therapist/counselors. The results of these analog studies, though based primarily on single interview experimental situations, are generally consistent with the findings of epidemiological and naturalistic research.

Several studies of outpatient psychotherapy of black patients with white therapists have shown that (1) blacks showed lower attendance in psychotherapy sessions and tended to terminate earlier than white patients (Krebs, 1971), and (2) in child guidance clinics, black parents reported less favorable therapeutic alliance, felt less understood, and perceived therapy as significantly less beneficial than white parents (Warren et al., 1973). Black patients are also less likely to be admitted to general hospital inpatient psychiatric units and, once admitted, are discharged earlier regardless of diagnosis (Steinberg at al., 1977).

Both clinical outcome studies and research analog studies indicate that racial differences affect treatment interaction patterns and treatment outcome for black patients.

TREATMENT PROCESS VARIABLES IN TRANSRACIAL PSYCHOTHERAPY

Although research literature sheds some light on several of the variables important in transracial therapeutic situations, there are other related psychological elements present in transracial therapy situations which should also be considered. Three central process variables in transracial therapy are level of expectation, degree of self-disclosure, and racial reactions of therapists.

Level of Expectation

Many studies have shown that a significant factor in the outcome of psychotherapy is the level of expectation of both therapist and patient in psychotherapy (Goldstein, 1962). These therapist/patient expectations of treatment outcome often correlate with the actual outcome. However, these prognostic assessments are influenced by the degree of perceived congruence between therapist and patient in respect to socioeconomic background, educational level, and cognitive and personality traits (Posthuma & Carr, 1975). Unfortunately, there is often little perceived congruence between therapist and patient in a transracial therapy situation. The special speech, dress, manner, and appearance of black patients may disguise psychological similarities. Often, in reaction, the non-black therapist may unconsciously stereotype the black patient as "hostile and not motivated for treatment, having primitive character structure, not being psychologically minded and being impulse ridden" (Sabshin, Diesenhaus, & Wilkerson 1979). With such expectancies and stereotypes, a psychological barrier can be formed between therapist and patient resulting in poor and inadequate assessment, treatment, and prognosis.

Degree of Self-Disclosure

The degree to which patients are able to freely discuss their thoughts, self-doubts, and concerns is a basic element in dynamic psychotherapy. However, self-disclosure is related to trust which, in turn, is dependent upon the degree to which the therapist and patient perceive themselves as similar and acceptable to each other. A therapist may more likely communicate feelings of warmth, understanding, and acceptance when the therapist views the patient as similar to himself with problems, goals, and coping styles with which he can identify (Shapiro, Struening, Shapiro & Barten, 1976). For example, Carkhuff and Pierce (1967) found that clients with counselors of similar race and social class tended to show greater self-disclosure than clients with dissimilar counselors.

Other elements which influence self-disclosure are language and styles of expression and communication. While some non-black therapists make it a point to attempt to understand the basic languages and vocabularies of various black subcultures, often little is atempted or known about the more subtle communication styles and values of various black patients. For example, black patients may have a tendency to communicate ideas and feelings by analogy rather than analysis. A black patient may be more likely to give examples of his or her experience of a problem rather than to isolate and analyze specific factors. Often, this information is dismissed as being too concrete and nonintrospective when, in fact, it may be a style of communication rather than an indication of degree of insight or ability to abstract.

Self-disclosure is also influenced by the perceived acceptance from the therapist. Even after the patient has begun communicating freely to a therapist, the reasoning and values expressed often appear to be foreign to the therapist. Indeed, in some instances, values inherent in two different subcultures may be realistically diverse and even conflictual, especially around racial and economic isssues. In such situations, expectations that a therapist function as a neutral value agent are impossible. Sensing this conflict, black patients often withhold information and feelings in important areas because they fear the non-black therapist may not be able to handle them. Also on this issue, unlike other patients, black patients tend to expect therapists to have certain values and opinions on issues that they present. In my experience, black patients tend to expect some of these value differences and anticipate interaction with these differences as a basic part of the therapeutic process. (Often the "neutral" therapist is experienced as one who cannot offer anything.)

Therapists' Styles in Reaction to Racial Differences

The position of a non-black therapist to the black client is often a very awkard one. In approaching the issue of racial differences, non-black therapists often make one of three kinds of errors in attempting to treat the black patients. The first error is "the illusion of color blindness" (Thomas & Sillen, 1972) whereby the black patient is viewed as just another client. As Sager, Brayboy, & Waxenburg (1972) have noted, the denial of color in a black patient disregards the central importance of color for the black person and, at the same time, attempts to ignore the undeniable impact of the therapist's whiteness upon the patient. A further consequence of this illusion of color blindness is to remove the black client from his or her social/racial environment and/or cultural mores which can also lead to identifying deviations from white middle class norms as pathological (Thomas & Sillen, 1972).

The second and opposite error is the assumption that all the black patient's problems revolve around the condition of being black in an oppressive society, and that a lifetime of oppression has produced a permanent crippling of personality — the "irreversible mark of oppression." As noted by Griffith (1977), the term "mark of oppression" originated by Kardiner and Ovesey (1951) can be updated to include "culturally deprived," "underprivileged," and even "minority" when these terms convey a permanent limitation in personality functioning as a result of environmental factors. Such a view severely limits a therapist's ability to focus on productive intrapsychic issues, and often fosters guilt and a need to offer the black patient special privileges and relaxed standards of treatment (Cooper, 1973). Like the "illusion of color blindness" the "mark of oppression" attitude results in a loss of clinical objectivity and an inattentiveness to the individual pathology that the black client may bring to treatment (Cooper, 1973; Grier & Cobbs, 1968; Griffith, 1977).

The third type of therapist error in a cross-cultural treatment situation is what Vontress (1971) has described as "the great white father syndrome." Here, the non-black therapist tries to communicate to the black client not only that he is somewhat omnipotent but that he means nothing but good for the patient. This view demands that the black patient totally disregard his reality testing while in the presence of a trained, benevolent, non-black therapist. It also assumes that the non-black therapist really knowns the intimate dynamics of black life. Since any questioning or criticism of the therapist is seen as resistance and/or ingratitude, opportunities for correction are limited and/or nonexistent.

Each of these approaches is a trap for the non-black therapist in that they provide a screen through which the black patient's actual feelings, desires, and actions are distorted in both the assessment and treatment phases of psychotherapy.

ASSESSMENT, DIAGNOSTIC, AND TREATMENT ISSUES FOR BLACK PATIENTS

Presenting Factors

Both the epidemiological and clinical research literature attest to the fact that race does make a difference in psychotherapy (Griffith & Jones, 1979). However, Griffith and Jones assert that the race difference has its greatest impact in the early phase of treatment, especially in the initial interview. Therefore, it is important to examine the special factors which black patients bring to psychotherapy and counseling. In my experience, most black patients present themselves differently in psychotherapy. Many black patients, having no family history with psychotherapy and counseling, are really uneasy and unsure of what to expect of the process, how much to talk, and what it is really important to talk about. Under these circumstances, they may appear to be "nonverbal." Most black patients expect questions and corrections from the therapist to help them explain their personal concerns. There is often a kind of subtle testing of the therapist to see if data are recalled, if inconsistencies are picked up, and if "outrageous" statements will really be addressed by the therapist (Gardner, 1972; Griffith & Jones, 1979). Often, too, the chief complaint is disguised. The patient may talk about his problems but want to see if the therapist can pick up where he is really hurting. Since traditional diagnostic techniques depend heavily upon self-disclosure, stated symptomatology, establishment of rapport, and the therapist's judgments of coping "adequacies," traditionally trained non-black therapists may be at a considerable disadvantage in diagnosing black patients.

Typically, after making a statement of his degree of concern and need for help by his very presence in the psychiatric setting, a black patient will proceed to verbally deny the depth of the problem and his need for help. These are part of the forces mentioned earlier as coping styles aimed at not appearing helpless and potentially dependent. This denial of the seriousness of the problem or the belief that psychotherapy can be of help serve the same purpose: to convey that everything is under control even when it clearly isn't. It is the patient's very presence, however, which states his intrapsychic understanding that everything is not under control. Here, a skilled therapist must pay more attention to the actions and implied meanings of these actions than to the spontaneous verbalizations of his patient.

Black patients also experience considerable impatience with delay in the start-up of the treatment process. A long lag between request for treatment and time of first visit is not acceptable to most black patients. The black activity style demands that one do something right away; and, if psychotherapy is not available within a relatively short period of time, another method for dealing with the problem will be sought. Similarly, long intakes with no interventions are viewed as a waste of time and as an excuse to withdraw from the treatment commitment. Often this dynamic is mistakenly viewed by non-black therapists as resistance by the patient. Similarly, black patients may also have different cultural expectancies about punctuality and frequency of sessions. Being unfamiliar with the rules of psychotherapy, many black patients may need to be instructed on the necessity for these expectations regarding time (Griffith & Jones, 1979). Even in the intake process, it is possible to offer both instruction and brief interventions from one session to another so that treatment is really begun within the first session.

Diagnostic Factors

Are there unique mental health problems for blacks and other minorities in this country? From clinical experience, there is little to suggest that black or other minority persons function basically differently psychologically from anyone else. Many of the same psychological rules apply. However, as in the large society, the end results of these rules are determined by the environmental factors encountered by the individual. Blacks and other minorities in this country undergo special environments which result in different expressions of strengths as well as psychopathology (Schneiderman, 1965). Black persons do develop different personality structures, defense hierarchies, and symptomatologies in response to their different personal and social environments. A brief discussion of several of these differences follows.

The issue of paranoia has many ramifications in the black patient. Several studies noted earlier have documented the increased wariness and reluctance to self-disclosure of black patients in transracial therapy situations.In many settings, paranoia, guardedness, and/or hyperalertness are necessary for black survival (Grier & Cobbs, 1968). The distinctions between this hypersensitivity, paranoid ideation, and paranoid psychosis may be especially difficult to determine in an initial interview and diagnostic session in a transracial situation. Often such wariness is accompanied by a deliberate blunting of affect as a further defensive posture. This may account for the high proportion of paranoid schizophrenia diagnoses reported for black patients seen in emergency and inpatient settings (Steinberg et al., 1977).

In dynamic psychotherapy, analysis of defense mechanisms is used to assess quality of personality functioning. Certain defense mechanisms, such as denial and repression, for example, are often termed primitive defenses in comparison with the more intricate defense mechanisms of sublimation and displacement. Thus, blacks observed using the defense mechanisms of denial and repression are viewed as being psychologically less well developed. But are denial and repression necessarily primitive for ethnic minority members in this country where opportunities for successful sublimation and areas of safe displacement are often artifically limited by the dominant culture?

The importance of activity as a physical and psychological defense or coping mechanism for blacks has been noted earlier in this chapter. Griffith (1977), in his review, has noted the tendency of early studies of black patients to focus on the issues of submissiveness and overcompliance by black patients in psychotherapy. As Griffith points out, it is not always clear whether this submissiveness is an intrapsychic stance or merely a ruse for keeping non-black therapists at a distance. Black patients have also been criticized for the frequent use of denial in coping with intrapsychic conflicts. This denial is often manifest to non-black therapists by the black patient's continuing concerns over environmental and racial difficulties. There is also a small but growing body of literature describing the denial of racial identification in black patients (Calneck, 1970; Grier & Cobbs, 1968; Griffith, 1977; Griffith & Jones, 1979; Jackson, 1973). This literature suggests that denial of racial identification can be a significant source of psychopathology for black patients.

Capacity for delay and degree of impulse control are also used to assess personality functioning and suitability for treatment. However, the assessment of these abilities is heavily culturally determined. "Acting out" is usually described in the theoretical literature as a less adequate, immature expression and working through of intrapsychic conflicts. But which conflicts for black Americans are truly intrapsychic? What are the reality factors? Is being active always "acting out?" What would have been the consequences for blacks in this country if activity and action were not used as a defense? Perhaps one can only be truly introspective when relatively free from outer reality pressures. Is a person a character disorder because he refuses to accept a value structure that excludes and limits him? Can an individual be correctly diagnosed as "an inadequate personality" because he has failed to develop certain standards of behavior in a culture which does not support his personal and social advancement? Many of these questions and others must be raised by any therapist looking at a black client for diagnostic purposes.

Symptomatologies

Black patients can develop special signs of psychological stress. For example, the reports of clinical depression in blacks appear to follow closely that observed in society as a whole. While the incidence may not vary, the expressions and intensity of their symptoms are varied for black patients. In addition to the classic signs of fatigue, loss of appetite and sleep, crying, and dejected mood, black patients are more likely to be active and self-destructive in their expressions of depression (Poussaint, 1972). Black patients may be more likely to act to confront the dilemma in ways that invite the feared outcome (Poussaint, 1972). (For example, a depressed mother may offer to give up her children when she is really afraid that they will be taken away.) Also, because the realities of black life and survival are different, some of the more common expressions of depression in the larger culture have a more life threatening value for minorities. For example, for a single black mother of four to stay home five days from her job is an almost suicidal gesture because she knows there is no rescue for herself or her family other than herself. Black patients are also less likely to show depression by loss of appetitite — it is more likely the opposite; also, crying is a less frequent symptom of depression. Activity or agitated depression is more common and at times can mask the depressive mood even to the patient. The true function of this activity can only be determined by looking at the possible self-destructive elements to black life. There is also a general tendency for blacks to express sadness and depression through anger. In a transracial therapy situation, this expression of anger and agitation may, in fact, make a non-black therapist more anxious than the patient. And in such a situation, it is often difficult for the non-black therapist to understand and interpret this defense while it is in evidence.

There is also a real concern about somatic complaints for black patients. Black patients do tend to express psychological stress through bodily concerns. Problems with headaches, stomach ailments, backaches, and general nervousness are frequently part of the presenting complaint. Often these are expressed without the apparent understanding that they may have any psychological determinants. While this may be due to a lack of sophistication regarding the relationship between psychological and body processes, many older urban black patients may have real physical difficulties. Blacks have been found to have more health problems than other groups. Since problems of hypertension, arthritis, obesity, and anemia are much higher in blacks (Mayo, 1974a), somatic complaints reported in psychotherapy may be the result of physiological irregularities.

Although there has been a recent rise in the suicide rate among black adolescents, black patients as a whole are still less likely to express suicidal ideation in a therapeutic situation. However, once they do, they do have a higher probability of being serious in intent rather than manipulative. Therefore, they should be treated with more caution. Both Bush (1976) and Poussaint (1972) theorize that a preponderance of black suicides may result when feelings of disenfranchisement from both black personal culture and the white culture occur simultaneously. Though the incidence of black suicide continues to increase, idle threats of suicide are not, yet, inherent in the black culture.

However, threats of homicide are frequently expressed in the black culture. Mothers and fathers use such threats to instill fear for disciplinary purposes. Men often use them with each other as methods of engendering self-protection and respect. Thus, expressions of homicide, of "I'm going to kill so-and-so," may be more righteous expressions of anger than actual intentions to kill. Homicides often occur when threats are challenged and weapons are used to back up threats. Several authors have discussed the concept of victim-precipitated homicide among blacks to explain the relatively low suicide rates among blacks (Bush, 1976; Hendin, 1969; Poussaint, 1972).

Psychological Strengths

A complete clinical evaluation of a black patient should include assessment of psychological strengths as well as expressions of psychopathology. Nonblack therapists may have difficulty understanding successful coping styles which do not fit white middle class norms. Because their environmental realities may be quite different, black patients' coping mechanisms may go unnoticed. Often, in the assessment of individuals and families, it is assumed that living through a stressful or traumatic experience has been overwhelming for the patient, and this experience is used to point to the low level of functioning of the patient. I would like to suggest the hypothesis that often the opposite is true. That to have survived and dealt with a particular stress situation may, in fact, be an indication of considerable ego strength (Boyd, 1977). For example, the ability to live in a multiproblem family may take more strength than many mental health professionals would have. The ability of a 14-year-old to carry through a pregnancy to term and to keep the child may be "a poor decision" in our opinion but, at the same time, may indicate a strong sense of ability to cope and master a hardship. Similarly, the ability to deal with single parenthood, poverty, and other environmental and social stresses is often an indication of ego strength which should be noted. Other strengths of importance in assessing black patients are quality and extent of interpersonal or family relationships, maintenance of strong support systems, and capacity to set and obtain goals (Boyd, 1977).

Therapeutic Process

Focusing on the process of psychotherapy with black patients, two factors emerge which have special import. The first is that, for a black patient, the issue of race continues to be a central theme interwoven into both maladaptive behaviors and ego strengths. At times, racial and cultural issues can be used as defensive or resistance measures, but the successful treatment of black patients usually must address racial issues at some key points, since the racial interface is a central part of a black person's life experience (Calneck, 1970; Griffith, 1977). In transracial psychotherapy, this may be difficult initially, but the successful treatment of a black patient must include his ability to express in psychotherapy his life as he experiences it.

A second factor in the process of psychotherapy is concerned with the nature of the transference phenomena for black clients. In my experience, though erotic transference may develop in a black client, it has rarely approached the degree of emphasis and explicitness depicted in much of the psychoanalytic literature. In fact, rather than being expressed in erotic terms, transference is generally conveyed in and focused on intellectual, authoritarian, and competence issues. In a transracial situation with black clients, some research has indicated that the erotic transference is especially subdued and perhaps even depressed, and that when an erotic transference has emerged in a black/white therapy situation, for example, it has resulted in reduced patient-therapist rapport. Another difference which seems to emerge for blacks in psychotherapy is the extent to which transference is used to increase productivity in psychotherapy for minority patients. This finding is somewhat dissimilar to early Freudian observations that transference material is primarily a method of resistance which slows down the work of the analysis.

There are also other obvious differences in dress, manner, language, and experiences which must be bridged in transracial psychotherapy patients. Any patient needs to be able to describe his or her concerns and feelings in the language that he or she experiences them. If he or she feels inhibited in that expression, a level of unreality will occur in the treatment process and potentially invalidate it. A particular area of difficulty often arises in the black patient's inability to express feelings regarding other whites with whom he or she must interact. Since the black/white interface is a very significant part of the black experience, these feelings should not be inhibited in order to spare the non-black therapist.

BLACK FAMILIES IN PSYCHOTHERAPY

While the major focus of this chapter has been on the dynamics involved in individual psychotherapy with black patients, there is a growing literature of the use of family therapy with black patients (Boyd, 1977; Minuchin, King, Auerswald, & Rabinowitz 1967; Sager, Brayboy, & Waxenburg, 1972). This literature has centered around poor, urban, black families whose life and survival systems have been found to be in sharp contrast to those of middle class, non-black therapists. Many of the treatment process variables noted earlier (self-disclosure, communication styles, etc.) are present and multiplied in transracial family therapy situations. However, since family members may outnumber therapists, the racial balance of the treatment is shifted for both therapist and patient. One study of family therapists with black patients noted that 74 percent of all clinicians felt that black families were more resistive to treatment (Boyd, 1977). Sager et al. (1972) noted the special factors in the black-white interface which make transracial family therapy especially difficult, but no new treatment techniques have been described for black families.

There are, of course, other variables in the initial treatment of black patients in transracial psychotherapy. A 300-year history cannot be erased simply because one is a psychiatrist, psychologist, social worker, or other trained therapist. To deny the racial differences and their 300-year history introduces a level of dishonesty and unreality into the treatment experience which is always antitherapeutic.

SUMMARY AND CONCLUSIONS

The provision of psychotherapy and counseling services for black Americans takes place against a historical background of racial and social oppression in general and a negative history of involvement in mental health in particular. The research literature strongly suggests that the physiological, sociological, and cultural differences which exist in transracial (cross-cultural) counseling and psychotherapy present significant obstacles to expectancies, self-disclosure, levels of trust, and degree of empathy necessary for successful treatment outcomes.

In the diagnosis and treatment situations, black patients tend to present themselves differently, emphasize different symptoms, express various psychological capacities differently, and express ego strengths in manners and situations which can be quite distinct from the dominant American culture. In general, the relative failure of cross-cultural treatment of black Americans is due to clinical inattentiveness and to misinterpretations of these differences. There are approaches to the successful understanding and treatment of black Americans which can be learned and managed by interested non-black therapists.

Just as one must acknowledge the difficulty in the establishment of trust in the early stages of treatment, in transracial treatment the difficulties presented by physical and cultural differences must be acknowledged and worked with. It is a special circumstance for a black patient to literally and figuratively put his head into the hands of a non-black therapist for help. It is like asking a Jew to be treated by a German, an Irish Catholic by an Irish Protestant, an Arab by a Jew, a white South African by a black. This is not to say that it cannot be done. However, the added difficulty the situation presents is real and must be addressed if therapy is to be complete.

REFERENCES

Adams, W.A. The Negro patient in psychiatric treatment. *American Journal of Orthopsychiatry*, 1950, *20*, 305-310.

Allen, S., Dubanoski, N., & Stevenson, H. Children's performance as a function of race of E, race of S, and type of verbal reinforcement. *Journal of Experimental Child Psychology*, 1966, *4*, 248-256.

Banks, G., Berenson, B., & Carkhuff, R. The effects of counselor race and training upon counseling process with Negro clients in initial interviews. *Journal of Clinical Psychology*, 1967, *23*, 70-71.

Banks, W. The differential effects of race and social class in helping. *Journal of Clinical Psychology*, 1972, *28*, 90-92.

Bernstein, A. Race of examiner as significant influence on based skin impedience. *Journal of Personality and Social Psychology*, 1965, *1*, 341-349.

Boyd, N. Black families in therapy: A study of clinicians' perceptions. *Psychiatric Spectator*, 1977, *41*, 21-25.

Bryson, S., & Cody, J. Relationship of race and level of understanding between counselor and client. *Journal of Counseling Psychology*, 1973, *20*, 495-498.

Bush, J.A. Suicide and blacks: A conceptual framework. *Suicide Lifethreatening Behavior*, 1976, *6* (4), 216-222.

Calneck, M. Racial factors in the counter-transference: The black therapist and black client. *American Journal of Orthopsychiatry*, 1970, *40*, 39-46.

Carkhuff, R.R., & Pierce, R. Differential effects of therapist race and social class upon patient depth of self-exploration in the initial clinical interview. *Journal of Consulting Psychology*, 1967, *31*, 632-634.

Cooper, S. A look at the effect of racism on clinical work. *Social Casework*, 1973, *54*, 76-84.

Cimbolic, P. Counselor race and experience effects on black clients. *Journal of Consulting and Clinical Psychology*, 1972, *39*, 328-332.

Gardner, L. The therapeutic relationship under varying conditions of race. *Psychotherapy: Theory, Research and Practice*, 1972, *28*, 87-89.

Goldstein, A.P. *Therapist-patient expectancies in psychotherapy*. New York: Pergamon Press, 1962.

Goldstein, A.P. *Structured learning therapy: Toward a psychotherapy for the poor*. New York: Academic Press, 1973.

Grantham, R.J. Effects of counselor, sex, race, and language style on black students in initial interviews. *Journal of Counseling Psychology*, 1973, *20*, 553-559.

Green, E.M. Psychosis among Negroes: A comparative study. *Journal of Nervous and Mental Disease*, 1914, *14*, 697-708.

Grier, W.H., & Cobbs, P.M. *Black rage*. New York: Basic Books, 1968.

Griffith, M.S. The influence of race on the psychotherapeutic relationship. *Psychiatry*, 1977, *40* (1), 27-40.

Griffith, M.S., & Jones, E.E. Race and psychotherapy: Changing perspectives. *Current Psychiatric Therapies*, 1979, *18*, 225-235.

Hendin, H. *Black suicide*. New York: Harper Colophon Books, 1969.

Hughes, R. The effects of sex, age, race and social history of therapist and client on psychotherapy outcome. Unpublished doctoral dissertation, University of California, Berkeley, 1972.

Hunt, W.A. The relative incidence of psychoneurosis among Negroes, *Jounal of Consulting Psychology,* 1947, *11,* 133-136.

Jackson, A.M. Psychotherapy: Factors associated with the race of the therapist. *Psychotherapy: Theory, Research and Practice,* 1973, *10* (3), 272-277.

Jackson, A.M. Mental health delivery systems and the black client. *Journal of Afro-American Issues,* 1976, *4* (11), 28-34.

Jackson, A.M., Berkowitz, H., & Farley, G. Race as a variable affecting the treatment involvement of children. *Journal of the American Academy of Child Psychiatry,* 1974, *13,* 20-31.

Jones, E.E. Social class and psychotherapy: A critical review of research. *Psychiatry,* 1974, *37,* 307-319.

Jones, E.E. The effects of race on psychotherapy process and outcome: An exploratory investigation. *Psychotherapy: Theory, Research and Practice,* 1978, *15,* 226-236.a

Jones, E.E. Black-white personality differences: Another look. *Journal of Personality Assessment,* 1978, *43,* (3), 244-252.b

Kardiner, A., & Ovesey, L. *The mark of oppression.* New York: Norton, 1951.

Katz, J., & Greenbaum, C. Effects of anxiety, threat and social environment on task performance of Negro college students. *Journal of Abnormal and Social Psychology,* 1963, *66,* 562-567.

Krebs, R.L. Some effects of a white institution on black psychiatric outpatients. *American Journal of Orthopsychiatry,* 1971, *41,* 589-596.

Mayo, J. The significance of sociocultural variables in the psychiatric treatment of black outpatients. *Comprehensive Psychiatry,* 1974, *15,* 471-482.a

Mayo, J. Utilization of a community mental health center by blacks: Admission to inpatient status. *Journal of Nervous and Mental Disease,* 1974, *158,* 202-207.b

Minuchin, S.E., King, E., Auerswald, C.H., & Rabinowitz, C. *Families of the slums.* New York: Basic Books, 1967.

Posthuma, A.B., & Carr, J.E. Differentiation matching in psychotherapy. *Canadian Psychological Review,* 1975, *16,* 35-43.

X Poussaint, A.F. *Why blacks kill blacks.* New York: Emerson Hall, 1972.

Puryear, C.R., & Mednick, M.S. Black militancy, affective attachment and the fear of success in black college women. *Journal of Consulting and Clinical Psychology,* 1974, *42,* 263-266.

Riess, R.L., Schwartz, E., & Cottingham, A. An experimental critique of the Negro version of the TAT. *Journal of Abnormal and Social Psychology,* 1950, *45,* 700-709.

Sabshin, M., Diesenhaus, H., & Wilkerson, R. Dimensions of institutional racism in psychiatry. *American Journal of Psychiatry,* 1970, *127,* 787-793.

Sager, C., Brayboy, T.L., & Waxenburg, B.M. *The Black Ghetto Family in Therapy.* New York: Grove Press, 1970.

Sattler, J. Racial "experimenter" effects in experimentation, testing, interviewing and psychotherapy. *Psychological Bulletin,* 1970, *73,* 137-160.

Shapiro, A.K., Struening, E., Shapiro, E., & Barten, H. Prognostic correlates of psychotherapy in psychiatric outpatients. *American Journal of Psychiatry,* 1976, *133,* 802-808.

Schneiderman, L. Social class, diagnosis and treatment. *American Journal of Orthopsychiatry,* 1965, *35,* 99-105.

St. Clair, H. Psychiatric interview experiences with Negroes. *American Journal of Psychiatry,* 1951, *108,* 113-119.

Steinberg, M.D., Pardes, H., Bjork, D., & Sporty, L. Demographic and clinical characteristics of black psychiatric patients in a private general hospital. *Hospital and Community Psychiatry,* 1977, *28* (2), 128-132.

Sue, S. Community mental health services to minority groups: Some optimism, some pessimism. *American Psychologist,* 1977, *32,* 616-624.

Sue, S., McKinney, H., Allen, D., & Hall, J. Delivery of community mental health services to black and white clients. *Journal of Consulting and Clinical Psychology,* 1974, *42,* 794-801.

Thomas, A., & Sillen, S. *Racism and psychiatry.* New York: Brunner-Mazel, 1972.

Vontress, C.E. *Counseling Negroes.* New York: Houghton-Mifflin, 1971.

Warren, R., Jackson, A., Nugaris, J., & Farley, G. Differential attitude of black and white patients toward treatment in child guidance clinic. *American Journal of Orthopsychiatry,* 1973, *43,* 384-393.

Wolkon, G.H., Moriwaki, S., & Williams, K.J. Race and social class factors in the orientation toward psychotherapy. *Journal of Counseling Psychology,* 1973, *20,* 312-316.

Yamamoto, J., James, D.C., & Palley, N. Cultural problems in psychiatric therapy. *Archives of General Psychiatry,* 1968, *19,* 45-49.

Chapter 9

Pluralistic Counseling and Psychotherapy for Hispanic Americans

Amado M. Padilla

The purpose of this chapter is to provide background information and techniques which will enable psychotherapists to communicate more effectively and to counsel more successfully with Hispanic clients. To achieve this, information which communicates the many ways in which Hispanic clients are similar and dissimilar to non-Hispanic clients is summarized. Following this, the basic tenets of pluralistic counseling are presented and it is shown how such a model can be implemented with Hispanics. The chapter is organized around the following topical outlines: Demographic characteristics of the target population, Ethnohistory and culture, Definition of pluralistic counseling, Implementing pluralistic therapy, Therapeutic modalities, and Communication styles in therapy.

DEMOGRAPHIC CHARACTERISTICS OF THE TARGET POPULATION

The term "Hispanic" is used here as a generic label to include all people of Spanish origin and descent. United States Bureau of the Census report (1977) indicates the existence of at least 11,200,000 Hispanic residents in the United States. While this figure almost certainly underestimates the current size of the Hispanic group, it appears adequate for our purposes. Analyzing the Hispanic group by geographic area of origin, and rounding by millions, population estimates as of 1976 are as follows: Central and South America, 0.5; Cuba, 0.7; Mexico, 6.5; Puerto Rico, 2.0; and "other," 1.5.

The census data further indicate that an absolute and relative majority of Hispanics are urban dwellers (82.5 percent) compared to 67.8 percent for the total population and 76.0 percent for blacks. Furthermore, locus of residence and Hispanic subgroup membership are related. More specifically, Chicanos are heavily represented in the southwest United States; 87 percent reside in Arizona, California, Colorado, New Mexico, and Texas. Most Puerto Ricans reside in Connecticut, New Jersey, or New York (76 percent); while most immigrants from Cuba are situated in Florida.

In addition to being urban dwellers, disproportionately large numbers of Hispanics are members of the lower income groups. The 1977 Census Report indicates that 2.4 million Hispanics, or 26.7 percent, were classified as living "in poverty." Closer examination of census data on personal and family income supports the inference that the standard of living among Hispanics is relatively lower than the general population. Although outdated at this time, it was noted in 1970 that median income for Hispanic males was $6,220 compared to $8,220 for non-Hispanic males. Examination of family income confirms the general trend: overrepresentation for Hispanics in the lower income groups and underrepresentation in the higher income groups. More specifically, 23.0 percent of the families reported income of less than $5,000 a year compared to 14.7 percent of the general population; while only 18.4 percent had incomes greater than $15,000 compared to 35.5 percent of the general population. There is no reason to believe that this situation has improved from 1970 to the present.

Difference in patterns of employment and unemployment between Hispanics and the non-Hispanic population exist; and these are interpreted as representing additional stress for Hispanics. With regard to status of employment, Hispanics are overrepresented in occupations which are menial and low paying; for example, 76 percent are blue collar workers. With regard to unemployment, a 1975 Bureau of Labor Statistics report indicates that during the third quarter of 1974 the unemployment rate among Hispanics was 8.0 percent, which is intermediate between the national level (5.0 percent) and that among blacks (10.5 percent). These data are somewhat deceptive, however, unless one considers the increase in unemployment during the preceding year was 29 percent among Hispanics, compared to 22 percent among the general population and 8 percent among blacks.

With respect to education, the U.S. Census reports the following for Anglos, black, and Hispanic males aged 25 years and older; median years of education: 12.2, 9.6, and 9.3 years; fewer than five years of schooling: 5.0,

13.5, and 19.5 percent; and, graduation from high school: 56.4, 34.7, and 32.6 percent. Thus, regardless of which of three educational criteria is examined, the interference remains unchanged. Hispanics are provided the least education compared to either the general population or to American blacks.

In conclusion, Hispanics are, on the *average,* urban dwellers, poor and low paid, menially employed and fearful of layoffs, and undereducated relative to age peers who are not Hispanic. Factors such as these are unquestionably significant sources of stress in U.S. society. It also follows that we would expect, because of increased stress, a relatively higher frequency of self-referrals for counseling and psychotherapy among Hispanics.

ETHNOHISTORY AND CULTURE

The demographic data presented above demonstrate how Hispanics differ from the general population. Here, we describe the Hispanic experience from a historical perspective as a means of documenting three major points. First, Hispanics may be thought of as members of a single cultural group in the sense that historically they share similarities in language, values, and tradition. Second, the Hispanic population is highly heterogeneous and, for some purposes, should be conceptualized as an aggregate of distinct subcultures, each possessing a recognizable pattern of unique traits. Third, information on ethnohistory and culture is important for non-Hispanic therapists who need to be able to differentiate between members of different Hispanic subcultures.

In terms of a common sense example, it may be argued that a particular counseling program designed to deal with a specific type of psychological problem might be highly successful with Chicanos, moderately successful with Cubans, and of only limited success with Puerto Ricans because of subcultural differences across groups.

The preceding argument is complex and subtle. What is involved is the identification of patterns of similarity among individual members of different subcultural groups, who are by definition unique in many aspects. The next step, of course, is to create "culturally relevant" programs of counseling and psychotherapy based upon intragroup subculture similarities which achieve maximum success rates in constructive behavior change and personal growth. The interested reader is referred to LeVine and Padilla (1980), and Padilla, Ruiz, and Alvarez (1975) for an analysis of culturally relevant counseling programs for Hispanics.

An ethnohistorical account begins with the Spanish explorers who arrived in the New World in the early sixteenth century, bringing with them a relatively homogeneous culture similar in language, values, tradition, and costume. In Mexico, they overthrew the Aztec empire, intermarried with the natives, and soon thereafter began to migrate north. The Rio Grande, or "Big River," current border between the United States and Mexico, was crossed in 1528. By the mid-sixteenth century, settlements had been created in what today is northern New Mexico. These original immigrants included Spaniards from Europe, native Americans from Mexico, and the *mestizo* (mixed blood) progeny of these two groups.

These events contribute to our thesis in three ways. First, genetic merger resulted in the gradual creation of a new Indo-Hispanic culture. Second, Spaniards as well as the *mestizo* offspring sought new lands to explore and colonize. Third, the settlers who reached northern New Mexico remained relatively isolated from Mexico and Spain, because of geographic distance and dilatory transportation. Later, they were outgrouped by the immigrants who came to call themselves the "Americans" of the United States. These Hispanics came to refer to themselves as "Spanish-Americans," or Hispanos, and, coincidentally, were the first people of European or European-Indian stock to settle in what is present-day United States.

This process of Spanish-Indian intermarriage and cultural fusion was occurring simultaneously in other parts of the New World. In some areas, native inhabitants were slain or driven off their land, and their cultures destroyed. Slaves from Africa were sometimes imported (Puerto Rico is a prime example) and the process of intermarriage and culture fusion continued for several hundred years. The net result, of course, was that a number of subculture groups were formed. As the ethnohistorical analysis reveals, Hispanics differ in genetic heritage (as indicated by observable physical characteristics), and in cultural tradition (the relative extent to which a given subculture is based on influences from Europe, and the New World, or Africa). A closer examination of some of these differences is in order to learn how they can determine need for, and response to, counseling intervention.

Skin color is one obvious physical characteristic with a genetic link which differentiates Hispanic subgroups. The range in skin coloration is from "white," through *mestizo* and mulatto "brown" to African "black." Considering the long-standing prejudice in the United States to people of color, it seems certain that darker Hispanics experienced greater discrimination than lighter-skinned Hispanics.

The types of subcultures formed were also influenced by original motivations for leaving their country of birth and migrating to a new country. Some Spaniards migrated for immediate personal gain with no thought of creating a new home. These people came to explore, colonize, exploit, and return. Others built new homes; they sought economic opportunity and personal liberty. Still others came because of interactions between complex social, political, economic, and personal factors. Today, Hispanics have migrated to the United States in waves: to seek employment and/or to escape periods of civil strife in their country of origin.

Thus, we can see that a large group of Hispanics can be identified on the basis of shared characteristics; primarily, language, values, and tradition. Further, this large group includes a number of distinct subcultures which share these characteristics, but to varying degrees. This variation is attributable to the degree of acculturation among Hispanics to the majority culture of the United States. Here, an examination of acculturation is required because it bears directly upon the kinds of social stresses experienced by Hispanics in the United States, which, in turn, is one factor which determines need for counseling.

One characteristic which determines rate of acculturation is fluency in English, yet the commitment to Spanish among Hispanics is so strong that 50 percent report it as their "native tongue," and as their preferred "home language." What this means, in effect, is that unlike many other ethnic groups, Hispanics overall have tenaciously held onto their Spanish language in spite of the fact that English is the language of the school, work, and play.

Hispanics also differ from mainstream Americans with regard to values (e.g., religious preference). The vast majority of Hispanics profess Roman Catholicism, with only a relatively small percentage professing Protestant faiths. In contrast, the dominant religious preference of the majority culture is reversed; that is, more professed Protestants than Roman Catholics.

The characteristic of Hispanic tradition is extremely complex and, therefore, more difficult to describe succinctly in terms of variation from the majority culture. The most prominent features, and those of greater significance for the counselor formulating programs based on cultural and subcultural differences, appear in the areas of family structure and attendant sex roles. The extended family structure is most common by far, but characteristically includes: a) formalized kinship relations such as the *compadrazgo* (godfather) system; and b) loyalty to the family which takes precedence over other social institutions. In addition, sex roles are traditionally more rigid and demarcated more clearly, males are granted greater independence and at an earlier age than females, and there are greater expectations for achievement outside the home for males.

There exists an additional pattern of behavior, which seems to stem from family structure and sex role, which differentiates Hispanics from non-Hispanics. Hispanics typically manifest *personalismo;* a term denoting a preference for personal contact and individualized attention in dealing with power structures, such as social institutions. Anglos, in contrast, seem to favor an organizational approach which follows impersonal regulations (the "chain of command"). Consistent with a preference for more personalized interaction is the observation of relatively more frequent physical contact among Hispanics. For example, handshakes between acquaintances and *abrazos* (embraces) among friends are the norm upon meeting and leaving. The influence of *personalismo* appears early and is reflected in play. Hispanic children, for example, have been observed to use less space between themselves and their playmates and to engage in more physical contact than Anglo or black children (Aiello and Jones, 1971).

The counselor interested in increasing his or her counseling skills by learning more about Hispanic culture will probably explore the social science literature. This may prove to be hazardous, however, because this literature contains a certain degree of misinformation concerning the "true nature" of the Hispanic character. Unsupported "findings" based on single-study research, or subjective opinions presented in the context of unsubstantiated essays seem to have been accepted by a segment of the scientific community. What may have occurred is that a certain degree of spurious "validity" has been created through constant repetition, rather than through the gradual accumulation of validating research. Without casting aspersions on the motivation of persons creating or perpetuating such myths, it does seem as if the most widely disseminated and firmly held are pejorative in nature.

It has been alleged often, for example, that Hispanics are fatalists. The belief that Hispanics adhere to predestination has been supported by a few studies showing, to use more technical language, higher "external reinforcement" sources on tests of "locus of control." This finding disappears, however, when socioeconomic status is controlled (Stone and Ruiz, 1974). Related to the myth of fatalism and belief in predestination is the idea that Hispanics possess distorted attitudes toward time. Specifically, Hispanics are presumably present-time-oriented, unduly emphasizing immediate gratification, and displaying underdeveloped skills in future planning. This tendency to enjoy the moment and to defer unpleasant responsibilities to some vague, indeterminate point in the future seems widely accepted despite a dearth of supportive evidence. What may be occurring is that some non-Hispanics translate common responses such as *manana* (tomorrow) or *Lo que Dios desea* (whatever God wills) into literal English equivalents. Any translation which ignores cultural and subcultural values runs the risk, of course, of communicating meaning inaccurately. It is at least conceivable that a Hispanic youngster who expends minimal effort in the pursuit of scholastic or academic goals is responding realistically to societal constraints based on discrimination and prejudice, rather than displaying any deficiency in "achievement motivation."

DEFINITION OF PLURALISTIC COUNSELING

With this broad overview of the demographic characteristics of Hispanics and their ethnohistory and culture as background, pluralistic counseling can be viewed as therapy which recognizes a client's culturally based beliefs, values, and behaviors. Further, this therapeutic approach is concerned with a client's adaptation to his particular cultural milieu. In essence, the pluralistic therapist is sensitive to all facets of a client's personal and family history, as well as social and cultural orientation.

As is true in all therapy, a pluralistic therapist holds the individual client as the prime concern; but on top of this, the pluralistic therapist is vigilant to all the ways culture affects the individual. The goal of pluralistic counseling is to help clients clarify their personal and cultural standards. To accomplish this goal, the pluralistic therapist needs awareness of both the minority and the majority culture, the points of contact of those cultures, and the process by which cultural standards influence the individual.

Cultures in Contact

In many parts of the world, people who do not share the same set of cultural values, beliefs, and traditions coexist side by side. Sometimes the coexistence is friendly and uninterrupted by conflict; more often, however, when cultures are in contact there is misunderstanding and domination of one group by the other. The United States is a good example of a country whose history is marked by people with different cultural orientations in contact with one another. Further, the sociopolitical climate of this country forces people to comply with the majority culture. The "melting pot" philosophy which has guided educational and social policy has profoundly affected the lives of children and adults who did not possess the cultural orientation of the majority culture. Although there have long been attempts by various ethnic minority communities to maintain their ethnic heritage through private schools, after-school language classes, and ethnic community encalves, it was not until recently that we began to notice the simultaneous upsurge of cultural pluralism from a number of ethnic minority communities. We hear a clear call to members of the majority to respect cultural diversity and to members of the ethnic minority community to manifest pride in their cultural "roots."

One of the central issues that must be dealt with by people who are members of ethnic minority groups is their perception of their own ethnic identification. Identification refers to a process resulting in an end-state by which an individual assumes a pattern of behavior characteristic of other people in the environment. Although identification clearly refers to the totality of self-experience, the term cultural identification refers to that part of the self which includes those values, attitudes, and standards which comprise cultural group membership.

When cultures are in contact, it is possible to identify with more than one culture. The child who speaks Spanish at home and English at school may experience dual culture identification. In many cases, this dual identification results in conflict and chronic anxiety, especially in that person who is only marginally familiar with the norms of one or the other of the cultures. The term "marginal" person stems primarily from the work of Stonequist (1937) and denotes bicultural membership combined with the relative inability to form dual ethnic identification.

The marginal person caught between two cultures in contact may experience particular difficulties which require therapy. The therapist must be understanding of the problems created for ethnic minority group members caught between two cultures. A person may see the relative benefits of acculturating to the values of the dominant group while undergoing pressure from family members and friends to remain ethnically "loyal" to the community. The degree to which the individual should acculturate or should remain a part of the minority group may be a major question in therapy. Problems of dual cultural membership make pluralistic therapy challenging.

Why is Pluralistic Therapy Complex?

When an ethnic minority group member is caught in a marginal life stance, the therapist must integrate understanding of values of the cultures and of the dual cultural experience into the therapeutic process. The therapist must view this knowledge flexibly allowing for clients' individual differences. The therapist must determine with the individual how much cultural separatism and/or acculturation to the majority group will facilitate personal growth.

Majority and minority group members differ in their opinions about the degree to which ethnic groups should remain distinct. Some perceive full assimilation as positive and inevitable. Others postulate continued conflict. Some envision that assimilation and pluralism will reach a balance (Dashefsky, 1976). The important thing about pluralistic therapy is that therapists should not make decisions that will affect the client's position or role in either culture. For example, the therapist should not conclude that the client's problems would be resolved if the person broke off relations with intimate family members and adopted a more "positive" attitude about acculturating to the majority group. These are decisions that must be worked through jointly by both the therapist and the client.

It is also important for the therapist to understand the cultural concepts of good and maladjustment so that the therapist will be able to work within the cultural framework of the client. Also critical is knowledge about environmental factors that operate to encourage good mental health or to produce emotional problems. For instance, stability of income is an important factor in minimizing psychopathology among ethnic minority group members. Similarly, the effects of rapid acculturation and intergenerational conflict affect adjustment. To elaborate on these points, majority group therapists may have little empathy for a situation where Hispanic girls are educated in English, acquire new life styles, and are trained for clerical jobs which then are not available. Traditional values are upset, intergenerational conflict may ensue, and for what economic advantage?

We have outlined only a few of the problems that make pluralistic therapy complex. Our purpose is to highlight these difficulties through a thorough examination of the life situation of one United States ethnic minority group (i.e., the Hispanic). We do not propose, however, to suggest that the points to be discussed throughout this chapter are specific only to Hispanics. It is our contention that many of the problems to be reviewed and solutions offered are applicable to other ethnic minority group members. Our approach can be used by the pluralistic therapist in working with minority group members other than Hispanics.

IMPLEMENTING PLURALISTIC THERAPY

Implementation of pluralistic therapy involves setting therapy goals, selecting environment and staff, and employing counseling techniques that facilitate clients' adaptation to their chosen cultures. In addition, it is important to ask ourselves how much separatism we believe cultural/ethnic groups of the United States should maintain. Some social scientists believe that full assimilation is essential for complete interpersonal understanding. Others believe that total assimilation is impossible, but without it there will always be conflict and misunderstanding between members of different cultural groups. Greely (1969) proposes that minority groups follow a sequence from culture shock, to assimilation of the elite, through militancy, to emerging adjustment and acceptance of ethnic and American identity. He warns, however, that too much pluralism increases prejudice. Unfortunately, he does not tell us what is "too much." Pettigrew (1976) sees assimilation and pluralism as part of the same social processes making up society in the United States, and proposes that a balance can be reached. Current literature suggests multiple answers to our question about the amount of separatism ethnic groups should maintain. What resolution to this issue can we draw from our study of Hispanics?

We have learned that marginality correlates highly with maladjustment. Self and ethnic identity can be confused when there is a lack of support in the family, when parents are not valued by the majority, and when a child feels conflicting loyalties to two cultures. The personal consequences can include anxiety, psychosomatic illnesses, addiction, neurosis, and psychosis. The majority institutions push for assimilation. My review of the Hispanic literature leads me to believe that the majority definition of deviance is often not objective but is, rather, a function of those in power. Thus, it is clear that marginality or pressure to assimilate can be destructive to the individual.

However, when ethnic minority people choose to assimilate or remain unacculturated, the effects may not be adversive. Some Hispanics are happily assimilated; others enjoy living unacculturated lives in rural settings or in urban *barrios*. Other Hispanics may try desperately to assimilate, but may be unable to do so. These individuals probably will experience feelings of rejection and be distressed. Similarly, those individuals who, out of fear or peer pressure, remain unacculturated may also experience personal pain. The critical factor is that individuals be aware of their options and free to choose whichever life style they want.

Part of the setting of therapy goals involves the therapist helping the client understand his or her life style options and the consequences of each. Research on Hispanics suggests that a therapist should lead a client out of a marginal life style. This ambiguous position in which the client feels inadequate to deal with the majority culture and disappointed with minority culture is probably associated with high stress for many individuals. The counselor should help other clients choose the identities they wish to play out. Clients' selection to move toward assimilation or biculturalism is a reflection of the variety and freedom of the human condition. By allowing the clients to set their own goals about life style, the counselor shows respect for varied cultures and maintains ultimate responsibility to the individual (Perry, 1969).

Another question that we must ask ourselves is "What principles can we employ to design pluralistic therapy appropriate to specific cultural groups?" Part of the answer to this question lies in determining if there are aspects of good therapy that are cross-cultural. Elsewhere, I have reviewed literature revealing success of both Anglo and Hispanic therapists with Hispanic clients, confirming the idea of common aspects of good therapy (LeVine & Padilla, 1980). Torrey (1972) emphasizes three qualities that are characteristic of all good healers — from witch doctors to psychiatrists — and these qualities are confirmed by our study of the mental health needs of Hispanics. First, good therapists exhibit a *personableness,* projecting warmth and empathy. In my research (LeVine & Padilla, 1980), one theme that emerges quite strongly is that Hispanic clients ask for counselors who were sensitive to their feelings, who did not overgeneralize, and who were accepting and nonprejudicial. Torrey explains that good healers in various cultures seem to display charismatic personalities. My study of Hispanic culture suggests that the charismatic qualities are not mysterious and can be operationalized. The effective pluralistic counselor exhibits a genuine caring for minority clients. Yet, genuine caring is only part of the nonprejudicial and accepting stance. An effective pluralistic therapist offers accurate empathic reflections—feedback—that demonstrate that the counselor understands the complexity and nuances of the client's feelings. Accurate empathic reflections and interpretations require practice and, also, full understanding of a client's culture. True, the counselor never knows precisely how any individual client feels, since each person's life and subjective experiencing are unique; but the more the counselor knows about a client's cultural, social, and familial environment, the more accurately the counselor can picture the client's roles and attitudes and the more sharply focused will be counseling feedback.

The effective pluralistic counselor offers accurate feedback, in part, by actively listening to the client. Counseling is seen as a growth process between the counselor and client. Pluralistic counselors listen to the client's feedback about the accuracy of their reflections and interpretations; and, in doing so, the counselors modify their misconceptions and broaden their understanding of clients' cultures.

A second characteristic common to all effective therapists, according to Torrey, is skill at *labeling a problem.* An effective therapist assists clients to interpret their emotional problems in terms of the client's world view. Naming the problem with the right language and appropriate sense of causality brings conflict and resistances to a conscious level. We have learned that many bicultural and unacculturated Hispanics prefer therapists to speak in Spanish. Therapists who do not speak Spanish are likely to interpret symptoms differently from bilingual therapists. Yet, language is only part of effective labeling. An understanding of the Hispanics' world view is as important as the language used. For example, with some traditionally oriented clients, it may be good therapy to incorporate folk beliefs and/or a folk healer into the helping process.

A therapist may be surprised by the wisdom of folk healers in recognizing the interaction of physical and psychological symptomatology (LeVine & Padilla, 1980). The system of folk illnesses is based on the belief that bodily fluids and mental processes must be in balance to maintain mental and physical health. Physical health requires a balance of warm and cold relationships, of intimacy and withdrawal. For example, *susto,* which is characterized by decreased appetite, restlessness, apathy, weakness, and withdrawal, is caused by fright. The folk explanation of *susto* states that certain experiences, such as seeing a car accident or being startled by a snake, precipitate this malady. *Mal ojo,* characterized by headaches, nausea, and irritability, occurs when one is looked upon with an "evil eye" by another who has "strong vision." According to folk theory, those who have "strong vision" should only look admiringly at others when touching them. If people with "strong vision" follow this touching code, they will not be feared or avoided. *Mal puesto* is characterized by severe psychological symptoms such as hallucinations, mania, and delusions. *Mal puesto* is considered to have a supernatural cause. The victim is *embrujado* (bewitched) by a witch. The witch is jealous of the victim's wealth or status and, therefore, hexes him or her by torturing effigies, using magic potions, or turning into an animal and attacking the victim. Another folk illness, *empacho,* creates symptoms of constipation and nervousness and is said to be caused by a bolus of food that is blocking the intestine (Torrey, 1972).

Psychological interpretations suggest that folk illnesses allow unconscious impulses to be expressed (LeVine & Padilla, 1980). The folk illnessess serve as ego defenses by suggesting that the causes of personal problems are external. For example, *susto* may be interpreted as distress about failure in role expectations, and the symptoms are similar to those seen in individuals suffering from extreme anxiety. In a similar fashion, *mal ojo* can be interpreted as a psychological disorder in which the individual projects the cause of illness onto others. In sum, the important thing is that the therapist recognize that some traditionally oriented Hispanics still adhere to folk beliefs and that they employ their own cultural specific labels to a variety of illnesses.

A third characteristic of good therapists is the ability to raise the client's *expectations for change.* Counseling mobilizes clients' hopes and trust so that they feel confident to lower their resistances and resolve their conflicts. The effective therapist recognizes which personal and social changes will create hope. Thus, the hope of many poor Hispanics will increase more when counselors guide them to a social service agency that can provide financial assistance rather than when counselors reflect clients' feelings about poverty. In other cases, resolving issues of how to cope with prejudice, how to appreciate one's psysiognomy, and how to live successfully within two cultures provides hope to particular Hispanic clients.

Given that skill at providing empathy, labeling a problem, and offering hope is critical to good therapy, how can we measure a particular counselor's effectiveness? An effective pluralistic counselor can describe the attitudes and feelings, points of stress, and system of maladjustments according to the clients' cultural conceptualizations (Torrey, 1972). The effective therapist holds a dynamic and open framework. The therapist embraces varied goals: assisting the individual to fit into his or her chosen society; changing the institutions and social systems to fit the client's needs. The therapist does not overract or assume all minority clients are alike. Therapy goals are set in accord with the clients' value systems (Casas, 1976). Our study of Hispanic culture suggests that paraprofessionals and ombudsmen from the community are knowledgeable about many of these factors and, thus, are vital additions to a pluralistic mental health team.

Broad appreciation of a culture is necessary but not sufficient to ensure effective pluralistic therapy. Our review of Hispanic culture reveals that Hispanic patients have avoided conventional mental health facilities — even though the facilities may have been planned to service them, and Hispanics on the whole express positive attitudes toward therapy and therapists. Yet, certain environmental conditions are necessary before services will be utilized. Services must be offered at reasonable rates within the ethnic community. Mobile crisis units are helpful. Research is inconsistent about the importance of the therapist's ethnicity, but professionals need to speak the language that their clients feel most comfortable using. Having the ethnic community participate by serving on boards and participating in the hiring of staff spurs use of mental health facilities. Services should focus upon crisis intervention. The traditional one hour for counseling may not be sufficient to ameliorate many crises, so time scheduling must be flexible within the effective pluralistic counseling model. Therapy should be offered for special groups. Among the Hispanics, counseling groups for *los tecatos* (drug addicts), alcoholics, women, the aged, and families may be particularly needed and, when carried out successfully, may fill a real void.

After the appropriate environment and therapeutic attitude is created, therapists must employ culturally relevant therapeutic techniques. Research about the most effective techniques with Hispanics is incomplete, but some specific recommendations are emerging. The therapist must be alert to different meanings of nonverbal communication across cultures. For example, Hispanics are more likely to touch than Anglos. Hispanics tend to sit and stand close together, while Anglos require more personal space. Thus, having seats placed fairly close together may facilitate comfort and trust when counseling Hispanics. Each client's attitudes about touching and spacing and particular meaning of nonverbal gesturing must be considered in effective pluralistic therapy.

The impact of directive versus nondirective counseling must be evaluated in terms of the client's cultural and idiosyncratic attitudes about authoritarianism, respect, and support. To some Hispanic clients, an older male therapist may be seen comfortably within an authoritarian role while a female therapist may clash with the cultural values of appropriate sex role behavior if she is very directive. A well-educated, middle class Hispanic suffering anxiety may respond well to supportive, nondirective counseling. An illegal and uneducated immigrant may need directive counseling and advice concerning his precarious residency in the United States.

The pluralistic counselor must recognize that the results of psychological tests differ across cultural groups. For example, results of projective tests such as TAT or Rorschach protocols differ in frequency and intensity of themes. Results of standardized tests demonstrate adaptation to majority group norms and may not reflect adjustment within an ethnic minority enclave. The pluralistic therapist employs results of standardized tests with discretion, seldom using results of a single test to diagnose clients for placement in institutional settings. When possible, culture-fair tests are employed. The pluralistic therapist strives to obtain and develop criterion-referenced tests, tests which measure behavioral adjustment within areas of concern that have been identified in the counseling process.

The pluralistic therapist will stay abreast of and employ new therapeutic modalities designed for the ethnic minority client. For example, group counseling games have been developed which build upon Chicano culture. Family therapy and psychodrama seem to be particularly effective approaches for Hispanic clients whose upbringing has involved strong family supports. Some specialized assertiveness training techniques may be helpful for Hispanic women who have been somewhat isolated in traditional settings and are beginning to interact with the majority culture. Bereavement counseling may involve different stages and more group catharsis with Hispanics than Anglo clients. My review of Hispanic literature has uncovered many new therapeutic techniques. Yet, the effectiveness of few of these techniques has been documented. Pluralistic therapists must exercise caution so that they do not become zealous of therapeutic approaches that are of little value with Hispanics. Therapists must assume responsibility for continued evaluation of their therapeutic approaches and research must be conducted to measure gain associated with each technique. With this, let us turn our attention to therapeutic modalities that have been shown to be effective with Hispanic clients.

THERAPEUTIC MODALITIES

Group Counseling

Group counseling has assisted Hispanic clients in ameliorating personal problems and expanding personal awareness (Maes & Rinaldi, 1974). Descriptive studies report success in group counseling with Hispanics of various ages, socioeconomic classes, and ethnohistories. For example, in a hospital in East Harlem, New York, group psychotherapy with blacks and Puerto Ricans was directed by a bilingual social worker. Review of individual case studies revealed many successes. Moreover, 75 percent of the group members followed through on referrals to other hospital units. Descriptive success of group counseling has also been reported with elementary school Hispanics. School counselors perceived group counseling as particularly effective for furthering children's skills in expressing their feelings in English, stimulating self-respect and pride in Hispanic culture, and clarifying personal values (Maes & Rinaldi, 1974). Successful group counseling with college students was reported by two Anglo student personnel deans who conducted a 15-hour encounter weekend with six blacks, four Chicanos, and four Anglos (Walker & Hamilton, 1973). Counseling techniques included teaching listening skills, focusing on feelings, and reinforcement of participants' interaction. The leaders cite as evidence for the success of the group the increased frequency of self-revealing statements and the stages passed through by the group which were congruent with healthy group process as posited by Rogers (1970). Some successful groups have been based upon behavioral principles. Members are asked to define behavioral goals, and are taught relaxation and contracting techniques. Group discussions assist clients in applying behavioral principles to their goals (Herrera & Sanchez, 1976).

The effectiveness of group counseling has been analyzed experimentally in several studies with young adults. In one study, ten blacks and Puerto Ricans ranging from 15 to 31 years of age who had been labeled destructive and aggressive and had been truant from school participated in group counseling, characterized by free expression of negative feelings and bombardment with positive feedback. The clients' self-reports about the group experience were quite positive, and truancy and aggressiveness decreased (Rueveni, 1971). In a second study of group counseling with young Hispanics, three groups comprised of Mexican Americans, Negroes, and Anglos joined encounter groups modeled after the National Training Laboratory (NTL) design. After ten weeks, significant changes in attitude toward self and others were reported on a semantic differential, Q-sort, and an index of social distance (Hamilton, 1969). Group processes are emerging that have been designed particularly for Hispanic clients. A number of group activities appropriate for the general Hispanic population (Ruiz, 1975) and for Hispanic drug addicts (Aron, Alger, & Gonzalez, 1974) have been described. The relative effectiveness of counseling groups that incorporate Hispanic cultural concepts versus counseling groups with no cultural content seldom has been studied. One investigator compared personal growth (as measured by academic achievement, self-concept on a semantic differential, and feelings toward nationality) of Mexican-Americans participating in a week of traditional group counseling with Mexican-Americans in bicultural group counseling (emphasizing pride in ethnic background). Change was not significant between treatment groups (Leo, 1972). With three experimental and three control groups of Puerto Rican sixth graders in an inner city school, addition of ethnic content (language and culture) did not facilitate group interaction (Ciaramella, 1973).

The generally positive trend of research about group counseling suggests it is a viable approach for facilitating growth among Hispanics. Much more research in which treatment approaches are clearly operationalized is needed to measure the relative effectiveness of various group counseling modalities, especially those built upon cultural premises.

Family Therapy

Family therapy offers particular promise with Hispanics because of the importance of and support inherent in kinship ties. A close family member can serve as a powerful auxiliary therapist (Ramirez, 1972) if goals and techniques of therapy are fully explained. If the entire family is interviewed in therapy, disturbances in the kinship support system can be identified. Once difficulties in the family system are rectified, the patient's symptoms may decrease significantly (Padilla, Ruiz, & Alvarez, 1975).

Success has been reported employing a "family group constellation" approach with lower and middle income Hispanic families (Pollack & Menacker, 1971). In this mode of family counseling, three or four families meet jointly with three to four counselors for weekly sessions of two hours duration. The counselors provide confrontation about family dynamics, and families attempt to help one another resolve their dilemmas. In addition to the family constellation meetings, counselors meet separately with each adult and child in efforts to improve communication skills that members will then employ in constellation meetings and in their private lives.

Family counseling has been effective in increasing academic performance of Hispanic children. A parent education program conducted for two years with families increased Hispanic children's performances on two IQ tests. In the first year of the program, the counselor felt that parents needed encouragement to participate in the program. Thus, the program was conducted in the families' homes. Mothers were taught home management, preventive health, and driver education. In addition, mothers and children were observed and recommendations offered for increasing children's curiosity and learning style. In the second year, fathers participated in a night program, and mothers and children joined in a daily nursery school program (Johnson, Leler, Rios, Brandt, Kahn, Mazeika, Frede, & Bisett, 1974).

Although research is sparse, limited findings show family counseling and therapy to be quite promising with Hispanic clients. The family can be included in the therapy hour in a number of ways: by asking specific family members to join in the counseling process; by working directly with the whole family; or by working with a member of the family as a consultant who will, in turn, work with the client (Christensen, 1977). The therapist should consider Hispanics likely candidates for family therapy and should be particularly alert for new methods of family counseling reported in the literature.

Another aspect of family counseling that needs consideration is counseling on parenting. Child-rearing practices among Hispanics is still a relatively unresearched area. Questions concerning punishment of children, insufficient or inappropriate sex education, degrading of one parent by the other or by other family members, and excessive attachment between mother and child combined with detachment between father and child are just a few of the questions that occur in counseling on parenting with Hispanics (Boulette, 1977). As yet, no models for counseling parents have been proposed. It is my conviction, however, that, because of the emphasis placed on children in the Hispanic culture, counselors must turn their attentions to counseling on parenting with greater vigor. This will require knowledge of the effects of acculturation stress, intergenerational conflict, and the implications of poverty in child rearing.

Assertiveness Training

Boulette (1976) has observed many Hispanic females respond to stress by *llorando* (crying), *rezando* (praying), and *aguantando* (enduring). Many Hispanic women try to hide their problems from their families and themselves. Assertiveness training may be effective in helping these clients increase appropriate behavior, protect their rights, and express feelings of anger, affection, and concern.

Pluralistic assertiveness training involves several steps. First, the person is educated about the relationship of their nonassertive behavior to their symptoms. Then, the therapist and client explore factors inhibiting assertion. The therapist provides advice as necessary. For example, the person may be advised about child care centers, womens' groups, etc. Then, the therapist models assertive behavior. Finally, behavioral rehearsal allows the individual to test out new assertive behavior (Boulette, 1976).

Research concerning effectiveness of assertive training with Hispanics is just beginning. With low income families, a combination of behavioral rehearsal, social modeling, and role playing were at least as successful as a varient of client-centered therapy on all outcome scales (Boulette, 1972).

The use of assertiveness training with Hispanics raises several issues. In the traditional Hispanic family, the female generally is not assertive. Would assertiveness training assist Hispanic females in adjusting to a traditional life style? Assertiveness training could disrupt a husband-wife relationship if it were built upon the female assuming an active role and the husband a more passive one. On another level, it is known that maladaptive responses to racism include withdrawal, psychosomatic disorders, and denial of ethnicity. Could assertiveness training be an effective tool in helping males as well as females to cope with discrimination? Hopefully, future research on assertiveness training will be conducted with various Hispanic populations and provide answers to these questions.

Vocational Counseling

Vocational counseling with Hispanics requires an appreciation of their attitudes about particular jobs. Hispanics may ascribe different statuses to some occupations than the general population. Responses of Anglo and Mexican-American post-high school students to a social status scale demonstrated few differences in the status ascribed to various occupations (Plata, 1975).

Hispanics have avoided government positions because of negative attitudes about the government, language difficulties on exams, low educational level, or fear of rejection and discrimination. For similar reasons, Hispanic representation in law enforcement agencies has been low. Despite a few differences, as a whole, Hispanics hold similar and not lower occupational aspirations than other Americans. For example, Mexican-American and Anglo college students responded to a questionnaire concerning occupational plans. Attitudes about occupations, college, vocational counseling, higher education, academic advising, study, themselves, and their counselors were similar for the two groups (Gares, 1974).

For some Hispanics, a discrepancy may exist between their occupational aspirations and educational plans. In one study, tenth grade Chicanos expressed vocational aspiration that matched Anglos. To some extent, the Chicanos expressed less realistic educational aspirations than the Anglos. Either the Chicano students expressed very high goals that would be difficult to attain or very low goals that underestimated their potential. Moreover, Anglos were more vocationally-oriented. Chicanos were more apt to aspire "to college," rather than a specific career (Cole & Davenport, 1973). In another study, Negroes, Mexican-Americans, and Anglos were interviewed by examiners of their own ethnicity. Educational aspiration was highest among Negroes and lowest among Mexican-Americans. In contrast, vocational aspiration was higher among Mexican-Americans and lowest among Negroes (Hindelang, 1970).

If Hispanics' educational and occupational aspirations are not congruent, an important facet of vocational counseling involves assisting them to bridge this gap. Very often, then, vocational counseling needs to be combined with educational counseling and tutoring. Considering Hispanics' socioeconomic history, experiences with discrimination, frustration with the educational system, and high vocational aspirations, the following recommendations for vocational counseling are offered: widen students' horizons about job possibilities; respect clients' values about occupations; suggest and help students to obtain special tutoring and summer programs when needed; maintain an employment pool to assist the Hispanic students in obtaining part-time employment; develop an extensive pool of financial aid programs for Hispanics aspiring to college; encourage more than one student to attend a particular college (Pollack & Menacker, 1971).

Group counseling may be effective in facilitating wise educational and career choices. In one program, university students studying for health careers chatted informally with high school Hispanics. The university students interpreted results of career inventories to the high school students and discussed the nature of various careers with the adolescents and their parents (Burstein & Kobos, 1971). A school counselor reported success in furthering high school Hispanics' educational goals by establishing informal meetings that continued over a three-year period. The Mexican-American high school students were invited to attend luncheon meetings. For a period of two years, students met with the counselor almost every day. The following year, they met biweekly; and the third year, talked occasionally. Issues such as the need for education, how to get accepted at a college, and how to obtain scholarships were discussed. This informal vocational counseling assisted 30 to 35 participants in entering and remaining in college (Klitgaard, 1969). One researcher (Ganschow, 1970) used films and videotapes to explore vocational and educational opportunities with tenth grade Anglos and Hispanics. Subjects who saw social models of their own ethnicity scored higher on measures of interest and occupation and engaged in slightly more information-seeking behavior. Another effective group activity for facilitating wise career choice involves students studying about Hispanic heroes. Familiarity with the lives of well-known Hispanics may increase students' awareness of career options and increase optimism about their own potential for occupation mobility. In recent years, two magazines for Hispanics, *La Luz* and *Nuestro,* have appeared which carry articles on successful Hispanics. Vocational counselors would be well advised to consult these magazines for ideas concerning career choices for Hispanic youth.

Group counseling may focus on developing skills needed for job interviewing. The importance of assertiveness in applying for a job should be explained. Finally, role playing may assist Hispanics in developing effective interviewing skills.

Counseling Addicts

Addiction is the most frequent diagnosis in mental hospitals for young adult Hispanic males (Bachrach, 1975). Counseling with drug addicts is generally a difficult process and may be more so with Hispanics. The therapist working with Hispanic drug addicts, *tecatos*, will confront issues true of all addicts and some special problems associated with ethnicity. The therapist must determine whether the person is primarily an addict who steals to support his habit or a criminal who, among other legal activities, takes dope. The focus of treatment will differ for these individuals. In the first case, the reason for and ways of "kicking the habit" will be emphasized. For the criminal addict, the basis of hostility and/or psychopathology will be considered.

Methadone offers limited assistance. Many addicts, Hispanic and Anglo alike, combine methadone and heroin or alcohol for a "super thrill." Probably, methadone works best with middle and upper class addicts, but these are a minority of the *tecatos* (Casavantes, 1976).

An important key in treating the *tecato* is to recognize the important role that the family and family members play in supporting the addict. It has been shown that addiction may be tacitly accepted by an Hispanic family (Scott, Orzen, Musillo, & Cole, 1973). The therapist must make certain that the extended family does not provide support inappropriately (Rivera, 1975), for example, allowing the *tecato* to live at home while still maintaining a drug habit is tacit support of the addict.

Another important key in treating the *tecato* is to minimize possibility for manipulation. New York conducts a number of therapeutic communities called Phoenix Houses. These centers are patterned after Synanon. The addict is subject to great pressure to "kick the habit" from peers and administrators (who are usually former addicts) and excuses are not accepted. Life is highly structured and controlled by members of the Phoenix House (Fitzpatrick, 1971).

Research conducted with Mexican-American drug addicts in a detoxification unit in California indicates that successful drug counseling requires intervention on two levels: counseling to increase self-image and to express feelings about discrimination and education and training so that rehabilitated clients can obtain employment after discharge. It is emphasized that Hispanic drug addicts need to be rehabilitated toward a goal, such as a career. Positive reinforcement, contracting, and group therapy were successful approaches with Hispanic addicts in the California detox unit. Rules were explained in group processes. Patients were allowed to express their views about the rules but could not veto a policy. Discipline was administered by a group of patients and staff. Therapy was divided into four phases. During Phase 1, of two to three months' duration, the *tecato* is involved in intensive therapy and has limited contact with individuals outside the center. In Phase 2, of another two to three months' duration, the patient lives in the center where educational and vocational training are emphasized. In Phase 3, also lasting about three months, the patient lives in the center and works outside. In the final two months, Phase 4, the patient lives outside and works outside but continues to visit the center for counseling (Aron, Alger, & Gonzalez, 1974).

Casavantes (1976) interviewed 26 counselors (most were ex-addicts) who reported success working with *tecatos* and gleaned a number of recommendations. Treatment programs must be individualized, recognizing patients' strength. For example, if the patient won't "rip off" his family, build upon this quality. Have the *tecato* help plan and administer the program. Many have been very clever manipulators in the underground world of drugs and can be equally successful working with their peers in an inpatient setting. Foster personal relationships with agency personnel. Take any progress as significant.

In general, successful therapy with addicts requires a combination of personal, family, and vocational counseling, vocational training, and patience. If a therapist is not equipped to provide a full range of services, including occupational guidance, referral to a drug clinic is appropriate. Contact with the therapist should be continued even after the patient has "kicked the habit." Organizations of drug addicts, such as LUCHA in Los Angeles, may help provide needed long-term support.

It is indeed difficult to "kick the habit" and more programs aimed at prevention are greatly needed. In New York, the Horizon Project has successfully offered widespread information about the hazards of drugs (Fitzpatrick, 1971). But the drug program cannot be rectified until the psychosocial stresses that lead to escape into drugs are confronted squarely. As long as psychosocial stresses confront minorities and the poor, the pluralistic therapist will encounter many *tecatos*.

Counseling Alcoholics

Research is badly needed about effective treatment for Hispanic alcoholics. Although not as widespread as drug addiction among Hispanics, nor as common as alcoholism among Anglos, alcoholism is a serious problem among Hispanics and involves more than 15 percent of the psychiatric admissions to state and county mental hospitals (Bachrach, 1975). Many alcoholics seek help from Alcoholics Anonymous. However, Madsen (1964) argues that association with this group is almost impossible for the traditional Hispanic since the required abstinence denies the individual's manliness and disrupts interpersonal relations. More recently, this argument has begun to be challenged by Hispanic-oriented Alcoholics Anonymous groups throughout the country. The current feeling is that A.A. can be effective with Hispanic alcoholics if the program is built on cultural strengths such as the importance of the family as a support system and the role of religion in aiding the individual to obtain the strength to abstain from alcohol.

The treatment of alcoholics is generally a difficult task. The therapist can expect some of the same difficulties with Hispanic alcoholics as those of other ethnicities, such as low recovery rates or frequent relapses. The exact ways Hispanic alcoholics differ from those of the other ethnicities has not been determined and, thus, specific treatment modalities cannot be recommended.

Geriatric Counseling

Since the 1950s, social scientists have attended increasingly to the aged as a quasi-minority group. Early forced retirement and other youth-oriented attitudes in our society stereotype against the aged and encourage them to "disengage" from many activities considered vital to the American way of life. Competitiveness, aggression, and doing are not sanctioned; rather, the aged are expected to be passive and cooperative. Yet, research has shown that, generally, persons who remain most active and engaged have the highest morale (Haven, 1968; Reynolds & Kalish, 1974). Because of stereotyping and forced disengagement foisted upon the aged, we recognize that this group has special psychological needs and may require specialized counseling techniques.

One wonders whether the plight of the Hispanic aged is similar to that of other Americans. Pluralistic counseling orientation has led to the tenet that one cannot assume any of the counseling techniques appropriate with majority Americans are directly applicable to particular ethnic groups. Do the Hispanic aged require a specialized kind of geriatric counseling? In traditional Hispanic culture, much support is gained through the extended family. The aged may live with their families and are afforded much respect and attention (Maldonado, 1975; Moore, 1971). Nevertheless, in an extensive survey in Los Angeles County, black, Mexican-American, and white residents, ages 45 to 74, were asked about their experiences with race and age discrimination in finding or staying on a job; and 60 to 88 percent of each ethnic subsample identified both ethnic and age discrimination.

Smaller percentages of each ethnic subsample (20-45 percent) stated that their own families and acquaintances experienced age and ethnic discrimination, and 8 to 34 percent identified personal experiences with age and ethnic prejudice. Blacks asserted the most discrimination, and Mexican-Americans reported more age and ethnic discrimination than whites (Kasschau, 1977).

Perhaps the discrepancy between the support one could expect for the aged in traditional Hispanic culture and the reported age discrimination cited in Kasschau's (1977) study can be explained by viewing the Hispanic aged as a bifaceted group. In their study of the aged in San Francisco, Clark and Mendelson (1969) describe some Hispanics as "community aged." The community aged maintain close contacts with family in the United States and Mexico. They base their self-esteem "not on those values which are models for young Americans, but on a contrasting profile, including congeniality, conservation, resilience, harmoniousness, cooperation, continuity, and an orientation on the present [p. 90]."

A second group of Hispanic aged are "disengaged" not only from employment and the larger American society, but also from family and friends. In a survey of the aged in Los Angeles, Reynolds and Kalish (1974) report that black respondents were significantly more likely to expect to live and want to live longer than Japanese-Americans, Mexican-Americans, and white Americans. The authors speculate that those wanting to live a long life feel that life is engaging them so that they are not ready to leave it. The disengaged Hispanic aged are products of the American mobile society. Their families move away from *barrios* with upward mobility and out of town with new employment opportunities. The isolated Hispanic aged are poorer than most Mexican-Americans and poorer than most Anglo aged. Their education is limited; and from census data, it is predicted that the next generation of aged will show an even wider gap in education between Mexican-Americans and Anglos. Many of these Hispanic aged are immigrants and experience added stress associated with the acculturation of their children (Maldonado, 1975; Moore, 1971).

The Hispanic community aged may require a different counseling orientation than the isolated Hispanic aged. Among the community aged, it would seem appropriate to deal with themes of fear of death or incapacitation, as it is appropriate to consider these issues among the elderly of other ethnicities. It will be important to foster family support and to include family members in counseling programs. A different counseling orientation is required for the isolated Hispanic aged. Here it would seem appropriate to deal with themes of poverty and loneliness. An important part of this counseling service is to help the isolated elderly Hispanic apply for social programs and financial support (de Armas, 1975). It is recommended that therapists reach out to this elderly population; most likely, they will not come to a mental health clinic. An effective place to reach this population is in church. Time can be set aside as part of the church service to discuss problems of the elderly. Advertising over television or radio has been quite effective. When conducting public relations, one can reach more of this population by speaking in Spanish than in English.

Thus, therapeutic recommendations specific to the aged Hispanic can be postulated. More research is needed to ascertain the particular needs of the isolated and community aged, and of Hispanic aged of other than Mexican origin. Then, counseling approaches for special groups of Hispanic elderly can be more fully developed and evaluated.

COMMUNICATION STYLES IN THERAPY

Nonverbal Communication

Therapists should be alert to special ways of communicating nonverbally that may be characteristic of Hispanics. A complete list of Hispanic nonverbal messages is impossible. Such a list would deny individual differences which must be at least as great as differences across ethnic groups. Moreover, much of the meaning of nonverbal messages is rendered by the context of the situation in which they are employed. Despite these difficulties concerning the meaning of an individual's nonverbal messages, several generalizations can be offered.

In the field of proxemics, the study of personal space, relatively consistent differences have been noted between the distancing of Hispanic speakers and speakers of other ethnicities. Parents of first- and second-grade, lower class Puerto Ricans and blacks and middle class whites were observed unobtrusively. The middle class whites stood further apart when communicating than either the poor blacks or Puerto Ricans (Aiello & Jones, 1971). In another study, pairs of Anglo, black, and Mexican-American adults, adolescents, and children were observed without their awareness. The Mexican Americans of all ages clustered more closely than the Anglos or blacks. Mexican Americans stood closer together indoors than outdoors. Thus, distancing varied with environment among the Mexican Americans, but not among the Anglo and black subjects (Baxter, 1970). Ethnic differences in distancing interact with sex of subjects. When lower class blacks, Puerto Ricans, and whites were observed in pairs and in social groups, females of all ethnicities stood closer together than males (Jones, 1971).

In the field of kinesics, the study of body movements, several differences have been noted between Hispanics and subjects of other ethnicities. For example, touch is common when Hispanics communicate. When pairs of Anglos, blacks, and Mexican Americans were observed without their awareness, Mexican Americans touched one another significantly more often than Anglos or blacks (Baxter, 1970). In contrast to this broad study with general populations of Anglos, blacks, and Chicanos, some data indicate less touch between Hispanic fathers and adolescent sons than between fathers and sons of other ethnicities (Pollack & Menacker, 1971).

Even though the precise meaning of each gesture cannot be provided, an awareness that the styles of nonverbal communication vary across ethnicities can prevent misunderstanding. In therapy, an awareness of possible differences in nonverbal communication may clarify miscommunication and prevent inappropriate confrontation. In addition, a study of proxemics and kinesics among Hispanics leads to several specific recommendations:

1. Shaking hands and placing an arm on the shoulder of an Hispanic client may increase the client's comfort and facilitate openness. In some cases, an embrace between the client and therapist is appropriate.
2. Chairs should be placed close together, probably closer than the Anglo therapist would be inclined naturally to place them. A distance less than two feet is preferred by many Hispanics (Hall, 1959).
3. The therapist should not attempt to maintain eye contact with an Hispanic who consistently avoids it. By forcing eye contact, the patient may assume that the therapist does not respect him or that the therapist himself cannot command respect.

Self-Disclosure

The style and rapidity of self-disclosure may differ between Hispanic clients and those of other ethnic backgrounds. During the standardization of his self-disclosure scale, Jourard (1971) observed that black and Puerto Rican college students disclosed less about themselves to significant others, such as parents and friends, than did Anglo students. When modification of Jourard's (1971) self-disclosure questionnaire was administered to white, Puerto Rican, and Mexican-American ninth graders residing in Louisiana, Mexican Americans were significantly less willing to disclose information about themselves than were Anglos and blacks; and Mexican-American males disclosed less than Mexican-American females (Littlefield, 1969). In these two self-disclosure studies, no mention is made of examiner ethnicity. In a third study, a Mexican-American examiner solicited Mexican-American and Anglo college students' attitudes about disclosing personal material to a model Anglo and a model Hispanic therapist represented through audio tapes. Although self-disclosure was high for all subjects, the Mexican-American students indicated significantly less willingness to disclose to either the model Anglo or Hispanic therapists than did the Anglo students (Acosta, 1975; Acosta & Sheehan, 1976).

These studies consistently reveal less self-disclosure among Hispanics than among Anglos of various ages. It follows that if an Hispanic client discloses personal data very slowly, the therapist should view this behavior as a normal, cultural response. Limited self-disclosure should not be employed as a single criterion to be indicataive of client resistance. Moreover, the therapist should press for self-disclosure only after careful determination that the client's normal ego protective functioning is being broken down. Clients uncover deep thoughts and feelings after a trusting relationship is established with a therapist. Total and immediate transparency is uncommon among clients of any ethnicity, and the individual's right to withhold painful material until ready to handle it is an important facet of an effective and trusting therapy relationship. The therapist must distinguish low self-disclosure associated with culture from low self-disclosure employed as a psychological defense or resistance.

Directive/Nondirective Styles of Therapy

It is common knowledge that clients differ in the degree to which they seek advice and direction from others; some clients are comfortable accepting advice from their therapists while others resent it. If the client's attitude about direction and advice is ignored, a power struggle between client and therapist may ensue, and communication will be hampered (Haley, 1963).

Several researchers suggest that Hispanics, particularly the poor, prefer therapists to communicate in a directive style (Abad et al., 1974; Torey, 1972). It has been observed that Puerto Ricans expect their physician to be active in a relationship with them and to offer advice, prescribe medication, and present tangible alternatives (Abad et al., 1974). Attitudes about therapy were elicited from a random sample of Mexican-Americans in Lubbock, Texas. Subjects were interviewed in Spanish or English, according to their preference, by a Mexican-American examiner. The vast majority of English-and Spanish-speaking subjects preferred a mental health professional to offer direct advice, to tell the client what was wrong with him, and to cheer up the client (Mack, James, Ramirez, & Bailey, 1974).

Behavior modification might be viewed as a directive approach in therapy and has been rated effective with Hispanics in several studies. For example, positive reinforcement and extinction were reported to be successful for modifying overall adjustment of drug addicts in an inpatient setting (Aron, et al., 1974).

Data is, however, also accruing which is not congruent with the thesis that Hispanics only prefer directive therapists. The client gain in directive group counseling, noninterventionist group counseling based on Rogers (1970), and no counseling control settings was compared with a sample of ninth- and tenth-grade Puerto Rican boys. Client gain was operationalized as increase in occupational aspiration, positive teacher ratings, gain in grade average, increased attendance at school, and decreased number of referrals to school administrators because of discipline problems. No significant difference in occupational aspiration or school behavior was noted across the three groups. The experimental subjects responded to a relationship questionnaire concerning their attitude about the group therapies. No significant difference in attitude about counseling was recorded for subjects in nonintervention and directive group counseling (Naun, 1971).

Recall Shofield's (1964) research about the YAVIS Syndrome which indicated that therapists prefer to work with young, attractive, verbal (basically middle class) clients. One can question whether Hispanics really want more directive therapy or if directive therapy is imposed by therapists. Directive therapy is swift and allows the therapist more time to work with preferred, middle class patients who are perceived as more amenable to insight therapy (Padilla, 1971).

Reviewing the preference for directive versus nondirective therapy among various cultural groups, Wallace (1970) explains that disillusioned groups favor control procedures such as confession, penance, and indoctrination. Secure groups prefer catharsis. Using Wallace's (1970) model, one can postulate that Hispanic clients prefer directive therapy when disillusioned about the possibility of changing external forces that precipitate stress. On the other hand, perhaps therapists are the "disillusioned," insecure group. Reliance on directive therapy by therapists working with Hispanic clients may reveal fear among these therapists about the behavior of Hispanics if they do not control them. At this point, it would seem premature to limit the mode of communication with Hispanics to the directive style. In many cases, intervention, advice, and reinforcement are appropriate; but research does not rule out Hispanics as good candidates for insight and nondirective approaches.

Initiating Therapy

The initial meeting is a powerful factor in establishing clients' trust in the therapist and in the therapeutic process (Hall & Lindzey, 1970). The therapist working with Hispanics must be cognizant of culturally specific factors to be successful in guiding a trusting relationship during the initial contact hours.

The therapist must be certain to pronounce clients' names correctly, making especially sure that both parts of a hyphenated name, such as Hernandez-Rodriguez, are included. For many Hispanics, especially Puerto Ricans, both mothers' and fathers' lineage constitute the family name (Christensen, 1975). For instance, in the case of Hernandez-Rodriguez, Hernandez is the last name of the father, while Rodriguez is the last name of the mother and is carried in respect for her and her family.

In essence, a warm and easy opening to therapy is one where *both* the client and therapist are at ease with each other. Pressure is not exerted for rapid disclosure and there is a mutual feeling of respect for each other.

CONCLUSION

I would like to conclude by asking "What will be the future direction of pluralistic therapy especially as it applies to Hispanics?" Ideally, the future will bring improvement and expansion in research and increased application of research to the delivery of pluralistic therapeutic services. With this, I would like to conclude with an overview of what I see as important directions in research and therapy.

Future research needs to focus on a number of unresolved issues in pluralistic therapy. More research is needed to determine the particular conditions conducive to directive and nondirective therapy. Research about the effect of therapist ethnicity on client gain is highly inconsistent (Cortese, 1979). Studies investigating this question should control a number of potential confounding variables, such as therapists' personality, sex, age, therapeutic modality; client's sex and age; and length of treatment. Moreover, means for measuring client gain must be sought. Another primary focus of research would be to increase the number of culturally revelant standardized and projective personality tests. The techniques for creating criterion-referenced and culture-fair tests are well established. We need to implement these procedures to develop tests of values, attitudes, and behavior appropriate to particular cultural groups.

Instead of assuming that therapeutic approaches are applicable to Hispanics, we must subject each tool and technique to a test of "cultural adaptiveness." We need to look at the way theories of personality and counseling interact with ethnicity. Are behavioral approaches more or less effective with Hispanics? Do Hispanics accept or reject humanistic counseling? Are individuals who desire advice and who are willing to assume responsibility for their own behavior similar or different in personality makeup across cultures? We need to investigate the dynamics of the counseling process across cultures. How do we establish rapport and project empathy and confidentiality across cultural groups? To what extent are empathy, positive regard, and genuineness universal traits of pluralistic therapy? Research about the effectiveness of various kinds of therapeutic leads (e.g., silence, reinstatement of ideas, reflection of feelings, reassurance, information giving,) with ethnic clients would be helpful.

We know that many individuals in need of help do not utilize mental health facilities. Research can offer possible explanations; and new proposals for increasing use by the target groups can be examined. Research about verbal and nonverbal communication styles in different cultures has been quite helpful in developing pluralistic therapy procedures. Continued research in this area will open new avenues for exploration in therapy.

As results of cross-cultural research are employed in clinics and by private professionals, pluralistic therapy will become increasingly effective. Ethnic minority clients will not be stigmatized or alienated by traditional majority group methods and techniques. Misunderstanding and confusion between counselor and client will decrease because of the counselor's knowledge of the client's preferred life style and world view. The intrusion of cultural stereotypes into the therapeutic process can be eliminated.

Hopefully, the future of pluralistic therapy will be not only the alleviation of human misery, but also the enhancement of human functioning. The highest priority should be given to preventive mental health. Study of Hispanic mental health reveals how prejudice, poverty, and marginality immobilize Hispanic-Americans with despair and defiance. In the future, pluralistic therapy should involve further redirection away from one-to-one therapy toward crisis intervention and social action. Some pluralistic therapists need to become involved in establishing local and national policies that foster mental health of ethnic minority groups. Needed are policies strengthening family and neighborhood life, accurate historical education about ethnic minority groups, public institutions recognizing the diversity of the American people, and educational programs designed to facilitate intergroup relations.

REFERENCES

Abad, V., Ramos, J., & Boyce, E. A model for delivery of mental health services to Spanish-speaking minorities. *American Journal of Orthopsychiatry,* 1974, *44,* 584-595.

Acosta, F.X. Mexican-American and Anglo-American reactions to ethnically similar and dissimilar psychotherapists. In R. Alvarez (Ed.), *Delivery of services for Latino community mental health.* Los Angeles; Spanish-Speaking Mental Health Research and Development Program, 1975 (Monograph 2).

Acosta, F.X., & Sheehan, J.G. Psychotherapist ethnicity and expertise as determinants of self-disclosure. In M. Miranda (Ed.), *Psychotherapy for the Spanish-speaking.* Los Angeles: Spanish-Speaking Mental Health Research Center, 1976 (Monograph 3).

Aiello, J.R., & Jones, S.E. Field study of the proxemic behavior of young school children in three subcultural groups. *Journal of Personality and Social Psychology,* 1971, *19,* 351-356.

Aron, W.S., Alger, N., & Gonzales, R.T. Chicanoizing the therapeutic community. *Journal of Psychedelic Drugs,* 1974, *6,* 321-327.

Bachrach, L.L. *Utilization of state and county mental hospitals by Spanish Americans in 1972.* Rockville, Md.: National Institute of Mental Health, Division of Biometry, June 1975 (Statistical Note 116).

Baxter, J.C. Interpersonal spacing in natural settings. *Sociometry,* 1970, *33,* 444-456.

Boulette, T.R. Determining needs and appropriate counseling approaches for Mexican-American women: A comparison of therapeutic listening and behavioral rehearsal. (Doctoral dissertation, University of California) Ann Arbor, Mich.: University Microfilms, 1972. No. 73-19, 146.

Boulette, T.R. Assertive training with low income Mexican-American women, in M. Miranda (Ed.), *Psychotherapy for the Spanish-speaking.* Los Angeles: Spanish-Speaking Mental Health Research Center, 1976 (Monograph 3).

Boulette, T.R. Parenting: Special needs of low-income Spanish-surnamed families. Psychatric Annals, 1977, *6,* 95-107.

Burstein, A.G., & Kobos, J. Psychological testing as a device to foster social mobility. *American Psychologist,* 1971, *26,* 1041-1042.

Casas, J.M. Applicability of a behavioral model in serving the mental health needs of the Mexican-American. In M. Mirada (Ed.), *Psychotherapy for the spanish-speaking.* Los Angeles: Spanish-Speaking Mental Health Research Center, 1976 (Monograph 3).

Casavantes, E.J. *El tecato: Social and cultural factors affecting drug use among Chicanos.* Washington, D.C.: National Coalition of Spanish-Speaking Mental Health Organizations, 1976.

Christensen, E.W. Counseling Puerto Ricans: Some cultural considerations. *Personnel and Guidance Journal,* 1975, *53,* 349-356.

Christensen, E.W. When counseling Puerto Ricans. *Personnel and Guidance Journal* 1977, *55,* 412-415.

Ciaramella, V. A comparative study of ethnic versus dominant culture group counseling: An interaction process analysis. (Doctoral dissertation, Fordham University) Ann Arbor, Mich.: University Microfilms, 1973. No. 73-26, 707.

Clark, M., & Mendelson, M. Mexican-American aged in San Francisco: A case description. *Gerontologist,* 1969, *9,* 90-95

Cole, S.G., & Davenport, K. Reported friendliness toward Mexican-Americans as a function of belief similarity and race. Paper presented at the Midwestern Psychological Association, Chicago, May 1973.

Cortese, M. Intervention research with Hispanic Americans: A review. *Hispanic Journal of Behavioral Sciences,* 1979, *1,* 4-20.

Dashefsky, A. (Ed.) *Ethnic identity in society.* Chicago: Rand McNally, 1976.

de Armas, E. The "supersystem" and the Spanish-speaking elderly. In D.J. Curren (Ed.), *Proceedings of the Puerto Rican conferences on human services.* Washington, D.C.: National Coalition of Spanish-Speaking Mental Health Organizations, 1975.

Fitzpatrick, J.P. *Puerto Rican Americans: The meaning of migration to the mainland.* Englewood Cliffs, N.J.: Prentice-Hall, 1971.

Ganschow, L.H. Stimulating educational information-seeking and changes in student attitude toward vocational education by videotape and film presentations. Final Report. August, 1970. (ERIC Document Reproduction Service No. ED 043 778).

Gares, V.D. A comparative investigation of the occupational counseling given to Mexican-American and Anglo-American students upon entering the community college. (Doctoral dissertation, United States International University) Ann Arbor, Mich.: University Microfilms, 1974. No. 74-14, 313.

Greeley, A.M. *Why can't they be like us?* New York: Institute of Human Relations Press, 1969.

Haley, J. *Strategies of psychotherapy.* New York: Grune & Stratton, 1963.

Hall, E. *The silent language.* Garden City, N.Y.: Doubleday 1959.

Hall, C.S., & Lindzey, G. *Theories of personality.* (2nd ed.) New York: Wiley, 1970.

Hamilton, L.S. *An experimental study of the effectiveness of small group discussions in facilitating interethnic group communication and understanding.* Unpublished doctoral dissertation, New Mexico State University, 1969.

Haven, B.J. An investigation of activity patterns and adjustment in an aging population. *Gerontologist,* 1968, *8,* 201-206.

Herrera, A.E., & Sanchez, V.C. Behaviorally oriented group therapy: A successful application in the treatment of low income Spanish-speaking clients. In M. Miranda (Ed.), *Psychotherapy for the Spanish-speaking.* Los Angeles: Spanish-speaking Mental Health Research Center, 1976 (Monograph 3).

Hinedelang, M.J. Educational and occupational aspirations among working class Negro, Mexican-American and white elementary school children. *Journal of Negro Education,* 1970, *39,* 351-353.

Johnson, D.L., Leler, H., Rios, L., Brandt, L., Kahn, A.J., Mazeika, E., Frede, M. & Bisett, B. The Houston parent-child development center: A parent education program for Mexican-American families. *American Journal of Orthopsychiatry,* 1974, *44,* 121-128.

Jones, S.E. A comparative proxemics analysis of dyadic interaction in selected subcultures of New York City. *Journal of Social Psychology,* 1971, *84,* 35-44.

Jourard, S. *The transparent self.* New York: Van Nostrand, 1971.

Kasschau, P.L. Age and race discrimination reported by middle-aged and older persons. *Social Forces,* 1977, *55,* 728-742.

Klitgaard, G.C. A gap is bridged: Successful counseling of college potential Mexican-Americans. *Journal of Secondary Education,* 1969, *44,* 55-57.

Leo, P.F. The effects of two types of group counseling upon the academic achievement and self-concept of Mexican-American pupils in the elementary school. (Doctoral dissertation, University of the Pacific) Ann Arbor, Mich: University Microfilms, 1972, No. 72-25, 740.

LeVine, E.S., & Padilla, A.M. *Crossing cultures in therapy: Pluralistic counseling for the Hispanic.* Monterrey, CA.: Brooks/Cole, 1980.

Littlefield, R.P. An analysis of the self-disclosure patterns of ninth grade public school students in three selected subcultural groups. (Doctoral dissertation, Florida State University) Ann Arbor, Mich.: University Microfilms, 1969, No. 30 (2-A).

Mack, C.N., James, L.E., Ramirez, J., & Bailey, J. The attitudes of Mexican American "non-help seekers" regarding help for personal problems: A pilot study. Presented at the meeting of the Southwestern Psychological Association, El Paso, Texas, May 4, 1974.

Madsen, W. The alcoholic *agringado*. *American Anthropologist*, 1964, *66*, 355-361.

Maes, W.R. & Rinaldi, J.R. Counseling the Chicano child. *Elementary School Guidance and Counseling*, 1974, *8*, 279-284.

Maldonado, D., Jr. The Chicago aged. *Social Work*, 1975, *20*, 213-216.

Moore, J.W. Mexican-Americans. *Gerontologist*, 1971, *2*, 30-35.

Naun, R.J. Comparison of group counseling approaches with Puerto Rican boys in an inner city high school (Doctoral dissertation, Fordham University) Ann Arbor, Mich.: University Microfilms, 1971. No. 71-20, 200.

Padilla, A.M., Ruiz, R.A., & Alvarez, R. Community mental health services for the Spanish-speaking/surnamed population. *American Psychologist*, 1975, *30*, 892-905.

Padilla, E.R. The relationship between psychology and Chicanos: Failures and possibilities. In N. Wagner & M. Haug (Eds.), *Chicanos: Social and psychological perspectives*. St. Louis: C.V. Mosby, 1971.

Perry, L. Moral and mental health. In S. Plog & R. Edgerton (Eds.), *Emerging perceptives in mental health*. New York: Holt, Rinehart, & Winston, 1969.

Pettigrew, T.F. Ethnicity in American life: A social psychological perspective. In A. Dashefsky (Ed.), *Ethnic identity in society*. Chicago: Rand McNally, 1976.

Plata, M. Stability and change in the prestige ranking of occupants over 49 years. *Journal of Vocational Behavior*, 1975, *6*, 95-99.

Pollack, E., & Menacker, J. *Spanish-speaking students and guidance*. Boston: Houghton-Mifflin, 1971.

Ramirez, M., III. Towards cultural democracy in mental health: The case of the Mexican-American. *Interamerican Journal of Psychology*, 1972, *6*, 45-50.

Reynolds, D.K., & Kalish, R.A. Anticipation of futurity as a function of ethnicity and age. *Journal of Geronotology*, 1974, *29*, 224-234.

Rivera, F. Motivation factors in treating Puerto Rican addicts. In D.J. Curren (Ed.), *Proceedings of the Puerto Rican conference on human services*. Washington, D.C.: National Coalition of Spanish-Speaking Mental Health Organizations, 1975.

Rogers, C.R. *Carl Rogers on encounter groups*. New York: Harper & Row, 1970.

Rueveni, U. Using sensitivity training with junior high school students. *Children*, 1971, *18*, 69-72.

Ruiz, A.S. Chicano group catalysts. *Personnel and Guidance Journal*, 1975, *53*, 462-466.

Scott, N.R., Orzen, W., Musillo, C., & Cole, P. Methadone in the Southwest: A three-year follow-up of Chicano heroine addicts. *American Journal of Orthopsychiatry*, 1973, *43*, 355-361.

Shofield, W *Psychotherapy: The purchase of friendship*. Englewood Cliffs, N.J.: Prentice-Hall, 1964.

Stone, P.C., & Ruiz, R.A. Race and class as differential determinants of underachievement and underaspiration among Mexican-Americans. *Journal of Educational Research*, 1974, *68*, 99-101.

Stonequist, E.V. *The marginal man: A study in personality and culture conflict*. New York: Russell & Russell, 1937.

Torrey, E.F. *The mind game: Witchdoctors and psychiatrists*. New York: Emerson Hall, 1972.

U.S. Bureau of the Census. Persons of Spanish origin in the United States: March, 1976 (Current Population Report, Series P-20, No. 310). Washington D.C.: U.S. Government Printing Office, 1977.

Walker, J.R., & Hamilton, L.S. A Chicano/black/white encounter. *The Personnel and Guidance Journal,* 1973, *51,* 471-477.

Wallace, A.F.C. *Culture and personality.* (2nd ed.) New York: Random House, 1970.

Chapter 10
Counseling and Psychotherapy with Japanese Americans
Harry H.L. Kitano

There is a current stereotype which labels the Japanese American as a "model American minority" (Kitano & Sue, 1973). The notion that a non-white immigrant group can be viewed as "successful" is an intriguing one, and provides a source of comfort to those who identify with the Horatio Alger tradition. The label is even more startling in light of the historical background of the Japanese in the United States — first an unwanted pariah group faced with systematic prejudice and discrimination, followed by a forced, mass evacuation into "America's concentration camps" (Daniels, 1971), then the recovery process leading to the present-day image. Or, as Ogawa (1971) writes, "From Japs to Japanese."

There appear to be a number of reasons behind the "success" stereotype. One factor is the desire on the part of the dominant group to point out to other struggling groups, and to the world at large, that American racism is not a completely closed system. Another is to provide a possible model for other nonwhite groups, with the inferred message, "you too can overcome some of the hardships and handicaps through working hard for acceptance and ignoring confrontation tactics." Less "successful" minorities are counseled to study the adaptive patterns of the Japanese, with the implication that a less obstreperous approach may be more helpful. But, as Katano (1976) writes, "measures of success not only are temporary, but ultimately based on value judgements, so what is success, based on one criterion, may not be so, based on another [preface]."

The success stereotype has also found its way into mental health, counseling, and thereapy circles. Here, the image is that of a group with few problems. There is assumed a strong family and community system with their ability to step in and take over when problems arise. The evidence that so few Japanese show up for mental health services is often interpreted as validating the impression of a group with few problems.

The evidence of the lack of use can be interpreted as a sign of good mental health, but there are also a number of other plausible interpretations why Japanese Americans are seldom seen in professional counseling services. The purpose of this chapter is to present a point of view that interprets the lack of use as a function of the inappropriateness of the current mental health delivery systems (Miranda & Kitano, 1976). By inappropriate, the reference is to the lack of knowledge, to the training, the personnel, and the therapeutic models which appear designed to serve the needs of groups other than the Japanese American. The expectation is to sensitize readers to the needs and cultural styles of this population so that current education, training, and services can be evaluated and modified.

The presentation will include: a) a brief historical background emphasizing generational stratification; b) problems of role identity in the context of Japanese American goals in the American society and the barriers that have limited goal attainment; and c) an analysis of the Japanese "culture" and the effects of acculturation. Finally, we will explore some therapeutic models which may be appropriate to Japanese Americans and some problems of evaluation.

DEMOGRAPHIC DATA

The 1970 Census showed that the great majority of the 588,324 Japanese Americans resided in California (213,277) and Hawaii (217,175). Other states with Japanese included New York (19,794) and Illinois (17,645). The heaviest concentration was in Hawaii where they made up about 27 percent of the population.

A summary picture of the group drawn from the 1970 Census is as follows: The median age was 29.5 years for males and 33.2 for females. More than 68.8 percent were high school graduates, and the rate of separation and divorce was 4 percent for the male and 6 percent for the female. The mean family income (male head) was $13,511. Seven and one-half percent had incomes below the poverty level, with the perponderance of low incomes in the 65 years and older category.

Generally, the Japanese ranked among the highest of all nonwhite minority groups in terms of educational achievement, income, and employment. However, much of their family income was based on the employment of more than one individual, and whites with the same education had higher incomes (Wong, 1974). Nevertheless, the demographic data does support the notion of a reasonably successful minority group in terms of education, employment, and income, especially when taken in the context of their historical past.

HISTORICAL BACKGROUND

The significant immigration of the Japanese to the United States occurred between 1890 and 1924. The passage of the 1924 immigration law effectively closed the door to Japanese immigrants (also to other Asians) until well after World War II.

The first immigrants were relatively homogeneous; they were generally young males from a rural Japanese background, with four to six years of formal education. They were soon joined by what has been termed "picture brides" because many of the couples had never seen each other except through photographs. It should be noted that very few of these marriages ended in divorce, which suggests that longer-lasting relationships can be built on variables other than love (Kitano, 1976). This group is called the Issei, or first generation Japanese immigrant, and conjures an image of "Meiji Japan," with certain values and ways of looking at the world which will be further discussed in the section on Japanese culture.

This group can also be called the "sacrificial generation," since many of them assumed that they themselves would never be able to "make it" in the American society so that their hopes and expectations lay with their Nisei, or second generation American-born children. The Issei generation is a dying one; those who survive are well into senior citizens status. The chances of any mental health professional working with this group are almost nil, although social workers and psychologists working in homes for the elderly may have extensive contact with them. They are apt to deal with "Issei" problems which are typical of an aging population, exacerbated by the Japanese values of ga-man (repression), enryo (deferential behavior, especially to those in authority), and language difficulties. Most are not used to prolonged verbal discussions concerning self, and many Issei residing in old people's homes are apt to feel deserted by their children. Conversely, feelings of guilt may be very strong among the Nisei for not caring for their parents in their own homes.

The Nisei were born between 1900 and about 1941. Most followed a model of acculturation with minimal interest in their Japanese cultural heritage. They acquired American ways — dress, language, mannerisms, organizations — although the critical variable of physical amalgamation eluded them so that most were Americans with Japanese faces.

The wartime evacuation (1942-45) disrupted the Japanese community. Homes and businesses were lost as the 110,000 Japanese residing along the West Coast were incarcerated in camps in Utah, Idaho, Wyoming, Arizona, Arkansas, and California. Many Nisei spent their adolescent, growing-up years behind barbed wire — older brothers fought for the U.S. Army, while selected others were able to "relocate" to cities in the midwest and the east.

The relocation broke up the ethnic west coast "ghettos" and affected family life. Government control became paramount so that "camp norms" took over. For example, "mess hall behavior" meant standing in long lines for food to be served in a central facility; food to be served impersonally on partitioned trays; eating with peers; gulping down food quickly for a chance at a possible second helping; picking at certain foods and leaving other foods untouched. These norms were in sharp contrast to family norms.

It is probably impossible to evaluate the effects of the mass incarceration on the Japanese American other than to assume that, if scars remain, they will remain hidden. Part of the reason for the lack of information is a common Japanese style of handling problems through internalization and their view of fate which encourages an "it can't be helped" orientation (shikata ga-nai). Friendships made during this era remain strong — Nisei who went through this experience will often use the "which camp were you in?" approach to greet fellow Nisei. Japanese Americans, especially from Hawaii, also served in the armed forces in the 100th Battalion and 442nd Combat Team which compiled impressive combat records. There is often much more than nostalgia associated with these groups—there are friendships and social networks where experiences and values are shared and reinforced.

The Nisei are now the parents of the college-age and over generation; many have achieved a middle-class status through their ability to do well in school and to work hard. The Nisei are a group that appears ripe for counseling; many have achieved a degree of affluence and independent means, have adequate education, and are conversant in English. They face problems of communication with older and younger generations; they have questions about acculturation, about bicultural orientation, and about cultural and ethnic identity; are often caught in the middle between white and black groups; and are experiencing the stresses that face all American families. Many have problems dealing with their "liberated children" (or for husbands, dealing with their "liberated wives"); one common issue is that of interethnic and interracial marriage. Some complain that the threat of banishment from the family is not as effective on their children and grandchildren as it was on themselves. Therefore, there are problems of communication, intergenerational misunderstandings, culture clash, and ethnic identity. Yet, very few Nisei go for professional counseling. Part of the problem no doubt lies in facets of the Nisei culture which hinder the use of professional counselors. But it may also be that counselors *do not understand,* and are therefore, ill-equipped to deal with these Nisei problems. At this stage, we hypothesize that an appropriate technique for helping this group will fall under the rubric of "education," rather than "counseling" or "therapy." Knowledge, information, and the awareness that there are professionals who can be helpful may have to be developed before counseling and therapeutic services are used.

The Sansei, or third generation, provide the majority of the current young adult population, while the Yonsei (fourth generation) can now be found entering the elementary grades. The great majority of these generations are American in terms of language, mannerisms, values, behavior, and attitudes; and their primary source of identification with their Japanese background lies in their physical identification. High rates of outmarriage for the Sansei (Kikumura & Kitano, 1973) indicate a process of assimilation and amalgamation which comes as somewhat of a surprise, given the historical background of discrimination and racism faced by the Japanese, and the early claims about their "unassimilability" (Kitano, 1976).

Other groups of Japanese in the United States include the Kibei, technically Nisei, but who were sent to Japan for early childhood training and education. This practice was most common in the 1930s so that the Kibei were exposed to the nationalism that was a part of Japanese education during that period. Many returned to their families in the United States with strong Japanese identifications. There is some evidence that the Kibei may not have found the level of employment of their Nisei peers, partly because of the years spent in Japan (Shiozaki & Shibusawa, 1977).

There are also new Issei who entered the United States after 1954 as a result of the change in immigration laws, including an estimated 25,000 war brides. There are also Japanese businessmen (*kai-sha*) and students, most on a temporary basis but bringing with them a number of problems that can be aided by counseling. Questions of immigration rules and procedures, of coping with loneliness and alienation, of establishing meaningful relationships, and of dealing with "culture shock" are problems that appear appropriate for professional counseling. The children and families of Japanese businessmen with a sojourner's orientation are another group that can use special consideration.

In summary, we have presented a broad picture of one type of stratification in the Japanese community. An identification of the different groups is important since they represent different experiences, perceptions, values, and behavioral orientations. In addition, there are other differences based on social class, goals, personality, and differential acculturation so that we are talking about many different individuals who have only one thing in common: their Japanese ancestry. However, this physical identifiability is important in shaping an ethnic identity.

PROBLEMS OF IDENTITY

The problem of an ethnic identity in a pluralistic society is a constant one. For the Japanese American, there are two major role definitions; one prescribed by the majority group, the other by the ethnic family and community. All physically identifiable groups face these definitions daily, especially where the "mark of race" categorizes a "less than equal status." This variable is shaped by experiences — it marks where one belongs, how high one dreams and expects of acceptability and of rejection, and is an "umbrella identity" in that it overshadows other identities. Perhaps it is the lack of sensitivity of majority group counselors to this variable that "turns off" many ethnics to standard counselors.

The factor of an ethnic identity in a pluralistic society is appropriate in a model developed by Newman (1976). His model (table 10.1), adapted for the Japanese American, includes: (a) the Japanese American's response to majority group definitions of his or her role; (b) the Japanese American's response to the definitions of his or her role prescribed by the Japanese family and community; (c) the compatability or incompatability of the role, or role conflict; and (d) the techniques to resolve the possible role conflicts.

Situation I

Although the meaning of being a Japanese American may differ between the two communities, the individual enjoys and accepts both of the definitions based on his or her ethnicity. Therefore, there is no basic conflict with being an American Japanese or a Japanese American so that there is a high degree of role compliance. It should be emphasized that, for most of their history, the Japanese seldom enjoyed positive role definitions from the majority community (i.e., sly, sneaky, tricky, unassimilable).

Those in the counseling professions should be especially aware of the power of majority group definitions concerning minorities. The usual sources of information (such as movies, television, and the mass media) generally reinforce ethnic stereotypes so that it would be difficult for a majority group counselor not to have preconceived notions unless he or she has developed a degree of intimate contact with Japanese Americans. How a counselor overcomes these stereotypes and helps a pariah group individual to develop a healthy self-concept and an appropriate role identity remains a problem.

Situation 1 (in table 10.1) approaches an ideal in that there is little role conflict in identifying with the role definitions of the two systems. For example, at the present time, being identified as a Japanese may be helpful in certain fields such as engineering, medicine, pharmacy, gardening, agriculture, and the secretarial field. There are other fields where a Japanese identity may serve as a handicap, such as in show business, public relations, the performing arts, and politics (in selected areas). The ideal is reached when the individual has a maximum number of voluntary choices and opportunities in all fields (including intimate social, business, and power contacts), without regard to his or her race and identity. The question of "Who am I" as a common theme of Japanese American conferences, seminars, and discussions, whether of the first, second, third, or fourth generations, indicates that Situation 1 remains an elusive goal.

Situation 2

Situation 2 is where the majority group definition of the Japanese is primarily negative (i.e., "Mr. Watanabe is only good as a gardener or laborer"), but where the ethnic role definition is perceived as positive (i.e., "Mr. Watanabe is an able and well-respected community leader"). It is a situation of role conflict since one identification is negative and the other is positive.

Several adaptations are possible under these conditions. One is for the individual to withdraw completely into the ethnic community and to live a segregated life. Many Issei either preferred or were forced into this choice so

Table 10.1. Role Choices and Pluralistic Identities for the Japanese American Individual's Response Individual's Repose

Situation	to Majority Group Role Definition	to Japanese Group Group Role Definition	Role Situation	Role Technique
1	+	+	Compability	Compliance
2	—	+	Role Conflict	Role Distance or Change
3	+	—	Role Conflict	Role Distance or Change
4	—	—	Multiple Role Conflict	Rejection & Role Change

Source: Newman, W. Multiple realities: The effects of social pluralism on identity. In Arnold Sashefskys (Ed.), *Ethnic identity in society*. Chicago: Rand McNally, 1976, p. 41.

that contact with the white world was minimal.

Nisei and Sansei, because of their exposure to the American system, did not withdraw as readily into an all ethnic world, even if the majority group definitions remained as negative and stereotypical as with the Issei. One possible adaptation under this condition is to employ "role distance," whereby the individual performs the role prescribed by the dominant community, even though it is not consistent with one's self-image. The individual retains a perceptual distance between self and the prescribed role when dealing with the majority community. There may be an exaggerated politeness ("so sorry, please"), a passive conformity and playing out of stereotyped role ("all of us are good at gardening") as a means of handling the majority group definition. Terms such as "playing up to whitey," "jiving and gaming," "dealing with the *goyim*," and putting up with the "dumb Haole" indicate role distance as used by various minorities to deal with the situation. There are occasions when the individual gets tired of "playing the game" and retreats into the ethnic community. There may be movements toward separatism, pluralism, or some other system where the individual can limit role conflict and develop healthier definitions of self.

It is a point of interest to note that the wartime evacuation of the Japanese set up a separatist structure. There were some Japanese who termed this period a "vacation from acculturation"; the implication was that they did not have to interact daily with Caucasians and, therefore, did not have to play the prescribed Japanese to Caucasian role as much (Kitano, 1976). The tragedy was that it was a forced and not a voluntary choice.

It is our belief that very few Japanese Americans under Situation 2 will turn to professional counseling, unless the agencies are a part of the ethnic community. The large number of Japanese clients who used the services of the social worker provided by the Japanese Chamber of Commerce in contrast to the non-use of dominant community agencies (Kitano, 1969) is an indication of this orientation. Those who do show up for professional counseling may be difficult clients because of the role distance. It would take a sensitive counselor to differentiate between an exaggerated politeness as a form of normal deferential behavior, and one based on hostility and role conflict.

Situation 3

In Situation 3, the individual accepts the majority group definition of his or her role while rejecting the definitions of the ethnic family and community. This was a common model among European immigrants, whereby rapid Americanization was achieved, often with rejection of the ethnic and "root" culture. The Nisei adaptation was often under this category with a strong attempt to identify with the Anglo community and its values, norms, and lifestyles. The basic hindrance to total "success" was physical identifiability, which was related to prejudice, discrimination, and less-than-equal status. Name changes and altering of physical features have historically been used by other groups caught in this situation of role conflict but were not that much used by the Japanese Americans. Terms such as *Uncle Tom* and *oreo* are black terms to describe this adaptation; and the term "banana" has been used by Japanese Americans (i.e., "Senator Hayakawa is a big banana") for those who may look Japanese or yellow on the outside, but are really white on the inside.

Japanese Americans under this orientation are more likely to show up for professional counseling and therapy than under any other situation. Yamamoto (1968) presents the case of Kimiko Marjorie caught in a crisis of the dual identities. Kimiko represents the Japanese identity as exemplified by her parents, the Japanese culture, and the choice of a marital partner of Japanese ancestry. Marjorie represents the desired American identity; Kimiko's choice was to reject Japanese boys and the ways of her parents by becoming Marjorie and dating an American boyfriend. As Yamamoto writes, Kimiko Marjorie was an example of an adolescent with a negative identity where the disadvantage of being a minority group member led to conflict.

The individual in this situation may also use role distance, but this time from the ethnic community and culture. He or she may learn a few Japanese phrases, be superfically conversant with the language and culture, and may even participate in a few ethnic ceremonies and celebrations. But he or she may resent being "forced" into a Japanese identity and retain a role distance.

The counselor who is too knowledgeable about the Japanese culture and comes across as "too ethnic" will have problems with Japanese Americans in Situation 3. Resistance in the form of dropping out or in the form of rationalizations and hostility will be possible outcomes. There may be a preference for a nonethnic counselor.

Situation 4

In Situation 4, the Japanese American finds little satisfaction and identity with the definitions of either the majority or the ethnic community. There are at least three adaptations under this position of multiple role conflict. One is to withdraw physically from the situation and to find a role in another culture. Sometimes the person might go to live in Japan. This was especially common among disillusioned Nisei prior to World War II, and is also seen among some Sansei and Yonsei. Another possibility is to identify with deviant norms and to join counterculture groups, mystical or religious sects, or delinquent cultures. The third possibility is to try to change the role definitions through new definitions of ethnicity, or to attack or embarass the system which has created the problem.

The Newman model is important because it helps to focus on the problem of an ethnic identity in a pluralistic and racially based society. It would be interesting to note how counselors perceive this model of ethnic identity. Until such time that physical identifiability is no longer an important factor in an identity, the model will have validity.

Japanese American identity will differ under different conditions. On the mainland, the question will be how they feel in a white dominated world; in Hawaii, how they feel in a Japanese American dominated system; and in Japan, to a Japanese dominated world. Very little research has been conducted in terms of these different situations.

THE JAPANESE CULTURE AND ACCULTURATION

It is important to emphasize the *difference* between Japanese culture and the Japanese American culture. A study of the culture of Japan, especially that of the Meiji era (1868-1912), is relevant for understanding some of the values brought over by the Issei from Japan; but the important factor has been the interaction of the Issei with the American system and the adaptations that have occurred. Greeley (1974) used the term ethnogenesis, which refers to acculturation in terms of the immigrant culture, the American culture, and most important, the product of the *interaction* between the two. There are many writings on the Japanese culture and the American culture, but very few studies have focused on the interaction. It is this interaction which makes for the differences between the Japanese in Hawaii (Ogawa, 1973) and the Japanese on the mainland (Kitano 1976), and also the commonalities between them.

A summary of some of the main psychological and behavioral orientations of the Meiji Japanese in contrast to basic American orientations is available from Connor (1977) and Kitano (1976). The Japanese system encourages collectivity, whereas the Americans prefer individuality; the Japanese emphasize duty and obligation, the Americans, will and freedom; the Japanese recognize hierarchial orders and dependency, while Americans rely on self, egalitarianism, and independence.

There are several terms which are important in understanding Japanese behavior such as *amae* (acknowledgement of dependency), *on* (ascribed obligation), *giri* (contractual obligation), *chu* (loyalty to one's superior), and *enryo* (modesty in the presence of one's superior). Many Japanese behavioral norms are based on a hierarchical structure so that prescribed norms for behavior include attitudes and interactive styles for those both above and below in terms of a status hierarchy. Other factors include a situational orientation (rather than one based on absolutes and universals); a preference for indirection (rather than direct confrontation); remaining less visible in public through conformity; giving priority to "means" (the process and etiquette of actions) over ends (the final product); and a hard work, high achievement (especially in education) orientation (Kitano, 1976, 120-136).

One hypothesized outcome of the Japanese system which includes the hierarchial structure, the cohesive family, and the ethnic community is that of "a child who is obedient, who relies on others, who recognizes, defers, respects and is polite to those in authority, who submerges individual wishes, needs and desires; who is generally non-aggressive; who obeys rules and can live in a world of restrictions and regulations." (Kitano & Kawakami, in press). However, the interaction between the Japanese and American culture may turn out to have many modifications from these projections.

Nakao and Lum (1977) surveyed the attitudes of 70 Asian American social workers in Los Angeles concerning the use of differential counseling techniques between Japanese and Caucasian clients. The respondents indicated that they would treat Japanese American clients differently from Caucasian clients by being more formal and less confrontal. They would also stay away from group sessions with the Japanese and would be quite careful in conveying the worker's credentials and knowledge.

Several other generalizations are drawn from discussions with professional counselors at the Asian American Counseling Center in Los Angeles. One general counseling technique deals with indirection, and the ability of the counselor to wait patiently while the client charts a circuitous route before talking about the problem. The indirect styles of communication are preferred modes for the Issei and older Nisei; a Sansei problem is related to separation and dependency. The norms for children leaving and living away from home are not clearly established among Japanese Americans so that breaking away becomes a problem.

Johnson and Marsella (1978) compared Caucasian and Japanese American college students and their attitudes toward verbal behavior. The Japanese Americans were concerned about male dominance, female subordination, and the propriety of conversation. For example, Japanese American girls showed concern about interrupting conversations, while it was considered to be shameful for boys to "show off" or to talk to get attention in class. The Caucasian sample endorsed aggressiveness, assertiveness, and egalitarian speech norms.

A special problem is that of newly arrived Japanese families and the experiences of their children in schools. The problem is often that of encouraging these children to speak up in classrooms. The question of cultural styles for the future is brought up since many of these children will return to Japan with their parents (often businessmen) and enroll in Japanese schools where speaking up may be discouraged.

Another problem is that of severe mental illness and the difficulty of getting Japanese American families to accept this diagnosis and to go for treatment. The current practice of discouraging hospitalization and leaving the ethnic community to take care of its own may not be the most helpful because the afflicted individual may very well end up in a closed, isolated room with moral pronouncements ("don't be lazy," "if you'll only try you'll get better") as the primary means of treatment.

JAPANESE THERAPEUTIC MODELS
AND TECHNIQUES

Until such time that therapeutic models based on the interaction between the two cultures can be developed, it is important to describe some Japanese models, since it is assumed that the audience is well aware of American models.

One interesting theoretical paper dealing with the mother-child relationship in Japan has been titled the "Ajase Complex" by Okonogi (1978). The term was developed by a pioneering Japanese psychoanalyst Kosawa (1897-1968), based on a figure who appeared in Buddhist scriptures. The basic theme is of strong mother-child ties, disillusionment by the child of the idealized mother image turning to hatred, guilt by the child since the mother remains the only one who stands by and is supportive under negative conditions, then a recovered sense of unity between mother and child. Hatred and guilt are all forgiven as the child returns to the mother. Okonogi contrasts the theme of forgiveness (when the child returns to mother) to the more punitive orientation of European psychology. For example, after the massacre at Lodz airport by a group of Japanese fanatics, the European press called for immediate punishment for the murderers. The Japanese position was one of forgiveness for the transgressors, provided they be returned to the motherland. The Ajase complex may be a more fundamental aspect of the Japanese culture than the more widely known Freudian Oedipal.

Morita therapy and Naikan therapy are two of the better known Japanese therapeutic systems. Miura and Usa (1974) describe Morita therapy as a "psychotherapy of neurosis" while Murase (1974) sees Naikan as a form a "guided introspection directed towards attitude and personality change [p. 431]." Both of the therapies are Japanese in origin and reflect their cultural stream which includes Buddhist and Confucian ideas.

Pedersen (1979) writes that Morita therapy emphasizes the acceptance of phenomenological reality as it is, rather than the "more Western notion of rationalistic idealism, wherein objective reality must be brought in line with the patient's needs and desires [p. 384]."

Naikan therapy focuses on the people who have molded the patient's life in the past with special emphasis on the mother. With the guidance of the "sensei" (teacher), the individual gains a better understanding of his or her relationship with these significant others and acknowledges his or her deep indebtedness. In the process, therapeutic gain can be observed as the individual becomes more sympathetic to the views of these others including the trouble he or she has "given to others" (Murase, 1974, p. 432).

Pedersen (1979, p. 384) mentioned that both of these techniques are indebted for their origin to Zen Buddhism, which emphasizes a nondualism and opposes a subject-object distinction. Zen teaches that both self and non-self are unified in the totality of existence.

It is difficult to evaluate the "effectiveness" of either of these therapies (as with most therapies) since very little research evidence is presented. The cross-cultural factor may provide further difficulties in evaluation since goals and objectives may be phrased, viewed, and operationalized differently.

ARE JAPANESE MODELS APPROPRIATE?

If one were to ask the question, "Are Japanese therapeutic models appropriate for Japanese Americans?" the overall answer would have to be a general "no," but with reservations. The Japanese therapies take place in a local context, within a local situation, and within the context of a specific culture so that, unless conditions for the Japanese in the United States are similar, the models may be less than appropriate. However, if someone were to ask, "Are therapeutic systems developed for Europeans appropriate for Japanese Americans?" the overall answer would also have to be a general "no."

For example, the problems of ethnic identity faced by Japanese Americans will find partial relevance drawing on knowledge of the Japanese culture. There may also be some ideas drawn from American therapeutic systems, but the primary theoretical and practical work remains to be done. The theoretical work contrasting and combining the two cultures is at a very primitive stage. When I first became interested in the relationship between the Japanese and American cultures and their interaction as examplified by the Japanese in America, the only theoretical statement I can remember was that of Caudill who noted the compatability, not the similarity of Japanese and American values. I'm afraid that we haven't progressed too much further in attempting to understand the interaction, although by now there are almost complete catalogs of different value, attitudinal, and behavioral differences between the two systems.

Our theoretical perspectives have been unable to handle much more than to be bewildered and to express surprise when dealing with Japan and its competitiveness with the Western world (and as a logical extension, the Japanese American). Perhaps it is the myopia that affects most Westerners when they deal with people from non-European cultures, for there is a tendency to look for the unique, the isolated, and the exotic, especially when these factors are so readily observable among the Japanese. But an understanding of an entire culture cannot be built on those variables, just as an understanding of the American culture cannot be based on perceiving some of the exotic practices seen in Los Angeles, although these also receive wide publicity and are readily observable; for an analysis of the dependent variables shows a high degree of similarity between the Japanese and the Western World including productivity, a work ethic, legality, competitiveness, literacy, and a comprehensive educational system. It is time to rethink and reformulate our theories and models to understand these phenomena better.

Our main hope is that material on the Japanese (and other Asians), their psychology, and their therapeutic models will be given equal exposure in the curriculum to that given to American and European writers. Until such time, it may be appropriate to label our current models as "Made in Europe" or "Made in America" and remember that these areas represent less than half the world.

REFERENCES

Connor, J., *Tradition and change in three generations of Japanese Americans.* Chicago: Nelson Hall, 1977.

Daniels, R. *Concentration camps, U.S.A.,* New York: Harper & Row, 1971.

Doi, T. Amae: A Key Concept for Understanding Japanese Personality Structure. In T. and W. Lebra, (Eds.) *Japanese Culture and Behavior.* Honolulu: University of Hawaii Press, 1974.

Greeley, A. *Ethnicity in the United States, New York: Wiley, 1974.*

Johnson, F., and Marsella, A. Differential attitudes toward verbal behavior in students of Japanese and European ancestry. *Genetic Psychology, Monographs,* 1978, *97,* 43-76.

Kikumura, A. & Kitano, H. Interracial marriage: A picture of the Japanese Americans. *The Journal of Social Issues,* 1973, *29*(2) 67-81.

Kitano, H. Japanese American mental illness. In S. Plog & R. Edgerton, *Changing Perspectives on mental illness.* New York: Holt, Rinehart, & Winston, 1969.

Kitano, H. *Japanese Americans.* Englewood Cliffs, N.J.: Prentice-Hall 1976.

Kitano, H. Mental Health in the Japanese American Community, In S. Korchin (Ed.). *Minority mental health,* New York: Holt, Rinehart & Winston (in process).

Kitano, H., Kawakami, C. Japanese Americans. In Julie Chan (Ed.), *Understanding and working with Asian students in the classroom.* New York: Charles Merrill (in press).

Kitano, H., and Sue, S. The model minorities. *The Journal of Social Issues,* 1973, *29* (2), 1-9.

Miranda, M. & Kitano, H. Barriers to mental health: A Japanese and Mexican dilemma. in C. Hernandez, N. Wagner, & M. Haug (Eds.), *Chicano social and psychological perspectives.* (2nd ed.) St. Louis; Mo. C.V. Mosby, 1976.

Miura, M., and Usa, A psychotherapy of neuroses: Morita therapy. In T. Lebra and W. Lebra (Eds.), *Japanese culture and behavior.* Honolulu: University of Hawaii Press, 1974.

Murase, T. Naikan Therapy. In T. Lebra and W. Lebra, (Eds.) *Japanese Culture and Behavior.* Honolulu: University of Hawaii Press, 1974.

Nakao, S., and Lum, C. *Yellow is not white and white is not right: Counseling techniques for Japanese and Chinese clients,* Unpublished master's theses, University of California, Los Angeles, 1977.

Newman, W. Multiple realities: The effects of social pluralism on identity. *In A. Sashefskys* (Ed.), *Ethnic identity in society.* Chicago: Rand McNally, 1976.

Ogawa, D., *From Japs to Japanese: The evolution of Japanese American stereotypes.* Berkeley: McCutchan, 1971.

Ogawa, D. *Jan Ken Po.* Honolulu: Japanese Chamber of Commerce, 1973.

Okano, Y., Japanese Americans and mental health. Los Angeles: Coalition for Mental Health (pamphlet), 1977.

Okonogi, K., "The Ajase Complex of the Japanese," *Japan Echo,* 1978, *5,* 88-105.

Pedersen, P. Alternative futures for cross-cultural counseling and psychotherapy, Paper presented at DISC Conference on Cross-cultural Counseling and Psychotherapy Foundations Evaluation and Training, Honolulu, June 12-19, 1979.

Shiozaki, L., and T. Shibusawa, *Kibei: The Untold Story.* MSW thesis, University of California: Los Angeles, 1977.

Wong, H.H., The relative economic status of Chinese, Japanese, black and white men in California. Unpublished Doctoral dissertation, University of California, Berkeley, 1974.

Yamamoto, Jr., "Japanese American Identity Crisis," In E. Brody *Minority Group Adolescence,* New York: Williams & Wilkins, 1968.

Chapter 11

Counseling and Psychotherapy with American Indians and Alaskan Natives

Norman G. Dinges
Joseph E. Trimble
Spero M. Manson
Frank L. Pasquale

INTRODUCTION

It is the primary goal of this chapter to place the theory and practice of counseling and psychotherapy with American Indians and Alaskan Natives in the context of programmatic mental health efforts.[1] In pursuing this goal, mental health programs will be discussed which are illustrative of the foundations, evaluation, and cultural themes of this volume. One section focuses on the collaboration of traditional Indian healers with Western-trained mental health practitioners. The second section provides an ethno-psychological analysis of the introduction of Western mental health principles and practices in an Indian culture. The third section describes the design and delivery of preventive mental health programs for isolated reservation families. The fourth section considers the evaluation of mental health training programs for Indians. The concluding section suggests a series of researchable questions, answers to which should provide much

---

[1] To conserve space, the term Indian will be used to apply to both American Indians and Native Alaskans in subsequent text.

needed insight into points of intersection as well as divergence which characterize the provision of counseling and psychotherapy to Indians.

It is by now common knowledge that mental health practitioners in the United States are currently serving a minor fraction of those identified as needing their services. Of this already statistically small group, a disproportionately smaller number are Indians. The reasons for underutilization of available mental health services for ethnic minorities have been analyzed previously and the explanations are reasonably plausible (e.g., Padilla & Ruiz, 1973; Torrey, 1970, 1972). These analyses, however, seem narrowly focused primarily on therapist and client variables and are of limited relevance to the concept of culture differences in a sociocultural context. There is a surprising lack of reference to other possible explanations for underutilization based on cultural boundary maintenance functions (e.g., Barth, 1969; Despres, 1975; Mitchell, 1974). There may be wisdom to the underutilization or nonutilization of alien mental health services, which is motivated by the desire to avoid erosion of the personal identity sustaining forces in the culture. From the standpoint of social ecology, there is justification for concern about the long–term consequences of making a service more attractive, if not more effective, at the cost of increased acculturative stresses to those served.

This is not to say that cultural and ethnic differences don't matter in counseling and psychotherapy, but, rather, to assert that such interactions may recapitulate the larger and, in the long run, more important cultural differences between Indian and other cultures. To the degree that Indian communities seek to maintain their cultural independence, while also wishing to enjoy the social and material rewards of contemporary society, Indians will continue to learn to manage their self-presentations to non-Indians. Negotiated identities will continue to serve worthwhile and socioculturally vital functions (e.g., Nagata, 1974; Vincent, 1974). Consequently, portrayals of the collective Indian personality, although useful in establishing dialogues that can lead to enhanced understanding, must be viewed as preliminary to more important awareness of contemporary Indian lifestyles. The reader is referred to already existing overviews of this type for an introduction (e.g., Trimble, 1976).

Some well-intentioned attempts to describe characteristics of the Indian client are so overgeneralized that it is possible to substitute the name of virtually any ethnic group in much of the text (e.g., Atkinson, Morten, & Sue, 1979). There are, already, too many stereotypes in the cross–cultural counseling literature (e.g., Navajo won't look you in the eye; Sioux aren't competitive) to mislead the non-Indian mental health practitioner. Minimal experience with either tribe would demonstrate the situational effects on eye contact or competitiveness and belie the collective personality absurdities.

Most aspiring mental health practitioners would be better left to overcome their ignorance through exposure and experience (resulting expertise not assumed as consequence of either) than to be falsely reassured by such blatant overgeneralizations. In support of this point, there is evidence (Tefft, 1967) that intertribal differences in values and attitudes are greater among Indians than between Indians and non-Indians.

Beyond asserting the general value differences between Indians and non-Indians, it must be recognized that Indians are a highly heterogeneous population. Census figures indicate that there are approximately two million Indians among over 250 federally recognized tribes, and at least nine distinct geocultural regions of the United States in which there are significant numbers of Indian peoples in urban, rural, and reservation settings. Trimble, Goddard, & Dinges (1977) provide a description of the richly varied lives of contemporary Indian peoples.

Recognition of the heterogeneity of Indians also suggests that it may be necessary to look beyond the individual in finding sources of therapeutic leverage. Moreover, attention and resources must be turned to the goals of preventive mental health so long as abuses of power exist, which create stresses among the poor and culturally different (Kessler & Albee, 1975). Otherwise, cross-cultural counseling and psychotherapy will continue to deal primarily with the casualties of the abuses of power, and an atypical few of those.

Irrespective of the sensitivity or effectiveness with which it is done, counseling and psychotherapy as currently practiced will very likely continue to be of limited significance for the overall emotional welfare of Indian peoples. This may be the most beneficial arrangement from the Indian standpoint. Limiting the role of the non-Indian mental health practicioner may be the most desirable course at this point, especially when different concepts of human psychology are introduced by counseling and psychotherapy, which, in turn, shape attributions for problems in a culturally erosive manner.

MENTAL HEALTH CARE DELIVERY TO INDIANS: SITUATIONAL CONSTRAINTS ON CROSS-CULTURAL COLLABORATION

The past importance of traditional healers among Indians is documented by a sizable literature (Ackernecht, 1943; Balikci, 1963; Jilek, 1971, 1974a,

1974b; Margetts, 1975; Murphy, 1964; Nieuwenhuis, 1924; Quinan, 1936; Straight, 1970; Torrey, 1970, 1972; Whiting, 1950). They have been alternatively labeled medicinemen, shamans, witchdoctors, native healers, or in indigenous terms such as *angakok* (Eskimo) and *wiscaca wakan* (Lakota). The nonacademic Western community has only recently become aware of its continuing role in present-day Indian mental health care (Bergman, 1973a, 1974; Sandner, 1978, 1979). Unfortunately, the prevailing view is more accurately represented by Michael Ansara's portrayal of Singing Rock, a fictional Sioux medicine man who joins Tony Curtis' supernatural battle with a *manitou* in a B-rated movie of the same title. As a context for the discussion to follow, it is instructive to consider the various ways in which the behavioral and medical sciences depict traditional Indian healers.

The image of traditional healers has gradually evolved from "crazy witchdoctors to auxiliary psychotherapists" (Jilek, 1971). Initially, they were thought to be mentally ill people whose cultures enable them to act out their particular psychopathologies in a prestigious role. More recently, they have been described as highly skilled therapists of sound mind and considerable acumen. This shift in perspectives engendered heated debate among social and medical scientists.

Outlining an argument about the cultural relativity of psychopathology, Kroeber (1948) unwittingly summarized the assumptions basic to the perception of traditional healers as "crazy witchdoctors":

> The primitive. . .recognizes, standardizes, rewards certain psychotic or neurotic experiences; the mentally unwell in modern advanced cultures tend to correspond to the well and the influential in ancient and retarded cultures [p. 300].

This view was offered repeatedly and, until the 1960s, characterized most treatments of traditional healers.

A wide range of psychopathology has been posited as the qualifying condition for their special status. Hambly (1926) suggested that the "primitive medicine man suffers primarily from a fear neurosis [p. 219]." *Angakok* trances were taken as evidence of clear "mental abnormality" (Weyer, 1962, p. 423), as an instance of arctic hysteria (Hambly, 1926, p. 237), and as self-induced hallucination (Jenness, 1922, p. 216). Devereux (1961) most vocally advocated viewing the traditional healer as "psychiatrically a genuinely ill person "(1961, p. 262). He sought to demonstrate that the Mohave healer is a fundamentally neurotic person," not unlike borderline psychotics in Western populations Devereux (1957, p. 1044). Devereux (1958) often referred to their "insanity" (1958, p. 364), and eventually came to see them as "outright psychotic" Devereux (1961, p. 285). Radin (1957) hypothesized that one must be "neurotic-epileptoid [p. 131]" to qualify as a traditional healer among the Eskimo. Boyer (1961, 1964a, 1964b), employing a psychoanalytic framework, identified impulsive and hysterical traits in a Mescalero Apache healer, and suspected latent homosexuality. Wissler (1931) was the least equivocal: all traditional Indian healers appeared to be "veritable idiots [p. 204]."

> What in shamanistic behavior may appear hysterical or psychotic to the Western psychiatrist is, to the people concerned, a time honored ritual through which practitioners heal sick people or divine the future. Hence, the "symptoms" of the shaman may in fact be the result of learning and practice [p. 351].

Opler (1936, 1946, 1959, 1961) seriously questioned Devereux's conclusions, noting that ethnographic data on Eastern Apache, Colorado Ute, and Southern Paiute healers do not significantly correlate with individual psychopathologies. Hallowell (1942, p. 13) reported his own inability to identify personality traits which distinguish traditional Salteaux healers from other members of their community. Discussing Northwest Coast tribes, Drucker (1965) categorically rejected the assumption that their healers are recruited on the basis of emotional instability. Similar observations were published about traditional healers among the western Nevada and eastern California Washo (Handelman, 1967). Coming full circle, Murphy (1964, p. 76) described Eskimo healers as "exceptionally healthy" and possessing a "high level of intelligence."

As one outcome of this changing image, United States mental health care delivery systems such as the Indian Health Service are exploring points of potential interface with the indigenous healing sciences. The first, tentative attempts suggest previously unanticipated barriers that require further investigation.

Indian Health Service

The Indian Health Service is the major federal agency charged with providing mental health care to Indians. In exchange for tribal lands surrendered under treaty agreements during the late 1800s and early 1900s, specific services—particularly health care and education—were guaranteed by the United States government. The War Department initially administered Indian health programs; this responsibility was later transferred to the Department of Interior's Bureau of Indian Affairs. Established in 1955 as a United States Public Health Service division, the Indian Health

Service currently provides both inpatient and outpatient care to more than 750 thousand Indians, urban and rural, through either direct or contracted services.

A mental health component was added to the Indian Health Service's primarily medical/surgical orientation, first as a demonstration project in 1965 on the Pine Ridge Reservation in South Dakota. Its early success prompted the establishment of a similar project for Alaskan Natives. Over the next five years, these two projects became a distinct program which rapidly grew in terms of service areas, staff, and budget.

Organizational structure The Mental Health Program is housed within an Indian Health Service-wide organization model. Certain structural features of the latter determine the former's shape as a delivery system.

Changing definitions in service populations have engendered a complicated array of eligibility criteria. Essentially, there are four types of Indian communities: 1) federally established reservations; 2) state established reservations (and reservations that have had specific responsibilities transferred from federal to state jurisdictional control); 3) off-reservation, rural tribal groups; and 4) urban organizations. The Indian Health Service was originally mandated to provide health care only to the first type of community: Indian persons residing on their respective federal reservations. All others were to be subsumed under state programs. The eligible service population eventually expanded to include people adjacent to federal reservations. As an artifact of earlier legal conditions, most Indian Health Service programs are located in states west of the Mississippi River, as are the vast majority of federally recognized reservations.

Administratively, the Indian Health Service is divided into eight areas in the United States. Each is administered by an area director, usually a physician, who in turn supervises a planning staff and chiefs of specialty services, e.g., medicine, nursing, environmental health, social service, and mental health. Care may be provided through hospitals, clinics, or health centers, referred to generally as service units. Local advisory boards, comprised of tribal representatives, monitor all aspects of the delivery program.

Traditional healers and Indian Health Service mental health professionals are most likely to interact at the service unit level. Clearly, their successful collaboration hinges, in part, upon the extent to which it is facilitated by the organizational structure. However, such collaboration also seems to be a function of a number of other factors: 1) one's sense of professional efficacy; 2) prior exposure to cross-cultural therapeutic practices; 3) the nature and means of personal introductions; 4) one's requirements for explanation; 5) patient involvement and expectations; and 6) community program support.

Past Collaborative Efforts

Successful collaboration between traditional healers and Indian Health Service mental health professionals has received considerable publicity. The Cornell-Navajo Field Health Research Project closely examined Navajo diagnostic and curative practices, attempted to identify the areas in which these practices are particularly effective, and elicited the views that traditional healers and Service professionals hold of one another (Adair & Deuschle, 1970; Deuschle and Adair, 1960; McDermott, Deuschle, Adair, Fulmer, & Loughlin, 1960). The former national chief of Mental Health Programs continued this interest, actively encouraging exchange between the two orientations (Bergman, 1971, 1973a, 1973b). Other collaborative efforts followed as a result of such emphasis. A number of Phoenix area service units established a policy that enabled traditional healers to serve and be reimbursed as medical consultants on a contract basis. An Eskimo village maintained a two-way referral system—without compensation—between Indian Health Service staff and traditional healers (Attneave, 1974). Yet, despite this success, *most* attempts to establish similar working relationships have ended in bitter failure. Recent examples provide some insight into the problem.

The examples cited here are organized in terms of questions about credibility, fee for service, professional efficacy, technical explanation, and patient expectations. Each was recorded during the past year based on discussions with traditional healers and Indian Health Service mental health professionals.

Credibility To be seen as credible and to act credible—for traditional healers as well as Service professionals—is a complicated part of establishing and maintaining a collaborative relationship.

At a midwestern clinic, a well-intentioned psychiatrist sought advice in treating a middle-age Indian female for an atypical depression. Having read a newspaper account about the local work of a traditional healer, he visited the nearby urban Indian center to obtain help. The psychiatrist recognized the man, introduced himself, and requested his consultation. Despite repeated overtures (perhaps *because* of them), no help was forthcoming. Later inquiries suggested the inappropriateness of this direct approach, which the psychiatrist believed to represent considerable personal effort and thus valued. In contrast, on a northwest coast reservation, a social worker established rapport and collaborated successfully with a local healer while counseling a client addicted to paint-sniffing. However, she was unable to interest other indigenous practitioners in subsequent cases. Unknown to

250   Cross-Cultural Counseling and Psychotherapy

her, they thought the original collaborator a charlatan; the social worker's references to this earlier relationship as a model to be emulated merely alienated the traditional healing community.

Similar examples indicate that credibility is more than impression management, for one is viewed simultaneously by multiple audiences: therapeutic counterpart, patient, family, staff, and peers. A protocol is implicit and seems common to these relationships. Introductions are critical: specifically, the person introduced, to whom he or she *can* be introduced, who introduces them, when and how they are introduced. One another's skills usually must be confirmed—frequently by independent testimony, often through personal experience. Skill sets are seldom represented as overlapping, but rather separate and complementary. "Credentials" remain negotiated and situationally applicable.

Fee for Service The issue of credentialing alone has raised several barriers to successful collaboration between traditional healers and Indian Health Service mental health professionals. Without some mechanism for confirming community recognition of a particular individual as a "legitimate" healer, area contract offices will not financially compensate them for their services. This particular obstacle was reported in six instances, across four different service areas. The same contractors did not offer definitive criteria for and could not agree among themselves as to what constitutes "community recognition." Furthermore, compensation is not necessarily a straightforward affair. A healer from the Great Basin related his embarrassment (and later anger for having been embarrassed) when insensitively given a consultant fee. Historically, his services were repaid in kind by patients, as part of a reciprocal and mutually supportive relationship.

Sense of professional efficacy Attneave (1974) describes a lack of critical perspective on one's own therapeutic competencies which precluded interaction between traditional healers and a Service professional:

"Look," he said, "I'm a careful, hard-working scientific physician. I don't prescribe medications I don't know about or use therapies that haven't got substantial evidence that they do some good. Besides, I'm willing to explain what's what to qualified colleagues—even to patients when they can comprehend. These medicine men aren't about to tell me what they do or how they do it. No! I can't refer my patients to them. That would be unethical" [p. 53].

Such righteousness was frequently cited by traditional healers as characteristic of failed attempts to work with their Indian Health Service counterparts. At another extreme, the same healers noted problems that stemmed from unbridled enthusiasm displayed by young, liberal professionals. Quick to recommend a sweat bath or herbal diet, they appeared uncertain of *their* skills and, hence, brought nothing to a presumably collaborative effort.

Technical explanation Therapeutic dynamics of traditional healing procedures generally are considered to be as complex and sophisticated as those in Western modes of psychotherapy (Bergman, 1973a, 1973b; Jilek, 1971, 1974a, 1974b; Miles, 1967; Torrey, 1972). Many aspects of the latter are not well understood nor readily explained. The explicable usually depends upon a particular set of philosophical assumptions. An Indian Health Service therapists's frustrated insistence that a collaborator "must have some way of talking about what he does" belied the explanatory limits to his own craft. Several traditional healers mentioned pressure (from their viewpoint) to reveal sources of "power"—including scrutiny of medicine bag contents. One woman described her struggle to articulate the principles which underpin the intensive kinetic and tactile stimulation that she employs as "picturing my power in boxes (words)." Conversely, she noted that her collaborator acted as if the theory for his practice was self-evident.

Patient expectations Patients ultimately determine whether or not traditional healers and Indian Health Service professionals collaborate in their care. As one healer pointed out, many of his people sense the competencies of each and accept help according to these predilections. Another healer illustrated: An elderly Indian woman from a southwestern reservation complained to the local social worker that she felt lonely and isolated. Her family seldom visited; they no longer helped with chores. The Service professional called an active traditional healer and cleared the woman's referral to him. She then approached her patient about seeing this healer. The woman staunchly refused. Her problem was transportation, not depression or senility, as the social worker had assumed to be the presenting complaint!

During a recent conversation with a major federal funding agency, a staff representative stressed the comparative study of cross-cultural therapies as a new and important research priority within her institute. She spoke of investigating their respective verbal and nonverbal dynamics, in summary, the face-to-face interactional process. The data resulting from such investigations is believed to represent the point of intersection among these therapies, and collaborative relationships are presumed to follow as a natural outcome of this knowledge. The examples presented above suggest otherwise.

New Directions

The view expressed by this funding agency representative is typical of narrowly conceived approaches to facilitating interaction between traditional Indian healers and Indian Health Service mental health professionals. In the early 1970s, Bergman (1971) and others called for federal funding to support an indigenous setting within which traditional healers could receive and train apprentices. The premise was that successful collaboration would increase as a function of a greater number of traditional healers. Two "medicine men" schools were subsequently established and are currently operating: one among the Navajo and another among the Rosebud Sioux. Both these schools are sponsored through the National Institute of Mental Health's Center for Minority Group Mental Health Programs. The original goal was to "bring these alternative practitioners into the overall health network (Mintz, 1977, p. 361)." However, simply adding to the number of traditional healers has proven to be a necessary, but *insufficient* condition. As a result, federal agencies are beginning to search for a more effective means by which to forge such a link. Current projects are being designed to achieve the goal noted above by complementing—not replacing—existing programs.[2]

These projects add an important dimension to past perspectives on cross-cultural approaches to psychotherapy and counseling. Theory is practiced in a sociocultural context—to divorce one from the other severely limits possible understanding of the therapeutic dynamics, particularly our ability to anticipate the appropriateness and to assess the relative effectiveness of different strategies of care.

POTENTIAL EFFECTS OF WESTERN MENTAL HEALTH CONCEPTS AND PRACTICE ON NATIVE ETHNOPSYCHOLOGY: THE NAVAJO

This section explores some of the broader effects of Western mental health

---

[2] A model project is currently being developed which is designed to train traditional Indian healers and Indian Health Service professionals in the mental health aspects of holistic health services for both their clienteles. It is predicated on the assumption that neither traditional healers nor mental health professionals deeply understand the other's purposes, objectives, abilities, or limitations. For a detailed description of the project, contact the National Center for American Indian and Alaskan Native Mental Health Research, Gaines Hall, University of Oregon Health Science Center, Portland, Oregon 97201.

principles and practice in Indian communities. Although introduced with therapeutic intent, the role of such services as an agent of social change must be carefully considered in the development and implementation of any programs. The overly enthusiastic introduction of Western therapeutic ideas and techniques, untempered and unguided by an adequate understanding of traditional psychological beliefs and social patterns, may tend to contribute only to the unwitting transformation of social beliefs, behavior, and problems in their own terms.

The Social Ecology of Western Psychotherapy in Indian Communities

The Navajo have developed an elaborate array of ceremonial events called "sings" which may last from one to nine days and nights (Sandner, 1978, 1979). The sing is a social event as well as a curative treatment. Often, all those who play a part in the patient's social life will gather together for the duration of the ceremony. Much of the curative power of traditional treatments has been attributed to the reaffirmation of social bonds between patients and social network, to the supportive presence of others intimately known to the patient, to the hope-generating power of the singer's chants and others' supportive comments, and to the general social expectation of cure (Bergman, 1973b; Leighton & Leighton, 1941; Pasquale, 1977).

Despite gradual movement toward a more "social" model of therapeutic practice, Western psychotherapy continues to be largely limited to the individual, the family (nuclear), the married couple, gatherings of strangers, or selected peers. Further, the role of involved others in Western social psychiatry is to enter into the analysis of the problem and to recognize the part they play in the development and maintenance of the problem. Traditional curing practices are *community*-based and nonanalytic. Those in the patient's social network are generally not involved in the treatment process. The relationship between patient and healer is a special one in which they have no direct part. While patient and singer are in a *hoghan* (traditional dwelling), family, friends, and well-wishing strangers would gather together outside, eating, dancing, and praying for the health of the patient. But they are not involved in analyzing the patient's ills, seeking to find partial cause of the disturbance in their own behavior toward him, or participating in an ongoing behavioral program designed to effect a social cure. The expectation on the part of the Western therapist that they should be so involved is based on a radically different conception of the nature of the problem and of the treatment process.

Attempts have been made to bridge the gap between native and Western healing practices by referring certain maladies to native healers or by bringing the native healer into the hospital or clinic (e.g., Bergman, 1973a). However, our observations indicate that most therapeutic practice continues to be removed from the community and from the patient's social and physical ecology.

Mental health workers have, in interviews, expressed frustration at their inability to get families involved in the therapeutic process. Often, clients will be brought to the clinic after traditional curing has failed. But the family that encouraged the client to seek Western help may have no intention of becoming actively involved in the treatment. Mental health technicians indicate that patients frequently arrive at the clinic alone, and subsequent efforts to involve family and friends are often unsuccessful.

The very presence of the mental health clinic may have a serious impact on the social ecology of mental disturbance in Indian communities. It provides a new "place" for the problem individual: alone and somewhere between the community and the clinic. In the effort to meet the needs of the individual client, an important component of a truly effective therapeutic process may have been lost: the family and community in which the client continues to live or to which he may return.

It is, indeed, ironic that many currently popular therapeutic techniques seem to stress the value of simply *being* and interacting with intimate others and of bringing the therapist *to* the patient in his own home. These are the very practices which may have been "lost" among Indian groups for a time through the overly confident intrusion of Western mental health practices. Before mental health technicians actively seek out these suspected thousands who currently go unserved, greater consideration should be given to the role and impact of mental health services within the larger social ecology of the Indian community.

Client Roles in Traditional and Western Therapeutic Processes

Most Western therapies demand the active and analytic involvement of the client as well as those within his or her intimate social network. The implications of this practice deserve closer scrutiny.

In traditional Navajo practice, once an individual has been identified by the community as in need of special treatment, he or she would be referred first to a diagnostician (e.g., Adair, 1963; Leighton & Leighton, 1941; Morgan, 1931; Wyman, 1936). The diagnostician typically would listen to a brief description of the nature of the ailment, begin to chant prayers and communications with supernatural "informants" (McNeley, 1973), move into a trance-like state during this supernatural contact, review all possible causes of the disturbance or ailment, and then emerge from the trance and reveal the primary cause of the illness. He would then either suggest an herbal remedy or, in the case of more serious problems, refer the individual to a "singer" who could perform a more elaborate sing appropriate to the malady.

At both the diagnostic and the ceremonial stages of treatment, *the client is relatively passive;* he takes a passively expectant and hopeful attitude toward the native practitioners. He may be directed to accept herbal potions, to answer questions about the nature of the ailment and about possible causes (e.g., personal improprieties, violations of ceremonial or moral prescriptions, or supernatural caprice), or to undergo physical cures. But all curative procedures, insight into the causes of the problem, and all curative powers lie with the *practitioner,* not with the patient.

Navajo mental health technicians have expressed frustration at the passively expectant attitude of many of their clients. One of their primary goals is getting the client *more actively involved* in their own cures. The passively expectant attitude taken by the traditional patient toward the healer is at odds with the demand for self-expression, introspective analysis, and self-conscious change of dispositions and behavior required by much of Western psychiatric practice. The Navajo disvaluations of preoccupation with self, introspection, and self-disclosure further contribute to a patients's resistance in therapy.

If therapy in the Western mold is to be successful, it must bring about some rather profound changes in the clients's way of thinking about himself and those around him. It is not terribly daring to suggest that the degree to which the Western middle class undulges in narcissistic self-scrutiny is, and has been for quite some time, comparatively extreme (Lasch, 1978). One of the hidden, but significant, lessons of Western therapy may be a tendency toward individualistic self-scrutiny and critical analysis of family and friends. This implication deserves careful consideration.

Effects of Western Concepts on the Therapeutic Functions of Traditional Beliefs

The displacement of potentially therapeutic functions of traditional beliefs by Western etiological reasoning is an important issue which has not received the serious attention it deserves. The following is a case in point.

It has often been pointed out that seemingly contradictory systems of etiological explanation exist within Navajo culture. On the one hand, there is explanation in terms of willful transgression of the canons of social behavior; and, on the other hand, explanation with reference to the operation of supernatural caprice (McNeley, 1973). Rather than view this as a problematic feature of the Navajo world view, it may be argued that two complementary, but logically incongruent, conceptual systems exist side by side, each fully and coherently developed and internally consistent, but operative within mutually exclusive contexts.

One of these belief modes, which might be called the "deterrent mode," is commonly invoked in everyday life. In this mode, disease, disturbance, or disruption of human life are viewed as the inevitable consequences of transgressions of moral or ceremonial rules. Thus, any impropriety or social misdeed may be considered the primary cause of subsequent disturbance or illness.

Within the treatment context, on the other hand, a "disengagement" belief mode may be invoked at times. The attribution of primary causal responsibility is frequently to capricious supernatural or natural events, or to accidental contact with primary causes (Pasquale, 1976). This attribution pattern may serve to relieve the individual of any preoccupation with possible personal responsibility for the illness, and of secondary anxiety in general.

Western etiological explanations challenge both the deterrent and the disengagement functions of traditional beliefs. Western psychiatry tends largely to see the causes of neurotic or psychosomatic disorder as embedded in the individual's basic core of personality traits, his "unconscious" dynamics, and in patterns of social relations. This aspect of Western belief might be termed the "social causative" and "individual rootedness" of psychoneurotic disturbance. The therapist's goal is to bring the patient and, if possible, those in his intimate social network to an awareness of the parts played by each relevant individual in the development of maladaptive behaviors and the abnormal dispositions underlying them (e.g., defense mechanisms, unconscious conflicts). Western psychiatric theory thus asserts, in essence, that the origins and maintenance of disturbance lie *within* the human individual and within the human group.

Western therapy does much more than attempt to bring its clients to a state of mental health. It contributes to a quiet, but radical, transformation of social and psychological beliefs. One may reasonably wonder if enough is known about the nature of this process to justify its presumed benefits for non-Western clients.

Overlooked Agents of Change: Native Mental Health Technicians

The Western practitioner has often been identified as the principal agent of social change in Indian mental health facilities. However, interviews and observations among primary contact personnel working in several clinics and schools suggest the critical role played by Indian mental health technicians among the Navajo. As of 1975, there were four psychiatrists, four psychiatric social workers, and seven mental health nurses, most of whom worked in hospital settings. There were, however, over twenty health para-professionals or technicians working in clinics located at nine points around the reservation. The paraprofessionals have a considerable amount of face-to-face contact with clients in the field.

Although most of the contact staff at the various area clinics are Navajo by birth, many were educated in American schools and do not speak the Navajo language fluently. During the summer of 1976, a program was underway to translate Western (English) psychiatric concepts and terms into Navajo, but there was no corresponding effort to translate Navajo concepts and terms related to mental health into English. This is in spite of the fact that several of the workers knew little Navajo and were not well-informed regarding traditional views of mental and emotional processes and disturbance.

All of the Navajo mental health technicians had been or were being trained in Western psychiatric principles and practice. Some of the techni-cians adhered rather dogmatically to some of the beliefs and technical con-cepts they had recently acquired. In discussions among several mental health workers, Western concepts and explanations (e.g., "unconscious" process, "defense mechanisms," "schizophrenia," "anxiety," "neurosis") were frequently employed.

In one situation observed at a mental health clinic, an adolescent boy was brought in for the first time by his parents. Three paraprofessionals were present, one of whom spoke with the father in Navajo (both parents were monolingual). The boy was alternately withdrawn and hyperactive, and occasionally acted in bizarre ways, such as urinating indiscriminately, shouting apparent nonsense, and so on. The parents had tried traditional cures, but without apparent success. After the client and his parents left, the technicians discussed their first impressions. Their comments were con-cerned with the father's apparent authoritarian attitude toward his son and his wife, the "defensive rationalization" of witchcraft, whether the prob-lem was organic or psychogenic, and with some of the ways in which they might bring about changes in the parents' behavior as well as the boy's.

The point is not that such explanations are inappropriate, but that the hiring of native-born staff does not ensure that bridges will be built between native beliefs and social values and those beliefs and practices which underlie Western psychotherapy. Paraprofessionals may often be hired for their ability to communicate and work effectively with psychiatric staff. This may mean that those hired will have less ability or inclination to work with their clients in a middle ground between traditional and Western beliefs.

Bridging the Gap: The Pitfalls of Ignorance

The gap between Indian and Western conceptions of psychological process cannot be bridged without sufficient knowledge about the nature of indigenous beliefs. Robert Bergman, first and former head of mental health services among the Navajo, provides an illustrative example of the pitfalls of generalizing about native beliefs when little is really known. Bergman (1973a) quotes a Navajo medicine man, Mr. Thomas Largewhiskers, as having stated that:

> . . .the most important thing I learned from my grandfathers was there is a part of the mind that we don't really know about and that it is that part that is most important whether we become sick or remain well [p. 8].

From this, Bergman concludes of Mr. Largewhiskers that: "he learned about *the unconscious* in 1886, seven years before Breuer or Freud published their studies in hysteria." (Emphasis added.)

Presumably, Mr. Largewhiskers is referring to either the concept of *honich'ih* "a person's Holy-Spirit-Wind" or *hwii'siziinii* "a person's instanding-one, soul" (Haile, 1943; McNeley, 1973). These are the only concepts which could be found through an exhaustive review of the literature on Navajo ethnopsychology and ethnopsychiatry (Pasquale, 1976) which might be considered to correspond roughly to the concept of the "unconscious." Although these entities seem to impart the power of motion and thought, and perhaps some aspects of personal character to an individual (e.g., Haile, 1943; McNeley, 1973), there is little in what is written about these concepts—or about Navajo ethnopsychology in general—to suggest that there are any concepts which truly correspond to the notion of the "unconscious mind," as it operates within the overall structure of Western psychological beliefs.

The dynamics of thought, behavior, and disturbance in traditional Navajo belief are quite distinct from those attributed to the operations of unconscious processes. The Navajo soul may impart movement and other animate capabilities to the human being, but it is not part of a self-contained personality system which revolves around inner conflicts. Rather, the "instanding wind" may better be likened to a "form," a "container," or a "conductor" of supernatural influences from outside the individual. Emphasis upon the influence of external forces upon behavior and thought is quite pervasive (McNeley, 1973; Pasquale, 1976). This is quite at odds with the individual rootedness, personality-permanence, and the self–containment of psychological processes embodied in the Western notion of the unconscious.

The speculative nature of cross-cultural analysis of concepts such as the unconscious is reason enough for caution and a search for greater understanding. Little is known, even at this date, about Navajo—or most other Indian—ethnopsychological beliefs. A comprehensive review of the literature turned up no truly systematic study of Navajo beliefs related to mental health and disturbance (Pasquale, 1976). This suggests a telling lack of interest in the issue. Although those who took the first therapeutic steps into Indian communities could plead ignorance and apply Western practices as directly as seemed effective, continued ignorance and unenlightened application of Western social and psychological beliefs is no longer defensible. This early approach was adopted partly on the assumption that Indian life would gradually and inexorably be absorbed into the American cultural mainstream. However, in view of the current resurgence of cultural self-awareness among Indian groups, this rationale is no longer tenable. A new conception of the relationship between Indian and Western mental health systems must be sought.

PREVENTIVE MENTAL HEALTH PROGRAMMING IN INDIAN COMMUNITIES: FAMILY-BASED INTERVENTION STRATEGIES

The previous section provided an introduction to Navajo ethnopsychology and cautioned against the potential for unintended damaging effects of introducing mental health services to Indian communities. This section will continue the theme of controlled collaboration by describing a preventive mental health program for geographically isolated Navajo families. The goal is to illustrate the cultural factors involved in conceptualizing and implementing programs of this type.

Program Background

As originally formulated, the primary goal of the program was to provide a preventive mental health program that focused on enhancing parent–child interactions through the provision of culturally appropriate interaction activities. A home-based delivery strategy for these activities was premised on the goals of building psychological strengths for both parents and children who face multiple stresses, some identifiable (e.g., going to boarding school), others vaguely defined (e.g., anticipating future culture contact demands). Interaction activities focused on the relationship between young Navajo children (infants to four-years old) and their parents.

The following discussion is distilled from naturalistic observations, survey results, ongoing evaluation of over 2,500 home interventions, and ethnographic materials on 60 families. There is no intention to generalize these outcomes to other Indian groups, but the experience may be useful for providing guidance in the introduction of similar programs in other Indian communities.

Cultural Aspects of Program Design

Although different in scale and content, introduction of a family-based preventive mental health program to the Navajo reservation presented many of the same problems as those described by attempts to introduce medical services (Adair & Deuschle, 1970). Just as Navajo views of the causes of disease do not (or did not) contain the concept of germ theory, there is no well-developed view of psychologically healthy functioning of adults and children. Adequate psychological functioning is primarily defined by the absence of negative indicators (i.e., stress symptoms) rather than the presence of well-defined positive behaviors.

By contrast with Western concepts of human development and the influence of the social environment on both adults and children, the Navajo view of what may be called "personality" is predeterministic in that the life course of the person is fixed at the time of conception or birth. What is already there gradually unfolds. According to ethnopsychological analysis (McNeley, 1973), this inner form is activated by "wind spirits" (nitch'i), elaborated into a composite of separable winds which account for a different aspect of the person (e.g., physical and behavioral traits). Personality, thus, may be seen as a gradual differentiation of the different winds which are united in the individual. Recent accounts have questioned the deterministic view of Navajo personality and suggest that the causes of disease or disturbances may ultimately reside in personal or freely chosen behavior, or may be the result of impersonal, supernatural sources. However, there is little argument that Navajo morality is consequence oriented (Ladd, 1957) with an overriding value placed on maintaining harmony within the social order. The pragmatic orientation to behavior which derives from these beliefs is not inconsistent with certain developmental models found in Western psychology (e.g., social learning theory).

An understanding of Navajo child-rearing practices was crucial to all elements of designing and delivering a preventive mental health program. Even though sanctions were obtained from local authorities and the program had been invited to the community on the basis of expressed needs, a great amount of time was devoted to gaining additional understanding in order to avoid doing damage, even if nothing helpful was done. This was motivated by the caveat so eloquently expressed by earlier students of the Navajo (Leighton & Kluckhohn, 1947):

A coherent culture represents a very delicate adjustment between people and environment which has been arrived at by countless generations of trial and error. If it be thoughtlessly and indiscriminatingly interfered with, the disruption and the loss to human happiness and human safety may sometimes be incalculable [p. 26].

Previous ethnographies of Navajo child-rearing practices were somewhat helpful, but the most comprehensive was dated by some 25 years. Since the project was to focus on interventions with parents and children under four years of age, both ethnographic and survey methods were used to obtain information on contemporary child-rearing practices.

Considering the many social changes on the Navajo reservation during the last 25 years, it might be expected that one would find the predicted changes and trends toward extinction of culturally distinct practices reported by Leighton and Kluckhohn (1947). Although space limitations do not permit full discussion, it will be of interest to students of culture change to find that, while some beliefs and practices had changed (e.g., adoption of contraceptive methods), others had remained virtually the same, (e.g., belief in the significance of the first breath as spirits entering the newborn—one of the holiest things that happens in the Navajo way), and still others had regained their vigor and were more prevalent than they were during observations made three decades earlier (e.g., cradle boarding). These results indicate that ethnographic materials as orienting guides for the aspiring preventive mental health practitioner must be used with caution, especially when the original observations on which they are based have become dated.

A major cultural issue involved the lack of general models of preventive intervention for the family, and those which might be more applicable for Indian families in particular. At the start of the program (1973), most previous research had focused on the dysfunctional family. Models of the "healthy" or "normal" family have only recently begun to appear (e.g., Kantor & Lehr, 1975; Lewis, Beavers, Gossett, & Phillips, 1976). Although the general goals of the program had been fairly clearly formulated, a conceptual framework for organizing the intervention activities of the project was still lacking. Almost all past preventive intervention programs for culturally different persons had focused on improving cognitive-linguistic-intellective behaviors and had concentrated on the individual child and not the parent-child interactions within family contexts as the intervention unit.

Lacking empirical data on contemporary Navajo family functioning, these conceptual difficulties were largely overcome by using a social systems approach which recognizes that within the family one is dealing with dynamic persons who are simultaneously family members and individuals (Nye & Berardo, 1966). This model was more compatible with Navajo family organization and reflected Navajo thinking about the relationship of the individual to the group (Leighton & Kluckhohn,

1947). Dinges, Yazzie, & Tollefson (1974) have previously described the advantages of this conceptual model from the standpoint of both cultural considerations and family functioning.

Equally significant from a theoretical standpoint were the assumptions of prevailing replacement-substitution acculturation models. This necessitated a framework within which preventive interventions could be provided under conditions of culture contact. Consequently, a guiding assumption was that it is possible for persons from Indian cultures to acquire the skills, knowledge, and material resources of another culture without sacrificing the identity-supporting elements of their cultures of origin. This assumption challenges the replacement-substitution models which assume that acquiring functional behaviors in one culture results in the loss of effective behaviors in the original culture.

Two other points are essential for adequate context. The first is the relatively "noninterventionist" orientation to influencing others in everyday interactions among the Navajo. Minding one's own business is a specifically valued behavior (along with quiet effectiveness and modesty) and extends to parents' relations with children of very young ages. This is reflected in the relatively laissez-faire and gradualism practices with regard to toilet training and weaning, which contrasts rather starkly with middle-class consciousness about schedules of development and parenting adequacy.

The second essential point is the profound significance of the land and the animals (predominantly sheep) to the Navajo, which is readily revealed in the choice of a family residence. While riding along heavily rutted clay and sand roads many miles from the nearest paved highway, one is often impressed with the beautifully solitary terrain, yet remoteness from human services that many urbanites regard as absolute necessities for their health and well-being (e.g., emergency medical services). When one inquires of some Navajo why they chose to live in such remote circumstances, the answers typically revolve around three main themes. The first refers to the family residence as the birthplace of parents or grandparents, and often includes comments about the navel cord of a significant family member being buried in the area. The second theme involves a complex description of the availability of water and the importance of this for the sheep herd. The third, less apparent theme often refers to the "view," meaning the historical and religious importance of much of the terrain. There are often comments about the significance of sacred mountains (the boundaries of the Navajo universe), and striking land formations which are associated with the Navajo origin stories. These three themes are recurrent and are always accompanied by expressions of deeply felt affection, which is apparent in the face and voice of the teller.

Similar observations have been reported by those who have conducted more systematic investigations among the Navajo (e.g., Shepardson & Blowden, 1970; Witherspoon, 1970, 1973, 1975). In summary, these analyses stress the relationship among the sheep, the land, and Navajo well-being. Witherspoon (1973) has probably done the most thorough analysis of the complex relationship in showing that:

> The sheep herd occupies an important place in Navajo thought and social organization. It provides the Navajo with both a material and psychological sense of security, contributes to the Navajo's physical and mental health, and is the object of considerable affective investment and moral responsibility. The residence group, the fundamental unit of Navajo social organization, is organized around and integrated by the sheep herd. At the residence group level, social groups correspond to the grouping of individually owned sheep in herds. The sheep herd also provides an interesting convergence of the concepts of egoism and individualism with those of altruism and communalism [p. 1441].

Culturally Appropriate Interaction Activities

One of the basic difficulties in developing culturally appropriate interaction activities was the family heterogeneity in terms of "acculturation," family size, and attitudes toward child-rearing and family processes. These aspects of the cultural context were repeatedly involved in developing interaction activities which reinforced positive family interactions. Activities which might change positive family interaction patterns or impose new life styles were carefully avoided. Rather, the goal was to develop interaction activities which reinforced existing strengths and which stimulated additional interactions compatible with the Navajo way.

Although Navajo parents are faced with the task of directing the development of their children in accordance with the generally accepted norms and values of the culture, it could not be assumed that Navajo culture was a homogeneous entity with clearly defined content and patterns that could be transmitted to future generations. This was most obvious in the variations of material and subjective culture (e.g., language, dress, living environment, religious beliefs) among program families. Acceptable interaction activities depended upon each family's beliefs about their proper forms. If similar activities were needed by families with different beliefs, ways had to be found to provide them.

The role of Navajo parents as mediators of culture contact required particular consideration. There were many stresses on them in terms of anticipating and preparing their children for both culturally unique and general life stresses which were compounded by their own coping demands. Their past intercultural experiences had a direct bearing on the ways in which they sought to train their children. This was the major reason that parent developmental tasks were also closely examined in developing interaction activities. Under conditions of culture contact, the roles typically assumed by parents were undergoing changes which often reduced their effectiveness as socialization agents, transmitters of culture, and identification models for their children. The structuring of the interaction activities, thus, aimed at incorporating elements that helped parents and children to interact in a qualitatively positive manner and reinforced parents as role models for their children.

The task of developing interaction activities with cultural relevance proved particularly difficult. Most available materials lacked cultural relevance in that the unique developmental tasks faced by children of different cultures had not been taken into account. Enhancing parent-child interactions in the Navajo culture required knowledge of cultural dynamics, which are often changing in ways that are difficult to anticipate. Culturally related perceptions of the ways in which psychological growth occurs, if it is perceived to occur at all, and culturally relevant means of influencing this process had to be taken into account.

The more culturally relevant of the interaction activities were also restricted by seasonal constraints specific to the Navajo culture. Coyote tales and other animal folklore could not be developed or used in any season other than winter (for Navajo, the period between the first frost in the fall and the first thunderstorm in the spring). This is based on the Navajo belief that in winter animals are hibernating and their spirits cannot be offended so they will not seek revenge. Navajo string games fall under the same seasonal restrictions, since a spider out of hibernation is angered by attempts to copy her intricate web patterns. There are other cultural restrictions regarding the types of activities considered safe for pregnant women. The unborn infant is seen as highly vulnerable and easily harmed by maternal behavior, such as contact with either real or symbolically dead or dismembered animals. This presented a problem in using a very popular interaction activity which involved making Navajo dolls. Many families' strong desire to have Navajo dolls for their children prompted a variety of solutions, including completion of the dolls by relatives beyond the childbearing years. Activities were eliminated completely where it was not possible to find culturally acceptable solutions to such problems.

Cultural Aspects of Program Delivery

A number of culture factors added to the difficulty of home interventions, particularly seasonal variations in ceremonial and social activities. During the summer months, ceremonial activity increases significantly, and neither the prevailing social atmosphere nor the heightened physical mobility of the families are conducive to consistent home visits. The annual pattern of physical mobility and accessibility revolves around both weather conditions and lambing among the sheep herds. In any competition for the families' time, the sheep herd came first and the program adjusted to their schedule.

Aspects of the Navajo belief system and the behavioral consequences of these beliefs also presented difficulties in maintaining continuity in program delivery. For example, a tragic accident occurred in which a preadolescent boy in one of the families shot and killed his younger sister. Among many Navaho, a place where death occurs is believed to be occupied by harmful spirits (Ch'iidii), which are particularly virulent in the case of the death of younger persons. When a death occurs, the immediate area must be vacated quickly and avoided. Several of the program families lived in the vicinity of the shooting; hence, they had to find other places to live which, along with the ceremonial activities required for restoring spiritual harmony to the families, precluded home visits for almost three months. In matters of death and dying, the Navajo way prevailed, and the program quietly receded into the background until conditions were more appropriate.

Probably the most critical cultural aspect of program delivery involved the selection of the Navajo staff to be involved in the face-to-face contact with the families. Since this type of program was unique to the reservation and lacked prior experience to draw upon, staff selection became a subjective process guided by a few concrete criteria. Although apparently obvious, a basic criterion was that the staff be full-blooded Navajo. Bilingualism was also imperative because a great deal of their job involved translating between project goals and the desires of the community. In addition to being valuable for project implementation, their reading, writing, and speaking fluency in Navajo—a highly valued ability among the people—directly influenced their acceptability for family contacts.

The division of male and female spheres of behavior among the Navajo are much less distinct than for middle-class whites. Although it seemed advantageous to have both male and female views of the Navajo family represented as the overall program strategy was being developed, the sex–typing of activities involving interaction with young children resulted in considerable role conflict for Navajo males associated with the program. Navajo mothers were selected for actual home interventions. They were more credible and acceptable because of lifestyle similarities, and could rapidly identify with the stress of the families.

Navajo respect age, and it was initially thought that older Navajo mothers might have more success with home visits. Early experiences proved differently. The Navajo do respect age, but they also respect quiet competence. One often observes interactions between older and younger Navajo women, especially between mothers and daughters, that are considered more typical of age peers. This is not an immature style of relating on the mother's part but, rather, is characterized by warmth and mutual respect. This also was true among the range of ages represented by program staff.

There is a prevalent but unwarranted assumption that indigenous paraprofessionals will automatically identify with and have empathy for the community of which they are a part. Where broad variations in acculturative status prevail, this assumption is particularly treacherous. Even though they came from the same relatively isolated area of the reservation and had roughly the same material resources as program families, one could not assume that staff would place equal value on the importance of maintaining both tribal and individual identity as Navajo. Staff were selected who represented a variety of values on these issues and who had also maintained continuity of contact with other families in the area. Absence from the reservation for long periods of time, particularly for formal education, often resulted in a person losing acceptance among those who had stayed. Consequently, the staff were chosen from those who had resided in the area from birth with minimal outside travel.

Interpersonal sensitivity in the Navajo way was an important characteristic for program staff. This criterion was particularly difficult to assess because it has typically been viewed as involving the articulation of another person's subjective state. Whether a Navajo will discuss another person's feelings or thoughts varies considerably with his or her acculturative status. However, there is general reluctance to make attributions about others, especially close relatives, unless that person has clearly expressed where he or she stands on an issue. This should not be mistaken for lack of empathy or interpersonal sensitivity; indeed, program experience proved quite the contrary.

Space does not allow full description of the many training experiences that the Navajo staff were provided or the various difficulties that were encountered in the actual interventions. It is important to note, however, that the Navajo staff were typically reluctant to visit families before they had perfected their skills in practice. This may be attributed in part to situations; but, it is also important to recognize the apparent Navajo need for subjective overlearning in a skill before it is performed publicly. Other cultures may see repeated failure as an inevitable part of learning, but Navajo are typically uncomfortable when asked to perform before having thoroughly understood the principles underlying action. However, if given sufficient time for internal rehearsal, which often far exceeds non-Navajo's frustration tolerance, the first performance is often near perfection. This approach to learning has been summarized by the artificial Navajo proverb, "If at first you don't think and think again, don't bother trying" (Werner &

Begishe, 1968).

In many regards, this program could be considered highly successful. The demand for participation far exceeded the available staff and resources, and both ongoing and outcome evaluation support a conclusion of positive mental health effects for the parents and children. Yet, one is left with lingering doubts about the application of psychotherapeutic principles and practices to the goals of preventive mental health programming under conditions of culture contact. Perhaps there is a wisdom to the Navajo approach to learning in new and unfamiliar situations which has been gleaned from centuries of culture contact.

EVALUATION OF COMMUNITY-BASED MENTAL HEALTH TRAINING PROGRAMS

An abundance of evidence suggests that conventional mental health training programs, in many instances, misperceive or never attempt to understand Indian community ethos (Beiser & Attneave, 1978; Manson, Medicine, & Funmaker, 1980). In response to the perceived insensitivities and inadequacies of formal training institutions, a number of Indian communities have constructed and implemented their own training programs. The relative effectiveness of many of these government-sponsored programs is undemonstrated, especially as it relates to client retention and recovery.

Although the content, philosophy, and techniques of training efforts may resonate with community needs, the importance of assessing their impact is critical. Evaluating training program effectiveness is all the more important in light of innovative community-based developments. Such developments are spot-lighted by federal government perceptions of Indian self-determination and a host of related topics. The phrase, "Let the Indian try it out this time around," has lost relevance as increasing congressional pressures call for full accountability. Quantitative outcome data, unbiased performance appraisals, costs per trainee, and post-training job placement are assessment variables which are often given more weight than the total impact on Indian mental health professional development.

Native Grounded Evaluation: Current Concerns

Although evaluation of innovative mental health training programs is an obvious need, its implementation is far less practical and feasible. Within the past two decades, resistance toward research has increased greatly in many Indian communities, often leading to the abandonment of program evaluations.

Community skepticism toward research and evaluation is not without basis. Some social science research findings have created an image of the Indian far removed from actual lifestyles (Maynard, 1974; Medicine, 1971). Negative, sometimes shocking mental health indicators are often presented in exaggerated journalistic style. The accurate and culturally sensitive studies are easily outweighed by the overwhelmingly negative portrayal of social disintegration and psychopathology among Indian communities.

Despite community reticence, many tribal and village leaders candidly acknowledge the importance of research and evaluation. Conventional research strategies, however, must undergo major revisions before they can be implemented in many Indian communities. Well-defined and appropriate research strategies are available which assert the need to work with community leaders from start to finish in assuring complete and mutual understanding of each phase of the evaluation effort (e.g., Ryan and Spence, 1978; Trimble, 1977).

Use of conventional research design to evaluate innovative programs has come under heavy criticism, largely because of the somewhat myopic restraints inherent in the methodologies (e.g., Guttentag, 1971). Hypothetico-deductive and some quasi-experimental designs often prevent capturing unusual phenomena and cultural subtleties. Moreover, their use is unusually cumbersome and inadequate in field and natural group settings.

Research designs must be more flexible, sensitive to cultural variations, and responsive to community dynamics. Community-based mental health training programs and academic-based cross-culturally oriented programs are innovations, and "all innovations must be seen in cultural context. . .[for] culture is in a constant state of change" (Adair & Dueschle, 1970, p. 64). Evaluations of the innovation process must account for and be responsive to the subtle yet important shifts in community organization produced by training and program implementation efforts. For example, the Navajo family mental health project described in the previous section encountered considerable difficulty in maintaining an uncontaminated comparison group for outcome evaluation purposes. Even though families from a separate geographical area had originally been selected to serve as a comparison group, the separation of 50-100 miles did not prevent indirect participation in the project. Nonproject and comparison group mothers would often visit project mothers *on the day and at the time of scheduled project visits.* Attraction to and interest in the project simply could not be confined to the target communities without disrupting established social networks.

Illuminative Evaluation

To evaluate Indian mental health training programs, the use of *illuminative evaluation* is recommended. This approach takes into account the *contexts* in which programs and innovations occur and is grounded in the orientation that "psychological knowledge is tied to the infrastructure of a society or socially defined groups" (Buss, 1975, p. 988). The existence of a dialectic is assumed between evaluator and a social system, with each assumed to have an impact on the other. These reciprocal influences are implicitly acknowledged; moreover, the use of this approach implies that one no longer has to strive for "value-free" and "purist" research and evaluation designs. Quite the contrary, *illuminative evaluation* is concerned with ethnographic descriptions and interpretations rather than pure measurement, prediction, and control. Advocates of illuminative evaluation specify that data sources should include the following:

1) how a program operates;
2) how the program influences the community and social institutions in which it is applied;
3) what those directly concerned with the program consider as its advantages and disadvantages;
4) how trainees and clients are affected by the program; and
5) peripheral influences on the maintenance of program activities (Parlett and Hamilton, 1976).

The primary aim of an illuminative evaluation is to describe and analyze what it's like to participate in the program, whether as a trainer, trainee, or client. A secondary and closely related aim is to identify and refine understanding of the program's most significant and salient features, recurring elements, commitments, effectiveness, and critical processes. Specifically, Trow (1970) argues that "research on innovation can be enlightening to the innovator and to the whole academic community by clarifying the process. . .and helping the innovator and other interested parties to identify those procedures, those elements which seem to have had desirable results [p. 302]."

Methodological Strategies

Illuminative evaluation is an amalgam of anthropological, sociological, and psychological techniques. Characteristic units of analyses (e.g., training or service environment) are identified *a priori* and techniques particularly suited to the units in question are selected. Technique selection is guided not only by the units under review, but also to permit investigators to triangulate data outcomes, i.e., to ensure convergent validation of outcome data and interview response patterns (e.g., Webb, Campbell, Schwartz, & Sechrest, 1966).

The units of analyses should reflect functions and operations of: (1) the training or service environment; (2) the training or service system; (3) application and implementation of skills; and (4) impact on training and community settings. Techniques should be identified which allow the evaluator to collect and aggregate information from the four spheres.

Armed with the appropriate (and, hopefully, culturally sensitive) assessment tools, the illuminative evaluator proceeds through four interrelated functional stages: (1) familiarization of the daily realities and occurrence of the environments relevant to the innovation and the program; (2) identification and selection of an assortment of situations, opinions, topics for discussion, and events for more intensive investigation; (3) identification and isolation of basic program components and characteristics intrinsic to program operation and delivery of services; and (4) establishing a network pattern relating the program to the components of the involved environments. The evaluator, using a levels of analysis approach (Sherif and Sherif, 1969), will typically depend upon observation, interviews, questionnaires, documentations, and records as primary data sources.

Illuminative Evaluation in Prospect

Like many academic and applied ventures, evaluation research is experiencing growth pains. Due largely to particular disciplinary origins, evaluation research has assumed a distinctive set of methods and procedures. Hypothetico-deductive orientations cannot be appropriately applied to a number of mental health training programs in Indian communities. The nature of such programs, their various sociocultural contexts, and differences in ethos argue for more culturally sensitive evaluation research paradigms.

The components of illuminative evaluation promise a more complete assessment of effectiveness of culturally different mental health training programs. Despite this promise, the approach is not without certain pitfalls and shortcomings. Specifically the efficacy of illuminative evaluation can be questioned on a number of grounds: (1) the subjective nature of data collection; (2) the relative position and presence of the evaluator; (3) applicability to large-scale programs; and (4) management of potentially large amounts of data gathered from field notes, interview schedules, and questionnaires.

Although illuminative evaluation as a method is itself an innovation, it certainly warrants comparison with scientifically proven evaluation techniques. With increasing experience and refinements, it offers considerably more sensitivity for evaluating mental health training efforts in the varying sociocultural environments of Indian communities.

SUMMARY AND CONCLUSION

The history of attempts to provide human services to Indians is littered with well-intentioned efforts that inadvertently produced more of the same problems they sought to eliminate. Although Indians may differ from other ethnic minorities in having a longer history of dealing with the United States government, the boundary-maintaining functions reflected by underutilization of mental health services by the culturally different are worth much closer examination. Indian and non-Indian alike, mental health practitioners who seek to apply their skills to the increased happiness and well-being of Indian peoples must be cognizant of and responsive to those therapeutic forces which are both their allies and their detractors. Lacking the ethnopsychology, ethnobehaviorism, and sociolinguistic research to support claims to the contrary, the most reasonable guiding assumption for the aspiring cross-cultural counselor therapist may be the superordinate role of individual differences in interaction with Indian clients.

The problems of providing effective mental health services to Indians may be alleviated to only a small degree by increasing the trained Indian mental health practitioners or giving non-Indian practitioners special training to enhance effectiveness. Moreover, there is precious little empirical basis for claims of superior therapeutic effectiveness of the Indian versus the non-Indian, or the interculturally trained versus the noninterculturally trained therapist. For every anecdotal horror story for an unsuccessful therapeutic intervention betweeen Indian client and non–Indian therapist, it is also possible to find a success story.

Mental health theory and practice constitutes a channel through which Western concepts of the individual, patterns of self-development and introspection, and attributions for many psychological problems are introduced to Indian communities. As attempts are made to have a salutary effect upon Indian clients, some of the broader, potentially unintended effects must be kept in mind. This does not mean that a "hands-off" policy is the answer. Rather, what is needed is more cautious and enlightened application of Western mental health practices and concepts.

The kind of enlightenment needed rests upon a balanced understanding of the strengths and weaknesses of *both* indigenous and Western systems and upon much more knowledge of non-Western beliefs than is currently possessed. Every therapeutic system may have both functional and dysfunctional effects upon the cultures in which it arises and to which it is introduced. What is important is the possibility that the hurried introduction of

Western mental health theory and practices among Indian cultures may contribute to the wholesale subsitution of Western cultural functions and dysfunctions for those of the host culture. As the problems which arise among Indian groups—partly as a result of the patterns of behavior and explanation encouraged by Western mental health theory—become progressively more Western in nature and etiology, practitioners would be able to respond to the problems which they shaped over time to fit their own therapeutic concepts and techniques. It must be asked whether this subtle cultural transformation is a deliberate goal and, if not, in what ways and to what extent it may be controlled.

Implicit in the theme of controlled collaboration expressed throughout this chapter has been the role of the Western mental health practitioner as both teacher and learner in providing remedial and preventive mental health services for Indian communities. Answers to the following general questions are suggested as a minimal empirical basis for future collaborations:

1. What are the positive and negative effects on the social ecology of Indian communities when Western mental health services are introduced and combined with traditional healing practices?
2. What competencies are required of both Western and Indian mental health practitioners for effectiveness with Indian clients, and how shall the criteria be determined?
3. What selection criteria shall be used and what training experiences shall be required for both Indian and non-Indian mental health practitioners working in Indian communities?

The provision of mental health services to Indians can probably be attributed in part to the belief that their cultures would be quietly absorbed into the "mainstream." The endurance of Indian cultures and the revitalization of cultural self-awareness in other American subcultures indicate that cultural absorption has not followed the course of self-fulfilling prophecy. This significant change in subcultural identity requires an equally significant change in intervention strategies.

REFERENCES

Ackernecht, E.H. Psychopathology, primitive medicine and primitive culture. *Bulletin of the History of Medicine,* 1943, *14,* 30-67.

Adair, J. Physicians, medicine men, and their patients. In I. Gladston (Ed.), *Man's Image in Medicine and Anthropology.* New York: International Universities Press, 1963.

Adair, J., & Deuschle, K.W. *The People's Health: Medicine and anthropology in a Navajo community.* New York: Appleton-Century Crofts, 1970.

Atkinson, D.R., Morten, G., & Sue, D.W. *Counseling American minorities: A cross-cultural perspective.* Dubuque, Iowa: Wm. C. Brown, 1979.

Attneave, C. Medicine men and psychiatrists in the Indian Health Service. *Psychiatric Annals,* 1974, *4* (1), 49-55.

Balikci, A. Shamanistic behavior among the Netsilik Eskimos. *Southwestern Journal of Anthropology,* 1963, *19,* 380-396.

Barth, F. *Ethnic groups and boundaries: The social organization of culture differences.* London: George Allen and Unwin, 1969.

Beiser, M., & Attneave, D.L. Mental health services for American Indians: Neither feast nor famine. *White Cloud Journal of American Indian/Alaska Native Mental Health,* 1978, 1 (2), 3-10.

Bergman, R. The importance of psychic medicine—Training Navajo medicine men. *National Institute of Mental Health Program Reports,* 1971, *5,* 20-43.

Bergman, R. A school of medicine men. *American Journal of Psychiatry,* 1973a, *130*(6), 663-666. a

Bergman, R. Navajo medicine and psychoanalysis. *Human Behavior,* 1973, *2,* 8-15. b.

Bergman, R. Paraprofessionals in Indian mental health programs. *Psychiatric Annals,* 1974, *4,* 76-84.

Boyer, L.B. Notes on the personality structure of a North American Indian shaman: Rorschach interpretation. *Journal of Projective Techniques,* 1961, *25,* 169-178.

Boyer, L.B. Folk psychiatry of the Apaches of the Mescalero Indian Reservation. In A. Kiev (Ed.), *Magic, faith and healing: Studies in primitive psychiatry today.* New York: Free Press, 1964a.

Boyer, L.B. Comparisons of the shamans and pseudoshamans of the Apaches of the Mescalero Indian Reservation: A Rorschach study. *Journal of Projective Techniques and Personality,* 1964, *28,* 173-180b.

Buss, A.R. The emerging field of the sociology of psychological knowledge. *American Psychologist,* 1975 (October), 988-1002.

Despres, Leo A. Ethnicity and ethnic group relations in Guyana. In John W. Bennett (Ed.), *The new ethnicity: Perspectives from ethnology,* St. Paul: West, 1975.

Deuschle, K., and Adair, J. An interdisciplinary approach to public health on the Navajo Indian Reservation: Medical and anthropological aspects. *Annals of the New York Academy of Sciences,* 1960, *84,* 887-904.

Devereux, G. Dream learning and individual ritual differences in Mojave shamanism. *American Anthropologist,* 1957, *59,* 1036-1045.

Devereux, G. Cultural thought models in primitive and modern psychiatric theories. *Psychiatry,* 1958, *21,* 359-370.

Devereux, G. Shamans as neurotics. *American Anthropologist,* 1961, *63,* 1088-1090.

Devereux, G. *Mojave ethnopsychiatry and suicide.* Smithsonian Institute, Bureau of American Ethnology Bulletin No. 175, U.S. Printing Office, Washington, D.C., 1961.

Dinges, N., Yazzie, M., & Tollefson, G. Developmental intervention for Navajo family mental health. *Journal of Personnel and Guidance Psychology,* 1974, *52,* (6), 390-395.

Drucker, P. *Cultures of the North Pacific Coast.* San Francisco, CA: Chandler, 1965.

Guttentag, M. Models and methods in evaluation research. *J. Theory Social Behavior,* 1971, *1,* 75-95.

Haile, B., Jr. Soul concepts of the Navajo. *Annali Lateranensi,* 1943, *7,* 59-94.

Hallowell, I.A. The role of conjuring in Salteaux society. *Publications of the Philadelphia Anthropological Society,* 1942, *2.*

Hambly, W.D. *Origins of education among primitive peoples.* London: Macmillan, 1926.

Handelman, D. The development of a Washo shaman. *Ethnology,* 1967, *6* (4), 444-464.

Jenness, D. The life of the Copper Eskimos. *Report of the Canadian Arctic Expedition, 1913-1918,* 1922, *12.*

Jilek, W. From crazy witchdoctor to auxiliary psychotherapist: The changing image of the medicine man. *Psychiatria Clinica,* 1971, *4,* 200-220.

Jilek, W. Indian healing power: Indigenous therapeutic practices in the Pacific Northwest. *Psychiatric Annals,* 1974a, *9* (4), 351-358. a

Jilek, W. Witchdoctors succeed where doctors fail: Psychotherapy among Coast Salish Indians. *Canadian Psychiatric Association Journal,* 1974b, *9* (4), 351-358. b

Kantor, D., & Lehr, W. *Inside the family.* San Francisco: Jossey-Bass, 1975.

Kessler, M., & Albee, G. Primary prevention. *Annual Review of Psychology,* 1975, *26,* 557-591.

Kroeber, A.L. Cultural anthropology. In M. Bentley & E.V. Cowdry (Eds.), *The problem of mental disorder.* New York: McGraw-Hill, 1948.

Ladd, J. *The structure of a moral code.* Cambridge: Harvard University Press, 1957.

Lasch, C. *The culture of narcissism.* New York: Norton, 1978.

Leighton, A.H. Cultures as causative of mental disorder. In A.H. Leighton & J.H. Jughes (Eds.), *Causes of mental disorder: A review of epidemiological knowledge.* New York; Milbank Memorial Fund, 1961.

Leighton, A.H., & Leighton, D.C. Elements of psychotherapy in Navajo religion. *Psychiatry,* 1941, *4,* 515-523.

Leighton, A.H., & Leighton, D.C. Some types of uneasiness and fear in a Navajo community. *American Anthropology,* 1942, *44,* 194-209.

Leighton, D.C., & Kluckhohn, C. *Children of the people.* Cambridge: Harvard University Press, 1947.

Lewis, J., Beavers, W.R., Gossett, J., & Phillips, V.A. *No single thread: Psychological health in family systems.* New York: Brunner/Mazel, 1976.

Manson, S., Medicine, B., & Funmaker, W. Training of American Indians and Alaskan Natives in mental health related sciences. *Practicing Anthropology,* 1980, *2,* (3) 4-5, 22-24.

Margetts, E.L. Indian and Eskimo medicine, with notes on the early history of psychiatry among French and British colonists. In J.G. Howells (Ed.), *World history of psychiatry.* New York: Brunner/Mazel, 1975.

Maynard, E. The growing negative image of the anthropologist among American Indians. *Human Organization,* 1974, *33,* 402-404.

McDermott, W., Deuschle, K., Adair, J., Fulmer, H., & Loughlin, B. Research in progress. *Science,* 1960, *131,* 3395, 3396.

McNeley, J. *The Navajo wind theory of life and behavior.* Unpublished doctoral dissertation, University of Hawaii, 1973.

Medicine, B. The anthropologist as the Indian's image-maker. *Indian Historian,* 1971, *4,* 27-29.

Miles, J.E. The psychiatric aspects of the traditional medicine of the British Columbia Coast Indians. *Canadian Psychiatric Association Journal,* 1967, *12,* 429-431.

Mintz, N. Health practices at the technological/folk interface: Witchcraft as a culture-specific diagnosis. *International Journal in Medicine,* 1977, *7* (4), 351-362.

Mitchell, J.C. Perceptions of ethnicity and ethnic behavior: An empirical exploration. In Abner Cohen (Ed.), *Urban ethnicity.* London: Tavistock Publications, 1974.

Morgan, W. Navajo treatment of sickness: Diagnosticians. *American Anthropologist,* 1931, *33,* 390-402.

Murphy, J.M. Psychotherapeutic aspects of shamanism on St. Lawrence Island, Alaska. In A. Kiev (Ed.), *Magic, faith, and healing—Studies in primitive psychiatry today.* New York: Free Press, 1964.

Nagata, Judith A. What is a Malay? Situational selection of ethnic identity in a plural society. *American Ethnologist,* 1974, *1* (2), 331-350.

Nieuwenhuis, A.W. Principles of Indian medicine in American ethnology and their psychological significance. *Janus*, 1924, *28*, 305-356.

Nye, F.I., & Berardo, F.M. *Emerging conceptual frameworks in family analysis.* London: Macmillan, 1966.

Opler, M. Some points of comparison and contrast between the treatment of functional disorders by Apache shamans and modern psychiatric practices. *American Journal of Psychiatry*, 1936, *92*, 1371-1387.

Opler, M. The creative role of shamanism in Mescalero Apache mythology. *Journal of American Folklore*, 1946, *59*, 268-281.

Opler, M. Dream analysis in Ute Indian therapy. In M. Opler (Ed.), *Culture and mental health —Cross-cultural studies.* New York: Macmillan, 1959.

Opler, M. On Devereux's discussion of Ute shamanism. *American Anthropologist*, 1961, *63*, 1088-1090.

Padilla, A.M., & Ruiz, R.A. *Latino mental health: A review of the literature.* DHEW Publication No. (ADM) 74-113, 1973.

Parlett, M., & Hamilton, D. Evaluation as illumination: A new approach to the study of innovatory programs. In G.V. Glass (Ed.), *Evaluation studies review annual,* Vol. 1, Beverly Hills, CA: Sage, 1976.

Pasquale, F.L. The interface between anthropology and social psychiatry in the analysis of indigenous concepts of behavioral and mental disorder: Navajo ethnopsychiatry. Unpublished masters thesis, Northwestern University, 1976.

Pasquale, F.L. A hypothesis on belief modes and psychosomatic cure among the Navaho. Unpublished manuscript, Northwestern University, 1977.

Quinan, C. The American medicine man and the Asiatic shaman: A comparison. *Annals of Medical History,* 1936, *10*, 508-533.

Radin, P. *Primitive religion—Its nature and origin.* New York: Dover, 1957.

Ryan, R., & Spence, J. American Indian mental health research: Local control and cultural sensitivity. *White Cloud Journal of American Indian/Alaska Native Mental Health,* 1978, *1* (1), 15-18.

Sandner, D.F. Navajo medicine. *Human Nature,* 1978, *1* (7), 54-62.

Sandner, D.F. *Navajo symbols of healing.* New York: Harcourt, Brace, Jovanovich, 1979.

Shepardson, M., & Blowden, H. *The Navajo mountain community.* Berkeley and Los Angeles: University of California Press, 1970.

Sherif, M., & Sherif, C. *Social psychology.* New York: Harper and Row, 1969.

Straight, W.M. Seminole Indian medicine. *Journal of the Florida Medical Association,* 1970, *57* (8), 19-27.

Tefft, S.K. Anomy, values and culture change among teen-age Indians: An exploration. *Sociology of Education,* 1967 (Spring), 145-157.

Torrey, E.F. Mental health services for American Indians and Eskimos. *Community Mental Health Journal,* 1970, *6* (6), 455-463.

Torrey, E.F. *The mind game: Witchdoctors and psychiatrists.* New York: Emerson Hall, 1972.

Trimble, J. Value differences among American Indians: Conerns for the concerned counselor. In P. Pederson, W. Lonner, & J. Draguns (Eds.), *Counseling Across Cultures.* Honolulu: University of Hawaii Press 1976.

Trimble, J. The sojourner in the American Indian community: Methodological issues and concerns. *J. Social Issues,* 1977, *33*, (4), 159-174.

Trimble, J., Goddard, A. & Dinges, N. Review of the literature on educational needs and problems of American Indians: 1971 to 1976. Seattle, W.A: Battelle Human Affairs Research Centers, 1977.

Trow, M.A. Methodological problems in the evaluation of innovation. In M.C. Wittrock & D. E. Wiley (Eds.), *The Evaluation of Instruction,* New York: Holt, Rinehart & Winston, 1970.

Vincent, J., The structuring of ethnicity. Human Organization, Winter 1974, *33* (4), 375-379.

Webb, E.J., Campbell, D.T., Schwartz, R.D., & Sechrest, L. *Unobtrusive Measures.* Chicago: Rand McNally, 1966.

Werner, O. & Begishe, K. Styles of Learning: The evidence from Navajo. Unpublished manuscript, Northwestern University, 1968.

Weyer, E.M. *The Eskimos—Their Environment and Folkways.* Hamden, NJ: Archon, 1962.

Wissler, C. *The American Indian.* New York: Oxford University Press, 1931.

Witherspoon, G. A new look at Navajo social organization. *American Anthropologist,* 1970, *72,* 55-65.

Witherspoon, G. Sheep in Navajo culture and social organization. *American Anthropologist,* 1973, *75,* 1441-1447.

Witherspoon, G. *Navajo Kinship and Marriage.* Chicago & London: University of Chicago Press, 1975.

Whiting, B. *Paiute Sorcery.* Chicago, Ill: Viking Fund Publications in Anthropology, 1950.

Wyman, L.C. Navajo diagnosticians. *American Anthropologist,* 1936, *38,* 236-246.

Part IV
Future Perspectives

Chapter 12

Counseling and Psychotherapy: Toward A New Perspective*

Allen E. Ivey

Counseling and psychotherapy in Western society have been based on highly individualistic person-oriented constructs and theories. Cultural and environmental considerations, while often given lip service, typically receive little attention in practice. Given this state of affairs, it is necessary to reconsider the counseling and psychotherapeutic literature and the implications a more culturally-based approach might have on theory and practice.

The purpose of this chapter is to consider a person-environment approach as central to a metatheory of counseling and psychotherapy. If we, indeed, are ever to answer that now almost tiresome question, "which therapy for which individual at what time under what conditions?" It seems basic to seek the answer from a person-environment perspective.

The classic formula $B = f(P,E)$, or behavior is a function of person-environment interaction (Lewin, 1935), may be considered a basic tenet of the psychological professions. Work over the years has expanded and clarified the importance of person-situation issues in counseling and psychotherapy (eg. Bandura, 1978; Berzins, 1977; Cronbach, 1957; Hunt, 1971; Hunt & Sullivan, 1974; Kohlberg, 1966; Rappaport, 1977). Yet the fact remains that person-environment constructs do not figure as prominently in the research and training literature as their import might suggest. Psychotherapy may be

*Portions of this chapter are taken from Allen E. Ivey with Lynn Simek, *Counseling and Psychotherapy: Skills, Theories, and Practice,* Englewood Cliffs, N.J.: Prentice-Hall, 1980, and are used by permission. This chapter also is the basis of the author's Presidential Address to the Division of Counseling Psychology, American Psychological Association, Montreal, September, 1980.

alive and well, but person-environment considerations have not yet reached center stage.

The first premise of this paper is that:

> Basic to the understanding of the client and the psychotherapy process is the person-environment transaction and the mutual effect each has on the other.

The Lewinian model of person-environment interaction tends to present a linear model. A circular model such as the following may describe the relationship between person and environment more accurately:

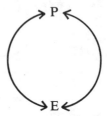

In this figure it may be seen that the person influences the environment and the environment influences the person. Equally important, however, are anticipations and expectations, i.e., what the environment demands of the person is likely to happen, but how the person sees her or his role and perceives the environment will determine eventual actions. The complex feedback loop between person and environment is omitted in most models of PXE interaction. The word *transaction* stresses the mutality of the feedback loop. There is as much need to study this transaction as the person and the environment.

This model can be made more complex by considering the counselor or therapist as an environment which the client experiences, and the several potential theories which may be applied for treatment as alternative environments. A large array of personal, situational, and cultural issues complicate the matter even further. A person-environment view demands that we view counseling and therapy as an incredibly complex interaction. Furthermore, when the environment provided by the therapist is that of a culture distinctly different from the client's, the likelihood of a successful transaction is naturally reduced. Cultural differences potentially underlie every interview — effective psychotherapy demands a full awareness of cultural dimensions.

Crucial to a person-environment view of counseling and psychotherapy is the fact that the actions in the interview and the theories which a therapist uses are primarily linguistic phenomena. Labov and Fanshel (1977) have noted:

As we study the many varied and rich approaches to the study of the therapeutic interview, we are struck by the fact that none of them concentrate on what is actually being said by the therapist and patient. It stands to reason that the primary data for the listener are the words spoken by the parties, and whatever interpretation he constructs will be based upon them. Paralinguistic cues, gestures, and postures may underline this verbal communication or even reverse its polarity, but they are relatively empty in themselves. . . .[We] are impressed above all by the complexity of the constructions which are built upon the words themselves and the complexity of response to those interpretations, [p. 21].

Thus, any serious examination of person-environment issues must consider the language of helping. The sentences generated by a client and the therapist are objects for study in their own right. In addition, it may be pointed out that the more abstract constructs generated by both are composed of sentences. As such, the personal construct theory of George Kelly (1955) and the study of linguistic and grammar (Chomsky, 1971, 1979) represent a foundation from which many theories of counseling and therapy may be examined. Again, the many variations among meanings of languages and cultures must be considered. Different cultures use different sentences and constructs to describe the world.

This chapter has been described as metatheoretical in orientation as it is concerned with theorizing about theory itself. Metatheory, or general theory, is a special type of construction or view of reality which attempts to find harmony among several seemingly opposing views or theories. The second premise of this approach is that:

All helping approaches and techniques are ultimately concerned with freeing people from immobility (e.g., tight or excessively loose constructs, polarities, splits, discrepancies between idealized and real self, irrational ideas). A common goal underlying all counseling and psychotherapy theories is an effort to assist clients to generate new sentences or constructs and to commit themselves more intentionally in the world.

Implicit in this statement is that there is potential value in all theories. The sentences and constructs generated in the Freudian, Rogerian, rational-emotive, and other modes have in common the quality of "newness" for the client, thus permitting new sentences, constructs, and eventually behaviors in the previously immobilized client.

Yet, the question remains as to the most appropriate type of sentence, construct, or behavior for a particular client. The popular adage "different strokes for different folks" sums up the issue nicely. Different clients exist in different personal, situational, and cultural contexts. The tendency at present is to rely primarily on Western theories of personality and psychotherapy and to overlook inherent cultural bias of primarily white, middle-class methods. The focus of this book is to bring together past and present research on cross-cultural issues in counseling and psychotherapy and to suggest directions for the future. Although perhaps overly ambitious, it seems appropriate to hope that a more culturally aware counseling and psychotherapy profession can result from our efforts.

The following pages summarize major points of a person-environment metatheoretical approach to counseling and psychotherapy. A series of assumptions are presented with accompanying corollaries for what is an evolving and developing conception of the helping process. Theories of counseling and therapy are considered as sets of sentences and constructs generated by those who have sought to "make sense" of the complex world of the counseling and psychotherapy interview. These constructs, in turn, are informed and explicated by skills, qualities, decision models, and verbal and nonverbal behaviors. The following pages offer the beginning of a metatheory of counseling and psychotherapy and summarize key research justifying this approach.

THE PURPOSE OF COUNSELING AND PSYCHOTHERAPY

Assumption I: All approaches to counseling and psychotherapy are ultimately concerned with freeing people to generate a maximum number of verbal and nonverbal sentences and constructs, thus freeing them for more intentional action.

Whether one is a behaviorist, an Adlerian, a strategic therapist, or an eclectic, the common task is to remove blocks and immobility and to encourage and teach new modes of responding and acting. Different therapies clearly have different goals. Behaviorists often talk about adding to the client's behavioral repertoire, humanistic therapists about self-actualization, and Gestalt therapists about removing splits and "doing one's own thing." Common to all these and other approaches is the desire to increase responding with the choice of response eventually resting with the client.

Outcome studies of psychotherapy are reviewed ably by Bergin and Lambert (1978) and in a series of papers in a review volume of Gurman and Razin (1977). Common to these reviews is the assumption that multiple criteria are needed for evaluation of therapeutic outcome and that different clients benefit differentially from similar processes. A unitary outcome or even a specified set of criteria no longer may be expected to define appropriate outcome. Bergin and Lambert note that situational assessment is more promising than present normative methods and emphasize the need to individualize criteria for effective psychotherapy. Parenthetically, it is important to remember that there is strong evidence that psychotherapy can harm clients if conducted in an ineffective and inappropriate manner (Bergin & Lambert, 1978; Lambert, Bergin, & Collins, 1977; Strupp,

Hadley, & Gomes-Schwartz, 1977). A common task may be to remove immobility and generate new responses, but there is evidence that some modes of helping are situationally inappropriate and damaging, even though it is possible that the same therapist or group leader may be facilitative to others.

It should be pointed that the generation of new sentences, constructs, and behavior is not designed to induce hypomania in the client. *Committing oneself to intentionality in the world requires decisions and selection from alternatives.* Intentionality may be defined as: 1) the ability to generate alternatives; 2) in a culturally relevant fashion; and 3) to select from and act on these alternatives with awareness of consequences.

> Corollary I.A.: Different theories are concerned with generating different sentences and constructs among clients. As a result of counseling or therapy with counselors of differing theoretical orientations, clients will tend to generate sentences resembling those of their therapists or counselors.

A single neurotic client may consult with numerous therapists of differing theoretical orientations over a period of years. Starting with a traditional Freudian therapist, the client may be expected to construct experiences with sentences such as "You're projecting," "I'm working through my mother relationship," and other similar verbalizations. If this client then moved to a transactional analyst, a new set of sentences and constructs would be generated (e.g., "Your parent ego-state is showing again that you're not feeling OK about yourself."). Moving on to a rational-emotive therapist, we might hear other sentences ("That's an irrational idea."). Each time the client changes therapists, the constructs and sentences change.

Meara, Shannon, and Pepinsky (1979) have well documented this phenomenon. Taking the film series, *Three Approaches to Psychotherapy* (Shostrum, 1966), the Computer Assisted Language Analysis Program (CALAS) (Pepinsky, Baker, Matalon, May, & Staubus, 1977) revealed major differences in stylistic complexity among Rogers, Ellis, and Perls. Number and complexity of sentences differed among the three, but more importantly it was found that the client, Gloria, converged or "tracked" the language style of each therapist.

The authors conclude:

> The evidence for concerted action, coupled with the client's statements, indicate that measures of linguistic structure might be helpful in predicting counseling outcomes or in training counselors to be aware of the effect of their speech on clients. Such measures might also be used to chart progress or changes in clients and be compared with other more traditional measures of improvement.
> The results also tend to support the speculation of others (Patton et al, 1977; Pepinsky

and Patton, 1971; Pepinsky, in press) concerning the instructive role of the counselor's speech in signaling clients the appropriate way to talk about themselves and their concerns In effect, Rogers taught Gloria to be her "feeling" self; Perls, her "fighting self"; and Ellis, her "thinking self." Through both syntactic structure and semantic content client and counselor are creating the ground rules for treatment or for establishing the common understanding necessary for accurate communication [p. 188].

Other work by this group (Bieber, Patton, & Fuhriman, 1977; Hurndon, Pepinsky, & Meara, 1979; Meara, 1976; Patton, Fuhriman, & Bieber, 1977) details the "tracking" phenomenon in more detail, also indicating that cognitive complexity may change as a result of different types of counselor interventions. Other relevant work in this tradition includes Labov and Fanshel (1977) and Weiner and Mehrabian (1968).

Corollary I.B.: Different cultures or groups of people may be expected to generate different sentences and constructs. Cultural differences in sentences and constructs may be found within subgroups in a culture. Further counseling and psychotherapy theories could be viewed as special types of temporary cultures which a client encounters.

Meara, Shannon, and Pepinsky (1979) have noted:

. . .an inability to change language may reflect the client's inability to relate to the "treatment policy" or "temporary culture". . .provided by the counselor. This could mean that it would be beneficial for either the counselor to change style or the client to change counselors. Counseling is a highly verbal enterprise and the style with which one communicates is part of what is communicated. . .Concern has continued to be expressed (e.g., Korman, 1976) about extending counseling and other psychological services to those from cultures other than white upper middle class, and to members of society who deviate from traditional roles and expectations. Perhaps, continued analysis of linguistic structures would provide a basis for addressing the problem and others related to counseling process and outcome [p. 188].

Approximately 50 percent of Asian-Americans, blacks, Chicanos, and Native Americans terminate counseling after the first interview. This may be compared with a 30 percent rate for Anglo or white clients (Sue, 1977; Sue & McKinney, 1975; Sue, McKinney, Allen, & Hall, 1974). However, Garfield (1978) presents more equivocal findings with varying results. Obviously, the temporary culture of counseling is not amenable to all clients, both white and non-white. And, as has been observed (e.g., Korman, 1976), this may be for the best, particularly if the tracking phenomenon described by Meara, Shannon, and Pepinsky (1979) were reconstrued as linguistic or cultural imperialism. Such imperialism could occur when a psychoanalyst tries to impose the culture of Freud on an inner-city client who suffers from racism and poverty, or even when a guru-type group leader imposes a culture of self-disclosure on a marginally functioning group member. Such tracking, of course, may be positive or negative. Effective therapy demands some linguistic tracking. What is needed is a more complete understanding of this issue.

For example, it is completely possible that therapists may consciously or unconsciously track the language of their clients, thereby putting themselves more fully in tune with them. In such cases, the term "cultural sensitivity" might well be substituted for cultural imperalism. Further, a mutual shaping process may evolve in which a new shared culture is developed.

From Bateson (1972) to Bandler & Grinder (1975) and from Hall (1959) to Diaz-Guerrero (1977), it is becoming increasingly clear that issues of culture and language are intricately intertwined. However, for the most part, counseling and therapy as elaborated codes in the sense of Bernstein (1964) are imposed on clients with little awareness of the power and meaning of what is happening. Chomsky (1979) has commented: "I would envision two intellectual tasks. One is to imagine a future society that conforms to the exigencies of human nature;. . .the other to analyze the nature of power and oppression in our present societies [p. 80]." Chesler (1972), Halleck, (1971), Ryan (1971), Steiner (1975), and Szasz (1961), have all, in different ways, pointed out the oppressiveness of the psychiatric and psychological status quo. Their comments and those of others have been distressing to the well-intentioned establishment, and efforts have been made to develop more culturally relevant procedures (e.g., Goldstein, 1973; Ivey and Authier, 1978; Pedersen, 1973). Yet, the primary thrust of the helping professions still fails to consider and take into account cultural variables. It is instructive to examine the major books, reviews, and training materials available in the field and search the index for the words culture, milieu, situation, or person-environment. Miranda and Kitano (1976), for example, decry present modes of service delivery as they relate to Third World people and discuss the rigidities and ultimate failure of present practice.

Thus, while all counseling and psychotherapy theories may, indeed, seek to increase the generative ability of their clientele, there is some evidence that this is in a relatively restricted linguistic model which is not suitable nor amenable for all. Tracking and convergence may be desirable in the early stages of helping as the client moves away from immobility; but later in therapy, one would hope that clients are encouraged to generate a greater array of sentences, constructs, and behaviors that one might associate with a single theory. Along with this would come the capability of the client to commit her or his self more intentionally in the world. Imposed on this problem is the issue of cultural imperialism, for our present theories represent pre dominantly white, middle-class approaches to human growth and change.

ISSUES IN PERSON—ENVIRONMENT TRANSACTION

The second assumption repeats the major premise of this chapter.

Assumption II.:   Basic to the understanding of the client and the psychotherapy process is
the person-environment transaction and the mutual effect each has on the
other.

As has been noted, much of counseling and psychotherapy focuses on treating the *individual* client in isolation from contextural factors. The extreme complexity of the individual and our many almost equally complex theories for understanding that individual often lead professional counselors and therapists to settle for some partial understanding of the person without even attempting to understand contextual and environmental factors. Current questioning of traditional assessment techniques (cf. Bergin & Lambert, 1978) has led Sundberg (1977) to project a model for the future which considers many group, community, organizational, and societal issues. He proposes a broad-based "assessment cube" and the use of social system indicators for the enhancement of everyday life.

Marsella (1980) has given special attention to cross-cultural studies of mental disorders. His careful review of the literature reveals that definitions of disorder vary markedly from culture to culture, and he has proposed a conceptual framework for understanding cross-cultural variations in depressive effect and disorder based on language patterns (metaphorical vs. abstract), codification of reality (imagery vs. lexical), and self-structure (unindividuated vs. individuated). This type of work is particularly important in the therapeutic field as the point of study *starts* with the culture or environment before turning to the individual client. Given Marsella's model, it is impossible to conceptualize a treatment plan for a troubled individual without first considering a broader context than individual psychology.

Corollary II.A.:   The counselor or therapist is an environment which the client experiences, and the client is an environment which the helper experiences. Through their interaction, client and therapist affect and change one another. For most effective counseling and therapy, it is desirable to match clients and counselors in growth-producing combinations.

The literature on matching clients and therapists has been well summarized by Berzins (1977) who concludes that background variables of social class, sex, and race, for example, may be as important or more important for matching than key personality variables. People seem to stay in counseling longer and enjoy it more with someone they like and can identify with. However, asymmetrical matching also seems promising. Differences in constructs, theories, and counseling techniques from those which the client expects may facilitate change in therapy. Berzins recommends matching models of therapy in which certain key varibles are similar, but others are dissimiliar. As one example of symmetrical and asymmetrical matching, it might be possible to match a counselor and client on the variables of age, race, sex, and past history with alcoholism or drugs. However, the lack of symmetry on key variables such as knowledge of counseling theory and no longer using drugs or alcohol may facilitate more rapid change.

Landfield (1971) used Kelly's REP Test to examine similarity in personal constructs between counselors and clients, and found that therapy was more likely to continue if their constructs were similar. However, outcomes for therapy were better if counselor and client organized their constructs differently and then developed converging construct systems during the course of therapy. Interestingly, in this study, the language system of the client did not change to match that of the therapist, although the construct system did change. Different methodological systems for examining language, however, may account for the variance from the Meara, Shannon, and Pepinsky (1979) study cited earlier. Work by others, such as Heck and Davis (1977), Hunt (1974), McLachlan (1972), and Palmer (1973), attests to the potential validity and importance of the matching model concept and the potential impact of the counselor or therapist as environment.

Corollary II.B.: Both counselor and client in their transactions also interact with the larger cultural and environmental context in which they work. Environmental interventions may be more important and effective in producing human growth and change in individual interview procedures.

Rappaport (1977) reviewed the expanding literature on system and environmental intervention and concluded that it may be more effective to use a "psychology based on values of person-environment fit rather than on changing all to fit into one 'best' environment (p. 139)." In particular, ecological psychology (Moos & Insel, 1974) is presented as an alternative where the target of the intervention is the organization or the system. In such efforts, system diagnosis (e.g., dormitory living group, hospital, prison) is conducted in an effort to determine where large-scale change may benefit the mental health of many. Followup action efforts are designed to provide major changes in living space, opportunities for personal interaction, or other activities which in some way change the "culture" of the organization.

A widely quoted work is that of Brenner (1973) who studied psychiatric hospital admission rates in New York State for the years 1841 to 1967 and has concluded that changes in numbers of patients admitted is heavily determined by changes in the national economy. Specifically, as the economy worsens, psychiatric admissions rise. As the economy improves, admissions decline. Patterns for women, blacks, and Puerto Ricans do not always follow the economic and admission curves as closely as white males, a result of cultural racism and discrimination (e.g., "When things are bad, no one can get a job. . .I guess it's not my fault after all," but "When things are good and I still can't get a job, maybe it is my fault.") Either way, those away from the economic center seem to be losers. Mental health efforts in terms of individual counseling and therapy sometimes seem but straws in the wind in the face of such economic and cultural constraints. Obviously, actions in the economy by politicians and business people may have more impact on mental health than years of individual therapy by the helping professions. The counselor or therapist who operates unaware of these larger system variables may be found guilty of "symbolic violence" (Bourdieu and Passeron, 1977) by implicitly supporting system status quo through individual therapeutic interventions designed to help clients "feel better" about conditions beyond their control.

BEING-IN-THE-WORLD: IMPLICATIONS OF SENTENCES AND CONSTRUCTS

Assumption III.: Our mode of being-in-the-world is represented by verbal and nonverbal sentences, constructs, and behaviors. Words and sentences drawn from key constructs form the core of most counseling and psychotherapy theories. The major theories of counseling and therapy may be considered systematic formulations for construing the world.

The concepts of Sigmund Freud, Carl Rogers, and B.F. Skinner may be considered the sentences and constructs generated by brilliant men. Chomsky (1965, 1971, 1979) has stated that humankind is capable of generating an infinite array of sentences, and Kelly (1955) has pointed out that the human scientist is capable of generating an infinite array of constructs from these sentences. Whether the theory is Freudian, primal scream, or trait and factor, all theories of counseling and psychotherapy can be viewed as constructions of one theorist or group of theorists representing their commitment or mode of being-in-the-world.

This assumption is basic to the metatheoretical model in that the argument about which theory or therapy is "best" or "true" is transformed into a statement that each represents a separate reality or alternative mode of construing the world. The sentences and constructs generated out of each theory are distinct and represent alternative world views.

Corollary III.A.: The client may be expected to come to the interview presenting a surface structure sentence describing a problem. A task of the counselor is to examine the surface structure sentences for both overt and covert meanings. In addition, the underlying deep structure may be examined to determine alternative meanings in the original client statement.

Language used by both clients and counselors can be only an approximation of reality (Ivey and Hurst, 1971; Vygotsky, 1962). To describe any single moment's thoughts and experiences may require thousands of words. "Reality" may be construed in an infinite array of patterns, although cultural and personal development history heavily determine the constructions which a client develops (Kelly, 1955). Examination of language patterns is critical, underlying client constructions of reality (Bandler and Grinder, 1975; Grinder and Bandler, 1976; Labov and Fanshel, 1977). Language analysis in counseling and therapy, at present only in infant stages, will be an important future direction in research and theoretical investigations.

Corollary III.B.: A useful way to measure movement in counseling and therapy is the examination of sentences generated by the client before, during, and after the helping process.

Research data relating to this point have been presented (e.g., Meara, Shannon, & Pepinsky, 1979). The client may appear for the first interview immobilized with repetitive variations of the same sentence (e.g., "My mother made me do it. It's her fault."). In such a sentence, the client has placed her or himself in a passive role as object and mother as subject. After successful therapy the statement may be expected to change (e.g., "I am responsible for my own actions. My mother acted as she did because of cultural expectations. No longer am I going to allow her to dominate me."). In the second example, the client is now the subject of the sentence and the word "responsible" has been substituted for "made me." The client has generated a new and potentially more useful set of sentences to describe the world.

While there is evidence that changes in client sentence structure converge or track with the counselor, this tracking is not necessarily inappropriate. The counselor has enabled the immobilized or blocked client to generate new, more useful sentences to construct reality. The client who generates new sentences will naturally use new words and constructs from the therapist. This is to be expected for we are a result of our interactions with the surrounding environment. In counseling and therapy, the counselor serves as a particularly potent environment and, if not fully aware of this issue and conducting an ethical practice, can produce clients who replicate and imitate the counselor rather than finding their own true direction. A critical and difficult aspect of therapy is to enable the client to generate her or his own sentences and constructs rather than those of the therapist. In sum, the temporary culture of the therapist ultimately may seek to destroy itself as the client becomes enabled and empowered to generate the infinite array of sentences and constructs which he or she is theoretically capable of producing.

Corollary III.C.:   The nonverbal language of the interview can be as important as verbal content and even override it in importance. The manifestions of nonverbal language in the interview vary from theory to theory and from culture to culture and from individual to individual.

Harper, Wiens, and Matarazzo (1978) have reviewed the extensive literature on nonverbal communication. Simply put, individuals, groups, and cultures differ markedly on a wide array of variables. When a message contains mixed nonverbal and verbal dimensions, it is most often the nonverbal message which is believed. Movement synchrony or harmony (Condon and Ogston, 1966, 1967) represents a particularly interesting aspect of nonverbal communication, and it has been found that therapists and clients who are communicating well exhibit synchronous body motions. People who don't communicate well manifest dissynchronous motions. A recent paper (Condon, 1979) discusses "cultural microrhythms" and the fact that different cultures have different patterns of movement in accord with their languages. Needless to say, those whose cultural microrhythms vary markedly have increased difficulty of communication. Just as counselors and clients converge in language patterns, so may they be expected to converge in nonverbal communication.

PROCESS DIMENSIONS IN THE INTERVIEW

Key elements of interviewing process include use of various communication skills, the empathic conditions, decision making, and examination of incongruities. Four assumptions are presented which examine these process dimensions of the counseling and therapy session.

Assumption IV.: All counselors and therapists (and other communicators) use basic communication microskills. However, therapists of differing theoretical orientations will tend to use different skill patterns. In addition, people of differing cultural groups will tend to use different patterns of microskills.

Microskills is the label which has been given to an array of communication skills (e.g., attending behavior, questions, paraphrases, summarizations) (Brammer, 1979). Ivey and Authier (1978) present a taxonomy of microskills (see figure 12.1) divided into attending and influencing skills. The system presented here was derived from videotape and typescript analyses using logical categories, and closely parallels the independent factor analytic work of Zimmer and Anderson (1968) and Zimmer and Park (1967). Numerous studies on the microskills are available attesting to construct validity (Kasdorf & Gustafson, 1978).

The microcounseling framework (Ivey & Authier, 1978) is most closely associated with microskills. In microcounseling training, beginning and experienced counselors and therapists study single skill units of varying types of verbal leads (skills mentioned earlier plus other attending skills, such as reflection of feeling, and influencing skills, such as directives and interpretation). Video demonstrations and self-observation practice sessions supplement the didactic-training. Microcounseling has been used to train beginning counselors, nurses, medical students, and a wide array of professional and paraprofessional populations. It has been used in many cultural settings ranging from the Central Arctic to Puerto Rico and from Hong Kong to Sweden.

Figure 12.1 reveals the now obvious point that different therapeutic schools have differing patterns of microskill usage. A psychodynamic counselor uses more interpretations, a Rogerian more reflections of feeling, a strategic therapist more directives, etc. Thus, if one wishes to use the microcounseling approach to teach a theoretical mode, emphasis on the specific skills as well as traditional theory is helpful in the learning process. Work in different cultures has revealed differing patterns of skill usage among groups. Just as different theories of therapy tend to use different skills, so do varying cultural groups. The precision of the microcounseling model forces one to recognize and identify differences in communication style, whether it be therapy or cross-cultural communication. Also portrayed in Fig 12.1 are patterned differences in qualitative (facilitatiave) conditions and focus (specific areas of content on which a therapist might center). Once again, cultural differences in these concepts consistently appear suggesting that process research in psychotherapy is greatly in need of more attention to cultural differences among populations served.

The importance of identifying patterns of skill usage among counselors and therapists is suggested by an early study of Blocksma and Porter (1947) who found that student trainees reported their in-therapy behavior inaccurately when compared to an actual study of what they did. Examining the literature on theoretical orientations of psychotherapists, Sundland (1977) concludes "Extremely important and lacking have been data showing that therapists' beliefs are matched by their behaviors (p. 215)."

However, data are clear that therapists of differing orientations use different skills. Early work by Strupp (1955a; 1955b; 1958) found that 1) experienced therapists drew from a wider range of responses than inexperienced; 2) experienced dynamic therapists used more interpretations and initiation than inexperienced; and 3) experienced client-centered therapists used more exploration and less reflection than inexperienced. Dudley and Blanchard (in press) found that experienced psychiatrists tended to ask open questions early in the interview and, then, as their diagnosis sharpened, would supplement their findings with closed questions to obtain key details. Inexperienced psychiatric residents, on the other hand, tended to ask many closed questions. Auerbach and Johnson's (1977) review of the literature on levels of therapist experience suggests strongly that more options are available as one learns more about the therapeutic process.

Examining typescripts of group therapists, Sherrard (1973) found wide differences in skill usage among group leaders devoted to human relations training (Carkhuff), client-centered growth (Lifton), psychodynamically-oriented "Bion process group" (Goldberg), and vocation (counselor unspecified). Fifty percent of Charkhuff's statements were directives, and he also used more expression of content — sharing information leads. Lifton reflected feeling and shared information, while the vocational leader primarily gave information (lectured) and paraphrased. Goldberg used interpretation as the primary skill and focused most heavily on group process.

Sloane, Staples, Cristal, Yorkston, & Whipple (1975) discovered that behavior therapists were willing to answer their patients' questions by giving information, while psychotherapeutically-oriented counselors tended to reflect back the question to the client. Behavior therapists tend to offer more directives telling their clients what to do. Interestingly, "In the psychotherapy group, patients receiving fewer 'clarification and interpretation' statements improved significantly more than those receiving many, but this paradoxical result did not hold true for behavior therapy patients (p. 222)." This tentative finding plus the studies summarized by Pope (1977) suggests that the content and timing of the interpretation may be important in determining its therapeutic value, and that behavioral interpretations may interfere less with the interview than certain psychodynamic types.

Cultural differences in skill usage need consideration. Using a technique similar to Strupp, Berman (1979) asked black and white men and women to write therapeutic responses to short client problems presented on videotape. She found that white men tended to ask more questions and use more interpretation, white women to use more reflections of feeling, and black men and women to give more advice and suggestions. Another illustration of cultural variations in communication patterns is supplied by the anthropologist Briggs (1970) who examined family life in the Central Arctic. Questions are considered rude and intrusive by many Inuit (Eskimo) populations.

Fig. 12.1. Twelve counseling and psychotherapy theories: Their use of quantitative, qualitative, and focus skills.

Theory	Closed Question	Open Question	Min. Encourage	Paraphrase	Reflect. Feeling	Summarization	Directive	Express. Content	Express Feeling	Inf. Summarization	Interpretation	Helpee	Others	Topic	Helper	Mutual	Cultural-Envir.	Primary Empathy	Additive Empathy	Positive Regard	Respect	Warmth	Concreteness	Immediacy	Confrontation	Genuineness
Psychodynamic		x	x			x					xx	xx	x					x	xx	x	x		x	P	x	
Behavioral	xx	xx	x	x	x	x	xx	xx			x	xx	x	xx			x	x	xx	x	x		xx	F	x	
Non-Directive		x	xx	xx	x							xx						xx		xx	xx	xx		H	x	x
Modern Rogerian		x	xx	xx	x			x				xx		x	xx			xx	x	xx	xx	xx		H	x	xx
Exist.-Humanist		x		x	x	x			x		xx	xx		x	x	x		x	x	x	xx	x		H	xx	x
Gestalt	x	x					xx	x			xx	xx								xx	x		x	H	xx	x
Transpersonal	x	x	x	x	x	x	xx	xx	x	x	xx	xx	x	x	x	x	xx	x	xx	xx	x	x		F	x	xx
Trait & Factor	x	xx	x	x	x	x	x	xx	x	x	x	xx		xx			x	x	x	x	x	xx		F	x	x
Rational-Emot.	x	x					x	xx		x	xx	xx		xx			x	x	xx	x	x		x	P/H	x	
Trans. Analysis		x	x	x	x	x	x	x	xx	x	xx	xx	xx					x	xx	x			x	P/H	xx	x
Reality Therapy	x	x	x	x	x	x	x	xx	x	x	x	xx	x	xx	x	x	xx	x	x	xx	x	x	x	P/F	x	xx
Strategic	x	x					xx				x	xx		x				x	xx	x			xx	P/H	xx	

Legend

xx Most frequently used dimension.

x Frequently used dimension.

☐ Dimension may be used, but is not a central aspect of theory.

P Primary emphasis on past tense immediacy.
H Primary emphasis on present tense immediacy.
F Primary emphasis on future tense immediacy.

Assumption V.: Empathy is considered a foundation stone of effective, intentional counseling and therapy. However, empathy and its subcomponents (e.g., immediacy, concreteness, genuineness) manifest themselves differently in the several theories of helping. Cultural expressions of empathy may also be expected to vary.

Early reviews of the literature on empathy concluded that it was basic to effective movement in therapy (e.g., Truax and Mitchell, 1971). More recent data, however, are more equivocal, and Mitchell, Bozarth, and Krauft (1977) suggest that the potency of empathy may not be as great as once thought. A landmark series of studies by Fiedler (1950a, 1950b, 1951) involved defining the ideal therapeutic relationship and systematic study of therapists of psychoanalytic, Rogerian, and Adlerian persuasions. He found that expert therapists of several types appeared more similar to each other than they did to inexperienced therapists with their same theoretical orientation. An equally important study was conducted by Barrett-Lennard (1962) who found higher level of facilitative conditions among experienced therapists. Other reviews (Anthony and Carkhuff, 1977; Auerbach and Johnson, 1977) support the centrality of the empathic constructs.

A review of negative effects in psychotherapy by Hadley and Strupp (1976) points out the importance of a solid relationship to meet the special need levels of each individual client (i.e., some clients need more warmth than others, some clients can accept a genuine therapist, while a greater distance and professional attitude may be needed by others). Strupp (1977) catches the essence of the argument when he says "the art of psychotherapy may largely consist of judicious and sensitive applications of a given technique, delicate decisions of when to press a point or when to be patient, when to be warm and understanding and when to be remote (p.11)." Strupp, then, has suggested that simple application of a few empathic qualities is not enough. These qualities also have to be in synchrony and rhythm with the client at the unique moment in the interviewing process. Too much of empathy research has focused on only the empathic environment provided by the therapist and has not considered whether this empathy actually is suitable for the client.

Given the above findings, do the empathic conditions really manifest themselves differentially in the different helping theories? The Sloan et al. (1975) study found that behavior therapists exhibited higher levels of empathy, self-congruence, and interpersonal contact than psychotherapists, while levels of regard and warmth were approximately the same. There was no relationship, however, between these measures and eventual effectiveness of the therapies. The Mitchell, Bozarth, and Krauft (1977) review suggests that the facilitative conditions are a part of the behavior therapy process. Ivey and Authier (1978) have redefined the facilitative conditions, relying more on linguistic frames than subjective five or seven point scales.

For example, immediacy is defined as the tense of a counselor or client statement (past, present, or future) and concreteness in terms of linguistic immediacy and specification of discussion (c.f. Weiner & Mehrabian, 1968). Bayes (1972) found body, head, and hand movements closely related to warmth ratings. Concepts of movement synchrony and cultural microrhythms (Condon, 1979) may be more suitable measures of genuineness than subjective scales. Toukmanien and Rennie (1975) found that training in the microskills was more successful in improving ratings of subjective empathy than direct training itself. Future studies will need to examine in more detail the relationship between skills and qualities of helping.

Empathic qualities manifest themselves differently in different cultures. Touching is appropriate in many South American cultures, but could represent instrusive and unwanted "warmth" in the North. Concreteness is highly desired in Western culture, but may be less relevant to more subtle Asian cultures. The Japanese and English concepts of the word "love" are an important illustration of this point. It would be argued that love represents the highest of the facilitative conditions. There is no direct translation for the word "love" in Japanese. The closest word is "anan" which describes a fondness, but also includes dimensions of dependency. In the United States, love implies a non-dependent, more equal relationship. This comparison illustrates the fact that our understandings from our own culture should not blind us to the fact that other people construct and construe the world differently.

Assumption VI.: The counseling and psychotherapeutic interview may be considered analogous to the decision-making process of problem definition, generation of alternatives, and commitment to action. Counseling and psychotherapy may be viewed as a creative act. The therapist with the client examines data from the client's life and together they reorganize pieces and create new sentences, new constructs, and new meanings. Appropriate decisions in one cultural setting may not be suitable in another.

Many alternative programs for teaching systematic decision making now exist (e.g., Brammer, 1979; Carkhuff, 1973; Prince, 1970). It can be suggested that the counseling process is centrally concerned with helping clients make more effective decisions. Ivey (1980) suggests that the counseling interview itself may be viewed as a decision analog, in that the early stages of the interview involve problem definition, the middle portion, generation of alternatives, and the conclusion, a commitment for action. Viewed from this perspective, the interview itself is structured similarly to the basic decision process. Clinical examination of ineffective interviews suggest either a rigid adherence to a single topic by a single-minded counselor or, more frequently, many topics are discussed with an inability to stay with the client on any subject for any period of time. Studies using the microskills concept of attending behavior have revealed consistently that inexperienced and beginning counselors find it difficult to structure an interview and stay on the topic whereas, after training, this ability is clearly manifested (Ivey & Authier, 1978).

Janis and Mann (1977) discuss the concept of vigilance as a mode of effective decision making. Seven specific criteria for vigilant decision making are posed which include canvassing the many possible alternatives, setting objectives, studying costs and benefits of alternatives, and examining positive and negative consequences of a proposed action. Omission of any of the seven steps leads to less effective and directed decision making. The parallels between Janus and Mann's vigilant mode and creativity are many. Tiedeman (1967) has described this mode of being-in-the-world as "tentativeness with commitment" or "commitment wth tentativeness" which results in a counselor who can act, but intentionally change her or his actions at the moment on the basis of new data.

Corollary VI.A.: The decision of a counselor or therapist to focus on or reinforce certain client utterances is critical in determining the content and flow of the interview. It may be anticipated that decisions as to appropriate topics for discussion are culturally-related issues.

Berman (in press) asked black and white, male and female counselors the question "What do you think is the problem?" after they viewed a videotape of culturally-varied client vignettes. Black clients focused on societal issues, whereas whites diagnoses were almost exclusively individual. For example, in response to a Puerto Rican woman experiencing difficulty in finding a job, blacks tended to say the "system" was at fault and to suggest ways for coping with racism. Whites, on the other hand, saw the problem as in the client and their helping leads focused on what the individual could do to change her attitudes and behavior.

Ivey and Gluckstern (1976 a and b) have identified six rough response classes as critical for beginning counselors and therapists, and indicate that given any complex client statement, the counselor could focus on (i.e., reinforce) client discussion of: 1) client; 2) significant others; 3) the objective problem or an external topic; 4) the counselor (through self-disclosure); 5) immediate interpersonal relationship (the counselor and client relationship); or 6) cultural-environmental-contextual issues. A common pattern in microskills research has been the finding that beginning counselors tend to focus frequently on significant others and the objective problem before microskills training. With successful training, the counselors tend to focus on the client and clients tend to talk more about themselves (Ivey & Authier, 1978). Clinical examination of films and typescripts of well-known therapists indicates a consistent focus on clients with relatively less focus on client's problems. Cultural-environmental-contextual focusing tends to occur rarely, although it is anticipated that black, female, or gay consciousness-raising groups would often center around this dimension.

Still another dimension of selective attention or focusing is attending, island, and hiatus behavior (Hackney, Ivey, & Oetting, 1970; Ivey and Oetting, 1966). The interview may be conceptualized as a series of conversational "islands" interspersed with periodic hiatuses where a topic ends and the client and counselor negotiate for a new topic. During conversational islands, therapists tend to appear quite similar in behavior almost regardless of theoretical orientation. They tend to stay on a single topic and listen carefully. However, at the hiatus point, marked differences in behavior may be observed. It is here that attentional patterns illustrating marked differences between theories will be manifested. For example, a female client may have spent some time discussing marital difficulties and a clear example argument may have just been presented. The hiatus calls for initiation in new areas. A nondirective therapist might simply wait for the client to initiate a new topic, a modern Rogerian might reflect feeling, an analytic therapist might direct attention to an early experience, a Gestalt therapist might suggest a role play through the "hot seat" enactment technique, and a feminist helper might offer consciousness-raising advice focusing on the cultural-environmental-context of the issue. Different counselors' constructs lead them to decide to reinforce different types of client talk.

Assumption VII.: Incongruities, discrepancies, and mixed messages may be considered to be the primary issue of therapeutic examination in all theories. The resolution of these incongruities may be said to be a major goal of all theoretical orientations. The resolution of these incongruities leads to "authenticity." However, what is authentic behavior in one culture may not be authentic in another.

The therapeutic hour is full of paradox and incongruity, and the true measure of an effective therapist is the manner in which he or she can confront and deal with this issue in a facilitative manner. Incongruity may be defined as the presence of incongruous or mixed messages from the client (in either verbal or nonverbal form), discrepancies between the client and significant others, discrepancies between client and counselor, and incongruous dimensions or conflicts among societal expectations on the client. Resolution of these incongruities leads to authentic behavior.

Fruedians talk about resolving polarities and unconscious conflicts, Gestaltists about resolving splits and impasses, client-centered helpers about synthesizing mixed feelings and discrepancies between real and idealized self, rational-emotive therapists about incongruent irrational thinking, and reality therapists about the desire to resolve the incongruity between what the client wants and the demands of the real world. Each therapeutic school works with incongruity as a major part of the helping process. However, the constructs they use and the sentences they generate vary widely.

Similarly, each culture or subcultural grouping may have its own way of conceptualizing what is incongruous or is a mixed message. The constructs of a culture may differ so much that what requires resolution in one may be the stuff of life in another. Nonetheless, it is suggested that the resolution of incongruity and the development of authenticity may be considered a goal of therapy in cross-cultural situations, just as authenticity is desired as a goal of typical Western psychotherapy. However, what is authentic in one culture may be incongruous in another.

Feminist and radical therapists (cf. Steiner, 1975) tend to focus on incongruities in the individual which relate to societal constraints. A woman concerned over her lack of interest in housekeeping has a basic incongruity between societal expectations and personal wishes. A psychodynamic helper may focus on the individual incongruities in this situation and assist this woman in adjusting to society as it is. A radical therapist, on the other hand, would tend to focus on social issues and seek to resolve the incongruities by changes in the woman's life styles and in society.

Cross-cultural counseling (Cf. Pedersen, 1973; Pedersen, Lonner, & Draguns, 1976; Sue, in press) demands that counselors and therapists take a still broader perspective, constantly focusing on the individual and the culture. Community counseling and community psychology (cf. Lewis & Lewis, 1977; Padilla, Ruiz, & Alvarez, 1975; Rappaport, 1977) suggest that interventions in the environment may be more important and effective in promoting mental health than continued emphasis on individual helping which, at its best, can reach but a few individuals.

Counseling and psychotherapy in Western society is individual-centered and concerned with clients generating "I-statements." A client who comes from a lower socioeconomic background often has difficulty with this verbally-oriented approach which in itself presents a discrepancy or mixed message for the client. Abad, Ramos, & Boyce (1974) comment:

> They [Puerto Ricans] expect to see a doctor who will be active in his relationship with them, giving advice, and prescribing medicine or some sort of tangible treatment. The more passive psychiatric approach, with reliance on the patient to talk about his problems introspectively and take responsibility for making decsions about them is not what the Puerto Rican patient expects. This discrepancy between the patient's expectations and his actual experience may well determine whether he continues in treatment [p. 590].

Traditionally verbally-oriented theories on which most research has been done tends to omit references to cultural and environmental variables. It is suggested that, for a full understanding of the individual, environmental incongruities may be as important or more important as those within the client. Authentic, culturally-appropriate behavior varies from culture to culture.

TOWARD AN APPLIED PERSON-ENVIRONMENT CONCEPTION OF COUNSELING AND THERAPY

Assumption VIII.: Different counseling and psychotherapy theories and approaches will be of varying degrees of utility with people who present alternative types of treatment problems, come from varying cultural backgrounds, or have special histories of person-environment transaction.

It may be noted that this assumption is but a slight rephrasing of the time worn "which therapy for which individual at what time under what conditions?" The rewording transforms the question into a statement which is often paraphrased as "different strokes for different folks." The importance of differential treatment for varying clients is made concisely by Authier and Lutey (1979) in their discussion of the "tearfully depressed client." Underlying the surface structure sentences ("I am sad" in its many alternative forms) may be a reaction to an immediate event, a delayed reaction six months later to the same event, suicidal ideation, hysterical reaction, or an antisocial personality "conning" the therapist. While the overt behavior may be the same, the treatment in each of these cases is different. When sex, age, ethnic background, and cultural setting are added, the possibilities for treatment expand exponentially.

Goldstein and Stein's (1976) *Perscriptive Psychotherapies* is an important addition to the differential treatment literature. Here, we find a careful review of the research on a wide array of clinical problems (e.g., obesity, smoking, hysteria, depression) with specific recommendations for treatment based on data. However, they were only able to find seven research studies on depression, and commented on the small amount of data given the extensive theorizing in this area. When one considers the many different ways in which depression may be manifested, one could question its value as a diagnostic category. A further implication which may be drawn from Goldstein and Stein and Authier and Lutey is that environmental and situational factors are as important as individual diagnosis in developing a treatment plan. Too often, therapists stop their thinking with "which treatment for which individual" and omit the environmental dimensions of "under what conditions." The valuable reviews of the literature on matching models (Berzins, 1977; Parloff, Waskow, & Wolfe, 1978) tend to focus on personal issues rather than environmental and situational factors, but these efforts represent major steps forward in developing a more flexible research and clinical stance.

The above comments are primarily in a context of individual therapy with relatively little emphasis on cultural factors. It is patently obvious that certain treatment modes are culturally inappropriate in certain settings, a point made repeatedly throughout this chapter. It may be anticipated that a major task of counseling and therapy for the future will be detailed examination of the appropriateness and effectiveness of alternative treatment modes given a wide array of individual and contextual problems. Further, it may be anticipated that the effective therapist of the future will demonstrate competence in several existing theoretical modes and be knowledgeable in several cultures. Further, this counselor, ideally, will be able to generate constructs and theories with clients who do not fit previously established modes.

The discussion thus far has focused on counselor and therapist choice of treatment modality with the assumption of prescribing "appropriate" or "correct" forms of treatment for the individual client. While such may be useful, in truth this is at best half the picture. From a true person-environment view, the client needs to have power to determine her or his own environment for therapy, just as the counselor needs to be able to provide multiple environments. Manthei (in progress) is currently investigating the relationship of client choice of therapeutic environment to satisfaction and outcome in therapy. He argues presuasively that a major issue in clients dropping out of therapy has been their relative lack of power in choosing what is "done" to them. In a community clinic such as that described by Sue et al. (1974) or in a college counseling center, clients are typically "assigned" counselors and given little or no choice in determining who works with them. Manthei's project entails assisting clients to choose their therapist and to give them some instruction in how to choose effectively. He points out that educated, middle-class patients often "shop" for a suitable therapist, thus reducing the likelihood of later drop-outs.

A particularly fascinating study illustrating the impact of person-environment transaction in the therapy hour is presented in an analog study by Fry, Kropf, and Coe (in press). They first replicated Berman's (1979) study and found that black and white counselors responded differently to standard vignettes. This was followed by the counselors interviewing standard black and white clients. Although black counselors were more effective with black clients, it was found that white counselors soon left preconceived counseling styles and adopted a more active and directive style more in accord with the linguistic frames of the client. With white clients, they tended to maintain their "natural" listening style. In this case, we find counselors learning to track the language of the client. This certainly is to be desired over the counselor imposing theory and language frames on the client, but clearly illustrates that better training in cultural differences for beginning counselors and therapists is needed. It seems a bit unfair to ask clients to teach counselors how to respond correctly!

Lorian's (1978) review of the literature on counseling and therapy with the disadvantaged is particularly relevant here. He points out that only six percent of more than 5,000 articles published between 1970 and 1975 focused on delivery of mental health services to the disadvantaged. He cites Goldstein's (1971) study on intake interviewer's attitudes and behavior which suggests that psychotherapy often stops rather than starts with the first interview due to the negative behavior exhibited in the first session. Lorian also summarizes data which indicate that special inservice training for therapists and pretraining instruction for clients may be helpful in developing a more successful approach. For effective therapy, the data would seem to suggest that *both* client and therapist benefit from instruction in how to cope with each other.

THE POLICY IMPLICATIONS OF A PERSON—ENVIRONMENT APPROACH TO COUNSELING AND THERAPY: RECOMMENDATIONS FOR FURTHER RESEARCH AND ACTION

The delivery of counseling and psychotherapy services in the United States and other parts of the world may be considered an exercise in social policy. Government, education, and business join to provide services for people. The way in which these services are constituted and delivered represents explicit or implicit policy. Pepinsky, Hill-Frederick, and Epperson (1978) have carefully traced the social and political conditions surrounding the development of the psychological specialty "counseling psychology." Influenced by government legislation and financial support (e.g., V.A. job counseling for veterans following World War II, National Defense Education Act [N.D.E.A.], licensing legislation and research contracts), new psychological developments (e.g., moving from a strict testing role to a more therapeutic mode with many new treatment alternatives, increased awareness of potential cultural bias in tests and treatment, tightened educational requirements and standards), and business (the testing industry and the selective marketing of books and training materials by commercial publishers in accord with government legislation and changing educational standards), it could be argued that counseling and clinical psychology have become part of the military-industrial-government-educational complex. The delivery of human services and counseling and psychotherapy has become "big business."

Unfortunately, counseling and psychotherapy have given relatively little consideration to larger issues of social policy although examination of the *American Psychologist, Professional Psychology*, and other relevant journals will reveal a constant examination of psychology's role in society. The failure to consider larger issues may be partly because of a tendency on the field's part to ignore the policy science approach (Lasswell, 1971). Policy sciences are concerned with studying the decision processes of public life. The government may make a decision regarding National Health Insurance. A policy science approach demands the profession do more than merely act on policy decisions made by others, but also be involved fully in the decision. Lasswell comments, "It is, for instance, unthinkable that . . . the central banks of Western Europe, Britin, and the United States would tackle the problem of monetary stabilization without benefit of economists (p.2)." Policy sciences require an awareness of the full context, a problem orientation, and diversity so that a wide range of methods of study and action may be employed. Power arrangements are particularly important in the implementation of social policy. Lasswell points out that policy planners are interested in *long-range compliance* more than they are in short-term consent. To build lasting compliance requires sharing power to build a base to continue power. Coercion must be kept at a minimum to maintain the public and private order of things.

What do the policy scientists say about the delivery of counseling and psychotherapy services? They first point out that the delivery of these services can serve as a form of social control. Through work with *individuals* within a primarily male, white, middle-class, Western psychology, counseling and psychotherapy have tended to obscure the systemic, cultural, and environmental influences on humankind. The individual client is often alienated from the social causes of her or his distress, and spends extensive time learning about the self, individual behavior, or personal psychodynamics. Environmental psychology, ecological psychology, community outreach interventions notwithstanding, counseling and psychotherapy remain primarily an individual, nonsystemic phenomenon.

Recent work by Bronfenbrenner (1977), Gibbs (1979) and Mishler (1979) points the way toward a more contextual psychology. All call for an awareness of the person in a social system context. Research and experimentation in psychology has tended to follow a simple, linear, causal model. While he have learned much from our simplifications of reality, this linear model has tended to result in thinking processes which fail to recognize the complexity of the phenomena we study. As Mishler (1979) has noted, "Scientific research is itself a social enterprise, subject to a variety of social forces other than its own declared imperative—the search for valid empirical knowledge and general understanding [p. 17]."

The time would seem to be ripe to examine our present delivery systems and theories, and our past research from a more contextual person-environment perspective. In addition, it seems central that we consider the policy science implications of this endeavor—*what do our methods and findings mean within a social context larger than the enterprise of counseling and therapy? What are our connections beyond the field?* The following would appear to be some beginning implications of a review of the counseling and psychotherapy field from a policy science and person-environment view:

1. Counseling and psychotherapy have traditionally been conceptualized primarily in Western individualistic terms. There is a need to reexamine theory and research literature from a person-environment perspective.

This recommendation suggests the need for a straightforward review of existing literature searching for existing interactions between person and environment, person and situation, and person and treatment. Berzins' (1977) and Goldstein and Stein's (1976) reviews of the literature offer two examples. A useful variation is the meta-analysis techniques of Smith and Glass (1977). In these reviews a large number of linear, cause and effect studies were examined for their interactional implications with immediate feedback and practical implications for professional practice. The data on counseling and therapy are extensive—what is needed is a conceptual map, a recasting of existing data in person-environment terms.

2. Counseling and psychotherapy must be recognized as cultural phenomena. Methods of helping another person vary from culture to culture and from setting to setting. An increasing awareness that culture in its broadest definition pervades and undergirds the helping process is imperative.

An examination of the many excellent major reviews of counseling and psychotherapy cited in this paper should include a search of the index of each for the words "culture," "environment," "milieu," or "person-environment." Although virtually all reviews give these concepts some emphasis, their lack of inclusion as a key index item speaks to their place in the field. Rappaport's *Community Psychology* (1977) is a happy exception to this general trend, but the title of his work suggests a vastly different approach to human change than ordinarily associated with counseling and psychotherapy. Until cultural issues assume a central place in our literature, the answer to the question "which therapy for which individual at what time under what conditions?" will always remain somewhat inaccurate. It may be anticipated that the sum and substance of this volume will do much to place cultural issues in the appropriate centerplace of counseling and psychotherapy theory, research, and practice.

3. Language must become a central object of study in a culturally relevant person-environment view of counseling and therapy. Although counseling and therapy are primarily linguistic phenomena, relatively little attention has been given to the immediately available language data in the interview as most research examines more abstract concepts. In addition, language forms the descriptors of culture and provides a base for culturally relevant counseling and therapy.

Psycholinguistics and sociolinguistics are fields which have much to offer systematic study of counseling and therapy. Through study of sentence structure, we can observe tracking or convergence between counselor and client or discover where miscommunication may have occurred. Abstract theories may be useful, but language is the data of change or failure to change. Sociolinguistics reminds us that language informs thought and our conceptual abstractions. The words, constructs, and sequences of thought we all use are heavily influenced by our culture. It is no longer appropriate to apply Rogerian or Freudian thinking to a culture indiscriminately without careful consideration of psychological and linguistic imperialism.

4. A major research and theoretical consideration of the future is the determination of appropriate and suitable constructs and theories which may be applied to different individuals, groups, and cultures. Different approaches are likely to be workable with different people under different conditions. Yet, this question itself has the danger of imperialism if the client population is not involved fully in choosing and influencing the mode of therapy to be used.

Important beginnings have been made in the study of matching models in counseling and therapy. However, it is, perhaps, even more important to involve client populations in determining not only their own goals for counseling and therapy. However, it is perhaps even more important to in-therapist might use to reach those goals. Not only *ends*, but also *means* in counseling and therapy should involve both patient and therapist. As different individuals from different histories of person-environment transactions generate certain sentences and key constructs, it is important that the counselor or therapist be fully in tune with their languages and representational systems and not simply impose the therapist's language and theory on the client.

5. It no longer seems appropriate to argue which counseling and psychotherapy theory is "true" or "best." A more relevant question to examine is what are the connections between and among theories? The search must be continued for a metatheory or general theory of helping which itself must recognize the centrality of culture, language, and person-environment transaction.

Castenada (1974), although far from a traditional psychologist or counselor, has made this point well:

The first act of a teacher is to introduce the idea that the world we think we see is only a view, a description of the world. Every effort of a teacher is geared to prove this point to his apprentice. But accepting it seems to be one of the hardest things we can do; we are complacently caught in our particular view of the world, which compels us to feel and act as if we knew everything about the world. A teacher, from the very first act he performs, aims at stopping that view [p. 230].

Theories are constructions of reality, sentences generated by our eminent thinkers. They are useful and can make a difference in the lives of many as they provide alternative views of life which remove immobility and blockages. However, their success should not blind us to the fact that they remain only views, alternative constructions of reality. Further, the constructions of our theorists to date have tended to underplay the importance of culture, language, and person-environment transaction. New, more culturally respectful theories and techniques are demanded for counseling and psychotherapy.

6. Process dimensions of the interview (microskills, empathy, decision process, dimensions of incongruity) thus far have been researched in primarily Western cultural terms. It seems imperative that future research on counseling process take into consideration cultural differences. Further, these constructs are developed in Western counseling and psychotherapy theories and may be irrelevant to other cultural groupings.

Early work in microskill research suggests that the communication skills of attending and influencing are used differentially among different cultural subgroups. It has been suggested that empathy and decision processes vary from culture to culture. Further, what represents an incongruity in one culture may be normal behavior in another. Witness, for example, Bateson's (1972) description of child-rearing practices in Bali which he describes as normal in that culture, and the essentially similar childrearing practices of "schizophrenic mothers" in the United States. What develops a healthy adult in Bali is quite similar to what produces a schizophrenic in the United States. The cultural context of our psychological objects of study must never be forgotten.

7. It is time for building awareness of the social policy implications of present modes of conceptualizing and delivering counseling and psychotherapy. Counselors and therapists have been so intently working with individual change that they have been unaware of larger social considerations impacting on their clients. New awareness of the comparative effectiveness of community, psychoeducational, and other alternative approaches toward building mental health is imperative. Culturally relevant primary prevention programs must become part of a newly operationalized social consciousness. These efforts, however, must consider larger sociopolitical issues beyond the usual scope of awareness of counseling and psychotherapy.

A preliminary scanning of the contents of this volume suggests that prime attention is given to individual counseling and therapy with relatively little consideration given to community, psychoeducational, and primary prevention programming. While such program efforts, themselves, sometimes tend to reflect white, middle-class efforts at maintaining the status quo, it seems critical that a culturally aware counseling and psychotherapy should give equal time and effort to more broadly-based efforts which may impact on many more lives than individual and group interviewing.

We must remember that counseling and psychotherapy are primarily individual phenomena characteristic of individualistic Western culture. Merely raising the question of culturally appropriate counseling and psychotherapy is itself potentially guilty of raising the spectre of unconscious cultural imperialism. Is individual therapy appropriate with group and family-centered Arctic populations? Are concepts of personal growth and change in accord with a stability-centered peasant culture? Are definitions of mental health and effective functioning derived from our constructions of reality suitable and meaningful in any consistent fashion in non-Western cultures?

Counseling and psychotherapy are evolving toward metatheoretical approaches which attempt to synethesize similarities and account for differences among theories and research discoveries as they apply to an ever-expanding array of populations. This particular paper is just one construction of reality among many. Most likely, the tast of the future will be to continue to generate new sentences, new constructs, and new realities for the helping process. As part of this task, it seems imperative that we remain aware of the social and political frames within which we work. Without that awareness and a consideration of social policy implications, even culturally-relevant counseling and psychotherapy is doomed to fail.

REFERENCES

Abad, V., Ramos, J., & Boyce, E. A model for delivery of mental health services to Spanish-speaking minorities. *American Journal of Orthopsychiatry,* 1974, *44,* 584-595.

Anthony, W., & Carkhuff, R. The functional professional therapeutic agent. In A. Gurman and A. Razin (Eds.), *Effective psychotherapy: A handbook of research.* New York: Pergamon Press, 1977.

Auerbach, A., & Johnson, M. Research on the therapist's level of experience. In A. Gurman and A. Razin (Eds.), *Effective psychotherapy: A handbook of research.* New York: Pergamon Press, 1977.

Authier, J., & Lutey, B. Clinical management of the tearfully depressed patient. *Journal of Psychiatric Nursing and Mental Health Services,* February 1979.

Bandler, J., & Grinder, R. *The structure of magic I.* Palo Alto: Science & Behavior, 1975.

Bandura, A. The self system in reciprocal determinism, *American Psychologist,* April 1978, 344-358.

Barker, R.G. *Ecological psychology: Concepts and methods for studying the environment of human behavior.* Stanford, Calif.: Stanford University Press, 1964.

Barrett-Lennard, G. Dimensions of therapist response as causal factors in therapeutic change. *Psychological Monographs,* 1962, *76* (43, whole No. 562).

Bateson, G. *Steps toward an ecology of mind.* San Francisco: Chandler, 1972.

Bayes, M. Behavioral cues of interpersonal warmth. *Journal of Counseling Psychology,* 1972, *39,* 333-339.

Bergin, A., & Lambert, M. The evaluation of therapeutic outcomes. In S. Garfield & A. Bergin (Eds.), *Handbook of psychotherapy and behavior change: An empirical analysis.* (2nd ed.) New York: Wiley, 1978.

Berman, J. Socio-cultural variables in counseling: Interaction effects of race and sex in responding to culturally varied client vignettes. Unpublished doctoral dissertation, University of Massachusetts, 1978.

Berman, J. Counseling skills used by black and white male and female counselors, *Journal of Counseling Psychology,* 1979, *26,* 81-84.

Berman, J. Individual versus societal focus in the problem diagnosis of black and white male and female counselors. *Journal of Cross-Cultural Psychology,* in press.

Bernstein, B. Elaborated and restricted codes: Their social origins and some consequences. *American Anthropologist,* 1964, *46,* 37-53.

Berzins, J. Therapist-patient matching. In A. Gurman and A. Razin (Eds.), *Effective psychotherapy: A handbook of research.* New York: Pergamon Press, 1977.

Bieber, M., Patton, M., & Fuhriman, A. A metalanguage analysis of counselor and client verb usage in counseling. *Journal of Counseling Psychology,* 1977, *24,* 264-271.

Blocksma, D., & Porter, E. A short-term training program in client-centered counseling. *Journal of Consulting Psychology,* 1947, *11,* 55-60.

Bourdieu, P., & Passeron, J. *Reproduction in education, society and culture.* London: Sage, 1977.

Brammer, L. *The helping relationship process and skills.* (2nd ed.) Englewood Cliffs, N.J.: Prentice-Hall, 1979.

Brenner, H. *Mental illness and the economy.* Cambridge, Mass.: Harvard University Press, 1973.

Briggs, J. *Never in anger: Portrait of an Eskimo family.* Cambridge, Mass.: Harvard University Press, 1970.

Bronfenbrenner, U. Toward an experimental ecology of human development. *American Psychologist,* 1977, *32,* 513-531.

Carkhuff, R. *The art of problem solving.* Amherst, Mass.: Human Resource Development, 1973.

Castenada, C. *Tales of power.* New York: Simon & Schuster, 1974.

Chesler, P. *Women and madness.* New York: Avon, 1972.

Chomsky, N. *Aspects of the theory of syntax.* Cambridge, Mass: MIT Press, 1965.

Chomsky, N. *Problems of knowledge and freedom.* New York: Vintage, 1971.

Chomsky, N. *Language and responsibility.* New York: Pantheon, 1979.

Condon, W. Cultural microrhythms. Paper presented at Interaction Rhythms Conference, Teachers College, Columbia University, March 1979.

Condon, W., & Ogston, W. Sound film analysis of normal and pathological behavior patterns. *Journal of Nervous and Mental Disease,* 1966, *143,* 338-346.

Condon, W., & Ogston, W. A segmentation of behavior. *Journal of Psychiatric Research,* 1967, *5,* 221-235.

Cronbach, L. The two disciplines of scientific psychology. *American Psychologist,* 1957, *12,* 671-684.

Diaz-Guerrero, R. A Mexican psychology. *American Psychologist,* 1977, *32,* 934-944.

Fiedler, F. A comparison of therapeutic relationships in psychoanalytic, nondirective, and Adlerian therapy. *Journal of Consulting Psychology,* 1950a, *14,* 435-426.a

Fiedler, F. The concept of an ideal therapeutic relationship. *Journal of Consulting Psychology,* 1950b, *14,* 239-245.

Fiedler, F. Factor analysis of psychoanalytic, nondirective, and Adlerian therapeutic relationships. *Journal of Consulting Psychology,* 1951, *15,* 32-38.

Fry, P., Kropf, G., & Coe, K. The effects of counselor and client racial similarity on the counselor's response patterns and skills. *Journal of Counseling Psychology,* (in press).

Garfield, S. Research on client variables in psychotherapy. In S. Garfield and A. Bergin (Eds.), *Handbook of psychotherapy and behavior change: An empirical analysis.* (2nd ed.) New York: Wiley, 1978.

Gibbs, J. The meaning of ecologically oriented inquiry in contemporary psychology. *American Psychologist,* 1979, *34,* 127-140.

Goldstein, A.P. *Psychotherapeautic attraction.* New York: Pergamon Press, 1971.

Goldstein, A.P. *Structured learning therapy: Toward a psychotherapy for the poor.* New York: Academic Press, 1973.

Goldstein, A.P. & Stein, N. *Prescriptive psychotherapies.* New York: Pergamon Press, 1976.

Grinder, R., & Bandler, J. *The structure of magic II.* Palo Alto: Science & Behavior, 1976.

Gurman, A., & Razin, A. *Effective psychotherapy: A handbook of research.* New York: Pergamon Press, 1977.

Hackney, H., Ivey, A., & Oetting, E. Attending, island and hiatus behavior: A process conception of counselor and client interaction. *Journal of Counseling Psychology,* 1970, *17,* 342-346.

Hadley, S. & Strupp, H. Contemporary views of negative effects in psychotherapy. *Archives of General Psychiatry,* 1976, *33,* 1291-1302.

Hall, E. *The silent language.* Garden City, N.Y. Doubleday, 1959.

Halleck, S. *The politics of therapy.* New York: Science, 1971.

Harper, R., Wiens, A., & Matarazzo, J. *Nonverbal communication: The state of the art.* New York: Wiley, 1978.

Heck, E., & Davis, C. The differential treatment model and drug counseling: An epilogue. In C. Davis and M. Schmidt. *Differential treatment of drug and alcohol abusers.* Palm Springs, California: ETC Publications, 1977.

Hunt, D. *Matching Models in Education.* Toronto: Ontario Institute for Studies in Education, 1971.

Hunt, D.E. A paradigm for developing and analyzing differential treatment programs. In C. Davis and M. Schmidt. *Differential treatment of drug and alcohol abusers.* Palm Springs, California: ETC Publications, 1977.

Hunt, D., and Sullivan, E. *Between Psychology and Education.* Hinsdale, Ill.: Dryden, 1974.

Hurndon, C.J., Pepinsky, H.B., & Meara, N.M. Conceptual level and structural complexity in language. *Journal of Counseling Psychology,* 1979, *26,* 190-197.

Ivey, A. *Counseling and psychotherapy: Connections and applications.* Englewood Cliffs, N.J.: Prentice-Hall, 1980.

Ivey, A.E., & Authier, J. *Microcounseling: Innovations in interviewing, counseling, psychotherapy, and psychoeducation.* (2nd ed.) Springfield, Ill.: Thomas, 1978.

Ivey, A., & Gluckstern, N. *Basic influencing skills: Leader and participant manuals.* North Amherst, Mass.: Microtraining, 1976.a

Ivey, A., & Gluckstern, N. *Basic influencing skills: Videotapes.* North Amherst, Mass. Microtraining, 1976.b

Ivey, A. & Hurst, J. Communication as adaptation. *Journal of Communication,* 1971, *21,* 199-207.

Ivey, A., & Oetting, E. Microcounseling innovations and analysis of interview process. Paper presented to the Convention of the American Personnel and Guidance Association, Dallas, 1966.

Janis, I., & Mann, L. *Decision making: a psychological analysis of conflict, choice and commitment.* New York: Free Press, 1977.

Johnson, F.A., & Marsella, A.J. Differential attitudes toward verbal behavior in students of Japanese and European ancestry. *Genetic Psychology Monographs,* 1978, *97,* 43-76.

Kasdorf, J., & Gustafson, K. Research related to microtraining. In A.E. Ivey and J. Authier. *Microcounseling: Innovations in interviewing counseling, psychotherapy, and psychoeducation.* (2nd ed.) Springfield, Ill.: Thomas, 1978.

Kelly, G. *The psychology of personal constructs.* Vols I and II. New York: Norton, 1955.

Kohlberg, L. Moral education in the schools: A developmental view. *School Review,* 1966, *74,* 1-30.

Korman, M. (Ed.) *Levels and patterns of professional training in psychology.* Washington, D.C.: American Psychological Association, 1976.

Labov, W., & Fanshel, D. *Therapeutic discourse.* New York: Academic Press, 1977.

Lambert, M.J., Bergin, A.E., & Collins, J.L. Therapist-induced deterioration in psychotherapy. In A.S. Gurman & A.M. Razin (Eds.), *Effective psychotherapy: A handbook of research.* New York: Pergamon Press, 1977.

Landfield, A. *Personal construct systems in psychotherapy.* Chicago: Rand McNally, 1971.

Lasswell, H.D. *A pre-view of policy sciences.* New York: American Elsevier, 1971.

Lewin, K. *A Dynamic Theory of Personality.* New York: McGraw-Hill, 1935.

Lewis, J., & Lewis, M. *Community counseling.* New York: Wiley, 1977.

Lorion, R.P. Research on psychotherapy and behavior change with the disadvantaged: Past, present, and future directions. In S.L. Garfield & A.E. Bergin (Eds.), *Handbook of psychotherapy and behavior change: An empirical analysis.* (2nd ed.) New York: Wiley, 1978.

Manthei, R. An examination of the effect of client selection of therapist. Study in process, University of Massachusetts, Amherst (in process).

Marsella, A.J. Depressive experience and disorder across cultures. In H. Triandis & J. Draguns (Eds.), *Handbook of cross-cultural psychology,* Vol. 6. *Culture and psychopathology.* Boston: Allyn & Bacon, 1980.

McLachlan, J. Benefit from group therapy as a function of patient-therapist match on a conceptual level. *Psychotherapy: Theory, Research, and Practice,* 1972, *9,* 317-323.

Meara, N.M. A computer-assisted language analysis system for research on natural language. Symposium presentation at the Interamerican Congress of Psychology, Miami Beach, Florida, December 1976.

Meara, N.M., Shannon, J.W., & Pepinsky, H.B. A comparison of the stylistic complexity of the language of counselor and client across three theoretical orientations. *Journal of Counseling Psychology,* 1979, *26,* 181-189.

Miranda, M.R., & Kitano, H. Mental health services in Third World communities. *International Journal of Mental Health,* 1976, *5,* 39-49.

Mishler, E.G. Meaning in context: Is there any other kind? *Harvard Educational Review,* 1979, *1,* 1-19.

Mitchell, K.M., Bozarth, J.D., & Krauft, C.C. A reappraisal of the therapeutic effectiveness of accurate empathy, nonpossessive warmth, and genuineness. In A.S. Gurman & A.M. Razin (Eds.), *Effective psychotherapy: A handbook of research.* New York: Pergamon Press, 1977.

Moos, R.H., & Insel, P.M. (Eds.) *Issues in social ecology.* Palo Alto: Consulting Psychologists Press, 1974.

Padilla, A., Ruiz, R.A., & Alvarez, R. Community mental health services for the Spanish-speaking/surnamed population. *American Psychologist,* 1975, *30,* 892-905.

Palmer, T. Matching worker and client in corrections. *Social Work,* 1973, *18,* 95-103.

Parloff, M.B., Waskow, I.E., & Wolfe, B.E. Research on therapist variables in relation to process and outcome. In S.L. Garfield and A.E. Bergin (Eds.), *Handbook of psychotherapy and behavior change: An empirical analysis.* (2nd ed.) New York: Wiley, 1978.

Patton, J.J., Fuhriman, A.J., & Bieber, M.R. A model and a metalanguage for research on psychological counseling. *Journal of Counseling Psychology,* 1977, *24,* 25-34.

Pedersen, P. A cross-cultural coalition training model for educating mental health professionals to function in multicultural populations. Paper presented to the Ninth International Congress of Ethnological and Anthropological Sciences, Chicago, September 1973.

Pedersen, P., Lonner, W.J., & Draguns, J.G. (Eds.) *Counseling across cultures.* Honolulu: University Press of Hawaii, 1976.

Pepinsky, H. & Patton, M. *The psychological experiment* Elmsford, N.Y.: Pergamon, 1971.

Pepinsky, H.B., Baker, W.M., Matalon, R., May, G.C., & Staubus, A.M. *User's manual for the computer-assisted language analysis system.* Columbus, Ohio: Group for Research and Development in Language and Social Policy, Mershon Center, The Ohio State University, 1977.

Pepinsky, H., Hill-Frederick, K., & Epperson, D. The *Journal of Counseling of Counseling Psychology* as a matter of policies. *Journal of Counseling Psychology,* 1978, *25,* 483-498.

Pepinsky, H. A meta-language of text. in H. Fisher & R. Diaz-Guerrero. (Eds.) *Language and logic in personality and society,* New York: Academic Press, (in press).

Pope, B. Research on therapeutic style. In A.S. Gurman and A.M. Razin (Eds.), *Effective psychotherapy: A handbook of research.* New York: Pergamon Press, 1977.

Prince, G. *The practice of creativity.* New York: Harper & Row, 1970.

Rappaport, J. *Community psychology.* New York: Holt, Rinehart, & Winston, 1977.

Ryan, W. *Blaming the victim.* New York: Vintage Books, Random House, 1971.

Sherrard, P. Predicting group leader/member interaction: The efficacy of the Ivey taxonomy. Unpublished doctoral dissertation, University of Massachusetts, 1973.

Shostrom, E.L. *Three approaches to psychotherapy.* Santa Ana, California: Psychological Films, 1966.

Sloane, R., Staples, F., Cristol, A., Yorkston, N., & Whipple, K. *Psychotherapy versus behavior therapy.* Cambridge, Mass.: Harvard University Press, 1975.

Smith, M., & Glass, G. Meta-analysis of psychotherapy outcome studies. *American Psychologist,* 1977, *32,* 752-760.

Steiner, C. (Ed.) *Readings in radical psychiatry.* New York: Grove, 1975.

Strupp, H. An objective comparison of Rogerian and psychoanalytic technique. *Journal of Consulting Psychology,* 1955a, *19,* 1-7a.

Strupp, H. Psychotherapeutic technique, professional affiliation, and experience level. *Journal of Consulting Psychology,* 1955b, *19,* 97-102.b

Strupp, H. The performance of psychiatrists and psychologists in a therapeutic interview. *Journal of Clinical Psychology,* 1958, *14,* 219-226.

Strupp, H. A reformulation of the therapist's contribution. In A.S. Gurman and A.M. Razin (Eds.), *Effective psychotherapy: A handbook of research.* New York: Pergamon Press, 1977.

Strupp, H.H., Hadley, S.W., & Gomes-Schwartz, B. *Psychotherapy for better or worse: An analysis of the problem of negative effects.* New York: Jason Aronson, 1977.

Sue, D.W., Counseling the culturally different: A conceptual analysis. *Personnel and Guidance Journal*, 1977, *55*, 422-425.

Sue, D.W. *Cross-cultural counseling: Theory and practice.* New York: John Wiley (in press).

Sue, S. & McKinney, H. Asian Americans in the community mental health care system. *American Journal of Orthopsychiatry*, 1975, *45* (1), 111-118.

Sue, S., McKinney, H., Allen, D., & Hall, J. Delivery of community mental health services to black and white clients. *Journal of Consulting and Clinical Psychology*, 1974, *42*, 794-801.

Sundberg, N.D. *Assessment of persons.* Englewood Cliffs, N.J.: Prentice-Hall, 1977.

Sundland, D.M. Theoretical orientations of psychotherapists. In A.S. Gurman and A.M. Razin (Eds.), *Effective psychotherapy: A handbook of research.* New York: Pergamon Press, 1977.

Szaz, T. *The myth of mental illness.* New York: Dell, 1961.

Tiedeman, D.V. Predicament, problem, and psychology: The case for paradox in life and counseling psychology. *Journal of Counseling Psychology*, 1967, *14*, 1-8.

Toukmanien, S., & Rennie, D. Microcounseling vs. human relations training: Relative effectiveness with undergraduate trainees. *Journal of Counseling Psychology*, 1975, *22*, 345-352.

Truax, C.B., & Mitchell, K.M. Research on certain therapist interpersonal skills in relation to process and outcome. In A.E. Bergin & S.L. Garfield (Eds.), *Handbook of psychotherapy and behavior change.* New York: Wiley, 1971.

Vygotsky, L. *Thought and language.* Cambridge, Mass.: MIT Press, 1962.

Weiner, M., & Mehrabian, A. *Language within language: Immediacy, a channel in verbal communication.* New York: Appleton, 1968.

Zimmer, J., & Anderson, S. Dimensions of positive regard and empathy. *Journal of Counseling Psychology*, 1968, *15*, 417-426.

Zimmer, J., & Park, P. Factor analysis of counselor communications. *Journal of Counseling Psychology*, 1967, *14*, 198-203.

Chapter 13

Alternative Futures for Cross-cultural Counseling and Psychotherapy

Paul B. Pedersen

Before we were born, culturally institutionalized patterns of thought and action were already prepared to guide our ideas, make many of our decisions, and take control of our lives. Culture was our inheritance from our parents and teachers who taught us the "rules of the game." Only later sometimes much later, sometimes never, did we learn that our culture was one of the many possible patterns of thinking and acting from which we could choose. By that time, most of us had already come to believe that our culture was the best of all possible worlds. Even if we recognized that traditional values were false or inadequate when challenged by the stress of radical social change, it was not always possible to replace the worn-out habits with the new alternatives.

There is a relevant story told by Claudio Naranjo (1972), a Chilean psychiatrist studying 150 different methodologies concerned with ways of personal growth. The story concerns four travelers—a Persian, a Turk, an

Arab, and a Greek—who were debating how to spend their last coin. "I want *angur*," said the Persian, but the Turk insisted that *uzum* was what he wanted, while the Arab argued for *inab*, and the Greek for *stafil*. A man came along, and, hearing their heated discussion, offered to buy what each wanted if they would only agree to give him the coin. The men distrusted him, but finally agreed to give him the coin. When the passerby, who was a linguist, bought a small bunch of grapes for each of them, the Persian, the Turk, the Arab, and the Greek were surprised and delighted to receive their "*angur-uzum-inab-stafil*." In Naranjo's interpretation, he points out that we all want the same goal of a "good life" but call it different names and insist on our own different ideas about where to find it, arguing for our own interpretation. Adjustment rather than liberation has become the theme of counseling and psychotherapy.

There are some clear indications that we are becoming more aware of the role of cultural alternatives in our mental health services, however. In the Report to the President from the President's Commission on Mental Health (1978) the authors point out how mental health services have been inadequate to meet the bicultural and bilingual needs of minority groups in this country. Likewise, the Council of Representatives meeting of the American Psychological Association of January 1979 asserted that social and personal diversity of faculty and students are highly desirable as an essential goal if trainees in psychology are to function effectively within our pluralistic society. The APA Council of Representatives voted the following resolution at its January 1979 meeting:

> It is the sense of APA Council that APA accreditation reflect our concern that all psychology departments and schools should assure that their students receive preparation to function in a multi-cultural, multi-racial society. This implies having systematic exposure to and contact with a diversity of students, teachers and patients or clients, such as, for example, by special arrangement for interchange or contact with other institutions on a regular and organized basis [p.5].

Forecasting the role of cross-cultural counseling in the future requires taking into account the goals which are generated by people rather than imposed on them. These goals are heterogeneous, diverse, and changing all the time. The guiding of cultural change is particularly difficult because the future is neither observable nor can it be easily predicted by extrapolating from the past. Maruyama (1973) provides a typology of attitudinal orientations for studying the cultural aspects of future society which is helpful for locating the role of counseling. The study of futures is divided into three basic approaches.

The descriptive studies deal with trends in social change from the past and the present, deriving guidelines for the future from the past. Descriptive studies are helpful to the extent that we can avoid past mistakes and learn from our errors but, otherwise, limited in helping us forecast the future.

The predictive studies tend to either extrapolate from the past rates of change and acceleration of change or speculate on the future effect of innovations without historical precedent. Predictive studies imply an inevitable course of events in which the person has very limited opportunity to respond.

The pragmatic studies look at what can and should be done to affect the direction of the future. Pragmatic studies are divided into three types: those which are reactive and conservatively defensive (e.g., how to preserve the old patterns, family structures), instrumental (how to use new tools for maintaining traditional institutions), or adaptive (how to modify culture to fit with technological changes). Those which are goal-generating ask what the goals of our society can be and, then, adapt technology toward achieving those goals in a humanistic liberal orientation. Adaptation may be either through a homogeneous design planned to emphasize our similarities or through a heterogeneous diversity of goals emphasizing diversities, differences, and the range of alternatives. The pragmatic studies of what can and should be done to affect the direction of social change seem to be the most promising in forecasting the future of cross-cultural counseling.

Before we consider the role of cross-cultural counseling, however, it is important to consider the three most popular alternatives for the future society in which that counseling would occur. Wilson (1979) suggests that we look at three scenarios to illustrate those alternatives, of an open, closed, or chaotic future.

THREE ALTERNATIVES FOR THE FUTURE

The three most frequently cited scenarios for the future are represented by the Club of Rome's (Mesarovic & Pestel, 1974) essentially pessimistic prediction of catastrophe, Robert Heilbronner's (1975) prediction of a closed society depending on authoritarian controls, and the Hazen Report (1972) of a more optimistic alternative for an open society in which modern society might successfully respond to the current crises.

The Second Report to the Club of Rome suggests that the world is headed toward a catastrophe, projecting current world problems in a consistently pessimistic trend. The only effective response suggested is world cooperation through a world economic order and global resource allocation system where nations and cultures would not be allowed to act independently of one another. The evidence is based on computer science technology and probability projections. The view of human nature considers man as self-destructive, able to act rationally and avoid the dangers of the future but unlikely to do so, preferring short-range, immediate benefits to long-range survival goals. The view of freedom is limited and projects the human struggle against nature for survival. The view of culture is global, reducing the variables to computer data probabilities that prescribe the only alternative to be immediate world cooperation as a community of utopian proportions. The only possibility for survival would be immediate world cooperation and an abrupt, but unlikely, shift from the vested interests of nationalism and the special interests of other cultural groups.

Heilbronner suggests a second alternative, that our society is headed toward an authoritarian alternative, building his arguments on an economic perspective. The view of human nature is essentially Freudian where we lapse into a reliance on authority figures in the present crisis because of man's essentially selfish self-interest. The view of freedom is negative and self-destructive, with a need to identify sources of authoritarian control who will make the necessary decisions on behalf of mankind. The view of culture is essentially political, modifying the existing cultures toward a more unified model of universal synthesis in a nationalistic power structure where survival becomes the criterion of truth. Human progress offers the alternatives of power to determine our survival as a species and to protect us from ourselves as well as from one another.

The Hazen Foundation report suggests a third alternative that begins from a sociological and educational perspective, building on the resources of a culturally pluralistic and essentially open society. The view of human nature is humanistic and evolves toward solutions for the problems we create, assuming the ability and capability of humanity to make the necessary compromises with shared responsibility for survival. The view of freedom is positive, and we are able to identify appropriate responses to modify selfishness toward universal goals motivated by spiritual priorities. The view of culture is diverse and heterogeneous, rejecting universal world culture uniformity as destructive, incorporating alternative cultural traditions as resources in a cooperative effort through voluntarily limiting destructive tendencies. The emphasis is on interdependencies and relationships between cultural identities without destroying cultural diversity.

In the three scenarios for the future, there is a sharp contrast between the view of humanity as basically selfish, authority dominated, and self-destructive; or the view of humanity as creator, innovator, and concerned about the welfare of species. Heilbronner's scenario is based on an authoritarian political model in contrast with the Club of Rome's scientific computer model and the humanistic alternatives of the Hazen Report on our capacity to cope with the future at all.

All of the scenarios agree that, unless we alter our commitments to nationalism, science, industrialization, and the other familiar "habits" of modernization which have taken over industrialized societies, we will not survive, at least not in our present form. First of all, we are confronted with a magnitude of problems that have created an immediate crisis requiring that we change our ways. Secondly, the problems are not institutional but the more basic elements of our own cultures which have created those institutions. If the problems of our immediate crisis are to be dealt with, there must be major changes in our cultural beliefs and values to provide the ultimate solutions to our problems (Fernandez, 1977). Cross-cultural counseling and psychotherapy has a role in making those changes.

Human futuristics is not a precise science, although there is a temptation in each of the scenarios to oversimply the variables. Engineers work from a goal where the variables are more clearly indentified while human needs are diverse and vary from individual to individual over time. The future crisis may seem more remote than it really is. In 1972, Goodman (1978) counted the predictions that Orwell made in his book *1984* and identified 137 specific predictions of scientific, technological, social, and political practices, discovering that 80 of those predictions had already been realized. Then, in 1978, returning to the same list he discovered that over 100 of the predictions had now come true. There is no doubt that the authoritarian regime of *1984* describes a future that is clearly possible in the near future.

There is a Messianic message in all three scenarios that reminds one of the Old Testament prophets, and the recurring crisis that has accompanied humanity throughout history. In our reponse, there is likewise a tendency to believe in a covenant favoring the most optimistic of the scenarios. Osgood calls that tendency "pollyannaism" (Triandis, 1979) where we find it easier to cognitively process affectively positive than affectively negative stimuli, accept congruent information, and reject incongruent information. It is important that we face our own future in realistic terms.

We know that our society is now in a condition of rapid social change which is accelerating and requiring more radical adaptation of our cultural habits. We also can well imagine that some of us will be unable to make the necessary adaptive changes to our own rapidly approaching future. Those who are unable to make the adjustment will not be able to survive the demands of the future culture. However, since the future is not knowable, how do we learn to adjust to the unknown? The answer would seem to be in the learning of process skills for adaptation to cultures and value systems different from our own which we *do* know and *can* study. Having rehearsed a variety of responses to different cultural value systems will provide the adaptive skills for coping with our own rapidly approaching future. The future of cross-cultural counseling would seem to be anchored in this task of increasing our adaptive ability and skill across cultural value systems, whichever scenario will finally describe our future.

INTERCULTURAL ADJUSTMENT TO THE FUTURE
AS A FOREIGN CULTURE

Toffler (1971) popularized the process of adjustment to the future in the concept "future shock," building on the principles of culture shock as the process of adjustment and adaptation to a future culture different from our own. Oberg (1958) first used the term "culture shock" to describe the anxiety resulting from losing one's sense of when to do what and how. When the familiar cues are removed and strange or unfamiliar cues are substituted, as might happen when visiting a foreign culture, our response is likely to range from a vague sense of discomfort until we have learned the new expectations, all the way to a profound disorientation which requires a complete reorganization of our lives. Any new situation, such as a new job, new friends, new ideas, new neighborhood, will involve some adjustment of role and change of identity. The functions of counseling relate to helping persons successfully complete such adjustments in a variety of crisis situations. If we generalize the principles of culture shock to the role of cross-cultural counseling, we can identify guidelines for adjusting to the future through cross-cultural counseling.

There are many positive opportunities to learn through culture shock in adjusting to other cultures. Like every other kind of learning, culture learning involves change and movement from one frame of reference to another. Culture learning is likely to result in a highly personalized experience of special significance, resulting in learning new self-identities which were previously unfamiliar, as well as learning new perspectives on the culture being studied. Change is provocative. The individual is forced into sometimes painful self-examination and introspection, with frustrating anxiety and personal pain likely to result if the cultural differences are significant. The individual is confronted with new relationships as an outsider looking in. The individual learns to try out new, tentative attitudes through trial and error until the right responses are discovered. As a result, however, the individual has learned about self, about the home culture, and also about new identities in the host culture.

By comparing familiar and unfamiliar values, the individual learns to grow toward intercultural perspectives and develop alternative futures from which to choose. The very frustrations of adjustment lead to self-understanding and personal development in a counseling context. The related phenomena of role shock, culture fatigue, and future shock present the same opportunities and difficulties to each individual experimenting with new ideas. The principles of counseling transfer naturally to the educational goals of culture learning in helping the individual cope with the new cultural system.

The events of culture shock go through a series of stages which apply to the cross-cultural counseling process. Peter Adler (1975) has summarized descriptions of these stages into five categories. First, there is the initial contact with another culture where differences are intriguing, experiences exciting, behaviors experimental, and the individual is isolated by the home culture. Second, there is disintegration of the old, familiar cues where perceptions are impactful, emotions are confused, behaviors are to withdraw, and cultural differences begin to intrude on self-esteem. Third, there is the reintegration of new cues, where differences are perceived selectively, emotional responses are stressful, behaviors are more hostile, and rejection of the host culture likely to occur. Fourth, there is gradual autonomy where differences are legitimized, emotional responses more self-assured, behaviors more controlled, and the individual is able to negotiate with the new culture. Finally, there is the independence stage, where differences are valued, emotional response covers the full range, behaviors are self-actualizing, and the individual functions with normal effectiveness. It is important to recognize that culture learning and culture shock, like counseling, do not progress neatly and orderly from one stage to another. Sometimes the experience of culture shock is delayed far beyond the actual intercultural contact itself, while in other situations the process may be compressed into a very short period of time.

We are all travelers through time and the future is our host culture. Coffman (1978) has described culture shock as having six identifying features where counseling techniques will help individuals adapt to an increasingly uncertain future. These features include cue problems, value discrepancies, an emotional core, a set of typical symptoms, adjustment mechanisms, and a pattern of emergence over time. Coffman and Harris (1978) applied these features to the transition shock and deinstitutionalization of the mentally retarded citizen as well as to the foreign traveler. These examples, again, provide guidelines for the adaptive benefits of cross-cultural counseling principles to a variety of boundary crossing behaviors in our society.

When the cues or messages we receive in another culture are confusing, it is usually because familiar cues we have learned to depend on are missing, important cues are there but not recognized as important, or the same cue has a different meaning in the new culture. Much of the problem in cross-cultural counseling and culture shock involves learning to deal with new cues.

Familiar values define the meaning of good, desirable, beautiful, and valuable for each individual. Each culture values its own behaviors, attitudes, and ideas. While visitors to the host culture do not need to discard familiar values, there is a need to recognize alternative value systems in order to adapt to the new cultural system. The counseling skills of empathic understanding become a bridge for transcending our own cultural boundaries.

Culture shock has an emotional core and produces a heightened emotional awareness of the new and unfamiliar surroundings, whether as a sudden and immediate event or as a gradual fatigue which occurs over a period of time. The emotional effect of this experience may include anxiety, depression, or even hostility ranging from mild uneasiness to the "white furies" of unreasonable and uncontrolled rage experienced by Europeans adjusting to tropical cultures.

The specific symptoms of culture shock focus on either dissatisfaction with the host culture or idealization of the home culture. The host culture is criticized as being peculiar, irrational, inefficient, and unfriendly. The visitor is likely to fear being taken advantage of, being laughed at or talked about, not being accepted, and wanting to spend more time around persons from the visitor's home culture. The visitor might develop a glazed, vacant, or absent-minded look nicknamed the "tropical stare," or withdraw for long periods of time by sleeping or being otherwise inactive. Minor annoyances in the host culture become exaggerated, and the few remaining links with the home culture become extraordinarily important.

Strategies for adjustment that worked in the home culture or familiar past might not work for the visitor in a new host culture, so that the visitor needs to spend a greater portion of energy in making adjustments and learning new strategies. Direct confrontation and openness might facilitate adjustment in the home culture but further complicate the problems in a new host culture. Defensive strategies might range from hostile stereotyping and scapegoating of the host culture to "going native" and rejecting the visitor's own home culture.

Culture shock is likely to extend over a long period of time, reappear in a variety of forms, and not be limited to an initial adjustment. As familiar cues are replaced by unfamiliar cues, the visitor experiences a genuine identity crisis, requiring either that the former identity be disowned or that the visitor create and maintain multiple identities for each of the several cultures encountered. In either case, the visitor is required to reintegrate, confront, and challenge the basic underlying assumptions of his or her personality.

Cross-cultural counseling suggests a variety of ways in which the visitor can learn to respond to a host culture and all situations of rapid social change or cultural disorientation. The applications of counseling techniques to intercultural situations, again, draws from Coffman's work on adjustment to culture shock situations.

First of all, the visitor needs to recognize that transition problems are usual and normal reactions to the stress of adjusting in a strange, new setting. The visitor can be helped to recognize, understand, and accept the effects of adjustment in the context of a host culture support system. The maintenance of personal integrity and self-esteem becomes a primary goal. The visitor often experiences a loss of status in the new culture where the language, customs, and procedures are strange or unfamiliar. The visitor will need reassurance and support to maintain a healthy self-image. The adjustment needs to be allowed time to take place without pressures of urgency. Persons adjust at their own rate, recognizing that their reconciliation with the host culture, while painful, will enhance their later effectiveness. Recognizing the patterns of adjustment will help the visitor mark progress in developing new skills and insights. Depression and a sense of failure will be recognized as a stage of the adjustment process and not a permanent feature of the new experience. Labeling the symptoms of culture shock will help the visitor interpret emotional responses to stress in adjustment in perspective. The problem will become more specific and less ambiguous as a result. Being well adjusted at home does not assure an easier adjustment in a foreign culture. In some cases, visitors might find it even easier to adjust to a foreign culture, although, in extreme cases of maladjustment, visitors at home are likely to carry their problems with them to the new culture as well. Finally, while culture shock cannot be prevented, preparation for transition can ease the stress of adjustment. Preparation might include learning about the host culture, simulating situations to be encountered, and spending time with persons who are familiar with the host culture way of doing things. In all instances, the development of a support system is essential to helping the visitor reconstruct an appropriate identity or role in the new culture.

In reviewing the literature about culture shock, the opportunities for learning it presents, the process or stages of adjustment, the identifying features, and suggestions for minimizing the negative effects of culture shock, there is a recurring theme. Throughout the process, the individual is required to reevaluate his or her individual identity. The key for understanding and controlling the effect of culture shock is in counseling the visiting individual as well as understanding the host environment.

ROLE DIFFUSION AND IDENTITY FORMATION GOALS OF FUTURE COUNSELING

Any change will require learning new roles. The normally stressful conflicts become magnified by cultural differences. The greater the cultural differences the greater is the likelihood that barriers to communication will arise and that misunderstandings will occur, particularly in conditions of stress. The skills of adapting to cultural diversity can become sources of great strength and an invaluable asset in helping persons learn from one another and about themselves. Intercultural encounters are likely to highlight otherwise hidden conflicts in our own behavior at a rate many times faster than when working within our own familiar culture. As indicated earlier in the three alternative scenarios, cultural diversity will have to be dealt with in one of three ways. Either the cultural diversity will have to be eliminated in a global synthesis, cultural diversity will have to be controlled in an authoritarian context, or cultural diversity will have to negotiate a balance of otherise conflicting cultural roles both on a global and a national scale.

Roles are normally defined as constellations of behaviors expected of an individual and appropriate to a particular social or cultural context. These roles are based on threads of continuous affect, perception, cognition, and values which define an order in the otherwise chaotic experiences of everyday life. To the extent that roles are diffusely defined and discontinuous with familiar values, the individual is faced with intrapsychic conflict. We can cope with our conflicting cultural roles because (1) we rank order them in terms of the importance of each role for our own identity, (2) most identities apply only in certain contexts and are constantly changing, and (3) these rankings and the identities themselves are constantly changing. The roles we value most highly define our "primary" identities that we have learned gradually since childhood or to which we have been "converted" as adults (Singer, 1977).

One of the most important issues of the future is, therefore, likely to involve role diffusion, experienced by the individual's adjustment in a variety of conflicting roles over a period of time. In the attempts to differentiate the cultural groups in our society from one another, the role of cultural identity has been a primary source of confusion, as pointed out by Atkinson, Morten, and Sue (1979). A variety of terms have been used to explain how and why these groups differ from one another. The term "race" or "racial" has been used to differentiate groups according to biological differences, physical characteristics, or genetic origin; but they do not explain differences in social behavior where similar patterns cut randomly across racial lines. The term "ethnic" is derived from social or cultural heritage a group shares among themselves relating to customs, language, religion, and habits from one generation to the next. The term "culture" is, again, different, where members of the same racial and/or ethnic group might still be "culturally" different or there may be many different cultures within the same ethnic group. A fairly recent controversy is whether age, life style, socioeconomic status, sex role, and other such affiliations should be referred to as "culturally" different from one another. In the relationships between cultures, one group will often tend to dominate the other. A variety of terms such as "culturally deprived" or "culturally disadvantaged" have emerged to identify the less dominant culture or "minority" culture group. In usage, these terms have tended to take on a pejorative meaning that is frequently offensive to the less powerful or exploited group. More neutral concepts such as "culturally different" or "culturally separate" have been used to avoid the offensive connotations.

Groups may coexist with little or no interaction between them in a mode of "separatism." Groups may benefit from one another in a relationship of "symbiosis." The relation may be such that what one group gains is what another group loses. This is "parasitism." One group may harm the other group in a relationship of "antibiosis." The ideal and most desired relationship between groups is symbiosis (Maruyama, 1973). There are two kinds of symbiosis, "organismic" and "mutualistic." In organistic symbiosis (Pribram, 1949) a hierarchical center of planning is set up and the component groups conform to directions from a central location. In the mutualistic planning alternative the ideas originate from the component groups and are pooled for mutual adjustment. Counseling has earned an unfavorable reputation in the past by aligning its resources with nonsymbiotic relationships between cultural groups in our society. Our task for the future is to facilitate intercultural symbiosis through counseling.

Until the mid 1960s, the counseling profession demonstrated minimum interest or involvement in the needs and problems of minority groups but, rather, focused on the needs of the "average" individual which was interpreted according to dominant culture norms and values (Atkinson et al., 1979). Likewise, in the delivery of mental health services, the needs of minority populations were frequently overlooked and underserved (Pedersen, 1977b; Atkinson et al., 1979), but during the decade of the 1960s it became apparent that the variety of cultural groups would require equal recognition (Aubrey, 1977). The number of articles related to minority group counseling in the 1970s increased dramatically, as did the special concerns of the aged, drug users, gays, handicapped, prison inmates, students, and women. The Civil Rights movement of the 1950s and political activism regarding the war in Viet Nam no doubt also contributed to the consciousness raising attention to minority groups. The power of these newly organized, special interest groups had a profound effect on the counseling profession by emphasizing the cultural-environmental contextual factors impinging on individual development (Ivey & Authier, 1978). Demographic data suggest that blacks and Hispanics are expected to increase their relative proportion of the population between now and 1990 at an accelerated rate (General Electric, 1978), and other special interest groups are, likewise, consolidating their combined influence to ensure a symbiotic relationship. This type of relationship between cultural groups is essential if intercultural harmony is to be preserved.

The idealistic promises of the Declaration of Independence regarding human rights and principles of equality have confronted us with a basic contradiction. Americans believe that while we are created equal the equality does not last. Those who make use of their opportunities and develop their skill can enjoy special advantages. The concept of equality is diluted to a doctrine of "equal opportunity" defending the right to become unequal by competing with one another. Instead of bringing individuals together, the equal opportunity doctrine sets one person against another. Our contemporary dilemma results from a social democratic trend bringing about a state of equality among nations, races, sexes, and generations. We have not yet adjusted to the impact of equality, with programs to ensure equality serving to increase expectations among all groups for higher standards of living, access to better housing, medical care, opportunities for higher education, guaranteed employment, and old age security.

The dilemma of our time is that we are not prepared to live with each other as equals (Dreikurs, 1972). Our traditions are based on inappropriate autocratic principles challenging the power and superiority of each group by the other. It is difficult to restrain our capacity to overpower and control one another regardless of race, creed, sex, and age. Only as equals can we live in symbiotic harmony as illustrated repeatedly throughout history. There needs to be a shift of emphasis from the intrapsychic adjustment model of dealing with culturally different clients to a recognition of the effects social oppression have had on the profession of counseling, and a more activistic interpretation of counseling functions through direct community involvment.

ALTERNATIVE ASSUMPTIONS ABOUT COUNSELING GOALS FOR THE FUTURE

Marsella (1978) reviews the literature on modernization that describes the prototype of modern man as synonymous with "Western man," incorporating the values and assumptions of Western culture. As Marsella also points out, however, the modern person of the future is going to be very different from contemporary modern persons. As we have already indicated, the modern person will have to live more harmoniously with nature and with other persons than has been the case in the past. There is some evidence that the value assumptions of Western society are less suited to guiding us toward harmonious relationships than the value assumptions of non-Western societies. In order to increase its effectiveness in a multicultural society, counseling will need to consider the full range of Western and non-Western value assumptions.

There is some evidence that many of the underlying assumptions of our contemporary mental health service delivery system reflect the social, economic, political, and cultural values of Western dominant cultures (Pedersen, 1977a, 1977b, 1979). In some cultures, the notion of "counseling" has gained a very negative reputation as the servant of a dominant majority seeking to maintain the status quo. Some activists who do carry out the functions of counseling would be offended to be labeled as "counselors." Part of the reason for this dissonance is in the dissonance between basic assumptions of Western and non-Western cultures. These assumptions have been based on models of "modernization" which have themselves been based on those Euro–American dominant culture values that have been idealized in Western and non–Western cultures alike. The future effectiveness of counseling will require that it accommodate the indigenous value systems of Western and non-Western societies in a wide range of available alternatives.

Increased attention to non-Western alternatives has resulted from the popularization of Asian philosophies and religions, adaptations based on Asian techniques such as meditation, increased interdisciplinary interest in Asian psychological functions, dissatisfaction with the culturally narrow assumptions of existing systems, and the increased political, economic, and social power of non-Western countries in a world perspective. Tart (1975), Diaz-Guerrero (1977), Sampson (1977), and others (Pedersen, Lonner, & Draguns, 1976) have pointed out the cultural bias in counseling. I would like to consider five examples of how non-Western psychology might be better suited to guide counseling in a multicultural environment than the assumptions of Western society.

1. Western culture emphasizes objectivity and the scientific method of discovering the truth as more valid and reliable than subjective and spiritual access to knowledge. The rules of logic and replication have helped sponsor technological advancement, but at the expense of oversimplifying the role of humanity in a cosmic and spiritual perspective in the view of many non–Western societies. The criteria of reality for Buddhism, for example, does not clearly differentiate between the actual and the ideal, fact and fantasy. Existence from this subjective perspective has been compared to a river whose source is birth and whose goal is death, winding through a continuous process of existence in which consciousness unites all persons with one another and brings together the different moments within our collective and individual experiences.

The components of this subjective view change in relationship to one another giving the illusion of constancy, of ego, or of an unchanging reality (Pedersen, 1977a). In looking at the issues of controversy which separate Western from many non-Western assumptions, it is useful to recognize the challenge of subjective, intuitive, and illogical access to knowledge eluding the logical categories of a rationally defined structure. The validity of cross-cultural counseling in the future will depend on accommodating both the objective and the subjective espistemologies. There are many kinds of logic and epistemology, and our choice of one epistemology over another is more likely based on factors outside, beyond, and independent from logic. Our social and historical environment generates specific feelings which generate goals and promote the purposes of our intramural world view to the exclusion of alternatives.

The favorite epistemology of Western dominant cultures is being challenged by alternatives preferred by a variety of minority groups favoring non-hierarchical mutualism rather than competition, harmonious balance in nature rather than technocentric development, and multiple truths rather than a single standard of reality. A modern theory of knowledge needs a series of alternatives which may prepare the cross-cultural counselor to include multiple epistemologies in preparing us to live and work in a multicultural future by being exposed to a variety of existing epistemologies, minimizing psychological dependency upon any single epistemology, developing a habit of questioning established theories, and inventing new cultural patterns that synthesize alternatives being applied in the cultures around us.

2. Not all cultures value the individualized perspective as definitive of human behavior but might even see attachment to individualism as a direct handicap to attaining enlightenment and a diversion from the attainment of more important spiritual goals. The notion of *atman* in India, for example, defines the self as participating in unity with all things and not limited by the changing manifestations of an illusory and temporary phenomenal world. From the corporate perspective, alternative to the individual perspective, identity is composed of a balance between self and non-self, internal and external, individual and relational components. In many non-Western cultures, identity is not one's private property but is attached to a web of human relationships to the extent that the personal pronoun in some languages, such as Japanese, is not even expressed (Pedersen, 1977a). English is, perhaps, the only language where the personal pronoun ''I'' is always capitalized. The locus of cultural change or resistance in many cultures is not the isolated individual but the circle of humanity through interpersonal relationships that are themselves situation centered and socially controlled. The emphasis of a counselor, then, would more appropriately be on the individual's appropriate role relationship to other persons and conformity to social reality rather than forcing reality to conform, emphasizing self-transcendence rather than self-assertion.

Through their emphasis on competition between individuals for status, recognition, and measured achievement, many of the rules of industrialized society impose an individualistic bias which conflicts with relational values. An adequate counseling strategy would need to accommodate either or both value systems as appropriate. By contrast, Western traditions are based on the self as ego, or the independent observer and potential controller of a world which is experienced as profoundly separate from self (Watts, 1963); while other traditions emphasize self-transcendence rather than self-assertion, harmony with nature, and integration into a social totality.

It is difficult to see the impact of our own cultural heritage on our point of view because, as Edward Hall (1966) pointed out, one's own cultural assumptions are best hidden from one's self. That perspective is particularly true for Western psychology (Diaz-Guerrero, 1977). There has been a tendency for counseling to search for the failing, evil, or disturbed personality to the neglect of the surrounding system. The person who requires a continuing system of supportive, interdependent relations is judged weak, sick, or failing without recognizing the mental health maintenance role of the collectives surrounding that individual as *part* of that individual's identity. One example of the self-contained, individualistic perspective might be establishing the androgynous individual as an ideal type, as a sign of good health where each individual is self-contained and self-sufficient. Sampson (1977) elaborates:

> In the present context, androgyny as self-contained individualism and morality as independence or transcendence from collective loyalties may be related to high self-esteem and personal success. But in the long run, how can a society manage its complex problems of energy and population policy and its welfare programs, for example, while supporting so individualistic an outlook? How can human welfare be based on people's detachment from others and their seeking to be self-contained? How can a democratic system of governance survive when collective interests and recognition of vital interdependencies are felt to be too constraining? Will psychology be in the forefront of tomorrow's problem solving or remain in the backwater, a chronicler of today's troubles and an ideological contributor to our cultural breakdown? [p. 780]

Our future will depend on the ability to go beyond individualistic assumptions in coordinating the relational perspective of other cultures with our own criteria of good mental health.

3. In many non-Western cultures, there is a greater acceptance of dependence among intrafamily relationships even as adults, without embarrassment or judgments of immaturity. The goal of maturity in India has been described as satisfying and continuous dependency within the family and society (Pedersen, 1977a). In Chinese society, when there is a fight between brothers, both are blamed. The older is blamed for not giving in to the younger, while the younger is scolded for not respecting the older, but both are punished for their aggressively independent behavior (Tseng and Hsu, 1971). In Hawaiian society, the term *ho'oponopono* ("to make things

right") refers to a system of counseling where all members of an extended family are assembled to resolve conflict in a ritualized format that emphasizes interdependency (Pukui, Haertig, & Lee, 1972). In Japanese society, the concept of *ie,* or family system, implies closely guarded family relationships in the context of total involvement, and the term *amae* emphasizes the model of dependence by a child towards parents for all ideal social relationships.

There is a tendency for adolescents in Western families to leave home to seek their fortune outside the family. The separation of family members from one another in this way has been adopted as the tragic theme of literature and film, and is not considered at all desirable. In Western cultures, adulthood becomes the symbolic goal of having achieved self-reliance, power, achievement, responsibility, and identity fulfillment. In the vacuum left by the "absent family" in the West, institutions have tended to take over the familial functions, sometimes displacing the family or competing with familial interdependency as final authority. Reality does not depend on an individual's mastery of others to advance and achieve. In an interdependent model, reality becomes, rather, a religiously defined experience where people interact with one another, past, present, and future, as well as with the indigenous spiritual belief system (Lambo, 1978). There is a unity of life and time which provides the necessary balance and foundation of mental health and social well being. Opposites are combined in a harmonious web of natural and supernatural, physical and mental, conscious and unconscious through a dynamic interdependency. By analogy, other non-Western cultures have found an acceptable model for interdependency in the family. In many ways, the "family" in many Asian and non-Western societies is as primary a social unit for their cultures as the "individual" is in many Western cultures. It may be useful, for the future of conseling, to reexamine the role of the family as a model for defining and maintaining mental health in the future.

In a study of Asian theories of personality, Pedersen (1977a) contends that the psychological construct "personality" is so dominated by individualistic assumptions that it can only be applied to cultures effectively where individualism is an important value priority. Westermeyer (1976), likewise, contends that personality has had an unjustifiably important role in defining mental health services from a dominant culture perspective with little demonstrated predictive or pragmatic value in cultures where individualism is not favored. More emphasis should be placed on interpersonal relations in relation to intrapsychic events to provide a balanced perspective for counseling in cultures where dependency relationships are a favored mode of maintaining mental health.

Counseling is likely to play an even more important role in the future than in the past, demonstrated in part by the recent popularization of mental health and psychological approaches to social problems. Psychology has become a new religion, ideology, and justifier for the full range of social programs. That trend is likely to increase still further as the stress of coping with our uncertain future increases, and as special interest groups compete even more vigorously for the world's limited resources. Counseling can serve to isolate, atomize, individualize, and alienate us from one another toward chaos and authoritarianiam, or it can help us refocus the necessary and fundamental interdependencies from within our various cultures.

4. There is an assumption that a "modernized" system is also a "Westernized" system which has distorted our understanding of indigenous mental health resources in non-Western cultures that define the problem and solution within their own cultural perspective. Some of the products of modernization, consequently, have resulted in increasing the distance between aspiration and achievement, resulting in dissatisfaction, frustration, low self-esteem, marginality, alienation, and social deviance from both traditional and modern values (Triandis, Malpass, & Davidson, 1973). The net result of equating modernization with Westernization has distorted history, and a continuation of this tendency would be disastrous for our future. It is ironic that, while non-Western thought and philosophies are having an increasingly profound effect on Western culture, non-Western cultures continue to emulate Western values through economic, political, and social forms (Marsella, 1978). From the Western perspective, there is a concern that the emphasis on technology has eroded spiritual values in society, while non-Western cultures are concerned that the benefits of modern technology be available to them as they are to the world's industrialized nations (Mundy-Castle, 1976).

There are many fundamental assumptions in Westernization which do not necessarily apply to modernization as we look to the future. For example, there is an activist orientation implicit in Western values that change is preferred to no-change when given a choice between the two alternatives. When confronted with a problem where the solution is ambiguous, the Westerner will be likely to *do* something. Under the same conditions, persons from many non-Western cultures would have been socialized to restrain themselves and avoid a direct response as the favored mode of dealing with the problem. A foreign student returned home to his non-Western family and, seeking to justify the expense of their sending him abroad, spoke at length about how much the experience had changed him. His more traditional family was horrified.

As another example, there is an emphasis in psychology on the covariance of cause and effect. In Hinduism, by contrast, the categories of cause and effect are not separated but are, rather, part of the same phenomena observed from a different perspective. In defining a psychological problem of delivering a mental health service, the effort of sorting out the cause and effect in each counseling interview may be the wrong approach. Perhaps a less mechanistic, alternative approach to the totality of a culturally different client's environment, which is less problem-oriented and more sensitive to the dynamic interrelationships of cause with effect, will increase our sensitivity to the essential role of both aspects in a balanced totality. It would be a serious mistake to reduce counseling to "problem solving" by disrupting the dynamic balance of social forces already existing in the client's environment.

In mental health as in other forms of development, there is a tendency away from independent and autocratic guidelines and increasing demands for more emphasis on interdependencies, joint ventures, and mutualism between partners in the development enterprise. There is a greater emphasis on viewing the social event from within the other person's perspective and acknowledging the importance of alternative values. Self-examination and testing of basic assumptions from a psychological perspective are likely to be included in most forms of modern development. Cultures where self-examination has been important have developed resources that favor introspection as an important, essential, and, in some cases, almost exclusive mode of mental health maintenance. Not only will we need to develop skill in this area to work with members of those cultures, but we may discover the validity of introspective approaches for dealing with counseling in a broad range of other cultures as well.

Triandis (1979) points out how the first two million years of human evolution emphasized the struggle with nature for survival where the man-nature relationship was central. This was followed by an industrial revolution where efficient production of material goods became essential. The future is likely to emphasize, as we have already discussed, the development of social structures that increase harmony where counseling will have a major role. The Western tendency has been to divide the world into categories and experience ourselves as isolated egos. This view contrasts sharply with the more mystical alternative view where all things and events are interrelated as different aspects of the same ultimate reality. A more holistic view of mental health will be required to cope with the future in a multicultural world.

5. Western cognition is based on objects of consciousness rather than consciousness itself, where religious and spiritual goals have a more dominant role. Non-Western psychologies have frequently been more comfortable with the teaching of spiritual reality unlimited by the physical and tactile world around us. Capra (1975) has popularized the radical notion that the spiritual explanation of the universe in non-Western thought provides a

more adequate basis for understanding our environment, as it is being revealed by advances in quantum physics, rather than the more materialistic teachings of Western thought.

Non-Western thought describes levels of reality external to our ordinary state of conscious perception which are dominated by illusion (Tart, 1975). By contrast, Western thought assumes more frequently that our behavior is determined by the physical processes of our nature and surrounding environment. If physics is leading us "back" toward mysticism of the early Greeks, where the assumptions of modern science have been said to begin, the difference is that the earlier mystical insights were intuitive while the more recent return to those insights is based on precise experimentation and rigorous mathematical formalism.

The emphasis on consciousness itself as the basis of reality describes a world where scientific discovery can be in harmony with spiritual aims and religious belief through the medium of the "unity" and "interrelation" of all phenomena in an intrinsically dynamic universe. The further science brings us into the submicroscopic world, the more apparent the reality of inseparable, interacting, and ever-moving components emphasizing the interrelationship of forces which hold our world together both physically and psychologically. As the evidence increases for this point of view from a scientific perspective, it will become easier to make applications of the principles in our psychological perspective.

Even Western thought, while discounting the reality of phenomena that cannot be observed or measured, will, in a somewhat contradictory mode, emphasize the importance of concepts such as love, charity, intelligence, and pleasure which are inferred from our behavior but which cannot, in fact, be measured accurately. There is a linear assumption in Western thought which moves ahead in a single direction. This linear view of time separates the past, which is dead and gone, from the future, which does not yet exist, leaving an infinitesimally narrow point on the continuum which fades from the future to the past with desperate urgency. A more adequate inclusion of spiritual insights into mental health will enrich the perspective of cross-cultural counseling by cosmic proportions.

PRIORITIES FOR PLANNED DEVELOPMENT OF COUNSELING RESOURCES

If there is a future for humanity, it will require us to reconcile our cultural differences and accommodate a variety of value alternatives. If we look at the range of relationships we describe as cultural and generate guidelines from cross-cultural research, we should be able to generate the insight and skill to facilitate increased harmony between members of different cultural groups through counseling. If we further extrapolate what we are learning from bringing cultural groups together to the large variety of other identities and special interest clusters in society, we might apply cross-cultural counseling insight and skill to the whole range of intergroup contact beyond ethnic and nationality differences.

There are two important implications that would follow logically. First of all, all intergroup or interpersonal relationships are, to some extent, cross-cultural with a variety of value perspectives that complement or contradict one another. If we consider the variety of roles each of us fills over a period of time, it might even be reasonable to consider the complete individual "personality" to be, to some extent, multicultural. In any case, there is a vitally important role for cross-cultural counseling in facilitating the harmonious interaction of cultures, groups, and individuals with different identities. Second, if the role of cross-cultural psychology and counseling is to be as pervasive as it would seem, the consequence would be termination of "cross-cultural" counseling as a separate area. The focus of cross-cultural counseling would more likely be absorbed into the fields of social sciences as an essential and definitive aspect. The net result, then, would be that all counseling would become cross-cultural, with deliberate attention to the cultural values dimension of mental health.

There is, already, a great deal of interdisciplinary cooperation in the areas of cross-cultural counseling with joint topics across fields and disciplines as an example. In the study of specific problems, we can expect more emphasis on multimethod, multicultural measurement of all theoretical constructs. Cooperation between disciplines and fields will increase the likelihood that our conclusions are not method-bound by the implicit assumptions of any single field or perspective. The result could be a total realignment of the traditional disciplines as we now know them. In many ways, the barriers between fields and disciplines function more rigidly than other cultural barriers and, by analogy, suffer from discriminatory attitudes as well. The application of counseling skills and the concerns of mental health might be integrated, then, into a wide range of legal, political, economic, and philosophical directions. The enormous vested interests by traditional fields and disciplines in their continued existence would prevent diversification from happening as long as possible, but the pressing problems of our survival in the future may force the issue.

Until recently, most mental health professionals have been trained in psychology, sociology, anthropology, or social sciences, and the topics of concern have been largely defined by past and present events. More recently, there is a tendency to apply existing knowledge from several disciplines toward solving community problems beyond the descriptive and explanatory levels of analysis and move on to *a priori* predictions based on what we already know to be true. There is likely to be more emphasis on prediction of future problems before they happen so that they can be anticipated and, if possible, avoided. Through technology, we have the capacity to apply systems analysis to future problems, and the accelerating rate of social change may well require accurate anticipation of problems. In order to accomplish that task, the input variables will have to be carefully defined and programmed to include biological, behavioral, and social phenomena in an analysis of the total system. The future of primary prevention in counseling will require accurate assessment of the cultural perspectives that define the total system in a multicultural society. The efficient mobilization of technology together with identification of culturally accurate perspectives promises greater capacity to anticipate and prevent mental health problems before they occur.

There has been a tendency to base our comprehension of human social behavior on historically located principles within cultures, rather than psychological universals that are fundamental to understanding human behavior across cultures. There will need to be networks and linkages between networks throughout the fields of mental health and the community, bridging the particularistic and limited special interests in our society. While pointing out the dangers of depending on "pseudoetic" characteristics, where the emic or particularistic character of a culture are generalized universally without evidence, Triandis (1979) highlights the search for cultural universals as a primary task of cross-cultural research in the future. While the study of particular cultures has helped protect counseling from *underestimating* the importance and impact of cultural values, the study of cultural universals will help protect counseling from *overestimating* the differences which is just as likely to result in racist policy.

Draguns (1977) emphasizes the importance of drawing practical implications from what we already know about culture and mental health, and applying those implications to the practical concerns of service and treatment with more precision than is now being done. Rather than focus research efforts on the "symptom," Draguns suggests that we expand our focus in two directions: inward, toward the subjective intrapsychic system of personal experience; and outward, toward the interpersonal network connecting patient, professional, institution, and community. Counseling procedures need to be modified to match the values of divergent cultures, rather than follow a unimodal generalization that incorporates all groups from a dominant culture perspective. Adaptive coping by members of one culture might be maladaptive when applied to another culture, especially if the coping is adaptive for dominant culture and applied to members of a minority group. At present, it is still unclear the extent to which psychological theory can be applied across cultures. While Vontress (1976) points out that rapport is a culturally generalized priority for all counseling, the appropriate techniques are likely to differ from one culture to the next. There is also no adequate procedure or instrument to measure counseling effectiveness in a variety of cultural environments.

Counselor education has been criticized by many minority authors (Pine, 1972) for not enrolling more minority students in courses of counselor training, causing many programs across the country to actively recruit minority students to their programs. Atkinson (1977) points out the difficulty of identifying sufficient numbers of minority candidates with academic grades and achievement scores equal to nonminority peers (Samuda, 1975). This difficulty has led programs to develop quotas or special selection criteria for admitting lower scoring minority group members. The Bakke decision in California successfully challenged the legitimacy of double standards for admission, and suggested that, in the future, a more adequate solution will need to be developed for increasing the numbers of minority group members in the mental health professions without discriminating against others. Atkinson (1977) suggests that, in addition to including more minority group members, we also need to examine the content of what is being taught in counselor education courses. More cross-cultural counseling courses need to be developed with more multiculturally sensitive content materials in the courses. The textbooks and teaching materials need to reflect a variety of cultural perspectives for training the adequately prepared counselor.

At present, there are very few opportunities to obtain a major, minor, or even a specialization in cross-cultural counseling. There are, perhaps, dozens of individual courses on cross-cultural counseling scattered throughout the counselor training programs around the country, but very few coordinated programs of cross-cultural counseling exist at present. The University of Utah offers a Ph.D. and the University of Washington offers a Masters degree in Transcultural Nursing, the University of Miami offers a program in the medical school for transcultural mental health, and McGill University offers a Masters degree in Transcultural Psychiatry. It seems incredible that the emphasis on culture and mental health has not resulted in more adequate opportunities for professionals in training to pursue a specialization in the field. In the future, universities will need to develop support for coordinated programs of study in cross-cultural counseling.

Cross-cultural counseling will need to be more activist in orientation through outreach and consultation programs, ombudsmen and change agent functions, and facilitators of indigenous support system roles to supplement and largely replace the office or clinic-centered, scheduled interviews. Likewise, training programs are going to need to involve more resources from the culturally diverse community. Experience with the Peace Corps training programs (Harrison & Hopkins, 1967) have demonstrated that training programs are often more effective vehicles of cross-cultural preparation than university-based alternatives. In addition to cognitive content, affective experiences need to be incorporated into the curriculum to increase awareness of cultural differences in personalized ways. Materials are available through simulation of case methods or experience-based human relations training programs (Brislin & Pedersen, 1976). In view of the multicultural composition of modern society and the mainstreaming tendencies of schools and societies, it is unlikely that any counselor will escape working with culturally different clients. However, as Spiegel (1976) points out, there is no established constituency for a program in ethnicity and mental health, and none of the mental health professions are actively pursuing multiethnic approaches (Aubrey, 1977).

Industrialized societies, according to a General Electric study (1978), are encountering a "new reformation" of individual and societal values shifting from uniformity and centralization toward diversity, pluralism, and decentralization; from the concept of independence toward the concept of interdependence; from considerations of quantity ("more") toward considerations of quality ("better"); from mastery over nature toward living in harmony with it; from the primacy of technical efficiency toward considerations of social justice and equity; from authoritarianism and dogmatism toward participation; and from the dictates of organizational convenience toward the aspirations of self-development in an organization's membership. In response to this predicted future of our society, the field of counseling has several alternatives (Toffler, 1971). The traditionalist will pretend that there is really no change occurring and that things will remain essentially as they have been, and risk becoming less and less relevant to a multicultural clientele. The specialist will focus in one or another area of mental health and gamble that the selected specialty will continue to be relevant in a period of rapid social change. The reversionist will seek to preserve the status quo by reinforcing modifications of existing methods and escape to the relatively tranquil past. The super simplifier will seek a neat equation or single solution to the complicated problems of coping with a multicultural future. The "encapsulated counselor" (Wrenn, 1962) will escape to a technique-oriented job definition that neatly avoids the problem altogether. All of these are victims of the future.

Alternatives discussed in this chapter suggest that we move toward symbiotic and pragmatic alternatives for the future, seeking alternatives to the authoritarian or catastrophic scenario in restructuring our society, building on the adaptive techniques now available to facilitate individual adaptation to culture shock, developing alternative assumptions from non-Western societies that might apply to our future condition, and, finally, identifying specific modifications that will be predictably required based on what we already know about the changes going on around us. There are alternative futures for cross-cultural counseling, with some more acceptable than others. It is important that we define our choices and declare our commitment to the rights of every individual from every culture for mental health.

REFERENCES

Adler, P. The translation experience: An alternative view of culture shock. *Journal of Humanistic Psychology,* 1975, *15* (3).

American Psychological Association, Council of Representatives. Minutes from the meeting of January 19-20, 1979.

Atkinson, D. Selecting counselor trainees with cross-cultural strengths: A solution to the Bakke decision crisis. Unpublished paper, 1977.

Atkinson, D., Morten, G., & Sue, D.W. *Counseling American minorities: A cross-culture perspective.* Dubuque, Iowa: Wm. C. Brown, 1979.

Aubrey, R. F. Historical development of guidance and counseling and implications for the future. *Personnel and Guidance Journal,* 1977, *55,* 288-295.

Brislin, R., & Pedersen, P. (Eds.), *Cross-cultural orientation programs.* New York: Gardner Press, 1976.

Capra, F. *The tao of physics.* New York: Bantam Books, 1975.

Coffman, T. Culture shock at home and abroad: A cross-culture model of psychosocial adjustment. Unpublished manuscript, Honolulu, 1978.

Coffman, T., & Harris, M. Transition shock and the deinstitutionalization of the mentally retarded citizen. Paper presented at the 102nd annual meeting of the American Association on Mental Deficiency, Denver, May 18, 1978.

Diaz-Guerrero, R. A Mexican psychology. *American Psychologist,* 1977, *32* (11), 934-944.

Draguns, J. Mental health and culture. In D. Hoopes, P. Pedersen, & G. Renwick (Eds.), *Overview of intercultural education, training and research,* Vol. I, La Grange Pk., Ill: Intercultural Network, 1977.

Dreikurs, R. Equality: The life-style of tomorrow. *The Futurist,* August 1972, 153-155.

Fernandez, R. (Ed.) *The future as a social problem.* Santa Monica: Goodyear, 1977.

General Electric Co. The U.S. through 1990: A most likely scenario with implications for human resources management. EDC 78-I Management Development Institute, 1978.

Goodman, D. Countdown to 1984: Big Brother may be right on schedule. *The Futurist,* 1978, *12* (6) 345-365.

Hall, E. *The hidden dimension.* New York: Doubleday, 1966.

Harrison, R., & Hopkins, R. The design of cross-cultural training: An alternative to the university model. *The Journal of Applied Behavioral Science,* 1967, *3,* 431-460.

The Hazen Foundation. *Reconstituting the human community.* New Haven: Author, 1972.

Heilbronner, R.L. *The human prospect.* New York: Norton, 1975.

Ivey, A., & Authier, J. *Microcounseling; Innovation in interviewing counseling psychotherapy, and psychoeducation.* (2nd ed.) Springfield, Ill.: C. Thomas, 1978.

Lambo, T.A. Psychotherapy in Africa. *Human Nature,* 1978, *1,* 32-40.

Marsella, A. The modernization of traditional cultures: Consequences for the individual. In D. Hoopes, P. Pedersen, & G. Renwick (eds.), *Overview of intercultural education, training and research.* Vol. III. La Grange Pk, Ill: Intercultural Network, 1978.

Maruyama, M. Toward human futurists. Paper presented at the Ninth International Congress of Anthropological and Ethnological Sciences, Chicago, September 1973.

Mesarovic, M., & Pestel, E. *Mankind at the turning point: The second report to the Club of Rome.* New York: E. P. Dutton, 1974.

Mundy-Castle, A. Psychology and the search for meaning. University of Lagos, Nigeria, inaugural lecture, 1976.

Naranjo, C. *The one quest.* New York: Viking Press, 1972.

Oberg, K. Culture shock and the problem of adjustment to new cultural environments. Washington, D.C.: Department of State, Foreign Service Institute, 1958.

Pedersen, P. Asian personality theories. In R. Corsini (Ed.), *Current personality theories.* Itasca, New York: Peacock, 1977.a

Pedersen, P. The triad model. *The Personnel and Guidance Journal,* 1977, *56,* 94-100.b

Pedersen, P. Non-Western psychologies: the search for alternatives. In A. Marsella, R. Tharp, & C. Cibrowski, *Perspectives on cross-cultural psychology.* New York: Academic Press, 1979.

Pedersen, P., Lonner, W., & Draguns, J. *Counseling across cultures.* Honolulu: University Press of Hawaii, 1976.

Pine, G.J. Counseling minority groups: A review of the literature. *Counseling and Values,* 1972, *17,* 35-44.

President's Commission on Mental Health. *Report to the President,* Washington, D.C.: Government Printing Office, 1978.

Pribram, K. *Conflicting patterns of thought.* Washington, D.C.: Public Affairs Press, 1949.

Pukui, M.K., Haertig, E.W., & Lee, C.A. *Nana I ke kumu.* Honolulu: Hui Hanai, 1972.

Sampson, E. Psychology and the American ideal. *Personality and Social Psychology,* 1977, *11,* 767-782.

Samuda, R. *Psychological testing of American minorities.* New York: Dodd, Mead, 1975.

Singer, M. Perception in international affairs. In D. Hoopes, P. Pedersen, & G. Renwick, (Eds.), *Overview of intercultural education, training and research,* Vol. I. La Granger Pk; Ill: Intercultural Network (1977).

Spiegel, J. Prospectus for the Brandeis/Heller School training programs in ethnicity and mental health. Waltham, Mass.: Brandeis University, September 1976.

Tart, C. Some assumptions of orthodox Western psychology. In C. Tart (Ed.), *Transpersonal psychologies.* New York: Harper, 1975.

Toffler, A. *Future shock.* New York: Bantam Books, 1971.

Triandis, H. The future of cross-cultural psychology. In A. Marsella, R. Tharp, & C.

Cibrowski, *Perspectives on cross-cultural psychology.* New York: Academic Press, 1979.

Triandis, H., Malpass, R., and Davidson, A. Psychology and culture. *Annual Review of Psychology,* 1973, *24,* 355-378.

Tseng, W.S., & Hsu, J. Chinese culture, personality formation and mental illness. *International Journal of Social Psychiatry,* 1971, *16,* 5-14.

Vontress, C. Racial and ethnic barriers in counseling. In P. Pedersen, W. Lonner, & J. Draguns (Eds.), *Counseling across cultures.* Honolulu: University Press of Hawaii, 1976.

Watts, A. *Psychotherapy east & west.* New York: Mentor, 1963.

Westermeyer, J. *Anthropology and mental health.* The Hague: Mouton, 1976.

Wilson, K. Comparison and critical appraisal of three perspectives. Unpublished paper, 1979.

Wilson, K. Comparison and critical appraisal of three perspectives. Unpublished paper, Honolulu, Hawaii, 1979.

Wrenn, G.C. The culturally encapsulated counselor. *Harvard Educational Review,* 1962, *32* (4), 444-449.

Subject Index

in intercultural therapy research, 41-44
  demographic characteristics, 41-42
  intercultural skills, 43
  knowledge of other cultures, 42-43
  other attitudes and characteristics,
    43-44
  prejudice and attribution, 42
Credibility
  of counselor
    as process variable, 104, 107-8, 114,
    117
  of traditional healers
    and Western therapists, 249-50
Crisis intervention
  as Hispanic need, 207, 223
Cross-cultural Coalition Training
  and expectancy effects, 98-99
Cross-cultural counseling
  educational specialization in, 331
  research overview of, 28-56
Cubans
  acculturation and alienation among,
    40-41
  client attitudes of, 39
  therapy problems of, 147-48
Cue problems
  in culture shock, 316
Cultural aspects
  of psychopathology, 32
Cultural differences
  in communications skills usage, 292-93
Cultural identity
  and role diffusion
    in future counseling, 318-21
Cultural imperialism
  and Western therapies, 284-85, 306
Cultural phenomena
  counseling and psychotherapy as, 303
Culture
  influence on psychological processes,
    159-60
  and psychosis expression, 163-68
  relevance in counseling and therapy, 16
  three future alternatives, 305-06, 314-16
Culture assimilator
  and expectancy effects, 99
Culture-bound values

as barrier to effective counseling,
  112-13
Culture brokers
  in cultural adaptations of psycho-
    therapy, 7
Culture-contact situations
  and psychotherapy needs, 11
Culture shock
  and future shock, 217-20, 335
  among Japanese, 232
  and psychotherapy, 11, 13

Death
  Navajo beliefs about
    and family interventions, 265
Decision making
  as counseling process, 295-96, 305
Deferential behavior
  as Japanese value, 230
Demographic characteristics
  of Hispanic Americans, 195-97
  of Japanese Americans, 229-30
Dependency
  socialization for
    and therapy expectancies, 91
Depression
  as Caucasian malady, 164-66
  cultural differences in, 36-37
  cultural effects on diagnosis, 160
  treatment of, 161
Desensitization
  in treating phobias, 133
Deterioration effect
  and psychotherapy effectiveness, 129
Developing Interculturally Skilled
  Counselors (DISC)
  in Hawaii
    and culture effects on diagnosis,
    160
Developmental variables
  in therapy interaction, 77-78
Deviant labeling
  cultural aspects of, 113-14
Diagnosis
  of Black clients, 184-87
  effects of culture on, 160, 171
Directive/non-directive styles

About the Editors and Contributors

Anthony J. Marsella is currently a professor in the Department of Psychology at the University of Hawaii in Honolulu, Hawaii and also Director of the World Health Organization Schizophrenia Research Center located at The Queen's Medical Center in Honolulu. He received his Ph.D. in Clinical Psychology from Penn State University in 1968. Following an internship at Worcester State Hospital in Worcester, Massachusetts, he was awarded a Fulbright Research Fellowship to the Philippines. He also received an appointment as an NIMH Culture and Mental Health Scholar at the University of Hawaii. Dr. Marsella has conducted extensive research on cross-cultural psychopathology in the Philippines, Korea, Sarawak and among various ethnic groups in Hawaii. He has published more than sixty books, book chapters, and journal papers and serves as a consultant for the World Health Organization and numerous human service agencies.

Paul Pedersen is currently Director of an NIMH funded training grant for *Developing Interculturally Skilled Counselors* located at the University of Hawaii, Honolulu, Hawaii. He is also an Affiliate Professor in the Department of Psychology and in the School of Social Work at the University of Hawaii and a Research Fellow at the East-West Center in Honolulu, Hawaii. Dr. Pedersen received his Ph.D. in Asian Studies from Claremont Graduate School in 1968. He has taught and conducted research in Indonesia, Malaysia, and Taiwan. He has published more than seven books and forty book chapters and journal papers. He has served as president of the Society for Intercultural Education, Training and Research (SIETAR) and as an officer with the International Association for Cross-Cultural Psychology and the International Council of Psychologists.

Carolyn B. Block, Ph.D., Department of Psychology, University of California, Berkeley, Berkeley, California.

Norman G. Dinges, Ph.D., East-West Center, Culture Learning Institute, Honolulu, Hawaii.

Juris G. Draguns, Ph.D., Department of Psychology, Pennsylvania State University, University Park, Pennsylvania.

Arnold P. Goldstein, Ph.D., Department of Psychology, Syracuse University, Syracuse, New York.

Allen E. Ivey, Ph.D., Department of Psychology, University of Massachusetts, Amherst, Massachusetts.

Frank A. Johnson, M.D., Department of Psychiatry, University of California, San Francisco, San Francisco, California.

Martin M. Katz, Ph.D. Department of Psychiatry and Behavioral Sciences, George Washington University, Washington, D.C.

Harry H. L. Kitano, Ph.D., School of Social Welfare, University of California, Los Angeles, Los Angeles, California.

Michael J. Lambert, Ph.D., Department of Psychology, Brigham Young University, Provo, Utah.

Spero M. Manson, Ph.D., National Center for American Indian and Alaskan Native Mental Health Research and Development Center, Portland, Oregon.

Amado M. Padilla, Ph.D., Department of Psychology, University of California, Los Angeles, Los Angeles, California.

Frank L. Pasquale, M.A., Communications Institute, East-West Center, Honolulu, Hawaii.

Derald W. Sue, Ph.D., School of Education, California State University, Hayward, Hayward, California.

Norman D. Sundberg, Ph.D., Psychology Clinic, University of Oregon, Eugene, Oregon.

Joseph E. Trimble, Ph.D., Department of Psychology, Western Washington University, Bellingham, Washington.

Pergamon General Psychology Series

Editors: Arnold P. Goldstein, Syracuse University
Leonard Krasner, SUNY, Stony Brook

UNIV